ISSUES IN INTERNATIONAL
ECONOMICS

(Oxford international symposia; v. 5)

IN THE SAME SERIES

International Aspects of the Provision of Medical Care
  Edited by P. W. Kent
Contemporary Aspects of Philosophy
  Edited by Gilbert Ryle
New Approaches to Genetics
  Edited by P. W. Kent
Modern Musical Scholarship
  Edited by Edward Olleson

ISSUES
IN
INTERNATIONAL ECONOMICS

edited by

PETER OPPENHEIMER

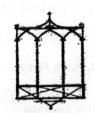

ORIEL PRESS
STOCKSFIELD
LONDON   HENLEY ON THAMES   BOSTON

Series Editor Dr P W Kent
© 1978 Board of Management of the Foster & Wills Scholarships
Oxford University, England
First published in 1980
by Oriel Press Ltd (Routledge & Kegan Paul Ltd)
Stocksfield, Northumberland, England NE43 7NA

Set in Baskerville and
Printed in Great Britain by
Willmer Brothers Limited, Rock Ferry, Merseyside

ISBN 0 85362 186 1

TO
THE MEMORY OF
HARRY G. JOHNSON

Contents

Preface

The growing complexity of international economic affairs, particularly as it effects the West, makes timely the production of an overview of some aspects of current problems as seen through the eyes of economists and others from various countries. Particular aspects in mind include North-South relationships, the needs of developing countries, and the appropriate extent and nature of government action in economic matters. The volume arises out of papers presented at the Oxford International Symposium held at Christ Church Oxford in September 1978 under the able and irrepressible general chairmanship of Peter Oppenheimer who was responsible not only for the liveliness of the meeting but also for the overall design of the programme.

The Symposia are held annually under the auspices of the Board of Management of the Foster and Wills Scholarships Committee of Oxford University and of the German Academic Exchange Service. These international academic occasions are made possible by the continued generosity of the Kulturabteilung of the German Foreign Ministry and by the organizational support which is provided by the Deutscher Akademischer Auschtauschdienst through Herr Franz Eschbach and his staff in London.

For the charming and efficient *venue* provided by Christ Church, thanks are extended to the Governing Body of the College and especially to the Steward and his colleagues.

The proceeds arising from this volume (like those before it) are dedicated to the Foster-Wills Scholarship Fund which exists to make regular provision for exchange of young scholars in any field, between German Universities and Oxford.

The index of the book has been prepared by Mrs R. E. B. Kent.

P. W. Kent
Van Mildert College
Durham

Editor's Introduction

The papers in this volume were presented at an international symposium at Christ Church, Oxford in September 1978. The symposium was one of a series sponsored each year in a different discipline (but always with international aspects in mind) by the Board of Management of the Foster-Wills and Theodor Heuss Scholarships, together with the German Academic Exchange Service. A full list of participants is given at the end of this volume.

Harry Johnson had died (at the age of 53) in May 1977, a few months before the list of invitations to the symposium was drawn up. It was natural, indeed automatic, that the symposium should be held in his memory. Not only had he been a committed internationalist and a dominating figure at economics conferences the world over, but his own most influential scholarly achievements lay in international economics, in both pure trade and balance-of-payments theory. No major present-day publication on these subjects can avoid copious references to his work.

Johnson's own astonishing list of publications – some 20 books and over 500 articles, plus numerous pamphlets, reviews and editorial contributions – has been followed since his death by an almost comparable series of tributes, surveys of his work and *in memoriam* articles and volumes, and there is little which the present introduction needs to, or can, add.[1] Since, however, the contents of this volume are on the whole slanted towards policy questions and empirical work, it is worth emphasizing that Johnson, though profoundly concerned with public issues, was first and foremost a theorist; and a theorist with two intellectual qualities in particular. First, he had a fabulous ability to synthesize in a brief compass a whole body of analytical work drawn from various corners of the subject, tidying up controversies, making order out of confusion and at the same time pointing the way to subsequent stages of investigation. To describe this as 'an ability' is to understate what it involved, unless the description call to mind Thomas Alva Edison's definition of genius as '1 per cent inspiration and 99 per cent perspiration.' Johnson's prodigious capacity for hard work and his driving zeal to familiarize himself with all research relevant to his own thinking were central to his professional accomplishments.

Secondly, Johnson sought to maximize the scientific element in economics and to minimize the element of ideology and propaganda.

Although his biting and even offensive criticism was famous, its intended targets were always weak argument, poor scholarship or untenable assertions, and not the political or cultural preference for one course of action over another. Economic nationalism was something which held no attractions for Johnson; likewise the belief that manufacturing industry is somehow economically superior to the service sector. Yet both attitudes received sympathetic analytical treatment at his hands, especially when they occurred in newly independent states.[2] On the other hand, his great admiration for Milton Friedman was qualified by his disapproval of Friedman's willingness to allow the propaganda motive to embroider his scholarship.[3]

Given these intellectual characteristics, it is not surprising that Johnson preferred to stay aloof from governments and official organisations and, when writing on economic policy, to delineate options and inter-relations rather than espouse some particular strategy. Charles Kindleberger once teased him with the fact that, in discussing the world monetary system, he had at different times expressed himself in favour of quite different and even diametrically opposed policies, such as a multi-currency reserve system, floating exchange rates, an increase in the price of gold, a new international reserve currency issued by the IMF, etc. Certainly Johnson had no consistent line on international monetary reform, compared for instance with his unfaltering commitment in later years to the monetary approach to balance-of-payments theory. But he did not regard Kindleberger's comment as a valid reproach. In his own words, 'In this area the tools of rational economic analysis can only illuminate the issues; ultimately politics has to resolve them.'[4]

In the policy sphere Johnson's talents came into their own when he undertook to survey a broad network of interconnected topics, emphasising their points of contact and at the same time identifying the distinctive features of each. This was pre-eminently true of his book on *Economic Policies Towards Less Developed Countries* (1967); it applied also to his three lectures on *The World Economy at the Crossroads* (1965) and, in a more popular vein, to the volume that he produced for the Trade Policy Research Centre on *Technology and Economic Interdependence* (1975). Chapter 6 of that book, on the 'Brain Drain', contains one of my favourite Johnson sideswipes at special pleading:[5]

'For example, in Britain it was widely believed in the 1950's and 1960's that immigration of coloured workers from other Commonwealth countries imposed serious costs of congestion on housing and social services, whereas the emigration of educated British people gave great gains to the United States and Commonwealth countries as recipients – to Britain's loss. One could well have taken the opposite view that the United Kingdom was over-supplied with educated people expecting to live in the style of an empire that no longer existed and under-supplied with humble folk willing to do an honest day's work for an honest day's pay.'

Vijay Joshi in his contribution to this symposium remarks (pp. 55–6 below) that 'The liberal sentiments of many people, even free traders, are apt to falter when they contemplate the horrors of free international movement of labour!' It is a fair comment; and one may properly add here that it was absolutely inapplicable to Harry Johnson.

*   *

*

Participants in the symposium who acted as principal discussants for one of the papers were given the opportunity (but not the obligation) to submit comments in writing for inclusion in the symposium proceedings. Accordingly, some but not all the papers that follow are accompanied by a discussant's comment.

The papers fall into three groups. The first group comprises essays by Jan Tumlir, Ryutaro Komiya, Ian Little and Helen Hughes on various aspects of the world economic order. The former two are mainly addressed to the advanced countries of the OECD area, the latter to the less developed countries (LDCs) or at least to participants in the North-South debate. In different ways these papers all emphasize limitations on the power of government in economic affairs. Public policy can achieve little of value in opposition to, or without support from, market forces (a point also highlighted in Donges's paper in Part II). And international co-operation cannot (nor perhaps should) be expected to run very far ahead of national public opinion.

Recognition of such constraints, however, still leaves major difficulties unresolved, not only in practice but in principle. For one thing, the constraints are liable to find themselves in conflict. Public opinion is seldom unanimous; and part of it may oppose the direction in which market forces are pushing. Secondly, as economists have long emphasised, even perfectly functioning markets cannot guarantee justice in the distribution of wealth and income. Distribution here encompasses both factor rewards in equilibrium and the costs involved in adjusting from one equilibrium to another. All this is true within countries, and still more so between them or in the 'world community' as a whole. Thirdly, unless one takes illegitimate refuge in tautology, national governments and electorates are not always good judges of their own national interest. Ample room thus remains for dispute over the aims and methods of economic policy. The extent to which governments should try to make up for shortcomings in real-life market mechanisms, or acknowledge an obligation to promote the economic well-being of poorer countries, or temper their policies to the wishes of foreign governments with different priorities from their own, are legitimate subjects for debate – as the comments by Andrea Boltho and Vijay Joshi both illustrate.

The chapters in Part II are concerned with trade, factor movements and commercial policies. Robert Baldwin's paper follows on directly from the theme of Part I, its subject being the interaction of economics with politics, and the weighting of producer relative to consumer interests, in the Articles of the GATT. In his conclusions Baldwin summarizes some desirable modifications of the GATT rules, but also brings out the problems of diagnosis and diplomacy that arise in efforts to secure an acceptable balancing of interests. In addition to Baldwin's, Part II contains six further papers. James Meade and his discussant Ronald Jones examine in a theoretical framework the impact of different personal tax regimes on international factor movements. Meade's paper stems from his leading role in the Institute for Fiscal Studies' Committee on Tax Reform; the Committee favoured a switch from income to expenditure as the main base of direct personal taxation in the United Kingdom. The paper also covers the subsidiary but nevertheless important issues of double-tax relief and savings incentives. Jones points out that, if individuals are free to migrate, potential world welfare is increased by the presence of different tax systems in different countries, enabling people to choose a tax regime that accords, relatively speaking, with their saving/consumption preferences.

Alasdair Macbean considers the extent to which future comparative advantage can be foreseen by planners anxious to diversify a country's productive structure. The case in point is that of an oil exporter, Iran – the Iranian political turmoil making no basic difference to the problem posed. Macbean's conclusion, unsurprising but instructive, is that such countries can do little by way of preparation for 'the day the oil runs out', apart from raising, by educational and other means, the quality of the labour force, including its entrepreneurial sections on whom the tasks of detecting and exploiting new production and export opportunities will sooner or later fall. The implication is that where present-day domestic investment by OPEC countries is designed as a matter of policy to diversify their productive structure away from oil, it is likely to involve considerable misapplication of resources.

The papers by Stephen Magee and Michael Michaely report on some attempts at empirical testing of well-known propositions. Magee (with Christopher Bliss as discussant) finds that lobbying for protection in the United States tends to be sector-specific rather than governed by the factor-identity of the lobbyist, i.e. by whether he (or she) represents labour or capital. On the assumption that lobbyists perceive their self-interest correctly, these findings cast doubt on the Stolper-Samuelson theorem about income-distribution and instead support the older Cairnes model, which asserts that protection will favour all factors engaged in import-competing production, at the expense of those in export production. Michaely investigates the structure of trade barriers in the advanced countries, particularly in relation to imports from LDCs. He finds that, contrary to some received opinion, trade barriers have not hitherto discriminated against the exports of low-income countries or against labour-intensive products. There is, however, a bias against imports of finished consumer goods; and although this may not have greatly handicapped exports of manufactures from LDCs up to the late 1970s, it is more likely to do so in future, if the existing structure of advanced-country trade barriers is maintained.

Michaely's findings are, on the face of it, consistent with the increased share of world exports (and world production) of manufactures achieved by LDCs in the 1970s.[6] At the same time, it must be remembered that tariffs and non-tariff barriers are seldom the most important influences on trade flows, and that in any case they tend only to make such flows smaller than they would otherwise have been in any particular period. As a matter of history, low trade barriers do not seem to have been a necessary condition for dynamically rising imports, as Arthur Lewis (1949) pointed out long ago. It is also unclear whether the data on trade barriers available to Michaely adequately captured the tendency observed during the 1970s towards 'informal' restrictive devices falling outside the framework of the GATT, such as voluntary export restraints, orderly marketing arrangements and the like.

More general surveys of the determinants of North-South trade flows are contained in the contributions by Juergen Donges and Stuart Harris, the former writing from a 'Northern', the latter from a 'Southern' (though not LDC) point of view. In relation to commercial policy these papers complement the earlier one by Baldwin, and provoke reflections on several aspects of the world trading scene. If the realities of the bargaining process as reflected in the Articles of the GATT mean that producer interests receive undue consideration compared with consumer interests, can it equally be said that the derogations permitted by the GATT from its own basic principle of non-discriminatory liberalisation of trade have favoured producers in the rich industrial nations at the expense of those in LDCs? This is probably true of the Long-Term Cotton Textiles Arrangement of 1962 and its successor from 1973 onwards, the Multi-Fibre Arrangement. On the other hand, the extensive protectionism practised, regardless of GATT, by many LDCs themselves argues in the opposite direction – even if such protectionism goes against the economic interest of the country adopting it, as is now widely believed. Moreover, the fact that the developed countries have tended increasingly to search for protective devices outside the GATT framework testifies to the latter's effectiveness as, at the very least, a source of embarrassment to any of its signatories trying to circumvent their commitments. Thus the case is far from clear.

The real difficulty anyhow is that the LDCs as a group have not hitherto supported the principle of non-discrimination, but on the contrary have demanded discrimination in their favour. The New International Economic Order, indeed, has been about little else, whether in the field of commodity agreements, market access for manufactures, transfer of technology or finance. The optimistic view is that this will gradually change, as third-world countries give recognition to their mutual divergences of interest. High oil prices and massive balance-of-payments surpluses in OPEC are not, after all, doing very much for the economic advancement of most oil-consuming LDCs (opportunities for migrant labour in the Arabian Gulf notwithstanding). The Integrated Programme for Commodities, to the extent that it gets off the ground, will not remotely enable OPEC's terms-of-trade gain to be matched by exporters of other primary commodities. And the Newly Industrialising Countries must already appreciate that non-discriminatory liberalisation of trade wherever possible is a more promising route than discrimination to widening markets for their manufactures.

Governments in the advanced countries, for their part, while facing stronger demands for protection from home industry, must also be aware of the significance for commercial policy of the volume and pattern of international debts. From the end of 1973 to the end of 1979 the non-OPEC third world and Eastern Europe added something like $200 billion to their combined external debt. Assuming that this debt can be viewed as a perpetuity bearing interest at, say, 10 per cent, the debt-service charge in 1980 came to $20 billion or about 10 per cent of the debtor areas' combined merchandise exports to the OECD countries. Of course these figures are excessively aggregated (for the major LDC debtors the debt-service ratio is much worse than this) and they give only a rough order of magnitude (ignoring *inter alia* the sizable debts already outstanding at the end of 1973). But they are getting bigger all the time, since the low-absorbing members of OPEC remain in massive surplus and the OECD countries are accumulating at best a fraction of the counterpart growth in indebtedness. In these circumstances advocates of extended protectionism by the advanced countries are playing with fire.

The third and final section of the book is on foreign-exchange and balance-of-payments questions. All four papers are concerned with the causes and effects of movements in (floating) exchange rates in a world of inflation. Ronald McKinnon's wide-ranging paper, with a comment by Max Corden, is a blend of theory and policy analysis. One of its principal themes is the role of the exchange rate as an indicator and transmission mechanism of monetary policy. Thus, a currency appreciation reflecting tight money tends to improve rather than worsen the trade balance – in some cases at any rate. The time-horizon of McKinnon's analysis is mainly short-term. Jürg Niehans's piece on the theory of purchasing-power parity complements this neatly. While also concerned with the impact of monetary disturbances, it chiefly examines the adjustment process by which an exchange rate reaches long-run equilibrium. Theoretical analysis of this process illuminates the difficulties of macro-economic stabilization under floating rates.

In the first of the two quantitative papers that follow, Robert Aliber investigates the behaviour of interest rates across countries and finds that on a quarterly basis arbitrage is not sufficiently reliable to keep real returns on assets in various currencies in line with one another as monetary conditions change. In the final paper Giorgio Basevi and Renzo Orsi present part of a larger study on the export-pricing policy of Italian industry. The point that particularly concerns them is the discrepancy between prices expected and realised in domestic currency when exports are invoiced in foreign currency and the exchange rate fluctuates. This discrepancy or 'customs conversion effect' is treated as one reason why *ex post* observed prices do not correspond to market-clearing prices, and the authors find it to be a significant element in the price equation for Italian exports. In response to

xvii

Marcus Miller's comment the authors agree that their approach presupposes that exporters do not correctly anticipate the movement of exchange rates when specifying contract prices. It also emerges from the exchange between authors and discussant that Italian exporters, in moving to more extensive use of foreign-currency invoicing during the 1970s, were able by taking forward rather than spot exchange rates for the Italian lira as the basis of price quotations to enhance their international competitiveness, inasmuch as forward rates tended to be lower than spot rates subsequently realised for the same dates.

*   *

*

A great debt is owed to the sponsors of the symposium for their generosity, and in addition to the German Academic Exchange Service under its Director, Franz Eschbach, for providing the bulk of the conference administration. Valued administrative assistance also came from the Trade Policy Research Centre, directed by Hugh Corbet, with which Harry Johnson had been closely associated since its inception in 1968; and from Sanjit Maitra, a graduate student in economics at Christ Church. Dr. Paul Kent, as convenor of the Oxford International Symposia, gave help and encouragement throughout, and Bruce Allsopp of the Oriel Press oversaw the publication process with few words and great efficiency. Acknowledgment is gratefully made to Messrs. Croom Helm Ltd., Publishers, for permission to reproduce in Stuart Harris's paper a table from L. N. Rangarajan, *Commodity Conflict: The Political Economy of International Commodity Negotiations.*

Christ Church, Oxford.
May 1980.

NOTES

1. Among the obituary notices see in particular Reuber and Scott (1977) Shils (1977) and Tobin (1980). For a full survey of Johnson's writings see *Journal of Political Economy* (1980), Special Supplement in Honor of Harry G. Johnson.
2. See Johnson (1965) and Johnson (1967) listed by Robert E. Baldwin on p. 93 below.
3. See Johnson (1971). Friedman has been taken to task in detailed fashion by Don Patinkin (1969) and (1974).
4. Johnson (1970), p. 120.
5. Johnson (1975), pp. 95–6.
6. In 1976–77 the share of non-OPEC LDCs in imports of manufactures reached 16 percent in North America (compared with 7 percent in 1963), 24 percent in Japan (compared with 6 percent) and 5 percent in the EEC and EFTA (compared with 3 percent). Data from GATT (1978), Table 5, p. 13.

REFERENCES

GATT (1978), *International Trade 1977–78*. Geneva: General Agreement on Tariffs and Trade.
Johnson, H. G. (1965), *The World Economy at the Crossroads*. New York: Oxford University Press.
Johnson, H. G. (1967), *Economic Policies Towards Less-Developed Countries*. London: George Allen and Unwin (for the Brookings Institution, Washington, DC). Especially Chs. IV–VI.
Johnson, H. G. (1970), 'The International Monetary Crisis, 1969' in I. A. Macdougall and R. H. Snape eds., *Studies in International Economics: Monash Conference Papers* (Amsterdam: North Holland), Ch. 7.
Johnson, H. G. (1971), 'The Keynesian Revolution and the Monetarist Counter-Revolution', The Richard T. Ely Lecture at the 1970 Meetings of the American Economic Association, *American Economic Review*, LXI, No. 2 (May), pp.1–14.
Johnson, H. G. (1975), *Technology and Economic Interdependence*. London: Macmillan (for the Trade Policy Research Centre).
Lewis, W. A. (1949), *Economic Survey 1919–39* (London: George Allen and Unwin), Ch. XIII, esp. p. 185.
Patinkin, D. (1969), 'The Chicago Tradition, The Quantity Theory, and Friedman', *Journal of Money, Credit and Banking*, I, No. 1 (February), pp. 46–70.
Patinkin, D. (1974), Keynesian Monetary Theory and the Cambridge School', in H. G. Johnson and A. R. Nobay eds. *Issues in Monetary Economics* (London: Oxford University Press), pp.1–30.
Reuber, G. L. and Scott, A. D. (1977), 'Harry Gordon Johnson, 1923–1977', *Canadian Journal of Economics*, X, No. 4 (November), pp. 670–677.
Shils, E. (1977), 'Harry Johnson', *Encounter* (November).
Tobin, J. (1980), 'Harry Gordon Johnson, 1923-1977', *Proceedings of the British Academy*, LXIV.

PART 1

Chapter One

INTERNATIONAL ECONOMIC ORDER: RULES, CO-OPERATION AND SOVEREIGNTY*

Jan Tumlir

> (International monetary reform must be) a movement to-
> ward greater responsibility toward the system as a whole on
> the part of the major countries concerned. Such a movement
> would have to be based on reciprocal understanding both of
> the system and of the position of the nations in it, and on the
> abandonment of nationalistic rivalries expressed in the pur-
> suit of mercantilist policies within the framework of the
> system. Harry G. Johnson, *On Economics and Society*,
> pp. 264–65.

C. P. KINDLEBERGER believes that for order in international economic
relations to exist, one country must assume the leadership function.
This happens to be true for the international socialist order, but
Kindleberger makes it a general proposition. Harry Johnson, on the
other hand, believed the liberal order to be a joint responsibility of the
countries composing it, the responsibility of each positively, though
perhaps only loosely, related to its size, and each having a proper
understanding of the nature of that order and of its own position in it.
He was increasingly sceptical as to whether the required degree of
understanding could exist among those on which that order depends,
the national governments and their electorates. Let me then talk, in
his memory, about the possibility of international order.

   We note how, as order declines, the calls for co-operation become

---

* I am grateful to Robert Aliber, Gerhard Bebr, Frieder Roessler and Larry
Sjaastad for helping to clarify my ideas on the issues discussed here. The views
are of course my own and in no way implicate these discussants or the GATT
Secretariat.

more strident and desperate. But 'co-operation' is a large word, and one of my questions is: What kind of co-operation, if any, do we need, and can realistically hope for, to maintain order?

There is also a widespread belief that the nation-state 'is about through' as an economic policy-making unit. Strangely, the governing establishments support this view by theorizing about the 'ungovernability' of contemporary democratic societies.[1] (To which Bertolt Brecht might have said: The governments have given their societies a vote of no-confidence. So now, presumably, they will elect themselves new societies.) My second question therefore is: Can we realistically expect supra- or international sovereignty(ies) to replace the increasingly ineffective national economic decision making?

Finally, I will indicate what seems to me a more realistic solution and a more likely development.

The Nature of Economic Order

An oblique definition of order must suffice for an opening. The conditions of economic activity are in constant flux. Rates of population growth, capital accumulation and technical change differ between countries and are changing within each. As the world economy grows, patterns of demand change, new sources of supply emerge, availability of certain materials may decline and substitutes must be developed. It is in the unceasing, uncontrollable, and sometimes radical change that human societies seek some overall stability; and such stability as they may hope for can only be attained through prompt adjustment by the economic agents affected to each manifestation of change. Attempts to block, postpone or slow down the adjustment – in the illusion that it is possible to avoid the social and political strains which it implies – only make the society and economy more vulnerable to the ongoing changes and set the stage for more violent instability later on. Such attempts are also the main – if not the sole – source of international friction. We can thus say, simply, that economic order exists when the required adjustments can proceed unobstructed.

To equate order with unobstructed adjustment has some interesting implications. I am thereby saying that we cannot imagine international order in any form that would not be essentially liberal. For only where economic activity is carried on by competing independent units can adjustment be sufficiently prompt, smooth and efficient for the world economy to remain in a state of order. This is so for several reasons.

The price system which such competition creates is a forward-

2

looking information device. As a rule, it informs about changes sufficiently far ahead so that the necessary adjustment to them can be gradual. At the same time it enforces the adjustment to the changes about which it informs. Competition forces large numbers of units to search simultaneously, but independently, for the best method of adjusting; and it ensures that any mistakes made in the process will be quickly revealed and appopriate consequences drawn from them. In these two ways, an effective learning process is maintained. Another advantage of the system based on competitive enterprise is that it tends to keep mistakes encapsulated or at any rate minimizes the possibility of their cumulation.

Only large organized groups, and government itself, have the power to obstruct adjustment – not to avoid it indefinitely, only to make it discontinuous, lumpy and costly. The adjustment costs thus caused flow from two main sources. One is the lack of adequate information due to the impairment of the price system. International repercussions of using the power to obstruct are the other, and they compound the costs from the former source.

In general, the efforts to block adjustment focus on preventing a given price (which may, in some cases, be the international price of national money) from rising or falling. As the efforts multiply, they progressively impair the information function of the price system. Both Adam Smith and Alfred Marshall used the metaphor of a watch to express the intricate nature of social economy. Yet the mechanistic metaphor may be misleading. A market economy is more of an organism evolved to cope with errors, and robust enough to take a lot of punishment. It is only when the price system is set aside that an economy begins to resemble a mechanism of enormous intricacy – one that does not operate automatically but requires an absolutely precise direction. But without market prices, that direction can only proceed on the basis of estimates of physical quantities which will be needed and available in the future (*not*, it is important to note, *demanded* and *supplied*). The number of widely varying recent forecasts of oil availability in 1985 indicates the degree of precision that can be expected in this respect. Education policy furnishes an even more graphic example. It is said to be a function of the government to see to it that the economy obtains the appropriate mix of skills. Can anybody (or any body) know what skills will be needed in what quantities five and ten years hence (or, for that matter, in six months)? All we can say is that *any* mix of skills is 'appropriate' as long as those skills are appropriately priced.

Relations between states are seldom analysed from the viewpoint

3

of adjustment and resistance to change. In particular, the theoretical work on socialist and other planning systems (and even most theories of macro-economic stabilization, from *The General Theory* until very recently) have paid virtually no attention to the international matrix. Socialism is an international movement *par excellence*; yet what has never been shown is how independent democratic socialist countries would plan their economic life including trade among themselves (since autarky is prohibitively costly) and still live in peace together. Such planning may work for a group of socialist economies surrounded by large, freely operating markets; for a group of economies, moreover, among which one is dominant and maintains discipline (exercises leadership function). Is it possible, however, to imagine a world socialist order? (Or, for that matter, a world of 'organized liberal trade'? The first question is, always: Who will do the organizing?)

Schumpeter's (or, before him, Lange's) 'proof' that rational economic calculation would be possible even with a central authority setting an arbitrary pattern of relative prices for consumer goods amounts to very little.[2] The planning of new investments would have to take the trade situation into account, and the evolution of the national patterns of relative prices would again come to be determined by the world market. Thus all the problems with which we are familiar would reappear. But where the authority wanted to *maintain* control over the domestic price structure (let alone over income distribution or industrial structure), a foreign trade plan would be necessary. And since foreign trade consists of a multitude of bilateral transactions, the plan could not be decided unilaterally. It would have to be negotiated; and in a world of sovereign socialist countries, there would have to be a multilateral negotiation of a world trade plan. The paradoxical result of this would be that the planning of national production (at least in the tradeable goods sector), through which the society had intended to liberate itself from the blind forces of the market, would become subject to international negotiation. We may well ask how long such a negotiation would take, in how co-operative a spirit it would be conducted and how costly it would be in terms of the uncertainty prevailing while it lasted.

The Nature of the Rules

The foregoing already indicates the nature of the rules on which international economic order depends. They are of two different kinds. There is, first, municipal law which makes possible the functioning of the markets; then there are the international rules regulating the con-

4

duct of public policy. These are predominantly in the nature of negative ordinances, specifying what governments are not to do lest economic relations between independent units in different countries, the true international co-operation, be unduly disturbed. In short, the purpose of these rules is to minimize governmental interference with the adjustment process. In this largely negative way the international rules define the legitimate rights of states within the order, in much the same way as national law defines individual rights. According to the classical conception of international law, only governments have rights and duties under the international rules, which in practice means that the rules are interpreted by diplomacy.

In general, rules increase welfare by reducing uncertainty. In an interdependent world, national policies interact and the effects that one society expects from a given policy may be offset, or transformed, by a given policy of another country. International rules proscribing certain types of policies, and prescribing others in specified situations, are a condition of effective policy planning by each participant in exactly the same way that municipal law constraining individual conduct makes foresight and planning possible for individuals.[3] The preoccupation of numerous economists in the past decade or so with the (ill-defined) concept of adjustment cost has given rise to the view that international rules entail costs for the nations complying with them.[4] The most important aspects of international order can best be explained by analysing this view.

The notion of cost implies that there exists some benefit, some welfare increment, which a society could secure if certain policies were not ruled out. Most economic objectives of governments can be attained by a number of alternative policies, and it is obvious that voluntarily accepted rules could not proscribe policies which were efficient in relation to legitimate objectives. Free trade is efficient, and where a society wants to protect an industry, the tariff is an efficient instrument. Quantitative restrictions, a third-best policy, are banned. Monetary policy and, perhaps, exchange rate policy, is the efficient means of dealing with an external imbalance. But capital controls and trade restrictions are inefficient in this context, and frowned upon. International rules cannot be considered costly because they constrain countries to use policies which are first-best even from the national viewpoint.

Furthermore, where a government may hope to gain something by pursuing a policy which the rules proscribe, the gain is always highly conditional. The hope of it is predicated on the usually implicit free-riding assumption that the government would be alone in using the proscribed policy – everybody else behaving in the way the rules were intended to promote. Here we are at the essence of law. The most general function of rules, international as well as municipal – indeed, the main reason why societies develop and enforce rules – is to prevent beggar-thy-neighbour conduct which might tempt individuals but would leave everybody worse off if generalized.

The parallel between municipal and international rules breaks down in one important respect. An individual infringing a municipal law may benefit if he is not caught. For a society, by contrast, which is the 'individual' of the international order, getting away with an infraction brings no corresponding gain. If only sub-optimal policies are proscribed by the international rules, it follows that only a subgroup can benefit from its government breaking a rule – at the cost, mainly, of the rest of the society. Here we can generalize the monoply theorem according to which the loss to society always exceeds the monopolist's gain. So also the costs of a government's interference with the market, when undertaken in defiance of international rules, always exceed the gain of the group on whose behalf the government intervened. International rules thus can be seen to protect the interests – one would like to say rights – of societies as wholes, as well as the position of governments against organized pressure groups. In this way, they protect the very authority and legitimacy of governments.

The ideal rules would be *comprehensive* (precluding the substitution for the proscribed policy of an equivalent one, 'legal' only by virtue of not being specifically mentioned by the rule), *general* and *abstract* (uniformly valid for all countries and all future instances) yet *precise* (clearly describing the context or situation to which the rule applies). They would be, it must be understood, designed not to maximize some cosmopolitan welfare in ways requiring sacrifices from individual countries but, primarily, so as to enable (and, why not, sometimes force) each country to effectively pursue long-term welfare-maximizing policies of its own. The ideal is, of course, unattainable; and the degree to which it can be approached differs from one policy area to another. The rules of trade policy approach it relatively closely. They regulate discrete government decisions (for example, periodic changes in levels of protection) which determine conditions of specific activities, affect particular groups, influence particular choices (for example, between domestic and foreign goods). The results of these decisions are, in the main, predictable on the basis of micro-economic analysis, an area of scholarly or scientific endeavour with two centuries of continuous development, cumulative accrual of knowledge, behind it. Monetary policy, on the other hand, is a continuous government activity, perhaps more 'proper' to the government than commercial policy in that it affects all decisions and all units in the economy without much possibility of discriminating (targeting its effects on particular areas). For a long time, international monetary policy was conducted – on the whole satisfactorily – with one rule only : maintain convertibility. The interwar period of monetary chaos was followed by almost a quarter century of stability based on a system of fairly detailed rules as to exchange market intervention, automatic and conditional credit transfers, and parity changes. Together, these rules effectively governed domestic monetary policies. Since 1973 international monetary policy rules have been so few, so far between, and so vague that it is difficult to speak of a system of rules. The reason for it is that in this area it has become unclear what optimizing behaviour is, and the relevant theory is undergoing repairs. In contrast to micro-economics, the development of macro-economic theory has been discontinuous. What in the 1930's and 1940's appeared a revolution, we are now discovering to have been much less. The recovery from a revolutionary illusion may take some time.

Co-operation

The word 'co-operation' has been sorely overworked in international economics of the post-World War II period. In those areas where governments act as organizations for the supply of particular public goods such as defence or pollution control, co-operation is unproblematic – it is a means of securing economies of scale. Problems with the concept arise in those areas where governments preside over an open-ended order to which no particular purpose can be ascribed except to enable individuals to effectively pursue purposes of their own.

The central problem concerns the relation between co-operation on the one hand and rules, or rule-oriented conduct, on the other. A number of alternatives is conceivable.

'Co-operation instead of rules' is often intended, but cannot work. Governments must at least agree on some very general principles indicating what they can rightfully expect from one another. Principles of this kind – non-interference in domestic affairs, for example – require interpretation in particular situations. Without more specific guidance, one can still imagine co-operation in the form of an active concern to avoid clashes. Such co-operation, however, can hardly be sustained for more than short periods, unless the breathing space which it provides is used to develop more specific rules.

7

This leads to another alternative: 'co-operation as willingness to negotiate rules'. It poses the least difficulty of all. In 1932, an international conference in Stresa concluded that 'decisions touching upon monetary policy belong exclusively to the sovereignty of each country'.[5] Barely ten years later the leading countries were willing to negotiate detailed sets of rules to constrain their sovereign decisions not only on monetary but also on trade (and hence domestic industrial) policy. That was indeed a significant if not revolutionary change.

A third alternative is, then, 'co-operation through observance of agreed rules'. The rules negotiated in the 1940's were certainly not perfect, but they were workable; and it would seem that given such rules, co-operation in this sense and in that of the preceding paragraph should have been secured. Yet today, decisions touching on monetary policy are in most countries again a matter of virtually unconstrained, though hotly contested, national sovereignty; and the rules of trade are being steadily eroded. What has gone wrong?

It is simply not enough to say that co-operation consists in observing common rules. The notion of a general rule implies the notion of an impartial authority to interpret it in specific situations. Sovereign democracies, subject to moods as all of them are, cannot interpret international rules co-operatively. Appeals to co-operation will be made in order to solicit agreement to a more permissive interpretation. 'They are not co-operative enough to see how hard it is for us to obey the rule in this particular situation.' Co-operative rule interpretation in this context amounts to giving the pickpocket and the man without his wallet an equal say in determining what the statute against theft was intended to convey.

This situation points to a fourth alternative, 'co-operation over and above the rules'. To ask a country to show its co-operativeness by doing more than observing common rules – by not insisting, for example, that another country observe a rule in a particular instance – is asking for favours. Co-operation as an exchange of favours might perhaps be sustainable among countries of equal power. In that case, favours granted and received might cancel out in the long run, leaving the underlying rules of the order intact. But countries being large and small, asymmetries must generate precedents; and 'co-operation' of this kind will ultimately destroy the rules.

The lesson to be drawn is this. Sovereign countries can agree – usually after some calamitous breakdown in mutual relations – on a set of enlightened rules to minimize conflicts among themselves and expeditiously to settle those that nonetheless remain. Being sovereign and democratic, however, they find it impossible to subject themselves to an independent authority adjudicating conflicts under these rules, and, in the long haul, they are equally unable to interpret and develop the rules co-operatively. The post-World War II order failed because it failed to provide for an authoritative interpretation of its rules.

International Sovereignty
This analysis of the notion and experience of international economic co-operation appears to lend some strength to the not uncommon view that the nation state is no longer effective as a unit of economic organization and policy making. It is increasingly believed that both national and international stability now require the cession of at least some economic policy functions to international authorities.

There are two main views as to the kind of authority needed. They differ in their respective conception of sovereignty.

Sovereignty can be conceived of as the power to create law, general and abstract in nature, ordering or making compatible the spontaneous behaviour of individuals. This is the concept on which European integration was launched. The European Community has provided for the essential institution lacking in the international order at large : authoritative interpretation of the rules. The provisions of the Treaty of Rome have become part of municipal law creating not only rights and obligations for governments but also rights for private persons. New law of the same kind is being created by the regulations and directives of the Council and the Commission. The Court of Justice of the European Communities controls both the legality of these acts and the interpretation of the European law by national courts. For the first time since the Middle Ages, sovereign governments are subjecting their societies to laws, the creation and interpretation of which they do not fully control.

The Treaty of Rome can thus be viewed as a constitution substantially limiting the economic policy-making powers of member governments. Through its provisions on trade and competition it effectively rules out those would-be predatory economic policies which in the past repeatedly led to conflicts of a particularly dangerous nature. Numerous conflicts remain, of course, but they are not dangerous, most of them being conflicts of opinion rather than 'vital interest'.

This legal or judicial approach to international integration is not, however, a promising model for global application. The alternative can be characterized as the executive approach. It informs, for

9

example, Sir Andrew Shonfield's model of European integration in which the governments of the Six have come together to control jointly what none could control individually.[6] The concept of sovereignty underlying this view emphasizes power in the direct sense: power directly to shape an economic system and control its results in the form of particular structures and distribution of activities and incomes. The supranational sovereignties envisaged in this approach are in the nature of international regulatory agencies.

The belief that national sovereignty is the root of international evil, and that the world's salvation lies in one global executive sovereignty (to be attained, perhaps, through several transnational ones), is generally considered a noble belief. There is at its core an elitist conviction, however, which I find demonstrably wrong and personally repellent. It says, in effect, that the mass of people are stupid – short-sighted as to their own interest and blind as to the legitimate interest of others; but that there is, in each people, an intellectual aristocracy which knows exactly which international policies will ensure peace and prosperity everywhere and, given the power, will institute them. The question is not really how to select the best individuals and secure for them the necessary power. No more than a superficial acquaintance with the problems, a shallow culture, is needed to see that no such elite and no such knowledge exist. In matters of peace and international prosperity we are still, and cannot but continue, learning how to cope, by experimentation, observing each other's mistakes. The progress of mankind is directly related to the number of mistakes it can make and from which it can learn. With one global sovereignty we would be limited to one big mistake at a time.[7]

Take, as an example, an international monetary authority whose functions could be defined either modestly as co-ordination and surveillance or ambitiously as those of a full-scale world central bank. Even for its modest functions, some criteria and guidelines derived from theoretical analysis would be indispensable. Let me briefly review what we do not know about the international monetary system we have, to suggest the likelihood of such guidelines becoming available in the near future.

Starting from the most general considerations, there is the unsettled question as to what causes exchange rates to move and what are the consequences of their movement. We are witnessing a contest of two theories, one emphasizing the exchange rate as an instrument of adjustment, the other relegating it to a symptom of the momentary state of the credit markets. Next, at the intermediate level of theoretical-empirical knowledge, we do not know the parameters and the lags. Thus we have no way of knowing what the equilibrium rate is at any moment; nor, indeed, what it was *ex post*. We do not know what effect central bank interventions have, whether they stabilize or only attract more funds into the market. Finally, we know little of what is actually happening beyond the movement of bilateral rates, for when we want to know how a currency fares against all others, we are up against the index number problem. What can international surveillance, co-ordination – or co-operation for that matter – mean in the face of this ignorance?

A world central bank issuing a single world currency would not, of course, face these problems. But economic opinion, if not equally groping in the dark, is at least clearly split in assessing first, the feasibility and, second, the welfare effects of this arrangement. Would there be the necessary trust in the decisions of an international agency not controlled by national governments given, for example, the wide differences of view on the harmfulness of inflation? The distribution of seignorage income would create clashing interests, especially if there existed the possibility of augmenting seignorage income by an inflation tax. The latter problem could be eliminated if it were agreed that maintaining a stable price level should be the sole and unconditional objective of the new institution. But with such an agreement among governments, a world central bank would hardly be necessary.

The intellectual fault of the executive approach to world integration can be summarized as follows. No matter how the international regulatory agencies arrived at their policies, most of them could not be executed directly. Execution would largely devolve on national administrations; and the error lies in believing that a policy which is essentially in the national interest but cannot be implemented by a national government will become politically feasible when it comes down as a decision of an international authority. A few exceptional instances can be thought of but they are makeshift in nature, cannot evolve into a reliable routine. In the long run, the national executive cannot be more effective as an agent of an international body than it would be if it were merely carrying out precise instructions of a national representative assembly whose preceding discussion would have demonstrated to the public the necessity, hence national interest, of the policy in question. The error involved here is one of believing that there are objectively 'right' policies which can be designed by engineers – that policies are effective or ineffective by virtue of their internal 'scientific' correctness, independently of what those affected by them think. That policies, in short, can be made without politics.

11

Self-Executing International Order

Even those demanding a world government tomorrow would probably agree that the judicial approach to it is more promising than the executive one. The central issue in the former, we have seen, is the arrangement for an authoritative interpretation of the rules. The experience is that rules binding governments only are interpreted by governments only. The International Court of Justice in the Hague, in its splendid isolation and majestic calm, is a monument to this discouraging truth.

The European integration model creating general laws which confer rights on private persons is too radical to represent a global solution. I do not mean that the world is not yet ripe for a good thing. It might not be a good thing for a world of many cultures, for two reasons. Below a certain level of detail, uniform laws would produce different results in different countries. One legislative assembly could not differentiate; one supreme court could not assemble the detailed, indeed intimate and even instinctive knowledge needed for judicious application and interpretation of the laws in different cultural contexts. There are optimum jurisdiction areas, even more clearly delineated than optimum monetary areas. The second reason has already been discussed. To the economist, a world structured into sovereignties is a competitive market in political ideas. Mankind cannot forego the arrangement promoting multiple search for solutions, experimentation, encapsulation of errors, and thus safeguarding the possibility of nations learning from each other.

The optimal solution must fall short of legal uniformity, and it seems eminently feasible. Nothing prevents governments, which continue to profess their desire for international discipline, from making an increased and increasing use of the legal device known as 'self-executing treaty provision'.[8] It consists in formulating the international commitments a government assumes in such a way that private persons derive rights from them. To give an example, Article 95 of the Rome Treaty and Article III of the GATT are practically identical as to their purpose, substantive content and even wording. Article 95 (1) of the Treaty states:

A Member State shall not impose, directly or indirectly, on the products of the other Member States any internal charges of any kind in excess of those applied directly or indirectly to like domestic products.

Article III (2) of the GATT provides:

12

The products of the territory of any contracting party shall not be subject, directly or indirectly, to internal taxes or other internal charges of any kind in excess of those applied, directly or indirectly, to like domestic products.

Under the former article, private persons can sue transgressing governments in the national courts of the Community countries. Under the latter, which is a conventional international treaty binding governments only and including no self-executing provisions, private suits are ruled out.[9] It can be seen that formulating an international commitment as a self-executing treaty provision represents the ultimate guarantee one government can give to another that it will honour the obligation. Society itself enforces the commitment on the government. National courts provide the authoritative interpretation of the obligation or the rule.

For the European Community, building a common legal system, uniform interpretation, application and efficacy of Community rules by national courts, has been of utmost importance – hence the need for the European Court of Justice. In normal economic relations among sovereign countries, however, legal uniformity is of low value; indeed, differences in national law can, by enhancing choice, have a positive value. What is much more important for firms engaged in international transactions is that the interpretation of the rules in each country be consistent over time. It has been the traditional function of national courts to provide this kind of predictability.

This is not a plea for specifying the rules of the international order in one grand treaty, the administration of which could then be turned over to national courts. It is an indication of a line of development which can be only gradual but which seems to me both logical and inevitable.[10] Even so, the opposition to the idea of providing more effective international rules through self-executing treaty provisions will be formidable. It will combine all those who conceive of sovereignty in the traditional sense of power to manage and control for, admittedly, self-executing treaty provisions severely constrain governments' room for manoeuvre. I wonder, however, how many people would, on reflection, go along with what seems to be the main assumption of contemporary economic diplomacy, namely, that the more options a government can keep open, the better it secures the welfare of its society. The freedom of action enjoyed by governments and the freedom of their citizens are not simply additive. If they were, why would so many societies feel the need for written constitutions? Why

13

indeed should so many governments now yearn for the lost discipline of fixed exchange rates?

To believe, as we did until recently, that governments' responsibility for the economy, their control of it, and their size relative to it, must continue to grow according to some preordained and inexorable law, is to violate logic. Not only are such over-extended governments bound to lose control domestically but, as I have tried to show, there is no way for them to co-operate, indeed to co-exist peacefully, in an interdependent world. It is to return to governments such control as they can effectively exercise that we need a more authoritative interpretation of international rules.

NOTES

1. See, for example, Crozier, Huntington and Watanuki, *The Crisis of Democracy*, Report on the Governability of Democracies to the Trilateral Commission (New York: New York University Press, 1975).

2. J. A. Schumpeter, *Capitalism, Socialism and Democracy* (New York: Harper & Bros., 1947), Chapter XVI.

3. For an extended treatment of these points, see R. Z. Aliber, 'Monetary Rules and Monetary Reform' in the volume (which he edited) *The Political Economy of Monetary Reform* (Montclair, N. H., Universe Books, 1977).

4. Usually, these costs are only indirectly attributed to rules, being considered rather the costs of interdependence (which has, of course, developed on the basis of rules). For references to this view see my *National Interest and International Order* (London, Trade Policy Research Centre, 178), ft. 16. Aliber, in the essay quoted above, attributes costs (borne by some countries only) directly to the rules.

5. Quoted by J. Viner, *International Economics*, (Glencoe, Ill, The Free Press, 1951), p. 193.

6. See his *Europe: Journey to an Unknown Destination* (Penguin Books, 1973), p. 14.

7. 'It is certainly more important that anything can be tried by somebody than that all can do the same thing.' F. A. Hayek, *The Constitution of Liberty* (The University of Chicago Press, 1960), p. 32.

8. The following discussion draws on G. Bebr, 'Directly Applicable Provisions of Community Law: The Development of a Community Concept', *The International and Comparative Law Quarterly*, April 1970, pp. 257–298. See also R. E. Hudec, *Adjudication of International Trade Disputes*, (London Trade Policy Research Centre, 1978), pp. 82–86.

9. Lawyers might rightly object to this drastic simplification. For some of the complexities, see J. H. Jackson, *World Trade and the Law of GATT* (Indianapolis, Ind., Bobbs-Merrill Co., 1969), pp. 106–108. Some GATT articles are considered self-executing by the courts of several countries; Article III, for example (with some minor exceptions) is so considered in Italy.

10. Many contemporary proposals for domestic reform aim in the same direction, expressing a preference for fixed rules and formal procedures over administrative discretion. One can mention here Friedman's monetary rule, Buchanan's con-

JAN TUMLIR

tinuing elaboration of the concept of 'fiscal constitution', and the recent political
moves in the United States to constrain quantitatively government spending and/or
taxing power. An extended, and excellent, general treatment of the issue is
T. J. Lowi's *The End of Liberalism* (New York, W. W. Norton & Co., 1969), an
analysis of a policy process in which decisions are bargained between individual
interest groups and the government, contrasted with 'rule of law by administrative
formality'. One of Lowi's key recommendations is: 'Encourage a more open
admi nistrative process and a closer approximation to real agency rule-making
by provisions in the law which would make possible group and taxpayer suits
enjoining agencies from further operation until they can provide the constitutional
basis and rule upon which a decision or a line of decisions is being made. The legal
notion of show cause is most profoundly needed in the relationship between
government and citizen'. ('Interest Groups and the Consent to Govern: Getting
the People Out, For What?', *Annals of the American Academy of Political and Social
Science*, June 1974, p. 99.)

Chapter Two

IS INTERNATIONAL CO-ORDINATION
OF NATIONAL ECONOMIC POLICIES NECESSARY?*

Ryutaro Komiya

WITHIN THE WORLD economy today, national economies are closely linked with one another, and a country's economic policies to cope with inflation, unemployment and trade and payments imbalance often have important consequences for other countries. In particular, economic policies adopted by the government of a major industrialized country have significant effects, both favourable and unfavourable, not only on neighbouring smaller economies but also on other major economies and hence on the course of the world economy. Thus, international co-ordination of national economic policies, particularly among major industrialized countries, has recently become an urgent issue.

In the later 1970's, strong inflationary pressures in some major economies and prolonged stagnation of domestic effective demand in some others resulted in the persistence of large payments imbalances despite floating exchange rates. This is said to have made it more difficult for deficit countries to improve their unemployment and inflation situations by their own efforts alone. The trends of economic performance among major economies have apparently tended to diverge. It is not surprising that in these circumstances countries are more and more frequently complaining about and criticizing other countries' economic policies which are thought to have unfavourable effects upon their economies or upon the world economy at large. International tension with respect to macroeconomic, trade and balance of payments policies appears to have increased substantially.

* Some of the themes developed in this paper were first set out in an article by the author and Miyako Suda published in *Nihon Keizai Shimbun*, October 31 and November 1, 1977, and another, *idem* February 6, 1978 (both in Japanese).

To cope with this situation, it is necessary for major countries to establish a set of rational rules which should govern the international effort to co-ordinate national economic policies. But such a set of rules has not yet been well established, and at present ad hoc approaches to co-ordination and arbitrary arguments seem to prevail, and national economic policies remain largely unco-ordinated. Unless participating countries more or less agree upon the rules of the game for international co-ordination, even a well-meant attempt may be resisted or even resented by individual countries which feel prejudiced by such an attempt, and is likely to be unworkable.

The purpose of this paper is to refute certain arguments for international co-ordination of national macroeconomic policies advocated by some officials of major governments and international organizations as well as by some policy oriented economists outside government. Specifically, I propose to consider the issue in terms of the so-called 'assignment problem' in the theory of economic policy, and ask: to what extent is international co-ordination of macroeconomic policies necessary and possible?

The paper first considers some basic points to be taken into account in developing the rules applicable to attempts at international co-ordination of economic policies in the conditions prevailing today.

1 Targets and Instruments

In discussing the rules of international co-ordination of national economic policies, the two principal macroeconomic policy objectives or targets for each country struggling with inflation, unemployment and payments imbalance may conveniently be summarized as:

(1) full employment and price stability, and

(2) overall balance-of-payments equilibrium. In addition,

(3) a reasonable degree of stability of employment in individual sectors

may need to be taken into account as a third objective subsidiary to the first two.

The first of these three objectives perhaps needs no explanation. As to the second, I consider that overall balance-of-payments equilibrium, in the sense of approximate equality of receipts from and payments to foreign countries for the country as a whole (excluding the transactions of the monetary and foreign exchange authorities), rather than the balance on current or on trade account, is of fundamental importance, for reasons to be discussed later. The third objective is concerned with a situation in which unemployment in a particular industry rises abruptly as a result of a sudden increase

17

in imports competing with its products[1]. The government may wish to help the industry in question maintain a higher level of employment than would prevail without assistance over a transitional period during which efforts for industrial restructuring and resource reallocation are made.

Now it is a well-known proposition in the theory of economic policy that when there are a number of policy targets to be achieved simultaneously, generally speaking there must be at least as many policy instruments as targets. Only in an exceptional case are all the policy objectives achieved by using a smaller number of instruments than the number of objectives (Tinbergen, 1952).

Since each country in an international economy must pursue the above three major objectives, each country must have at least as many effective policy instruments. This is the first point of fundamental importance that I wish to emphasize.

An obvious qualification to the above general rule arises from the fact that when there are n countries there are only (n–1) independent balances of payments. It is inappropriate for each country to set its balance of payments target, or to make decisions on the balance of payment policies, without due regard to their impact on other countries.

The second point I wish to emphasize is that the problem must be considered as an 'assignment problem'. When there are plural policy targets and at least as many policy instruments, one must solve the problem of how to use each of these instruments in relation to each target. When, in addition, the structure of the economic system is not known precisely, the 'system works best if variables (policy instruments) respond to the markets (policy objectives) on which they exert the most direct influence' (Mundell, 1968, p. 169). In other words, the system of economic policy works most effectively when for each policy objectives one selects an instrument (or instruments) which exerts the most direct influence, and 'assigns' that instrument to it. This principle, named by its author Robert Mundell (1968) as 'the principle of effective market classification', is highly relevant to the problem of international co-ordination of macroeconomic policies, since it essentially addresses the problem of how to achieve plural interrelated policy objectives simultaneously with the use of plural instruments.

2 *Sovereignty and International Co-ordination*
When attempting to co-ordinate economic policies among major industrialized countries it is important to distinguish between those

areas which are by and large to be left in the hands of individual governments and those in which actions of individual governments need to be more or less co-ordinated or restrained internationally. Matters related to international trade, tariffs and other barriers to trade, the balance of payments, exchange rates and international investment obviously belong to the second category.

The distinction cannot be a clear one, since policy actions in the former areas often have important international consequences. Yet certain matters have traditionally been considered as primarily domestic affairs for which each country as a sovereign state has exclusive responsibility. Under normal circumstances it is not advisable for outsiders, whether another state or a multilateral body, to put strong pressure on a national government to take a particular action with regard to such domestic affairs.

In the second category, on the other hand, efforts to harmonize actions of individual governments have long resulted in international agreements and multilateral organizations. It is most important that the governments of major countries fully respect the existing international agreements when attempting to co-ordinate economic policies among themselves.

3 *Policies towards Full Employment and Price Stability*

Decisions related to the first of the two principle policy objectives of national economic policies given above, namely full employment and price stability, should be considered as essentially domestic affairs of individual countries, in my view.

First, decisions to set national targets for the rate of growth of real GNP or the rate of unemployment in a particular year or over the medium term should be relegated to individual countries. It would be highly useful for major countries to exchange information and views on these matters. When determining its own targets each country should take into account other countries' targets and probable international repercussions of its own actions. But they should not try to put pressure on a particular country so as to change its target rate of growth or of inflation in the interest of the international community. These targets should be regarded as a matter lying outside the domain of international co-ordination.

This is because the national preference as between full employment (or growth rate) and price stability differs from country to country, and each nation is entitled to choose its own domestic targets according to its own preference, so long as it does not give inconvenience to other countries.

19

Moreover, these targets are often subject to political and social constraints within the country. Suppose, for example, that the target rate of growth of a particular major country, say the German Federal Republic or Japan, is viewed by other governments as too low and that the latter wish the former government to raise it. Fear of possible resurgence of inflation in the country in question may be so strong and prevalent that the government risks losing the next election if it proposes more expansionary fiscal and monetary policies.

Or there may be an influential political party as well as public opinion which is strongly opposed to higher public debt as a source of government finance, and the political fact that such an opinion cannot be ignored may set an upper limit to an annual increase in public expenditure.

On the other hand, a country's rate of inflation may be considered too high by others, and the rate of depreciation of its currency resulting from that rate of inflation as unacceptably fast from an international point of view. But its government and public opinion may give priority to a reduction in unemployment in the immediate short run over a reduction in the inflation rate, and in that case there may be no combination of policy instruments which brings about an inflation rate and a degree of stability in the exchange rate acceptable to other countries.

Or looking from the outside, a country's high rate of inflation may appear to result mainly from its government's lenient attitude towards the labour unions which demand unreasonably big wage increases. But the government in question may not be able to take the political risk of open confrontation with the powerful unions.

Political and social factors such as these may be crucial considerations in determining national macroeconomic targets. In a democratic society the government cannot be expected to pursue in the interest of the international community policies which are unpopular at home and therefore likely to weaken its political position.

Second, the appropriate instruments to be used to achieve each country's target rates of growth, unemployment and inflation are its own macroeconomic policy weapons, of which the most important are fiscal and monetary measures. This is a straightforward application of the 'assignment' principle. Since especially under the floating exchange rate system fiscal and monetary policies of a country exert the most direct and powerful impact upon its own employment and price levels, each country should rely primarily on its own fiscal and monetary policies in order to attain its growth, employment and price targets. It is not within the scope of the present paper to discuss what kind of policy measures are to be used by individual countries for the above purpose. Readers are referred to a report (OECD, 1979) of an OECD expert group in which I participated[2].

When each country sets its targets for growth of real GNP, unemployment and inflation, the figures may differ substantially among countries. But the difference in the targets itself should not give rise to an international difficulty. For example, it is possible that the target rate of inflation in the GNP deflator over the medium term be 3 per cent in one country and 7 per cent in another, and that inflation does not accelerate beyond the target rate in either country. Then the latter country's currency would depreciate at an annual rate of 4 per cent in relation to the former's, and its nominal short-term interest rate would be higher by 4 per cent. So long as inflation is non-accelerating the situation contains nothing inherently unstable or destabilizing, or detrimental to international trade and investment.

Similarly, the target rate of unemployment may differ substantially between countries, reflecting the difference in the voters' preference as well as differences in employment practices and customs. There is nothing in this situation to worry about from an international point of view, provided that such a difference in targets does not give rise to balance-of-payments difficulties.

In short, in the broad area of demand management policies, both target setting and implementation of policies to achieve them cannot but proceed on a country-by-country basis. It is unrealistic at this stage to try to adjust, from an international point of view, an individual country's growth, employment and inflation targets, or to request it to apply its fiscal and monetary policies to promote the interests of the international community at the expense of its own interests.

Also, in the area of macroeconomic policy, it is advisable to maintain a degree of decentralization, as in many other fields. Within the world economy, international co-ordination generally means centralization of decision making, and is likely to increase the danger of synchronization of booms and recessions among countries.

4 Balance-of-Payments Policies

Since the balance of payments is obviously an international affair, policy targets in the area of the balance of payments cannot be left entirely in the hands of individual countries pursuing their respective national interests. Here it is important that each country aim, as a first approximation, at an equilibrium in its overall balance of payments. In other words, the policy target of each country should be

21

approximate equality of international payments and receipts. This is a target which is compatible internationally. So long as each country aims at an approximate balance of overall payments and receipts, there will be no further need to co-ordinate balance-of-payments targets among countries.

For major countries the chief instrument to be 'assigned' to balance-of-payments equilibrium is the (floating) exchange rate. If the government of a country avoids intervening in the foreign exchange market strongly in either direction and lets its exchange rate move flexibly under the influence of market forces, then total payments will be approximately equal to total receipts over a period of weeks or a few months. I am not necessarily advocating a completely laissez-faire policy in the area of foreign exchange and balance of payments, but the recent experience of major countries in this area seems to indicate that there are only a few reasons for which active intervention in the exchange market or rigid exchange controls can be justified.

First, it may be desirable, if possible, to smooth out fluctuations in the rate over a period of, say, several weeks to a couple of months, by means of official intervention in the foreign exchange market. But the exchange rate between any two currencies cannot be confined within a narrow band over an extended period, so long as each country's central bank pursues independent monetary policies.

An attempt to stabilize the exchange rate over an extended period is likely to generate intolerably large purchases or sales of foreign exchange. This is incompatible with balance-of-payments equilibrium. Any attempt to diminish fluctuations in the exchange rate must satisfy the condition that over a short period the amounts of official selling and buying be approximately equal, or else that net selling or buying be equal to an amount agreed upon beforehand by other countries concerned. Otherwise, the latter will rightly complain that the government in question is pursuing a balance-of-payments target which is unacceptable to the international community.

Market expectation of the future exchange rate often changes abruptly as a result of a shift in factors affecting the balance of payments, and when it does a fairly large change in the exchange rate is unavoidable. If the government intervenes in such a situation to slow down the speed of adjustment, it must buy or sell large amounts of foreign exchange until the adjustment in the exchange rate is completed. Such prolonged one-directional intervention intended to slow down the speed of exchange-rate adjustment is bound to result in an ex-post disequilibrium in the balance of payments, and serves no useful purpose.

22

Second, an exception to the above rule is government intervention for the purpose of correcting the external portfolio and indebtedness position of the national economy as a whole. For a non-key-currency country one of the motives for holding foreign assets, especially liquid ones, is precautionary, namely to use them to maintain the level of imports when there is an adverse movement in the country's terms of trade or when its exports decline as a result of some unexpected event. From the same 'financial prudence' point of view it is not advisable for a country to be too heavily indebted at short term in a normal, non-emergency situation. Hence the government may wish to steer the portfolio and indebtedness position of the country as a whole towards some sort of optimal position. For this purpose, the government may change its own holding of liquid foreign assets (official reserves) and/or influence the portfolio and borrowing behaviour of the private sector. This is very similar to stockpiling of foods, oil or certain raw materials for security reasons. But since the action of a major government for the above purpose is likely to affect exchange rates substantially, and to have a considerable impact on other countries, such actions need to be co-ordinated internationally.

Third, although I am not dogmatically opposed to all types of exchange control under any circumstances, I am sceptical about the usefulness of most exchange controls currently in force for balance-of-payments purposes, as far as major developed countries are concerned. As a result of liberalization of trade and long-term capital movements – especially direct investment – enterprises in these countries operate more and more on a world-wide basis. They are bound to own assets and claims and owe obligations in different countries, both denominated in a variety of currencies and with maturity of varying length. When exchange rates are floated, management of claims and obligations denominated in different currencies for such enterprises is very similar to portfolio selection for an investment fund; the manager must try to find an optimal combination of various assets and debts taking into account the expected yields or interest costs, the risks attributable to each type of asset or debt, and the cost of converting one type into another. In an international economy in which a large number of such enterprises operate, it is by and large meaningless to try to stop a certain type of financial flow between countries or to prohibit a certain type of financial transactions which is considered as 'speculation', while leaving current account transactions as well as direct investment liberalized.

If one defines exchange speculation as the activity of willingly taking exchange risks in the hope of making pecuniary gains from it, any enterprise operating internationally today has to speculate extensively as a part of its ordinary business. This is because it is often impossible or too costly to cover all the exchange risks in which it is involved. If the government attempts to maintain the exchange rate at a level much different from that dictated by expectations prevalent in the market, then leads and lags alone could give rise to a large swing in the official reserves whether or not some form of exchange 'speculation' is prohibited.

In other words, so long as we wish to keep trade and investment basically liberalized, and so long as each country wishes to maintain its own central bank, there seems to exist no better alternative to letting exchange rates move freely under the impact of market forces, without much government intervention or exchange control. In this way, the balance-of-payments problem is readily solved. It may lead to uncomfortably large swings in the exchange rate, but this is a cost, so to speak, of liberalizing trade and investment and of having independent central banks. Moreover, floating does not seem to have discouraged international as compared with domestic trade and investment.

5 *Safeguard Against a Sudden Increase in Imports*
The policy instrument to be 'assigned' to the third objective, namely maintenance of a degree of stability of employment in individual sectors, especially in the face of a sudden increase in imports competing with the products of a particular industry, is that of safeguard mechanisms temporarily restricting the trade flow in question, combined with adjustment assistance to the industry affected to encourage restructuring and resource reallocation.

I will not go into this specialized subject in this paper. I wish to emphasize, however, that import restriction for the above purpose should be allowed only on a temporary, and preferably non-discriminatory, basis for as short a period as possible consistent with industrial restructuring policy, if the free, multilateral world trade system is to be preserved.

6 *Bilateral or Overall Trade Balance as Target*
Some readers may find nothing new in the above argument, and may think what has been proposed is no more than simple common sense. But current thinking on international co-ordination of economic policies often deviates from the general principles outlined. In the following I will take up some of the current arguments which are in conflict with the principles proposed here.

In recent bilateral and multilateral discussions of economic policy co-ordination, the bilateral or overall trade balance has often been the subject of attention, as something on which internationally co-ordinated action is supposedly required.

(i) In a bilateral trade relation, a country having a large deficit on bilateral trade account often complains about it, and requests its trading partner to reduce the deficit by increasing imports. This is an unreasonable mercantilist request, however. Members of GATT ought to follow the principle of free, multilateral, nondiscriminatory trade, and it is in no way unnatural or undesirable for a particular bilateral trade surplus to accompany a large deficit within the free multilateral trade system.

(ii) Attention is sometimes paid to the overall trade balance. A country having a large deficit on merchandise account often wants to 'improve' its trade balance, and one having a large trade surplus is urged by others to reduce it. From a balance-of-payments or macro-economic policy point of view, there is no reason to distinguish between visible and invisible trade, and it is more meaningful to look at the balance of payments on current account rather than just the visible trade balance.

7 Balance on Current Account as Target

Recent discussion of international policy co-ordination has quite often focused on the size of the balance of payments on current account of individual countries. Specifically, the so-called 'stronger' countries having a large surplus on the current account, such as the Federal Republic of Germany and Japan, are urged by others to take effective measures to reduce the current account surplus. This amounts to regarding the size of the current account balance as a major target of macroeconomic policy. The 'stronger' countries are requested by others to revise the target rate of growth upwards and to stimulate domestic demand by expansionary fiscal and monetary policies in order to reduce the current account balance.

The argument put forward by those who attach great importance to the current account balance may be summarized as follows. In the present stagflation situation the change in the current account balance has a direct effect on the size of unemployment in each country. An improvement in the current balance has a positive multiplier effect on GNP in the same way as an expansion in domestic investment or in government expenditure. Therefore, a country having a surplus on the current account is thought of as 'exporting' unemployment at the expense of other countries having a current account deficit. Thus the current account surplus of the former increases the burden of the latter in their struggle with stagflation. This is unfair; the burden of unemployment must be borne equitably, so that countries with large current account surpluses must reduce it and bring the current account into an approximate balance as soon as possible.

The above argument represents, in my view, an erroneous solution to the macroeconomic assignment problem under consideration. As explained earlier, in order to attain whatever the level of employment each country desires, it must use its own fiscal, monetary or other measures. Each country's policy instruments should be assigned to each country's target for employment.

The reason why balance-of-payments equilibrium is regarded as the macroeconomic policy objective of primary importance is that a prolonged deficit eventually puts a country into a position in which it cannot make unrestricted payments to other countries, and hence has to place undesirable restrictions on international trade and investment *for balance-of-payments reasons*. On the other hand, persistent surplus, particularly of a major country, is unacceptable from an international point of view since it generally means that some other country's balance of payments is in persistent deficit. It is also undesirable from a national point of view, since accumulating unnecessarily large liquid reserves is wasteful investment of national resources. At any rate, equilibrium in the balance of payments is sought for by each country, solely because by maintaining it the country can get along without unwanted restrictions on free, multilateral international trade and investment.

When one views the balance-of-payments problem in this perspective, it should be obvious that not much importance can be attached to the equality of payments and receipts within a particular category of transactions, such as current account transactions or visible trade. What is important is that the country always remain reasonably liquid and ready for any international transaction which has merit of its own.

The Articles of Agreement of the International Monetary Fund as recently amended explicitly state in Article IV that 'the essential purpose of the international monetary system is to provide a framework that facilitates the exchange of goods, services *and capital* among countries'. The IMF's *Surveillance over Exchange Rate Policies*, which deals with the implementation of Article IV and came into effect simultaneously with the amended Articles of Agreement, is based upon the idea that a member country's exchange rate must be such as to bring about an overall equilibrium in the balance of payments which reflects 'underlying economic and financial conditions including factors affecting competitiveness *and long-term capital movements*' (italics supplied).

In the IMF Agreement, in IMF Executive Decisions or in any other international agreement currently in force, there is no clause which calls for a balance on current account transactions, nor one which attaches special importance to the current account balance.

On the other hand, it should also be obvious that a government must not manipulate the balance of payments for purposes other than maintaining the Country's international liquidity. Since the balance of payments and the exchange rate are an international, not a purely national, affair, it is unfair for a country to further its national interests at the expense of other countries through manipulating its balance of payments or exchange rates. Thus the IMF's *Surveillance over Exchange Rate Policies* states that 'a member shall avoid manipulating exchange rates or the international monetary system in order to prevent effective balance-of-payments adjustment or to gain an unfair competitive advantage over other members'.

A policy of maintaining the exchange rate artificially undervalued under managed floating, which leads to a large current account surplus and is sometimes called beggar-my-neighbour policy, is clearly improper in the light of the *Surveillance*. But it is possible that underlying market forces are such that a large capital outflow out of a country, especially of a long-term nature, persists, and that its current account therefore develops a large surplus corresponding to the capital account deficit without the government intervening in the foreign exchange market persistently in one direction or otherwise manipulating the exchange rate or the balance of payments. Such a state of a country's balance of payments should be considered perfectly acceptable to the international community.

It may well be difficult, or indeed impossible, for a country to achieve a particular target for the current account, such as equality of payments and receipts or a deficit of a particular amount, unless its government 'manipulates exchange rates in order to prevent effective balance of payments adjustment,' or 'introduces for balance of payments purposes of restriction on, or incentives for, the inflow or outflow of capital.'[3] Under the floating rate system, in the absence of active government intervention the overall balance of payments including both the current and capital accounts is brought into equilibrium, and there is no mechanism within the market system which works to bring the current account alone into equilibrium.

8 *Sharing the Burden of Oil Deficits*

It is sometimes argued that the basic principle set forth in the previous section cannot be applied in the present world payments situation, since it is an abnormal emergency situation in which the OPEC countries as a whole are running a large current-account surplus, and hence many other countries slid into severe and prolonged payments difficulties. The size of the 'oil surplus' resulting from the quadrupling of the oil price, although diminishing much faster than expected at first, still amounts in the late 1970's to thirty to forty billion dollars annually. This means roughly that the current-account balances of all developed countries and non-oil-producing developing countries add up to a total deficit of approximately the same size. Since many of the non-oil-producing developing countries and some of the 'weaker' developed countries have already accumulated debts to an unacceptably high level, they will soon find it difficult to finance current account deficits through further borrowings.

Hence the major developed countries, especially the 'stronger' ones with better payments records and international credit standing, must 'share the burden of the oil deficits' – the counterpart of the current-account surplus of the OPEC countries together. In other words, 'stronger' countries should develop current-account deficits which add up to thirty to forty billion dollars annually, allocated appropriately among them. Thus the target for the current-account balance of a 'stronger' major developed country must be set at a sizeable negative figure, in order to relieve the balance-of-payments difficulties of the 'weaker' developed countries and non-oil-producing developing countries.

This argument is based, in my opinion, upon a wrong view of the role of finance in an economy. Whether in a national economy or in an international economy, there always exist surplus financial units which save more than they invest and deficit ones which invest more than save. The basic function of the financial system is to play the role of intermediary between surplus and deficit units, and to transfer the surplus funds of the former to the latter's use. In addition to simply transferring the funds, the financial system changes the maturity structure of the funds supplied from the surplus units before channelling them to the deficit units. In particular, one of the functions of the financial system is to change short-term funds supplied to it into long-term funds offered by it.

From a financial point of view, the emergence of the OPEC countries as very substantial surplus units posed two fundamental problems for the world economy. First, it meant a decline in effective demand, since a major part of the funds used to purchase oil is absorbed into the 'oil surplus' and is not spent on goods and services. To cope with this problem, each country should establish a target for its own growth rate or employment and 'assign' its demand management policy to achieve it, as stated earlier. The existence of the oil surplus makes this national task more difficult, but the oil surplus must be taken for granted as a datum for the policy-making of each country as there is no other way out.

Second, the surplus funds of the OPEC countries must be channelled to deficit financial units. It is desirable that a considerable part of these funds be transformed into long-term funds through the international financial market, making it possible for deficit units to borrow and invest the funds on a long-term basis.

The international financial market mechanism seems to have functioned remarkably well since the emergence of the 'oil surplus'. The oil surplus has been 'recycled' quite smoothly, perhaps much better than expected immediately after the oil crisis.

Those who argue that the burden of the oil deficit of a given size must be shared by 'stronger' non-OPEC countries seems to ignore the facts that OPEC or other countries with a surplus on current account have no choice but to acquire whatever assets are available on international financial markets or to lend the surplus directly to borrowers, and that under the floating system the oil deficit is allocated among countries primarily by the working of market forces. By 'the working of market forces' is meant those factors which influence and determine the demand and supply of goods and services as well as financial assets.

In principle, there is no reason to worry about the 'sharing' of the oil deficit among countries, just as there is no reason within a country to worry about the 'sharing' among deficit financial units of the total deficit which is a counterpart of the total surplus of the household sector. This is not to deny that some companies, local governments or countries may go bankrupt by borrowing beyond a reasonable limit. The fact that there may exist such financially unsound units does not lead, however, to the necessity of a plan to share the 'burden' of a given total deficit in either a national economy or an international economy.

9 The 'Locomotive' Approach

In view of the divergent trends in economic performance among major countries, it has been argued that the 'stronger' countries which have already overcome severe inflation and the balance-of-payments difficulties following the oil crisis should play the role of a locomotive to pull the 'weaker' countries and the world economy out of depression. This is the so-called 'locomotive' or 'engine-countries' approach. The Federal Republic of Germany, Japan and the United States, or the former two, are singled out as engine countries. A 'convoy approach' which argues for a joint effort of moving together, with the 'stronger' countries leading and escorting the 'weaker' ones, seems to be based upon essentially the same idea.

This argument is not acceptable, in my view, as a basis for international co-ordination, since it again represents an erroneous 'assignment' solution to the macroeconomic policy problem. The engine-countries approach or the convoy approach implies that there are two types of countries: the locomotive countries to pull and the passenger or frieght-car countries to be pulled, or the warships to lead and escort and the transports to be escorted. In other words, the 'stronger' countries are expected to take expansionary measures not (only) for their own domestic reason but in order to help the 'weaker' countries get out of depression.

But, as discussed earlier, each country should use its own demand management policy to attain its own employment and growth targets. The notion that a country can rely upon some other country's expansionary measures in order to attain its own employment or inflation target is a typical example of a wrong way of assigning policy instruments to policy targets.

Each country is trying to move along a 'narrow path' back towards higher employment and a lower inflation rate: if the expansion of demand is too fast there is a danger of rekindling inflationary expectations, and if it is too slow the economy may slide back into deep depression. Each country should set the pace of recovery at a rate which makes it possible to return progressively to a reasonably high level of employment and at the same time to wind down inflationary expectations. In view of the difficulties encountered in moving forward within its own 'narrow path', it is not surprising that each country finds little room for adjusting employment and price targets upwards or downwards, in order to help other countries.

Moreover, the favourable 'cross' effect of a country's expansionary measures upon another country's employment is usually very small; it is much smaller than the 'own' effect of the latter country's expansionary measures on its own employment, even between neighbouring countries closely related to each other. This is more so under the floating than under the fixed exchange rate system.

It is sometimes argued that a 'weaker' country which suffers from a high rate of unemployment may find it difficult to take expansionary measures because these will accelerate domestic inflation and worsen the balance of payments which is already in heavy deficit, or lead to further depreciation of its currency, thus again adding to inflationary pressures. If, on the other hand, some 'stronger' countries take expansionary measures, this will have favourable effects both on employment and on the balance of payments of the 'weaker' country and moreover will reduce inflationary pressures within it through appreciation of its currency. So again, it is argued, the 'stronger' countries should play the role of an engine to help the 'weaker'.

It may be pointed out, however, first, that while it may be convenient from the weaker countries' point of view to have the stronger countries expand demand sufficiently to help the former, the latter may be simply unable to do so, for their own domestic economic and political reasons. In a world economy consisting of sovereign democratic states it is asking too much to request one state to use its demand management policy for the purpose of achieving another's employment and inflation targets.

Second, the above argument seems to contain some misunderstanding about the working of the fixed and floating rate systems. Consider an international economy consisting of two countries A and B. Under the floating system a favourable 'cross' effect of A's expansion on B's employment level – which is normally much smaller than the 'own' effect even under the fixed rate system – is diminished by appreciation of B's currency. If it appreciates to such an extent that the current-account balance between the two remains unchanged, then there will be no favourable effect on B's employment. B enjoys a favourable effect on prices, but not one on employment. On the other hand, under the fixed-rate system there is no favourable price effect, and, moreover, if B cannot take expansionary measures by itself for fear that it will accelerate inflation, then any favourable effect on B's employment of A's expansionary measures will have the same unfavourable inflationary effect as B's own expansionary measures.

Thus under managed floating, which is a sort of compromise between the fixed rate system and pure flexibility, the benefits which the 'weaker' countries enjoy in the form of favourable effects on employment, the balance of payments and prices when the 'stronger' countries take expansionary measures are likely to be rather narrowly circumscribed.

To overcome world-wide stagflation, it is essential that each country, whether a stronger one or a weaker one, set its growth, employment and inflation targets appropriately and use the policy instru-

31

ments at its disposal to achieve them. The extent to which the stronger countries can help the weaker seems to be limited in a world consisting of sovereign, democratic states.

10 *Summary*

International co-ordination of national economic policies, particularly among major industrialized countries, which has recently become an urgent issue, should be viewed as an 'assignment problem' of applying plural policy instruments properly to achieve plural policy objectives. Also, it is important to distinguish between those matters which are to be left in the hands of individual governments and those which need to be co-ordinated internationally. Decisions to set national targets for rates of economic growth, unemployment and inflation should be regarded as a matter lying outside the domain of international co-ordination, since they depend crucially on domestic political and social factors with which other governments or a multilateral body are not familiar, and the latter are not responsible for the political consequences of choosing a particular set of targets. The policy instruments to be assigned to each country's targets for growth, employment and inflation are its own macroeconomic instruments, of which the most important are fiscal and monetary measures, since especially under the floating exchange rate system they exert the most direct and powerful influence on the targets in question. On the other hand, balance-of-payments equilibrium, another major macroeconomic target, should be attained primarily by letting the exchange rate move flexibly under the influence of market forces affecting both current and capital account transactions.

Viewed in this perspective it should be obvious that one cannot attach any importance, in international co-ordination, to the bilateral or overall trade balance or to the balance of payments on current account. These balances are not to be considered as targets which need to be co-ordinated. Only the overall balance of payments matters. This position is the only one consistent with the amended Articles of Agreement of IMF and its *Surveillance over Exchange Rate Policies*.

The argument that the burden of oil deficits of a given size must be shared by the major developed countries is based upon a wrong view of the role of finance in an economy, and is not acceptable as a basis for international co-ordination. Another argument, the so-called locomotive-countries approach, or a convoy approach, is not acceptable either, as it represents a wrong solution to the international macroeconomic assignment problem.

RYUTARO KOMIYA

NOTES

1. Such a situation could arise whether the overall balance of payments is in deficit or not.
2. It might be argued that fiscal and monetary policies alone are not sufficient to achieve the growth, employment and price targets. Even so, each country should find additional policy instruments which it can use effectively. It should be obvious that a country cannot rely upon other countries' policy instruments to achieve its own targets.
3. Quotations from IMF, *Surveillance over Exchange Rate Policies*.

REFERENCES

Mundell, Robert A. (1968), *International Economics*, New York: Macmillan, 1968.
OECD (1977), *Towards Full Employment and Price Stability*, A Report to the OECD by a Group of Independent Experts, Paris: OECD, June 1977.
Timbergen, Jan (1952), *On the Theory of Economic Policy*, Amsterdam: North Holland Pub. Co., 1952, Rev. ed., 1956.

A COMMENT ON PROFESSOR KOMIYA'S PAPER

A. Boltho

PROFESSOR KOMIYA has given us a very well argued defence of national sovereignty and the virtues of free floating. His arguments lead him to discard the current balance of payments as a policy target, to dismiss 'locomotive' theories for world expansion and, in fact, virtually to do away with international co-ordination of economic policies. One can have considerable sympathy for a thesis which firmly places responsibility for domestic economic management in the hands of democratically elected governments and lets the balance of payments be determined by the free flow of demand and supply of foreign exchange – provided, however, that one can trust the foreign exchange market to do the job properly and domestic governments (which are now free, at least in theory, from external constraints), to respond to exchange rate changes in ways which maintain total output growing at target rates.

The experience over the years 1975–78, particularly in Europe, casts some doubt on the validity of both these suppositions. Exchange markets have behaved unpredictably, forward exchange rates have provided little guide to spot developments and the short- to medium-term impacts of depreciations and appreciations upon trade flows have been disappointing. More importantly, government reactions to exchange rate changes have not necessarily been appropriate for the maintenance of the inflation/unemployment trade-offs ostensibly favoured in each country.

Let us take as an example the reactions of both 'strong' and 'weak' countries over the last few years. Assume at the outset that the 'strong' countries (say Germany, but also Japan), decide on a relatively slow growth path for fear of inflation, while the 'weak' countries (say the

34

United Kingdom and Italy), give priority to the fight against un-employment. The latter then go into incipient balance of payments deficit and their currencies depreciate. In theory, this could be the end of the story: the price mechanism should ensure a reallocation of resources towards the balance of payments, the current account should improve and growth should continue at a sufficient rate to prevent unemployment from rising. In practice, however, things seem to have moved differently. Short-run J-curve effects and the sluggish reactions of traders in the face of erratic and unpredictable exchange-rate changes (mentioned by Professor McKinnon[1]), lead to an over-shooting of the exchange rate. More important, domestic inflation responds rapidly to depreciation in countries in which real-wage re-sistance and trade-union structures are strong and inflationary ex-pectations rife. To stop accelerating inflation and a growing deficit (or a continuous depreciation), the weaker countries are forced to resort to restrictive measures (aided and abetted by the IMF). Over the medium-term, these countries will re-establish equilibrium in their balances of payments thanks mainly to the squeeze on demand, and hence at the cost of low growth and unemployment. Floating has not provided them with the freedom to chose their preferred position on the trade-off. One consequence, among others, is strong pressures in favour of protectionism.

Let us turn now to the 'strong' countries. Appreciations go beyond what was originally anticipated because of usual J-curve effects and also undue depreciations in the 'weak' countries. But more import-antly, the growth of domestic absorption decelerates as multinational investment leaves the country in view of the rise in labour costs (cfr. again McKinnon's arguments), and as domestic investment in the tradeables sector falls because of lower profit opportunities. Invest-ment in non-tradeables either does not increase at all (because many non-tradeables are supplied by the public sector), or does so only with long lags. And governments do not off set this shortfall in private absorption mainly for fear of large budget deficits. The rate of growth of the economy falls below forecast levels and external surpluses re-main high (or appreciation continues) because of the sluggishness of domestic demand.[2]

In other words, floating seems to have forced 'weak' countries to restrict demand and has, at the same time, induced deflationary effects in 'strong' countries which are not fully offset by policy action. Over the medium-term, balance of payments equilibrium may be achieved (in 1979, for instance, payments imbalances between major areas and also within Europe turned out considerably smaller than in previous years), but at the cost of much slower growth in the world economy as a whole. Floating, therefore, at least in the form in which we have seen it recently, has had an asymmetrical demand-deflationary bias. It may in addition also have had an asymmetrical price-inflationary bias if there is any truth in the Mundell–Laffer 'ratchet-hypothesis'[3]. Given governments' preoccupations with inflation and the likelihood that the latter deters rather than stimulates private demand, the depressing impact of floating on the growth of output and employment may have been compounded. There are no doubt many reasons why the world has been kept in an underemployment equilibrium since the oil crisis – floating exchange rates, contrary to expectations, may well have been one of them.

If this is so, then a 'locomotive' approach may still make sense, and not only from the point of view of the 'weaker' countries. Germany and Japan should take determined expansionary action to offset the deflationary effects of appreciations on their economies, and to help lessen the pressures for protectionism which persistent excess capacity and unemployment are inevitably strengthening in many countries. More generally, a co-ordinated approach to international demand management would seem to be inevitable in a world in which the nation-state has lost much of its sovereignty in the economic policy making area. Relatively free floating may be appropriate between the three large blocks (the United States, Western Europe and Japan), but it would not seem to correspond to the needs of a progressively more unified Europe.

NOTES
1. R. I. McKinnon, 'Exchange Rate Instability, Trade Imbalances and Monetary Policies in Japan and the United States', this volume, pp. 225–50.
2. This picture fits the experience of both Germany and Japan in recent years—cfr. the increasing direct investments made abroad by German and Japanese multinationals, the sluggishness of manufacturing investment in both countries (sluggishness which in Germany goes back to the beginning of the 1970s), or the record of over-optimistic official forecasts in the last few years.
3. A. D. Crockett and M. Goldstein, 'Inflation Under Fixed and Flexible Exchange Rates', *I.M.F. Staff Papers*, November 1976.

Chapter Three

DISTRIBUTIVE JUSTICE AND THE NEW INTERNATIONAL ORDER*

I. M. D. Little

I *Introduction*

I believe that equality of rights, and freedom from coercion, is of value even to the poorest people, if they have ever experienced them. But many socialists have argued that economic equality is a condition of equality of rights, thus linking distributive or social justice to political and legal justice. Nevertheless, so far as I am aware, a full theory of distributive justice – ironically a theory which might in principle justify great inequality – has been only recently elaborated by John Rawls. He states : 'a conception of social justice, then, is to be regarded as providing in the first instance a standard whereby the distributive aspects of the basic structure of society are to be assessed', (Rawls, 1972, page 9). A still more recent work by Robert Nozick (Nozick, 1974) challenges the view that justice has anything to do with the size distribution of income or wealth.[1] These works relate essentially to justice as between members of a state. But the new International Economic Order (NIEO) also bases its claims largely on the concept of distributive justice. Before examining these claims, I thought it of interest to consider the theories of Rawls and Nozick, and see how far they carry over to the international sphere.

II *Justice and Egalitarianism within States and Societies*

Both Rawls and Nozick start from the inviolability of human rights. Rawls makes liberty, and equality of liberty, lexicographically prior to

* I am indebted to Robert Skidelsky, A. K. Sen, and P. M. Oppenheimer for some valuable comments. Many of the issues addressed in this paper are also considered by A. K. Sen (1978), a paper I saw only after writing this. Sen provides a far more extensive bibliography than I do.

37

anything else. But his conclusions imply that it is just for the state to coerce some to aid others. Nozick denies that the state has a right to do so. It is therefore important to understand how redistributive taxation, or other restrictions on a person's liberty to do what he will with what he has or earns, can be justified within the framework of Rawlsian theory.

Rawls's first principle of justice is that 'Each person is to have an equal right to the most extensive total system of equal, basic liberties compatible with a similar system of liberty for all', and there is a 'priority rule' such that 'the principles of justice are to be ranked in lexical [= lexicographic] order and therefore liberty can be restricted only for the sake of liberty. There are two cases: (a) a less extensive liberty must strengthen the total system of liberty shared by all, and (b) a less than equal liberty must be acceptable to those citizens with the lesser liberty'.

Rawls's second principle is that social and economic inequalities are to be arranged so that they are to the greatest benefit of the least advantaged (p. 83). This is called the difference principle (there is also a second part to the principle not relevant to my argument).

These principles are claimed to result from the 'original position' in which the parties are rational, self-interested, people called upon to produce the principles of justice. They operate behind 'a veil of ignorance', which means that they do not know their own position in society, nor their own preferences or abilities. I shall refer to them as the 'veiled participants'. Each is assumed to try to maximize the minimum outcome for himself, in accordance with the maximin principle of game theory choice under uncertainty. I shall not add to the considerable criticism which has been directed at this assumption about how rational people would actually behave if put into a situation which would make them perfectly impartial. Given this assumption, Rawls can derive principles which he claims to be normative, since he regards them as rules for the design of just social institutions.

The first principle of justice makes it clear that basic liberties cannot be arbitrarily circumscribed. But are property rights, including the right not to have property (which includes earnings) removed for the benefit of others, among the basic liberties? Rawls lists the basic liberties as 'political liberty (the right to vote and be eligible for public office) together with the freedom of speech and assembly; liberty of conscience and freedom of thought; freedom of the person along with the right to hold (personal) property; and freedom from arbitrary arrest and seizure as defined by the rule of law' (page 61). But evidently this right to hold personal property does not exclude the state's right to take some of it away to give to others. For Rawls's 'distributive branch' of government is there 'to preserve approximate justice in distributive shares by means of taxation and the necessary adjustments in the rights of property' (page 277). For many people, there may seem to be no difficulty in arguing that the state is justified in restricting some persons' rights for the sake of material benefits to others. But Rawls's lexicographic principle puts him into the position of either defining some rights as non-basic and therefore tradeable in the above sense, or else of justifying restrictions of property rights by the priority rule.

Property rights are fundamental to the proper working of any state. But it might be argued that they are created by the state, and are not 'basic', i.e. 'natural'. As against this, it seems that they are fundamental to any known society; people generally have some belongings even in the most communist communes, and also in the most natural of all social units, the family. Furthermore, it is difficult to draw a clear line between personal rights and property rights. My right to my hand is not morally very different from another man's right to his artificial hand. And what about a pacemaker? As against this, the difficulty of defining boundaries cannot be taken as a compelling argument against drawing distinctions.

I have found no guidance from Rawls on this point. I shall assume that restriction of property rights must be justified by the priority rule, and therefore ask whether either case of the priority rule can be held to justify redistributive taxation.

Under the first case, the total system of liberty must be strengthened. In defining liberty, Rawls does not count poverty as a constraint. A person's liberty is not constrained by his purchasing power; although the value of his liberty is (page 204). Where then do we find the increase in liberty which offsets the various restrictions on spending their gross income (or dealing with their gross wealth) which are placed on the rich?

It might be argued that redistributive taxation is necessary to hold society together, and the system of liberty would certainly suffer if it broke down. Rawls does indeed justify his principles on grounds of stability. He connects stability with 'publicity' (page 177). Publicity is one of the 'constraints of the concept of right' (page 130 f.). The concept of right is prior to the original position in that it constrains the deliberations of the veiled participants. They must choose principles for a *public* conception of justice. 'They suppose that everyone will know about these principles all that he would know if their acceptance were the result of an agreement. Thus the general awareness of their universal acceptance should have desirable effects and support the stability of social co-operation' (page 133). One could read this as saying that the desirability of designing cohesive principles does not spring from veiled maximin logic, but is an imposed injunction. But this may be an incorrect reading. Knowing, despite his veil, the laws of social psychology, each participant may alternatively argue that anyone who is going to be rich in the society he votes for must be coerced to aid the poor, because otherwise the poor may upset the applecart, thus reducing the total system of basic liberties, and he would not choose to be an apple in so unstable a cart. This sounds to me more like expediency than justice.

Under the second case of the priority rule, we have to suppose that all the veiled participants accept the restriction of property rights, and that the subsequent actual rich are therefore deemed to have contracted in. Thus Rawls writes: 'then having chosen a conception of justice, we can suppose that they are to choose a constitution and a legislature to enact laws, and so on, all in accordance with the principles of justice initially agreed upon. Our social situation is such that by this sequence of hypothetical agreements we would have contracted into the general system of rules which defines it' (page 13). This, which recalls Rousseau, might seem to be a recipe for an overbearing state to those lovers of liberty who would find the notion of a hypothetical 'contracting in' a monstrous pretence.

This brings one to Nozick. His preface begins with the resounding sentence: 'Individuals have rights, and there are things no person or group may do to them (without violating their rights). So strong and far reaching are these rights that they raise the question of what, if anything, the State and its officials may do' (page ix). His answer to that question is 'very little', and this very little certainly excludes redistributive taxation, or any interference with property rights. He rejects the idea that different patterns of distribution can or need be justified. Any end-state is just if it is arrived at by just historical processes. These include taking possession of anything that was not scarce, and transfers by gift or exchange contract. Only holdings thus acquired are entitled. A distribution is just if everyone is entitled to their holdings under it. Unjust distributions can arise only by unjust acquisition of holdings. Redistribution is just only if it 'rectifies' such unjust distributions – e.g. undoes the results of aggressive acquisition in the past (page 151).

This constructive theory is accompanied by a destructive attack on any end-state conception of justice, including that of Rawls. One of Nozick's powerful arguments is that any just distribution, as perceived by any end-state theory, can and will be upset by transactions which the parties are entitled to make, that is by just transactions. The preservation of the particular pattern of a just end-state distribution (supposing that such a concept makes sense) requires continuous intervention by the state, and a continuous infringement of people's rights. In principle, any gift, except to the most disadvantaged, made in a state which is just by Rawlsian standards is necessarily unjust. Gifts, I suppose should then be outlawed, if that were possible.

With Nozick gifts present no problem. Anyone is entitled to make a gift. Furthermore, in certain circumstances, people ought to give. There is no reason in Nozick's philosophy why a person should not regard one distribution as better than another, although neither is unjust. If so, it could certainly be argued that he ought to bring about an appropriate redistribution in so far as he can. The obligation may be especially strong where there is a special relationship, e.g. a family relationship, between the donor and potential recipient. There is also no reason why non-familial redistributive communities should not be formed within a state, such as Kibbutzim, provided persons are not coerced to join them and are free to leave them (it is too difficult to leave a state – even one without a wall, or exchange controls). Such a community could establish a right for its members to receive their basic needs.

I think I have said enough to show the essential similarities and differences between Nozick and Rawls. While both proclaim the priority of rights, Rawls theorizes that the concept of justice requires the supposition that people have traded away many rights for the sake of not risking relative or perhaps absolute deprivation; all, in fact, except the basic rights (and here I have failed to find the principle which separates basic rights from others). Nozick stands much firmer on rights. These are the natural rights of Locke – ' "no one ought to harm another in his life, health, liberty or possessions". Some persons transgress these bounds "invading others' rights and . . . doing hurt to one another" and in response people may defend themselves or others against such invaders of rights' (page 10). For the sake of security, people transfer to a minimum state most of their rights of defence and punishment. There is nothing else they can transfer. The state is a protective association with monopoly powers, but these powers 'are merely the sum of the individual rights that its members or clients transfer' (page 89). Thus people cannot, it appears, create new rights for the state when they create a constitution. This would inevitably transgress against the rights of members. The state is being created to protect people against immoral aggression against their rights. A

41

state with powers to transgress the rights of innocent people would be perpetrating the moral crime it is being created to prevent. Everything in Nozick follows, I think, from this.

Rawls and Nozick are, however, united in opposition to utilitarianism. I suppose most economists are rather unthinking utilitarians. When pressed, they would perhaps admit that some rights are inviolable, and that it is unsatisfactory and implausible to derive the inviolability of all rights from utilitarianism itself. But then why not maximize (average?) utility subject to some moral side constraints? Unless combined with the assumption that all persons have the same utility functions, this still produces inegalitarian and possibly unacceptable results, as A. K. Sen has emphasized. (Sen 1973, pages 15–18). Thus imagine two persons with equal real wealth, but one is physically or mentally handicapped in such a way that the marginal utility of money is lower for him.[2] Then the utilitarian takes money from the cripple and gives it to the robust fellow, which is anti-egalitarian and possibly wrong. Perhaps economists slide over this difficulty, tending to forget it, because they think in terms of representative men, who do have the same utility functions. But this will not do either, at least in rich societies, because the poor are precisely the old and the sick, or have other atypical disadvantages. In other words, the above 'difficult' case may be typical.

Brian Barry makes the same point forcibly against Rawls, whose maximin principle is made to apply to a representative person of the most disadvantaged class, somehow but quite broadly defined. (Barry, 1973, pages 49–51). Why should not the veiled participant want to guard against his turning out to be a manic-depressive cripple? Rawls does not seem to see this as a problem, since he regards the laws of justice as applying only to the basic structure of society. A counter-view is that justice is essentially a matter of human detail, and that a theory of justice must be able to deal with these atypical cases which nevertheless abound.

Even in cases where it seems legitimate to think in terms of averages – the general shape of the distribution – it may be asked (as Nozick does – page 204 ff) whether one can be comfortable with a macro-theory which produces nonsense at the micro-level. In other words, can one be comfortable with a theory that produces institutions which are fair as between similar people, but which also produce unacceptable guidance in dealing with particular cases. If one does not see this as an objection, then the case of the cripple is also no objection to utilitarianism. Moreover, given a broad sweep – and rough justice – utilitarianism by quantitative aggregation produces more plausible results than Rawls. Who would not want to benefit 99 per cent of Indians by 100 Rs a year per head, at the cost of further impoverishing the poorest 1 one cent by 1 rupee?

I can only conclude from all this that there is no acceptable theory of justice. It seems to me that Rawls's theory has been seriously undermined. The entitlement theory of Nozick (which he admits is underdeveloped) is very appealing in many ways; but for most people it produces, I think, unacceptable results. Most people would probably think that some liberties can be *justly* curtailed if the material gain for the poor is great enough. Or am I wrong about this? Those in doubt should read his Chapter 10 – entitled (to use the mot juste) 'A framework for Utopia'.

III *Inter-state and World Distributive Justice*
  (1) The Applicability of Political Philosophy.

Despite the doubts about Rawlsian theory, it is worth asking whether it could be applied beyond the state. His veiled participants are already members of some society. Provided one can conceive of a society of states, there is no reason why one should not imagine that the veiled participants represent states, without knowing, of course, which state. Rawls does indeed adopt this device and argues that 'justice between states is determined by the principles that would be chosen in the original position so interpreted'. (page 378). Without further argument, he simply goes on to say that the principles of self-determination, self-defence, forming defensive alliances, and respecting treaties, would emerge. He makes no attempt to apply the difference principle. Why not? A veiled participant would know that he might be an Indian. Since he is assumed to want to apply the maximin principle within a state, why not also between states? Brian Barry asks the same question, again forcibly (Barry, Chapter 12). I suppose Rawls assumed that international society has insufficient institutions with insufficient powers for it to make sense to talk about *distributive* justice between just states. (Justice, he says, is the first virtue of social institutions.) The veiled participants are not allowed to start designing a world state which could impose an international income tax. Justice presupposes a society. There is, as it were, enough of an international society for some rules of justice, but not enough for rules of distributive justice. It is also worth noting that it appears to be impossible to apply Rawls's priority rule internationally. This implies that property rights cannot be regarded as 'basic' if the Rawlsian system is to work internationally, since the restriction of basic liberties can be justified only by application of the priority rule.

We could also imagine that the veiled participants were designing the world, without it being presupposed that they were representatives of states. The whole world order would then be in question. Perhaps they would opt for empires, not nation-states. I will not pursue this deviant thought ! In any case, if it is true that the states of the world do not form enough of a society for Rawls to apply his concept of distributive justice to them, it would also seem that human beings in the world at large cannot be regarded as forming enough of a society either.

Nozick would, I presume, attach no meaning to inter-minimal-state distributive justice. But his philosophy leaves room for considering the world distribution, because individuals' entitlements have nothing to do with states. The distribution of world income is unjust, in so far as property was obtained by aggression or fraud in the past. Nozick could thus agree with the claim that aid should be considered as (inadequate) reparations for unjust colonial expropriations and exploitation; this being the USSR line on aid. How this should be assessed, and who exactly should pay, I do not know. Nor is it even clear who should receive. The case of Latin America would, for instance, be peculiar, for most Latin Americans have little Indian blood. Nozick calls this the principle of rectification, but himself raises many more questions as to how just rectification could be carried out than he gives answers. No good theory of justice can, presumably, be as inapplicable as this seems to be.

Nozick also has two particular criticisms of Rawlsian arguments, which may throw a faint glimmer of light onto the international stage. He takes issue with Rawls's claim that the increase in production resulting from social co-operation creates the problem of distributive justice. He imagines ten Robinson Crusoes, some richer than others, whether because they work harder, or are cleverer, or have chanced to land on better islands. They suddenly discover each other. Nozick suggests that the poor might make claims on the rich in the name of justice, although there is, and has been, no social co-operation. A theory of justice would then be needed, Nozick suggests, to show that these claims are without merit. He has furthermore provided such a theory. But it seems to me that Rawls could argue that the claims were without merit on the grounds that the ten Crusoes in no way constituted a society, and that justice presupposes a society. This might be the reason why the claims lacked merit, and not that the Crusoes were entitled to their holdings, and that no one's entitlement can be justly removed.

Rawls's also seeks to show that well-endowed people (who are coerced to aid the poor) have no cause for complaint. They need the co-operation of the poor. He writes 'we can ask for the willing co-operation of everyone only if the terms of the scheme are reasonable. The difference principle, then, seems to be a fair basis on which those better endowed could expect others to collaborate with them ...' (page 15). Nozick correctly remarks that the 'then' in this sentence is mysterious. We can imagine two Crusoes with, respectively, incomes of 10 and 2. Then they are given an amnesia drug, and veils of ignorance. On Rawls's principles they might proceed to set up a nation state and constitution, which gave the better endowed Crusoe 8 and the worse endowed Crusoe 7 (allowing a 25 per cent gain from the division of labour). Would this be fair? One would have thought that Rawls must answer 'yes', because the new situation has emerged from his veil of ignorance, etc. But he cannot say, as he does, that it is a fair division of the spoils of co-operation, for this is appealing to the outcome of an historical process, as a result of which one lost 2 and the other won 5. What would happen when the effects of the amnesia drug wore off? One of them would be very unhappy that he had not remained a Crusoe.

In principle these arguments can also be related to aid and the gains from trade. The Crusoes may merely be setting up a trading-cum-aid system, not a state. Rawls's principles would then (in my opinion) result in free trade, and aid on an unimaginable scale. But, again, this could not be represented as a fair division of the gains resulting from the opening up of trade.

It seems clear that distributive justice requires a moral community, in which individuals accept at least some mutual obligations. It would be futile to say that the distribution of wealth between the wholly isolated Crusoes was unjust. Even if they formed a mere system (for the concept of a system, presupposing much less contact and assumption of obligation between members than in a society – see Bull, 1977, pages 9–15), being aware of each other and having some occasional contact, but still not entering into obligations or having any way of settling disputes etc., it would still be close to futile to talk of distributive justice. If, in such circumstances, one Crusoe made demands in the name of justice he would be presuming, perhaps hoping to create, a community which did not exist, but which, if it did exist, would perhaps recognize an obligation to aid him. We must therefore ask what sort of a community exists in the world – and perhaps what sort is embryonic if not born.

(2) Current Claims

It is clear that a society of states exists, and that many claims to interstate justice are both made and recognized. Most of interstate justice is concerned with sovereignty, with the right to conduct wars claimed to be just, with equality of treatment in international organizations and international law, and so on. This is what Professor Tucker refers to as 'the old equality' (Tucker 1977).

But claims of the Third World to transfers of resources, and to special treatment in trade, are made it least partly in the name of *distributive* justice. Nevertheless, there seems to be no doubt that the political leaders of developing countries are primarily demanding justice as between states. Many still lack confidence that their sovereignty is secure, and believe that they are excessively dependent. So they are demanding greater equality of liberties, and equality of respect. They want to be more powerful, and better able to exercise the right to defend themselves. Most of this can come only with an increase in wealth. So greater material equality is closely bound up with the aspiration to be able to play a more significant role in the world political order. This is also no doubt a large part of the reason why so much stress is put on industrialization, and why there is a lingering belief that more people is no bad thing.

We economists (including myself) are too prone to assume that a country's objective function to be maximized is the (weighted) present value of consumption per head. We know really that it is not so, but we still often forget it. Equality of states, not people, is what the NIEO is about. This is implied by the tremendous stress on sovereignty in the various NIEO declarations. For the reasons that follow, it is also implied by the fact that commodity agreemests are the most stressed of the desired economic reforms. The aim here is surely to raise commodity prices, and not merely to stabilize them. By now, many Western economists have pointed out that the poorest people in developing countries would be likely to lose by such further cartelization of world commodity trade. But such arguments seem to cut no ice in the tropics. It is true that sometimes developing country spokesmen invoke distributive justice in the name of mankind. But this, I think, has to be regarded as rhetoric if at the same time they insist, as they do, that internal equality is their own affair. One cannot convincingly say at the same time 'you have an oligation to help our poor' and 'our poor are our own concern'.

But none of the reasons produced by political philosophers as to why some should have their liberties restricted in order to benefit others apply to states. With utilitarianism, it is the utility of individuals that is the final arbiter. Utility cannot be enjoyed by states. For non-utilitarians, redistribution is justified by giving the status of a right to adequate access to the means of securing health etc. Again, it is human beings who are deemed to have such rights. Certainly, states (and other collectives) admit to moral rights and duties by seeking to justify their actions, in terms of both international law and international justice. But Nozick would clearly maintain that no state has the right to incur international obligations which require it to tax its citizens for the benefit of other states (or indeed, individuals in other states).

Many, including Rawls, would agree that the value of an individual's political and legal rights increases with his wealth. There seems to be a clear analogy in this respect between individuals and states. Formal equality in terms of international law is already granted to states; but substantive equality in the exercise of these rights demands material equality. Substantive equality would require that all states had nuclear weapons, and so were equally capable of fighting a just war. But redistribution between states on such grounds is clearly not accepted as part of international morality; which implies, of course, that the desirability of substantive equality of states in the world order is not admitted either. Not only is it not admitted. The very idea of substantive equality of states is in hopeless conflict with nation-states and the idea of self-determination. The analogy breaks down. There is normally no compelling reason why any one person should not be as wealthy as any other. But divergence of numbers is a compelling reason why the Welsh cannot be equal to the Russians.

The strongest claim I have seen to a community of states among whom distributive justice might be said to apply has been made by Professor Ali Mazrui. To quote : 'The Nuremberg trials helped to redefine aspects of morality and gave coherence to the idea of "crimes against humanity". The formation of the United Nations signified that new global institutions were needed. The anti-colonial movements in Asia and Africa heralded new triumphs for the principle of self-determination. And racism based on color all over the world found itself increasingly on the defensive. We were witnessing the birth pangs of a new international moral order. It is partly on the basis of that new moral order that we now hear demands for a new international economic order. Indeed the latter hardly makes sense without a redefinition of international morality itself. The demand for a new international order is a culmination of a quest for appropriate norms to govern relations among collectivities – a quest that goes back to the Treaty of Augsburg of 1555 and far beyond' (Bhagwati, ed. 1977, pages 373–4).

It seems to me that this passage confuses two different concepts, a universal humanistic morality and interstate morality. The Nuremberg trials were based on the concept of humankind. Since only the defeated suffered for their crimes against humanity, the trials have also to be seen as emanating from great power politics; but nevertheless the morality claimed was humanitarian and universalistic. The issue of racism is similarly based on the idea of human equality. But self-determination is concerned with the creation of nation-states (a nation being, ex ante, any community which has claims to be a state; ex post, any community whose claims have succeeded). The twentieth century idea that those particular communities which can be deemed to be nations should be self-governing can certainly be seen as a change in international morality, although, of course, this morality is overlain with the expediencies of power politics, which often determine whether a claim to nationhood is recognized. But in any case, the stress is on nations, not persons. The political rights of persons may (or may not) be better served in a world of nation-states – and this possibility may have supported the change in international morality: but distributive justice seems to have very little to do with the ideal of self-determination. It is thus difficult to see that those parts of the NIEO which are concerned with distributive justice are based even partly on the humanistic foundations cited by Mazrui. If they were, it would not be true (as it is true) that the NIEO 'hardly makes sense without a redefinition of international morality itself'.

This implied or proposed redefinition consists of a set of imperatives obliging richer states within a society of states to help poorer states, without questioning their behaviour towards their own citizens, or towards those of other countries. I can see no moral theory backing up the development of such obligations. Still less can one say that they are now accepted by the richer states. Developed countries have, of course, accepted aid targets, thereby putting themselves in a position in which they can be (rightly) berated for their failure to take their promises seriously. But what sort of obligation have they accepted? Certainly not to give regardless of the recipients' behaviour. The assumed obligation is only to transfer a certain volume of purchasing power to developing countries in general. This is no different from rich men accepting that they ought to give so much to charity, or to charitable organizations whose policies they approve. They are far from accepting any such notion as an international income tax. A state does not tax its own citizens in order to help their enemies. These transfers are essentially political, although helping the poor (or development) can enter (lexicographically?) as another objective. The preservation of peace comes before international justice, or at least has a bigger weight, if there is any conflict between the two. (On order versus justice see especially Bull, Chapter IV, and Tucker, Chapter III.)

Most Western liberals are treading a different path. Tucker refers to the 'regnant intellectual elites' and calls the movement 'the new political sensibility'. There is a continuous outpouring of books and articles which are essentially trying to arouse the conscience of people in the West towards the appalling poverty of hundreds of millions of people in the developing countries. The appeal of such books and articles is universalistic and in the name of humanity. Many liberals would claim that Western governments have a duty to support basic needs and to reduce inequality in the World. If governments do not accept this, or anyway do not fully accept it, it is because they do not dare to spend much on programmes which have little popular appeal. And that they have little popular appeal is an unfortunate fact. Sympathy depends on knowledge, contact, and familiarity. Many intellectuals, but few of the electorate, travel to developing countries. To this extent, the regnant intellectual elite seems to be appealing to a community which hardly exists. Some of the same elite try desperately to create a sense of community by stressing 'growing interdependence', a phrase that is seldom given a factual content. Some authors have expected that the concept of the Welfare State would spread outwards to embrace mankind. If anything, the opposite is happening except possibly in a very few countries. This is not surprising, for egalitarianism at home, implying high taxation, may surely be as easily competitive with as complementary to the idea of helping foreigners.

Humanitarian appeals tend to ignore many difficulties. Most particularly, they tend to ignore the fact that states (or, more strictly, the changing governments of states) come between the donor and the recipient; or else they assume that donors can impose conditions which will ensure that poverty will be reduced. If the appeal is humanitarian, there must be some assurance that the aid reaches the poor to a reasonable extent. This assurance has been undermined in recent years by exaggerated, even false, statements to the effect that the mass of the poor have gained little, or even lost, as a result of the growth of the developing countries.

The international organizations tend to fall into the same category as Western liberals. Thus the ILO submission to the World Employment Conference is entitled *Employment, Growth and Basic Needs*, with the sub-title *A One World Problem*. The delegates' accepted declaration of principles speaks of ensuring 'full employment and an adequate income to every inhabitant of this one world in the shortest possible time'. Since this can be read as implicitly going over the heads of nation-states, and carries overtones of interference with the policies of developing countries, it is not altogether surprising that the concept of basic needs has since run into criticism from a number of developing country spokesmen. A further reason is that meeting basic needs might slow down the industrialization which is almost everywhere preferred by leaders in developing countries. Mr. Macnamara has also, of course, been vociferous in his appeals to increase aid and to direct it, and development in general, towards the mass of the poor. He has spoken of 'a global compact'. Similarly the Development Assistance Committee of the OECD has endorsed the idea that basic human needs should be a central purpose of development co-operation. Making aid dependant on human rights (more or less the same basic rights as those, for example, listed by Rawls – see above) gets a still worse reception in developing countries.

Moreover, it is not only political leaders and foreign office spokesmen in developing countries who think this way. Even very westernized and liberal academics from developing countries are usually nationalists first and egalitarians second. This is not, of course, to say that they are usually unconcerned about inequalities and poverty in their own countries: but, not surprisingly, they get irritated when Westerners criticize the elites of developing countries both as self-serving and as far more interested in nationalistic objectives than in the poor. Few, I suspect, would support a compact of increased aid if it went with an effective surveillance of policies to ensure (suppose this were a possibility) that development was wide-spread and human rights respected.

A serious conflict of values has thus become evident. It has often, in the past, been argued by liberals that one of the defects of aid was that Western governments tended to impose their values on developing countries, and thus distort their development plans. The implication was that the values of developing countries should be respected. I never thought myself that this was a very serious argument: the conflict of values was exaggerated, and the fault of donors lay more in such things as aid-tying which had nothing to do with values. But now that 'the development community' is promoting the idea of redistribution, and Mr. Carter the idea of human rights, there is a serious conflict. Both equality and liberty are Western ideals; very few developing countries have embraced that of equality, and still fewer, if any, both ideals. If the DAC countries, or the World Bank, proceed very far in the direction of trying to impose redistributive policies, or refusing aid to countries whose policies do not seem to be directly poverty-regarding, conflict will surely be exacerbated.

Conclusions

What I have said and surveyed in the preceding section leads to no obvious conclusions. So I shall jump to a few.

The most serious recent efforts to define an acceptable general theory of justice having failed, one seems to be driven to echo Hedley Bull who writes '... justice is a term which can ultimately be given only some kind of private or subjective definition ... My starting point is simply that there are certain ideas or beliefs as to what justice involves in world politics, and that demands formulated in the name of these ideas play a role in the course of events' (Bull, page 78). But this does not imply that 'distributive justice' must be treated purely as an emotive term. One can at least discuss the boundaries of its legitimate use – boundaries which are changing as they have certainly changed in the past. Nozick has denied that it can simply be applied to an end distribution. I would agree with this, and always have (cf. Little 1957, pages 65–6). One cannot judge a distribution without knowing how it arises – what historical deserts and rights it satisfies. But I find it difficult to agree with him that rights cannot be watered down by the state for the sake of alleviating poverty. Not all rights, but some. Similar views are expessed in a recent paper by Deepak Lal (Lal, 1978), which examines the issue of liberty and basic needs, very rightly pointing out that in India, which contains the great majority of the world's poorest people, both ends must be served and that they may conflict.

On the international stage, the meaning and extent of community seems vital. I think the idea of justice requires a moral community. Those who appeal to the community of man seem to be going beyond what exists. One can perhaps see their efforts as trying to further the idea.

This idea, however, conflicts with the thrust of the NIEO. The international economic order is an order of states, an order with very many new members. What is being claimed, as a matter of justice, is no interference with the fullest sovereignty, equality of opportunity (e.g. that trade negotiations should in practice be fair to all states) and of equal participation in international economic decision-making. But transfers and unequal treatment (e.g. preferences) are also claimed as a matter of distributive justice. The primary desire is to strengthen the nation, and to reduce inequalities of power. (Whether

51

or not this would be conducive to world order is examined by both Bull and Tucker.)

It seems to me that few in the West would yet agree that the poverty of a state gives it a right to receive, regardless of its policies. Some want political strings, and others want to promote redistributive policies. The combination of the NIEO and the new liberal egalitarianism have produced a more serious dilemma for aid than when I wrote about it in the mid-sixties (Little, 1965).

The difficulty is that strengthening weak states, and aiding poor people, are both respectable aims. My own view is that, in the case of most countries, the poor will benefit from interstate transfers without trying to exercise major leverage on the governments' policies, and benefit enough to justify large increases in aid. I would not tell British or German citizens or politicians that poor countries have a right to receive aid. I would tell them that aid does good, despite the unjust behaviour of many developing country governments. I think that donors are entitled to choose their projects, and that they can increase (a little) the impact on the poor this way.

They are also entitled to favour countries whose policies they like, and to refuse aid to some. But I think it is dangerous to try to exert leverage on major thrusts of internal policy. A compact (Alliance for Progress!) in which redistributive policies, or respect for human rights, was promised on one side, and more aid on the other side, would be honoured in the breach, and give rise to recrimination. By attaching strings, it might avoid the complaint that developing countries do not want charity: but I do not set much store by that argument; developing country leaders do not ask for alms for themselves, but for international aid in the name of states, or nations, or people. Finally, I would oppose discriminatory trade arrangements; and the increasing political management and cartelization of trade, which increases dependency, is unlikely to help the poor or the poorest states, and promises to be disruptive of world order.

NOTES

1 I recall that Harry Johnson once asked me to join a seminar to discuss this work which he believed to be very important. Unfortunately I could not find the time.

2 It could perhaps be argued that this sentence is self-contradictory, and that equality of marginal utility of money is a sufficient condition of equality of real wealth It is difficult indeed to define 'equal real wealth', but I do not think it is quite the same as 'equality of marginal utility of money', although this is a position

I. M. D. LITTLE

one might want to take up if one regarded marginal but not total utility to be interpersonally comparable (See Little 1967, Chapter IV; and Sen 1973, pp. 44–6).

Brian Barry, *The Liberal Theory of Justice*, 1973, Clarendon Press, Oxford.
Jagdish N. Bhagwati (ed.), *The New International Economic Order: the North–South Debate*, 1977, MIT Press, Cambridge, Mass.
Hedley Bull, *The Anarchical Society*, 1977, Macmillan, London.
Deepak Lal, *The Basic Needs Approach and the Third Development Decade*, March 1978, mimeo.
I. M. D. Little, *A Critique of Welfare Economics*, 2nd edition, 1957, Clarendon Press, Oxford.
I. M. D. Little and J. M. Clifford, *International Aid*, 1965, Allen and Unwin, London.
Robert Nozick, *Anarchy, State and Utopia*, 1974, Basil Blackwell, Oxford.
John Rawls, *A Theory of Justice*, 1972, Clarendon Press, Oxford.
A. K. Sen, (1) *On Economic Inequality*, 1973, Clarendon Press, Oxford. (2) 'Ethical Issues in Income Distribution: National and International' (mimeo), paper presented to the Saltsjöbaden Symposium on the Past and Prospects of the Economic World Order, August 1978.
Robert W. Tucker, *The Inequality of Nations*, 1977, Basic Books.

53

DISTRIBUTIVE JUSTICE AND THE NEW
INTERNATIONAL ORDER : A COMMENT

Vijay Joshi

PROFESSOR LITTLE's paper is a sophisticated analysis of the philosophical foundations of the New International Economic Order. The central question to which he addresses himself is whether less developed countries (LDCs) have a claim on the wealth of developed countries (DCs) on grounds of *distributive justice* as distinct from grounds of *charity*. The legitimacy of such a claim may be denied at three different levels. It could be asserted that:

1. Even within a community, poor persons do not have a just claim on the wealth of rich persons.
2. Poor persons do sometimes have a just claim on the wealth of rich persons within a 'community' but the world is not a community.
3. The world is a community but it is divided into states which are not themselves just in their internal policies. Inter-state redistribution of wealth will not in fact lead to redistribution of wealth from rich persons to poor persons.

I shall discuss these propositions *seriatim.*

1. The first denial is obviously the most fundamental. In assessing it, one is inevitably drawn into basic questions of moral and political philosophy. Unfortunately, as Little shows, attempts by philosophers to provide a single organising principle for distributive justice have not succeeded. It seems to me, nevertheless, that the case for increased redistribution from rich persons in DCs to poor persons in LDCs is 'strong' – and perhaps stronger than the tone of Little's paper suggests – in the sense that it can be based in a reasonably well-founded way on several *different* (and competing) theories of justice.

For utilitarians, justice consists in maximising the sum-total of

54

utility. Reducing the present enormous disparities in incomes between rich people in DCs and poor people in LDCs must surely increase total utility – unless we are prepared to assume that the extra dollar is worth more to the very rich than to the very poor. For believers in Rawls-type theories, justice consists in maximising the welfare of the worst-off representative individuals, welfare being measured in terms of exogenously specified 'primary goods' or 'basic needs'. Leaving aside various obvious objections such as who is to do the specifying of these 'primary goods' and how, it again seems plausible that the worst-off representative individuals in the world are poor persons in LDCs. There are of course incentive arguments for inequality in both utilitarian and Rawls-type theories, but it strains the imagination to believe that a reduction in present disparities between the rich in DCs and the poor in LDCs would be likely to lead to a smaller sum-total of utility or to lower welfare for the poorest as a result of adverse effects on the supply of effort by the rich.

Nozick's entitlement theory, on the other hand, defines justice solely in terms of the observance of certain procedures which respect individual rights. Can a case for redistribution from the rich in DCs to the poor in LDCs be made on Nozickian grounds? I shall consider this question in some detail because Little, although suggesting that it is generally unacceptable, shows some admiration for this theory; and also because the theory is apparently highly conservative on the question of redistribution. One possible line would be to follow Nozick's 'principle of rectification'. I am not inclined to reject this approach altogether, but I can see that going further and further back in history produces absurdities and it is not clear how far back one should go. Perhaps there *is* something unjust about visiting the sins of people on their far-off descendants if these descendants cannot even be identified! I shall, instead, propose a different argument for redistribution, based, surprisingly perhaps, on Nozick's premises.

Start with Locke–Nozick natural rights possessed by all human beings. The poor from LDCs (say India) have a natural right to move freely to the DCs (say the US) and try and make a living there. US employers have a right to hire Indians at any mutually agreed wage rates. The current situation could be described as follows: the US government, acting on behalf of some or all people of the US (not wearing their employer-hats), has enacted immigration laws which infringe the natural rights of Indians to live in the US and the natural rights of US employers and Indian workers to enter into voluntary contracts. (The liberal sentiments of many people, even free traders, are apt to falter when they contemplate the horrors of free inter-

55

national movement of labour!) It would follow from Nozickian principles that US employers and Indian workers must be paid compensation adequate enough to induce them not to undertake these contracts. Of course, many questions remain. For example, who should be taxed? How should compensation be divided between US employers and Indian workers? The principle, however, is clear enough and provides an argument for increased foreign aid based on an entitlement theory of justice.

I conclude that the case for a transfer of wealth from rich people in DCs to poor people in LDCs can plausibly be based on several different theories of justice.[1] Of course, some of the arguments apply equally to redistribution from rich to poor within DCs and within LDCs and even to redistribution from the rich in LDCs to the poor in DCs.

2. I now turn to the second ground on which the justice of redistribution from DCs to LDCs may be questioned, viz. that the world is not a community. This argument is of course not open to believers in universal natural rights. Nevertheless it has some force. Even if we accept the case for redistribution from rich persons to poor persons within a community, it is not clear that these individuals would have any mutual obligations if they are not part of a community – if they are, say, a collection of Robinson Crusoes who have just discovered each other. But it would surely be tendentious to describe the world as a collection of individual Robinson Crusoes, given the many links that now exist between these individuals, not least through mutually beneficial trade and commerce. Even if we accept for the sake of argument that the world is not yet enough of a community to permit meaningful claims in the name of justice for redistribution of all wealth including 'initial endowments', it is surely enough for a community to permit claims for just redistribution of the 'gains from trade'.

3. The third ground for rejecting the justice of redistribution from DCs to LDCs is the most powerful one. The argument is that there is no moral basis for redistribution from rich *states* to poor *states*, since nation-states are founded on the principle of self-determination which includes the right to be unjust within their boundaries. If DC governments try to ensure that aid transfers reach the poor in LDCs they interfere with national sovereignty; if they give aid without asking such questions, aid may not reach the poor.[2] As Little correctly observes, there is at present no easy way out of this dilemma. Aid can only be defended, as he defends it in his conclusion, on a (controversial) consequentialist judgment that it does reach the poor, to a

56

greater or lesser extent, in one way or another, in spite of some unjust behaviour on the part of LDC governments.

I agree wholeheartedly that the fundamental moral unit is the individual, not the state, and that it makes no sense to talk of the principles of *inter-state distributive justice* without reference to the welfare and rights of individuals. I would add, however, that Little does not apply the same stringent test to the principles of *inter-state commutative justice* (or the principles of 'the old equality' as he, following Tucker, calls them) which have come to be accepted by the international community and which he appears to accept as reasonable. So-called commutative justice (or 'old equality') between states may often involve gross injustice to individuals. For example, the principle of non-interference in internal affairs may lead to condonation of serious violations of individuals' rights. Similar results may follow from the generally accepted principle that states should repay previously incurred debts. An international debt may have been incurred by a former government against the wishes of the people, for purposes contrary to their interests; nevertheless, the present government may tax its people to service or repay it.

If the welfare of individuals and the preservation of their basic rights are the primary aims of the world community, the nation-state system can be justified only on the ground that, on balance, it promotes these aims. The principles of inter-state commutative and distributive justice can be seen, in this sense, as being on the same footing. Neither set of principles is self-evidently correct; neither can be accepted without an (in part empirical) demonstration that it fulfils the primary aims of the world community better than feasible alternatives. The conclusion, contrary to the spirit of Little's paper, is that the moral case for redistribution from rich to poor states is *a priori* no weaker (though no stronger) than the moral case for 'non-interference in internal affairs' or other currently accepted principles governing inter-state relations.

NOTES

1. In the interests of brevity, I have not dealt with Marxist entitlement theories which would make the case for redistribution from the rich in DCs to the poor in LDCs using the concepts of 'labour entitlements' and 'exploitation'. On this question see A. K. Sen, 'Ethical Issues in Income Distribution, National and International', Saltsjöbaaden Symposium on the Past and the Prospects of the Economic World Order, August 1978. Professor Sen's paper presents a beautifully

57

clear taxonomy of the moral theories underlying controversies concerning income distribution.

2. As Sen points out, while it is important to ask whether more foreign aid to LDCs would *actually* benefit their poorer citizens, is it not equally important to ask whether less foreign aid by DCs would actually benefit *their* poorer citizens? (A negative answer to the latter question would improve the case for redistribution from DCs to LDCs) To say that DCs should be exempt from such scrutiny since it is *their* wealth which is being disposed of is to beg the moral question of their entitlement to that wealth. See Sen, *op. cit.*

Chapter Four

NORTH-SOUTH ECONOMIC NEGOTIATIONS:
A PROPOSAL FOR A MORE CONSTRUCTIVE AGENDA*

Helen Hughes

AN UNPRECEDENTED effort has been devoted to the discussion of 'the new international economic order'. Since the introduction of the resolutions seeking a new relationship between low and high income countries in the Special Session of the United Nations Assembly in May 1975, dozens of meetings of the U.N. and its specialized agencies (including the month-long UNCTAD IV and ILO World Employment Conferences held in 1976), the 1976–7 meetings of the Paris Conference on International Economic Co-operation (CIEC), and the 1978 U.N. General Assembly Committee of the Whole meetings, a large number of other international meetings and hundreds of national conferences have been concerned with 'the new international economic order', focusing largely on commodity, energy, debt moratoria, transfer of technology, shifts in manufacturing location, and more recently 'international interdependence' issues. The research and information effort backing these meetings and conferences has led to a vast, if largely repetitive, literature. It is not for the lack of words or resources that the 'new international economic order' negotiations have run into sand. Nor is it because the framework of international economic relations can not be improved. Rather it is because the wrong agenda has been discussed in the wrong forums. This is in turn related to the analysis of the underlying economic issues.

* I am grateful to Isaiah Frank, Karsten Laursen and the staff of the Economic Analysis and Projections Department of the World Bank for helping to clarify my ideas on problems in the international economy, but the views expressed in this paper are of course my own. They do not necessarily reflect those of the World Bank.

I. *The Economics of Confrontation*

The call for a 'new international economic order' did not arise from an analysis of present international economic relations, but from the evolution of the international economy in the 100 years or so from the early 19th century. Whatever the ultimate view of the economic developments of this period may be,[1] it seems clear that while inequality was reduced quite markedly within industrializing countries, it grew between the countries of north-western Europe, northern America and Australasia and the rest of the world. And whatever precise explanations for this process might be given, the structure of the international economy, backed by corresponding political relationships, was both cause and effect. Foreign investment apparently contributed more to the overall economic development of the United States, Canada and Australasia than to the other temperate countries of 'new settlement' and the tropical colonial and semi-colonial countries. In the latter most of the foreign investment was in export-oriented agricultural and mineral enterprises, and exports came to be controlled by entrepreneurs and investors in the industrial countries. These foreign investors, and through multiplier and trickle-down effects the other citizens of the investors' home countries, appropriated a large share of the rich resource rents that followed the opening up of new lands and mines. The enclave nature of many of the foreign enterprises together with population pressures contributed to their relatively small impact on their 'host' economies. Politically backed imperfections in the production and marketing of commodities as diverse as bananas and copper and in accompanying services such as shipping, also led to high monopoly rents. However, such imperfections also applied to Australia, Canada and New Zealand and the contrast between their growth and the inability of such countries of 'new settlement' as Argentina and Chile to sustain broad-based economic development in the twentieth century remains unexplained.

It is reasonable to argue in broad terms that until the colonial and semi-colonial world was shattered in the late 1940s and 1950s, international markets were not only highly skewed, but skewed toward the interests of the industrial countries. But the years since the early 1950s have seen unprecedented economic growth in the industrial countries, and the former colonial and semi-colonial countries and in world trade and capital flows.[2] (There have also been very large permanent and temporary labor movements.)

Although the GNP growth of the developing countries has averaged a little over 3 per cent per capita per annum (or about the same as the market economy industrial countries), it has been very uneven, ranging from countries whose annual real GNP growth has barely exceeded population increases to countries with real per capita income growth rates of 6 per cent to 8 per cent. It seems that it takes some time for a country to reach an infrastructure, administrative and entrepreneurial capacity that enables it to grow rapidly, so that growth tends to accelerate with rising income per capita (and decline again at relatively high per capita income),[3] but a country's policies and their implementation are critical to its rate of growth. Countries which were very poor in the 1950s have been among the most rapidly growing, and some of those which had relatively high incomes and advanced entrepreneurial and administrative structures have had a very poor growth record. Nor is there any one model of policies for growth. Some of the countries with highly regulated economies such as Japan, Korea and Taiwan have grown as rapidly as such laissez faire economies as Hong Kong. The People's Republic of China's centrally planned economy has apparently achieved a healthy long-run growth rate of around 4 per cent per capita despite serious political upheavals.[4] The developing countries today represent a wide range of per capita income levels and development from the small, least developed countries of Africa south of the Sahara and the large poor countries of South Asia at one extreme, to semi-industrialized relatively high-income countries of southern Europe, Latin America and East Asia at the other end of the spectrum.

The structure of the world economy and patterns of trade and capital have changed accordingly. In the 1950s, the developing countries were predominantly primary, often one commodity, exporters and manufactured goods importers. Some, not necessarily very poor, countries remain dependent on one primary product, but most developing countries have diversified among primary products and into manufacturing and service exports. More than 25 per cent of the developing countries' merchandise exports are now manufactures. On the rather conservative assumption that the developing countries' exports of manufactures grow at about 12 per cent a year in the 1980s (compared to 15 per cent in 1965–75), and assuming that their total exports grow at about 6.5 per cent (compared to 7.5 per cent in 1965–75), this ratio would be over 55 per cent by 1990. Starting from very low levels in the 1950s, non factor service exports accounted for $56 billion compared to merchandise exports of $177 billion in 1975; this 1:3 ratio can be expected to be maintained or increased.

The terms of trade (in so far as this phase has any meaning for groups of products or countries) for the primary commodities pro-

61

duced by the developing countries have not turned against them despite the 1950s and 1960s' expectations to this effect. Over the long-run they appear to have remained stable if petroleum is excluded. If pretroleum is included, they have improved substantially.[5] If quality improvements in capital equipment and other manufactured products are taken into account, it seems likely that even the non-petroleum primary producers' terms of trade have improved. There have been two major commodity booms since World War II (during the Korean war in 1951 and with the co-ordination of European and north American economic upswings in 1972–3), but the commodity related crises feared by those who experienced the 1920s, and the 1930s depression did not follow because of the changed structure of international trade with its heavy emphasis on manufactures.

Primary product price fluctuations have occurred, but the amplitude has not always been greater for commodities largely produced in developing countries than for commodities largely produced in industrial countries, or indeed than for some manfactured products. While such price fluctuations have caused very considerable balance of payments and government budget problems to countries dependent on the export of one product, export diversification and the improvement in many developing countries' economic management capacity has meant that price fluctuations have had a declining impact on fluctuations in export earnings, and on growth. Rapidly growing economies have managed to handle price and export income fluctuations, and price fluctuations have not been an important cause of slow growth, although they have, of course, complicated growth and development problems. Despite fluctuations price trends have, moreover, proved to be useful signals to countries wishing to diversify their domestic production and exports.[6]

Although the Dillon and Kennedy rounds of trade negotiations resulted in substantial reductions of tariff barriers by industrial countries, significant areas of protection remain, particularly in agricultural goods. However, with a few exceptions, notably sugar, textiles and footwear, these barriers are as much, if not more, intended to deter exports from other industrial countries than from developing countries.[7] Developing countries have been given privileged access to some of the restricted markets, and they have benefited from the industrialized countries' liberal attitude to their export incentive measures. It is not clear that the remaining industrial country tariffs on 'processed' primary products represent an escalation of effective protection of primary product imports,[8] and again they are directed at other industrial countries as well as at the developing countries.

The main restrictions introduced specifically against developing countries are in a relatively small area of labor intensive manufacturing production; they represent an attempt to control the pace of increase in the imports of textiles and footwear, and do not prevent entry. The bulk of the industrial countries' recent trade and trade related measures, such as employment subsidies, has also been aimed at restricting imports from other industrial countries. At least until late 1978, major industrial countries managed to hold the line fairly successfully against protectionist lobbies wishing to restrict imports from developing countries.

There are of course imperfections in international markets. They range widely from horizontal and vertical control of significant shares of primary commodity and manufactured goods markets by transnational corporations to the 'conferences' of shipping cartels. Commodity and service market structures shift from time to time, and the developing countries are now not only playing a role in petroleum but also in coffee and tin. Market imperfections are of course not synonymous with a total absence of competition. Like administrative trade barriers, they are not necessarily turned against developing countries *per se*, but rather tend to discriminate against the producers of such products as bauxite, or against countries like Australia and New Zealand that are situated at the end of transport routes.

The rapid increase of capital flows to developing countries during the past 10 years has been another striking feature of the changing structure of the world economy. Capital flows in the form of aid (grants, technical assistance and concessional credits and loans) from industrial market economy countries have increased from about $5 billion in the early 1960s to $14 billion by the mid 1970s, that is a growth rate of some 3 per cent a year in real terms. However, on average this only represents about 0.35 per cent of the industrial countries' GNP although the Scandinavian countries, the Netherlands and Canada have reached substantially higher levels. The OPEC countries have shown greater sensitivity to the problems of the poor developing countries since their incomes rose in 1973, with aid and concessional transfers of about $5 billion representing about 3.5 per cent of their GNP. Socialist countries' contributions are still below $1 billion, and represent less than 0.1 per cent of GNP. Commercial markets, beginning with direct foreign investment and export credits in the 1950s, and expanding to include direct flows from financial institutions in the 1960s, have proved to be highly responsive to those developing countries desiring foreign capital inflows. Total commercial capital flows rose from about $3 billion in the early 1960s to

63

$28 billion by the mid 1970s, with about $3 billion coming from OPEC countries.[9]

Private capital flows, and particularly private direct foreign investment by transnational corporations and associated technology transfers, have generated more discussion than any other aspect of international economic relations. Foreign investors probably continued to reap high monopolistic rents on their investments well into the 1960s. The transnational corporations' monopolistic practices no doubt contributed, but the developing countries' weak resource, agricultural and industrialization policies were primarily responsible. 'Import substitution at all costs' by a combination of over-valued exchange rates, high tariffs, quantitative import restrictions and subsidies to capital led to particularly high rents. But as the developing countries improved their policies, monopoly rents have been reduced and the transnational corporations have adapted to their hosts' desire for greater equity and management control. This has led to some movement from direct investment to indirect flows through financial intermediaries. Increased financial flows are also an indication of the growing economic strength and management capacity of the developing countries. While some developing countries, paradoxically particularly mineral rich countries, have borrowed excessively and unwisely, most developing countries have matched borrowing to their absorptive and repayment capacities, and used the capital markets wisely.

But borrowing of course leads to debt. The developing countries' external medium- and long-term debt grew from about $8 billion in 1955 to $16 billion in 1960 and some $35 billion in 1965. By 1977 it totalled $210 billion. In real terms the growth was about 14 per cent in the 1950s (as many developing countries became independent and colonial transfers were transformed into lending), 12 per cent in the 1960s, and about 10 per cent in the 1970s. Although the donor countries have moved toward grant assistance for the very poor countries, 40 per cent of the developing countries' debt is still from official sources, mostly with a substantial concessional element. The 60 per cent borrowed from private sources is principally owed by the more advanced, higher income developing countries. Countries which borrow beyond their capacity find themselves in difficulties, but this is not true of the bulk of the borrowers. Debt has overall grown at roughly the same rate as exports, so that debt servicing capacity in terms of export income has been maintained.[10] Inflation has of course substantially reduced the debt burden by implicitly transferring income from lenders to borrowers.

The movement of labor, mainly in the form of temporary migration to the United States, north western Europe, and more recently to the Middle East, on a scale not experienced since the 1900s, has also had a marked impact on developing country growth. Like capital flows, labor flows have not been without problems. The effect on the 'home' developing countries has sometimes been disruptive, and the migrants themselves have suffered from the personal and cultural traumas that migration entails. The industrial 'host' countries used migrant labor to even out employment fluctuations, reducing inflows sharply from 1974. But in general the migrants were able to improve their living standards, and their remittances have made substantial contributions to their home countries' growth. Conservative estimates suggest that workers' remittances to developing countries were about $15 billion in 1975, equalling aid flows.

The proponents of 'the new international economic order' have consistently lagged behind the changes taking place in the international economy. Their first major push, for the Generalized Scheme of Preferences (GSP) for manufactured exports, was in an area of expanding interest to developing countries, but it was doomed to have a trivial impact by the industrial countries' tariff reductions. Whereas the halving of a 12 per cent tariff could give developing countries an advantage, the halving of a 3 per cent tariff has practically no impact. When the transnational corporations' petroleum 'monopsony' began to be replaced by the petroleum producing countries' 'monopoly' in 1971, in terms of the economics of confrontation, this seemed the first breakthrough of a 'new international economic order'. The sharp rise in petroleum rents and prices underlined this view in 1973–4. In fact the shift in the incidence of a considerable share of petroleum rents from the consumers in industrial countries to the producing developing countries was one of the last steps in the demolition of the 'colonial' order of economic relations.

Unfortunately, just as the economics of confrontation were becoming outdated by economic events, they were given a boost by the apocalyptic visions of The Club of Rome.[11] It was claimed that with the exhaustion of its mineral and other resources, Spaceship Earth would crash at the turn of the 20th century! Although developing countries were growing rapidly, the heritage of the past was still strongly reflected in their actual living standards and per capita consumption of non-renewable resources, so that the industrial countries, with a small proportion of the world's population, still used the bulk of non-renewable raw materials produced. If natural resources were running out very quickly, only quick and radical measures could give the developing countries an adequate share. The 'Meadows Report' paradoxically had the beneficial effect of leading to the demonstration, once again, of the symbiotic relationship between the demand for non-renewable resources, changing technology (in mineral and energy exploration, exploitation and processing) and supply conditions. An emerging consensus of views on the outlook for energy and for mineral supplies indicates that the problems likely to be faced in matching supply and demand are manageable without very substantial increases in real cost (that is, in relative prices) well into the 21st century.[12] But considerable damage was done to relations between industrial and developing countries, and the overtones of scarcities remain to haunt international and national policy formulation in spite of the strong evidence to the contrary.

The global population prospects have also become somewhat calmer. The initial impact of the rapid growth in living standards in many developing countries, combined with the near elimination of such diseases as smallpox and cholera, led to a lag in the reduction of birth rates behind death rates, but this lag is now being overcome. While the current structure of the population, reflecting the rapid growth of the past 20 years will lead to major further increases, population growth rates are declining, and a stationary world population early in the 21st century is in prospect.

II. *The Economics of Interdependence*
The implicit recognition of the emptiness of the economics of confrontation (and of the dangers of the accompanying politics of confrontation), and the almost total lack of practical results, have led to a new approach to 'the new international economic order' through stress on economic interdependence. The intellectual origins lie in the neo-classical trade-oriented stream of advice that economists from market-oriented industrial countries have been giving to developing countries. The industrial countries' failure to put their own house in order, and the potential impact of relatively low growth and relatively high unemployment in industrial countries on exports from developing countries, has triggered the debate. And whereas the confrontation debate was, naturally enough, led on the developing country side by petroleum rich countries, it is the semi-industrialized group of developing countries which is most interested in the economics of interdependence.

The concept of interdependence does have an economic basis. The growth of economic relations among countries is a concomitant of economic development. Differences in resource endowments within and among countries lead to trade, capital, labor and technology movements with corresponding output gains from specialization. Specialization does not have natural political boundaries. International flows are complex, and thus cannot be given a simple quantitative expression, but whatever indicators are used – the ratios of trade to GNP, or the growth of trade, capital and labor flows – confirm that international economic relations have grown. The developing countries have shared in the increased pace of international economic relations as part of their post-World War II development. In some senses this can be taken to mean that there has been an increase in international 'interdependence'. In the short run national economic growth becomes dependent through various economic linkages on what happens in other countries. This is reflected in the greater sensitivity of countries to economic developments and policy changes in other parts of the world. But this is only one side of the coin. International economic relations do not mean interdependence in the sense that any countries' or group of countries' welfare and growth is dependent on what other countries do. The pace and nature of a country's development is largely determined by its own policies, including those that react to the international economic environment, and while it takes time to adjust to changing domestic or external conditions, national policy is the critical element even in the very short run. Many developing countries, in spite of their relative economic weakness, demonstrated the importance of such 'independence' in being able to absorb the impact of the increase in petroleum prices and the recession of 1974–5 by internal policy reactions and borrowing on international capital markets.[13] Their average growth rates for 1974–6 were below 1968–73 levels, but they were higher than industrial country growth rates and they have remained higher. The poorest countries which are not yet highly integrated in the world economy were scarcely affected by the relative price changes and depressed markets. Their growth is still very low, and it remains largely dependent on harvest conditions.

International economic relations, moreover, like those that take place within countries, have costs as well as benefits. Because increased participation in the international economy increases uncertainty and makes economies more vulnerable to arbitrary action or unanticipated development in other countries, the reaping of the full benefits of international economic relations requires the international acceptance of 'rules of the game' which reduce a country's exposure to adverse developments abroad. This in turn means that a country's freedom to pursue strictly national objectives is constrained by its acceptance of such international rules. Countries have to make sophisticated policy choices to benefit on a continuing basis from their participation in the international economy.

While growing trade and other international economic relationships are usually welcomed as yielding a mutual gain to the participating countries, the gains may not be evenly distributed among them. Within countries particular groups are likely to benefit more than others. Indeed, some groups are likely to lose, at least for a transitional period of unpredictable duration. Although larger flows of goods and factors across national boundaries would contribute to a more efficient utilization of the world's resources with gain to all countries in conditions of full employment, it does not follow that such flows necessarily contribute to a higher level of utilization of the world's resources in conditions of unemployment. Trade liberalization and similar improvements in the international economic framework have to be considered along with domestic fiscal and monetary policies as means of alleviating unemployment; they may not be the most efficient mechanisms for the achievement of full employment.[14]

Pump-priming in Developed Countries by Increasing Capital Transfers to Developing Countries.
The argument that industrial countries have a self-interest in increased capital flows to developing countries has been revived on the basis of some very simplistic assumptions.[15] It is argued that if capital transfers are increased, the developing countries will grow more rapidly and therefore import more from the industrial countries, thus stimulating their growth.

The view that OECD countries are dependent on a type of pump-priming which involves a real transfer out of their countries rather than to their own citizens seems to rest on the assumption that conventional domestic pump-priming is more inflationary than expansionary, and consequently it either will not be undertaken at all, or that it will be relatively inefficient. Conversely, an increase in developing countries' demand for industrial country products is assumed to be expansionary rather than inflationary. Many industrial country governments fear that domestic pump-priming will involve exchange rate depreciation, and that this will be inflationary. There is considerable danger at present that the difficulties said to face industrial countries' pump-priming will become self-fulfilling prophecies simply because action is not taken. But the arguments for pump-priming remain at least as strong as those against it.

There is, of course, nothing in economic theory to substantiate the view that developing countries' demand for industrial country products is more expansionary than domestic demand. There is no empirical evidence that excess capacity in export industries is greater than those producing for the domestic market. On the contrary, some of the greatest bottlenecks in industrial countries at present appear to be in industries that export capital goods such as earth-moving equipment and chemical/fertilizer plants for which developing country demand is strong. Even if such evidence were available, the case for increased transfers could not be argued as a long-term proposition on the grounds of economic self-interest in the industrial countries. Their long-term interest then would be to remove existing bottlenecks to domestic expansion. For the second round multiplier effects the under-utilized versus over-utilized capacity would be the same whether the original increase in demand affected export or domestically-oriented industries; the argument for pump-priming aid largely rests on a political sleight-of-hand. It is assumed that the industrial country electorate can be persuaded that (a) export-led growth is 'good' at all costs and (b) only export-led growth is sound as a basis of additional aid flows. Neither of these assumptions is likely to be persuasive to labor which would be foregoing the transfers that would go to the developing countries instead. Indeed, politically such arguments are likely to have serious 'backlash' effects because many labor leaders are aware that the alternative to pump-priming through transfers abroad is to make transfers to the poor at home.

An analogous case has been made for non-concessional (direct and indirect) capital flows from industrial to developing countries. One may certainly argue that both investors and recipients gain from such flows. Indeed they have gained, because marginal returns to capital in developing (particularly rapidly growing) countries have been relatively high. However, it is not clear that the middle income countries' absorptive capacity for private capital flows is not being met by the market mechanism. The middle income developing countries have continued to increase their borrowing at almost 10 per cent per year in real terms, with mineral rich, principally capital deficit petroleum exporting countries, such as Indonesia, Nigeria and Mexico, increasing their borrowing much more rapidly. The liquidity of capital markets is enabling well managed developing countries to refinance old loans and contract new ones on favorable terms, with relatively low interest rates and medium-term maturities of 5 to 7 years.

However, the mutual interest of the individual lender and borrower does not necessarily apply to the countries which export and

69

import capital. The capital intensity in the former countries presumably goes down (or fails to increase) as a result of the transaction, and this has a depressing effect on wages. Thus, even if capital from an industrial country is invested in a developing country at a high rate of return, given unemployment in the former country, its citizens are likely to be better off if the investment takes place at home even at a lower rate of return. The impacts on the future technological capacity of the country and its economic structure should be discounted to present values and compared to the benefits of investment abroad. The benefits of such investment are likely to be low in comparison to the costs. The gains to the industrial country are likely to be even lower when the distributional impact of an investment abroad is compared to that of an investment at home.

Export Goods Aid
It is also being argued (mainly in the European Economic Community) that since developed country governments are anxious to preserve and protect export industries in the current unemployment and recession situation, additional aid can be obtained for developing countries by subsidizing stagnant export industries through purchases of their goods for aid transfer to developing countries.

Excess capacity is proved by definition. Only those exporters with excess capacity would be (in some cases already are) eligible for such programs. Here the difficulty is of a somewhat different nature. Firstly, if the industry in question is not merely temporarily embarrassed by a lack of demand, then helping it to stay in business is inimical to the long-term interest of the industrial country. Unless firms use such orders to finance a move out of the industry, this type of action becomes 'adjustment resistance'. Such resistance would adversely affect developing countries whose competitiveness in that particular industry has improved, and may in fact be contributing to the difficulties in the industrial country. Shipbuilding, one of the most seriously embarrassed industrial country industries, for example, is suffering both from a drop in demand and from sharply increased competitiveness of Korean and other developing country shipyards.

All the programs relying on excess capacity in industrial countries' manufacturing export industries would be likely to increase capital intensity biases in developing countries. (They would also be limited largely to assisting middle income developing countries because low income countries have low absorptive capacity for such goods.) Surplus food transfers to developing countries often proved to be costly

70

to them by undermining the development of local agriculture; those of surplus capital intensive goods could be higher.

Commodity Prices and Inflation

It is now being argued, as part of the interdependence argument, that the stability of commodity prices would have a positive impact on the world economy in general, because stable commodity prices are believed to be counter-inflationary and because inflation is believed to be counter-expansionary. Both effects are largely speculative. Price fluctuations largely affect relative prices, unless they reach the dimension of a commodity boom, such as that of 1972–3. But it is doubtful whether any reasonably cost-effective buffer stock scheme could contain price increases of that magnitude. As the real issue for the producers appears to be how to 'stabilize' prices above their market trend, 'stabilization' that would be successful from that point of view would hardly be counter-inflationary. There are also of course resource allocation objections to such a policy. In any event, the industrialized countries are not dependent on the developing countries for price stability. They can, indeed, must, use monetary management, and other policies and controls, unilaterally to achieve price stability. One may of course argue that such policies are difficult to implement: so is commodity price stabilization.

Import and Export 'Dependence'

In a curious twist of the case for increased trade, it is now being argued that industrial countries are 'dependent' on the developing countries for their imports, particularly of raw materials, and for their exports. The industrial countries do, of course, trade with developing countries, and rising trends of trade between industrial and develop-

Table 1: Share of Developing Countries in Industrial Countries' Imports and Exports in 1976
(per cent)

	USA	Japan	Germany	France	UK
Share of Imports from Developing Countries in Total Imports	44	55	20	26	25
Share of Exports to Developing Countries in Total Exports	35	41	16	23	25

Source: U.N. *Yearbook of International Trade Statistics,* 1976.

71

ing countries reflect the upswing in the developing countries' share of developed country exports that followed the increase in oil-rich countries' imports, and other developing countries' borrowing policies to sustain output in the 1974–75 recession. If the middle income countries continue to grow rapidly, as seems likely, the developing countries as a group will have a greater weight in world trade, and hence in industrial country imports and exports by the late 1980s. But it does not follow in any sense that industrial countries are 'dependent' on imports, particularly imports of raw materials from developing countries.

Industrial countries draw a large share of their tin and petroleum consumption from developing countries, but otherwise less than half their mineral consumption comes from developing countries. On balance developing countries are winning a larger share of the mineral

Table 2: Share of Total Mineral Consumption in Developed Countries Imported from Developing Countries, 1960 and 1976 (per cent)

	1960	1976
Petroleum	40	60
Gas	—	2
Coal	—	—
Nickel	25	40
Iron ore	20	30
Copper	40	45
Tin	80	95
Bauxite	70	40

Source: Estimated from industry sources.

market, but the shares have fluctuated in the past, and are likely to do so again in the future, depending on developing and industrial country attitudes to mineral rents, political alliances, and so on. Trade in minerals illustrates the costs and benefits of trade in broader terms, and the benefits are generally expected to far outweigh the costs for both parties. The severance of a source of mineral supplies would lead to adjustment problems, but even in the medium-term these would be likely to be larger on the suppliers' than on the consumers' side. The reduction of petroleum supplies by developing countries to industrial countries would be likely to stimulate alternative energy technology. The capital deficit, highly capital absorptive petroleum exporters that need high export incomes are not likely to favor such a reduction in supplies, and the capital surplus petroleum countries

are now heavily dependent on the industrial countries for im̧
and investment income. Disruption of supplies is not in their interest
either.

Industrial countries are now said to be 'dependent' on developing
countries for exports, and in particular jobs in those countries are
sometimes regarded as being 'dependent' on exports to developing
countries. But employment in industrial countries remains dependent
on their own economic policies. Exports, and increases in exports, can
not simply be translated into employment and increases in employment. While a growth in exports leads to increases in employment,
these may be offset by the declining employment in import-competing
industries. The calculation of direct and indirect employment in exporting and importing industries is difficult, but in general export
industries in industrial countries are more capital intensive than industries that compete with imports from developing countries. A
dollar gained in exports thus could lead to less employment creation
than would be lost in employment if a dollar's worth more goods were
imported. The employment adjustment that is necessary as a result
of the continuing growth of imports from developing countries is only
a small proportion of total employment adjustment that is continually
taking place in industrial countries. But the employment displacement effects of trade with developing countries are difficult to handle
because they tend to affect the least skilled workers and most disadvantaged groups. Moreover, in the political context it is relevant
that whereas increased trade in manufactures benefits the factory
workers who are among the higher income groups in the developing
countries, the costs are generally paid by the lowest income groups in
the industrial countries.

III. *A More Constructive Agenda*
The so called 'north' and 'south' groups in 'the north-south dialogue'
are as spurious as the economic interests they are said to represent.
There is a wide spectrum of 'industrial' and 'developing' countries,
and a significant group of 'transitional' countries which also vary
markedly among themselves, in between. The centrally planned economies can not be ignored. All these countries have an interest in stable,
long-run development, but within this very broad concept, their
economic interests cut across the north-south categorization. This has
been demonstrated on both the industrial and developing country
side whenever specific attempts have been made to come to grips
with 'north-south' issues. Neither the economics of confrontation nor

73

those of interdependence are a sound basis for long-run political alliances.

The international economic debate has unfortunately been pushed, for political reasons, on both the industrial and developing country side, to deal with problems which can only be effectively handled nationally.[16] The maintenance of full (or other) levels of employment, of desired rates of growth, and of welfare levels is only meaningful and possible on a national basis, because it depends on the use of national policies. There is no 'world community' in which distributional issues could be meaningfully settled.[17] International economic relations are important for a high level of economic activity, and countries obviously have to limit 'beggar-my-neighbor' policies if the international economy is to grow. But within this limitation, on both the industrial and developing country side, there is much more need for unilateral, national policy improvement than for international debate. Given the weight of the OECD countries in the international economy, and in particular the importance of high employment levels in those countries for further international specialization and growth, national action to reduce their unemployment is of higher priority than any new international initiative. For developing countries, domestic policies are likely to continue to be the principal determinant of growth rates.

The common long-term interests of north, south, west and east lend themselves to general commitments to international economic co-operation in international forums. But the adjustments that are necessary for the long-run benefits to be reaped require, in the short-run, the resolution of quite sharp conflicts which reflect the interests of groups that would be losers from such adjustments. If adjustment is to be a politically viable policy, some compensation generally has to be offered to those that are displaced both in developing and industrial countries. Such conflicts can only be resolved, and compensation can only be worked out, in highly specialized forums by detailed, technically backed, negotiations.

Aid

Despite the cries of interdependence and long-term self-interest of industrial countries in accelerating developing country growth, perhaps the most marked failure of international exhortation has been in increasing the flow and quality of aid to developing countries. Overall aid transfers have barely kept up with the industrial countries' growth. There has been some increase in the ratio of grants to official loans in aid flows, and some donors have written off the debt owed to

74

them by small, very poor countries, but there has been little untying of aid. Project rather than program aid remains sacrosanct among the large high income country donors and the multilateral aid and lending institutions they influence, despite the patent absurdity of giving aid for say, school buildings rather than teachers' salaries.[18] The only industrial country donors which have increased the flow and quality of their aid are small countries with serious domestic welfare commitments and little direct political or economic interest in aid. Their motivation is moral and humanistic, and it is for this reason that the share of their GNP that they devote to aid is approaching 1 per cent rather than hovering at 0.2 per cent.

Capital Markets and Debt

It would not be altogether a caricature to suggest that the objectives of the 'new international economic order' were to increase the developing countries' access to capital markets while at the same time reducing their indebtedness. In practice, of course, the middle income countries have repudiated most of the 'new economic order' capital flow proposals because they represent a threat to their creditworthiness. It soon became evident that a major move toward debt moratoria that went beyond 'forgiving' the official debt of small, poor countries, would penalize countries that borrowed carefully and well to benefit those which had borrowed excessively and used their loans badly, as well as undermining the middle income countries' creditworthiness.

The principal issue that remains on the international capital flow agenda is the creation of new instruments and institutions that would enable developing countries to borrow at longer maturities than those available in the capital markets. But if such measures were to be subsidized, this would mean an increase in aid to middle income countries, and as the volume of aid appears to be limited in total, less aid for low income countries. Alternatively the borrowers would have to pay the additional costs of longer maturity borrowing. It is not at all clear that such extra costs would be worth their while. Loan maturities of 5 to 7 years give the well managed country considerable freedom in managing its debt so as to prevent the bunching of repayment obligations. Refinancing has, by and large, reduced debt service obligations to interest payments, and when the market is highly liquid, as it is at present, many developing countries find that they are able to negotiate very favorable borrowing terms. Indeed some developing countries now borrow on more favorable terms than some industrial countries. The real long-run cost of capital appears to have been about 2 per cent per annum for some time, and the supply of funds still appears to be growing with high savings rates in some industrial and in the capital surplus petroleum exporting countries. Some developing countries are obtaining lower interest rates from the market than from multilateral lending institutions, and prefer the 'program' nature of loans from the former to project ties.

There is no doubt that some borrowing countries need to put their houses in order, and that lending countries must insist that their lending institutions exercise proper lending criteria. It is evident that the high liquidity of international capital markets leads to undue pressures by lending institutions for developing countries to borrow, albeit on very favorable terms. There is also some danger that the persistent doomsday predictions of the 'domino' effects of failure either by developing (and socialist) countries or of potential lending institution bankruptcies could become self-fulfilling prophecies. But short of disasters born of 'crying wolf', the capital markets are likely to be able to continue to function reasonably well with borrowers and lenders exercising judgment born of experience.

There has also been much talk about codes of behavior for transnational corporations, particularly in the transfer of technology, in recent years. It is not likely that such codes will do much good, although they are also likely to do little harm. The critical factors in the impact of direct foreign investment and technology transfer on developing and industrial countries are those countries' domestic policies. There is also room for bilateral taxation collaboration between host and home countries, particularly during transition periods before policies are improved, but international debate is not likely to be effective in increasing the benefits and reducing the costs that accompany international direct investment flows.

Trade

Trade accounts for the bulk of international economic relations, but the 'new international economic order' and 'north-south dialogue' discussions have set off on the wrong foot by focusing on commodity issues, and north-south trade. The principal barriers to trade at present lie in the quantitative restrictions and high tariffs imposed by developing countries, mainly on manufactured imports, and the associated implicit overvaluation of exchange rates. Present north-south trade is complementary and inter-industry, rather than competitive and intra-industry. The major gains in the next 25 years are likely to come from a further liberalization of trade in manufactures, predominantly by the developing countries, and from the impact of such liberalization on inter-developing country trade and the associated growth in productivity in developing countries. If such trade liberalization were to come to the forefront of developing country policy, it could begin to affect their growth markedly by the mid 1980s, and to have a major impact on the scale and competitiveness of total international trade, by the late 1980s, and early 1990s similar to that of the Dillon and Kennedy multilateral trade negotiations. New trade opportunities would then be opened up for the low income countries.

The extent to which protective measures were necessary to establish manufacturing in developing countries remains a matter for debate, but there is increasing agreement that after some point the gains from reducing protection through increased competitiveness and the associated welfare gains are greater than those from maintaining or increasing it. Such semi-industrialized countries as Singapore, Taiwan and Korea have unilaterally reduced or are currently reducing their protection levels. Others, notably Brazil and Mexico are considering how to implement such a reduction in protection. Lower income countries would probably require assistance in the shape of program loans for the restructuring of their economies to reduce protection. For all these countries the principle of reciprocity in bilateral and multilateral trade negotiations is an important instrument in persuading those groups in their own countries on whom the brunt of the adjustment process will fall that it is necessary to take adjustment measures.[19] The developing countries were ill advised to insist on exemptions from the reciprocity approach to international trade negotiations and largely to ignore the Tokyo round of multilateral trade negotiations. They have also failed to pay adequate attention to introduction of safeguards against the turning of temporary protective measures taken to avoid disruptions in the domestic economy as a result of increased imports into permanent barriers, yet these are critical in holding the line against the threat of protection.

The international treatment of subsidies to production is becoming increasingly important as industrial countries seek to maintain employment by production subsidies, and developing countries seek to win exports without the restructuring of highly protective regimes. While moderate and temporary subsidies for exports can play the same role in overcoming initial export difficulties as moderate protection does in overcoming problems of 'infancy' in production for the domestic markets, the high level of export subsidies in many developing countries is a burden on the economy. Where excessive protection has been followed by excessive export incentives, there has

77

been little structural change to make exports genuinely competitive, and foreign consumers are being subsidized by the population of the poor exporting country. The developing countries have also been ill served by their de facto exemption from GATT rules against export subsidies.

The diversity of development levels among developing countries is being recognized in the need for 'graduation' procedures that would differentiate among countries according to their levels of income and economic development. A range of procedures ranging from giving the poorest countries privileged market access to those for accepting semi-industrialized countries into such organizations as the European Community are required. As part of this graduation process, and because of the need to pace adjustment in industrial countries if severe protectionist measures are to be avoided, it may pay developing and industrial countries to negotiate agreements on the rate of market penetration for selected particularly sensitive products. Such agreements have been described as cartel attempts with all their attendant ills,[20] and they are of course, 'second best' solutions. In practical terms, however, carefully negotiated agreements could ensure at least modest overall growth and quotas for small, new producers. The textile agreements, for example, while representing barriers to developing country exports, have assured new comers access. Some of the major, poor textile producers (notably India and Pakistan) have not always been able to meet their quotas, but overall there has been a steady 7 per cent to 8 per cent annual growth in developing country textile exports.

The dubiousness and the tendentiousness of the argument for the 'international commodity fund' has now been stated so frequently and at such length that it does not have to be repeated.[21] The continuation and extension of commodity by commodity discussions and agreements on the basis of the reconciliation of the interests of producers and consumers is, however, likely to continue to be rewarding. Such negotiations have a role in improving the operation of markets through the exchange of information and hence the reduction of extreme price fluctuations and by the increased competitiveness of prices. In some cases producers' control over supplies, or the creation of buffer stocks may prove desirable. It must, however, be recognized that the lack of commodity by commodity agreements largely reflects not only conflicts between consumers and producers, but among producing countries themselves. There are, in addition, income distribution issues within countries. Trade-offs between price and volume increases may elicit different responses from large scale and small scale producers, particularly in agriculture. These are not issues that are likely to be settled quickly and real progress again depends on detailed, careful, technically supported negotiations.

The industrial countries' desire for security of raw material, including energy, supplies is merely a special case of the conflicts of interest between consumers and producers. With the decreased role of 'gunboat diplomacy', security of supply is increasingly reflected in prices, and negotiations over the distribution of the rents accruing to mineral production. Long-term contracts are one approach to the problem. Investment by consuming country firms or governments may be a solution in some cases.

Arenas of political rhetoric will not nurture the economics of negotiation. Where demagogy reigns, there is a tendency towards political accommodations at economic cost. Industrial countries may agree, for example, to some form of an international commodity fund, in part because they consider that a reduction of price fluctuation is likely to work more in favor of consumers than producers, but mainly because they consider the cost of such a fund to be low and deductible from aid flows and trade adjustment measures. Capital market subsidies to lengthen maturity terms for borrowing may similarly be acceptable because they will subsidize industrial country lending institutions. But in international economic relations, as in international political relations, easy fixes do not lead to lasting accommodation. The greatest damage done by the proponents of the 'new international economic order' is the expectation that the developing countries' situation can be changed by a few bold measures. Following such messianic promises, the spelling out of the dull, technical steps that are necessary for real progress in international economic relations comes as an anti-climax.

NOTES

1. For some current insights, see W. Arthur Lewis, *The Evolution of the International Economic Order* (Princeton, 1977). The analysis of international economic relationships already engaged the interest of the Victorians (see A. K. Cairncross, *Home and Foreign Investment, 1870–1910* (Cambridge, 1953), Chapter 10 and became an important component of political economy with C. K. Hobson's *The Export of Capital* (London, 1914). A comprehensive and balanced assessment, however, remains to be written.

2. D. Morawetz, *25 Years of Development* (Washington, 1977).

3. For an econometric illustration see Martin Paldam, 'Bliver Verdens Indkomstfordeling Skaevere?' (Is the World's Income Distribution Becoming More Skewed?), *Nationaldekonomisk Tidsskrift*, No. 2, 1977.

4. The economists' predictive record of growth and development has accordingly been very poor. Countries which in the 1960s were expected to grow very rapidly included India, Burma, Argentina, Chile, Egypt, Ghana and Jordan. Countries which performed much better than expected include Brazil, Kenya, Korea and Taiwan. Overall growth projections have proved to be too low. See Morawetz, *op. cit.*, pp. 17–22.

5. C.f. World Bank, 'Commodity Trade and Price Trends' (Washington, 1977) for actual price trends, and for developing country expectations Raul Prebisch, 'Commodity Policy in the Underdeveloped Countries', *American Economic Review*, May 1959 and K. N. Raj and A. K. Sen, 'Alternative Patterns of Growth Under Conditions of Stagnant Export Earnings', *Oxford Economic Papers*, February 1961.

6. See Karsten Laursen, 'The Integrated Programme for Commodities', *World Development*, Vol. 66, pp. 423–435 for a discussion of price fluctuation issues.

7. Michael Michaely finds only a systematic bias against developing countries on rather extreme assumptions in 'The Income Level of Exports and Tariff Discrimination', this volume pp. 156–177.

8. D. Wall, 'Industrial Processing of Natural Resources', World Bank Commodity Working Paper No. 4, April 1979.

9. Organization for Economic Co-operation and Development, *Development Co-operation, Review, passim*. Note: the aid figures exaggerate the aid component because they include loans with a 25% or more grant element. Such loans accounted for 20% of aid flows in 1975–76.

10. World Bank, 'Prospects for Developing Countries, 1978–85', November 1977, Annex 1 and more recent estimates.

11. Donella H. Meadows, Dennis L. Meadows, Jorgen Randers, William W. Behrans II, *The Limits to Growth: A Report for the Club of Rome on the Predicament of Mankind* (New York, 1972).

12. The Massachusetts Institute of Technology Workshop on Alternative Strategies directed by Carroll L. Wilson, *Global Energy Prospects, 1985–2000* (McGraw–Hill Book Company, 1977), and the World Energy Conference, Conservation Commission's *World Energy, Looking Ahead to 2020*, IPC Science and Technology Press, 1978, both found on the basis of detailed global supply and demand studies that the problems of providing adequate energy were manageable. L. Gordon, 'Environment, Resources and Directions of Growth', and M. Radetzki, 'Metal Mineral Resource Exhaustion and the Threat to Material Progress: The Case of Copper' in *World Development*, February–March 1975 pointed out that exploration of non-renewable resources was running well ahead of likely demand trends, so that shortages were highly unlikely.

13. 'Prospects for Developing Countries, 1978–85, *op. cit.* Chapter IV discusses the developing countries' adjustment to the shocks of the mid-1970s.

14. There is thus no conceptually sound basis for the measurement of 'international interdependence'. Ex-post, and ignoring the distributional effects of their impact on economic growth, it is possible to estimate the share of growth attributable to an increase in international trade (and with even less certainty to labor and capital movements). In shorthand this takes the form of the impact growth in one group of countries has on growth in another group of countries. John A. Holsen and Jean L. Waelbroeck argued in 'The Less Developed Countries and the International Monetary Mechanism', *American Economic Review*, May 1976, that the developing countries had a small but not negligible impact on sustaining demand in developed countries in 1974–75. But the distributional effects alone make the estimation, and particularly the projections, of such impacts very dubious indeed.

HELEN HUGHES

15. See The Organization for Economic Co-operation and Development 'Elements of a Programme of Stepped-Up Investment to the Third World in the context of interdependence: Key Issues and Choices', May 1978 and United Nations Conference on Trade and Development, 'Trade Prospects and Capital Needs of Developing Countries, 1976–80', April 1976.

16. It has been argued that self-interested international civil servants and academic and other lobby groups are largely responsible for escalating the new international economic order discussions beyond the levels they merit. See for example, H. G. Grubel, 'The Case Against the New International Economic Order', *Weltwirtschaftliches Archiv*, No. 2, 1977.

17. See I. M. D. Little, 'Distributive Justice and the New International Economic Order', this volume pp. 37–53.

18. Isaiah Frank, 'Reciprocity and Trade Policy of Developing Countries', *Finance and Development*, March 1978.

19. See David Wall, *The Charity of Nations* (New York, 1973), for a discussion of aid quality issues.

20. Bela Belassa, 'World Trade and the International Economy: Trends, Prospects and Policies', World Bank Staff Working Paper No. 282, May 1978.

21. Laursen, *op. cit.*

PART 2

Chapter Five

THE ECONOMICS OF THE GATT

Robert E. Baldwin

As INTERNATIONAL trade in goods and services continues to expand at a considerably more rapid rate than the growth of world output, the institutional arrangements for maintaining order in international trading relations take on added significance. The main international organization established to promote this order, the General Agreement on Tariffs and Trade (GATT), was highly successful in the early post-World War II years not only in resolving international disputes but in facilitating significant tariff reductions by the industrial nations. However, since the mid-1950s and especially since the conclusion in 1967 of the Kennedy Round of trade negotiations, the influence of the GATT has declined. So-called 'voluntary' export constraints and 'orderly marketing agreements' covering trade in such items as footwear, steel, and TV sets have been introduced entirely outside of the GATT framework. Such trade distorting measures as domestic production subsidies, government purchasing policies that favor domestic producers, and state-trading on a non-commercial basis have also been used more extensively in recent years. Furthermore, the consultative and reporting roles of the GATT have diminished in importance.

Many had hoped that the decline in GATT's role would be reversed as a result of the Tokyo Round of trade negotiations. But it is now evident that, although some important improvements in behavior codes have been made, these negotiations have not completely removed the danger of a breakdown in the international trading order through the continued introduction of trade distorting measures. Given this possibility, it is important for economists and others to examine closely the economic and political basis of the various rules of GATT with a view towards again attempting to re-establish the basis of an open and stable international trading order. In both his academic role and as Director of Studies of the Trade Policy Research Centre, this is a subject that occupied many hours of Harry Johnson's time and on which he made many significant contributions, e.g., Johnson (1960, 1965, and 1967).

The Political Basis of the GATT

Economists tend to judge the rules of organizations such as the GATT on the basis of whether they promote economic efficiency, growth, and stability. Trade economists are somewhat ambivalent, however, as to whether it is world efficiency, growth, and stability they wish to promote or only the economic welfare of their own country. Analysts of domestic issues by and large act as if income redistribution will be undertaken to offset any losses to particular income groups when there is a net gain to the community as a whole. Trade economists, on the other hand, cannot even pretend that redistribution among countries is likely to occur, and this may be the reason why they often adopt a nationalistic viewpoint.

Maximizing the collective economic welfare of individuals making up either a country or the world is, however, not the main policy objective of the GATT. The GATT is an international legal document whose primary purpose is to promote or protect certain political goals of nation-states. Economic factors influence these political goals but to the extent that economic interests are promoted in GATT rules and procedures, it is mainly the interests of the more politically effective producers rather than of consumers. In the GATT, as in such other postwar economic organizations as the International Monetary Fund and the World Bank, the broad objective is to help to maintain international political stability by establishing rules of 'good behavior' as well as mechanisms for settling disputes.

Those who played the major role in shaping these agreements, especially the Americans, placed great importance on economic factors as the cause of World War II. These factors include the 1930s depression itself, the uncertainty about the international financial system, the burden of reparations payments, and – what is of concern here – the many restrictions introduced on international trade. In the trade field, it was a policy act by the United States, namely the passage of the Hawley–Smoot Tariff Act of 1930, that initiated trade retaliations in the 1930s and worsened the trade contraction associated with the depression. To try to prevent this from again happening, Cordell Hull and his colleagues at the State Department pressed for an international trade organization that would facilitate the type of liberalizing negotiations held successfully under the U.S. Trade Agreement Act and that would provide a set of rules minimizing the use of discriminatory measures, quantitative controls, and other government trade-distorting policies that are especially irritating to other nations. A very broad agreement (the Havana Charter for an International Trade Organization) covering, in addition to traditional trade issues, commodity agreements, restrictive business practices, and international investment was proposed but the ITO was not approved by key governments and a more limited organization covering only trade matters (the GATT) emerged from the discussions.

The Economic and Political Rationale of Reducing Trade Distortions
The tariff cutting mechanism and safeguards rule of GATT illustrate the relationships between political and economic objectives in this agreement. On the basis of the type of first-best economics usually taught introductory students, a country should unilaterally reduce its import duties, since this will increase its economic welfare. The possibility that the country's terms of trade might deteriorate so much as a result of the cuts that the nation's net welfare in fact declines is mentioned but this is usually not dwelt upon very long, since it raises the question as to why tariff increases are not being recommended. However, if pressed on this latter point, economists generally argue that any potential terms of trade gains are likely to be lost through retaliation, though Harry Johnson (1953–4) pointed out long ago that this is not necessarily true and economists are quite vague on the politics of retaliation. Reciprocal tariff-cutting is thus presented as a process by which all the participants can obtain the kind of gains possible to any one country facing fixed terms of trade, and the troublesome issue of choosing between a nation's welfare and world welfare is avoided. Still another economic argument used to support reciprocal duty reductions is that, compared to unilateral reductions, these cuts have less unfavorable effects on such macro-economic variables as aggregate employment and the balance of payments or exchange rates.

Even if the above reasoning by trade economists is valid in most cases, it seems to be more the result of a happy coincidence of economic and political objectives rather than of foresight and deliberate choice by the founders of GATT. These latter individuals viewed tariffs, especially the high ones existing at the end of World War II, as trade barriers that antagonize foreign producers and lead to big-power economic domination of small countries for marketing purposes as well as to coalitions of the larger powers. Such developments, in turn, increase the possibilities of international political instability and its ultimate manifestation, military conflict. The framers of the GATT believed that cutting duties multilaterally would reduce these international political tensions without significantly disturbing existing power relationships. However, where these power relationships were very unequal, as was the case between the developed and developing countries or between the United States and the other industrial countries at the end of World War II, they were prepared not to insist upon reciprocity.

Since the reduction of international political tensions is a public good, its provision in society involves the free-rider problem. All wish to enjoy greater international political stability but hope to get others to pay the costs involved in obtaining it. Moreover, except when international relations among nations are strained, the benefits of an alleged marginal improvement in political stability are generally perceived to be very small by any one individual, as are the economic benefits from reciprocal tariff reductions. Because of this and the fact that political action involves costs, active domestic support for reciprocal tariff-cutting by the gainers of this policy tends to be weak whereas opposition can be very strong from import-competing industries that fear significant producer-surplus losses as duties are cut. Thus, while there may be unambiguous political and economic gains for individual nations as a whole, the losers may be able to block the achievement of these gains through active political opposition. The framers of GATT attempted to prevent this occurrence by permitting exceptions in any tariff-cutting negotiations and by allowing the withdrawal under Article XIX of tariff-concessions previously granted. They recognized, in other words, the pressure-group nature of international economic policy-making and established a safeguards rule as a means of moderating the major source of opposition to trade liberalization.

On the basis of economic efficiency criteria, taxes and subsidies on imports and exports all have the same type of distorting effect. The rate of transformation between exports and imports is equal in production and consumption but differs from the transformation rate in international exchange. Consequently, in terms of the economic objective of achieving an efficient allocation of world resources, one would expect the GATT to have one statement recommending the elimination of all direct trade taxes and subsidies. However, this is not the case. Export subsidies are banned outright as of a particular date

(Article XVI), while import and export taxes are to be reduced only gradually. No mention at all of import subsidies is made in either the GATT or the ITO.

The rationale for these differences rests on the political nature of the GATT and the economic forces that shape political objectives. The 1930s experience with export subsidies as well as with competitive devaluation, which has the effect of a general export subsidy and import surcharge, apparently convinced the GATT founders that export subsidies exacerbate international political tensions and should be eliminated. Though consumers in the importing country gain from export subsidization by other nations, domestic-producer groups in the importing countries are forced to curtail output and incur a producer-surplus loss. The greater ability of these latter groups to make their views the determining ones in national policy is what increases the likelihood of increased international tensions as various counter-restrictions or subsidies are urged on the government of the country receiving the subsidized goods. While eliminating export subsidies may improve international relations, their removal can also cause serious injury in the subsidized industries much as tariff reductions can. However, the political power of domestic producers in insulating themselves from possible injury-causing actions by their government is much less when the government's actions affects the income they earn in foreign markets in contrast to their earnings based on domestic sales. The view that domestic producers are somehow more entitled to domestic compared to foreign markets is still widely held by the general public. Thus, in the case of export subsidies, it was not necessary for the founders of GATT to implement their international political objective with regard to this distortion only gradually (as with tariffs) and export subsidies were banned outright.

Export taxes, like tariffs, are permitted under the GATT, although the preamble of the Agreement implies that they are to be reduced along with tariffs through trade negotiations. However, there did seem to be less concern by the GATT founders over the international political dangers associated with controls over exports than over imports. In part this was probably due to a recognition that the political power of domestic producers, who tend to be hurt by export taxes, acts as a strong restraining force on the imposition and level of such taxes. The international political danger from these taxes arises mainly because of the antagonism of foreign producers who use taxed products as intermediate production inputs and who therefore are hurt by their increased cost. At the time GATT was established, however, the extensive political dependency of many raw-material suppliers on the developed industrial nations made the likelihood of significant price-increasing export taxes much less than at the present time.

Interestingly, the general prohibition of quantitative restrictions under GATT rules is lifted for exports when critical domestic shortages arise. The quantitative controls over exports are to be administered in a non-discriminatory manner, however. This GATT rule recognizes that the sharp price increases often associated with domestic shortages can cause consumers to modify their usually passive role on trade matters and exercise their basically greater domestic political strength over both local producers of the products in short supply and those concerned with the foreign-policy implications of supply restrictions.

While export subsidies are prohibited and warnings raised about possible adverse effects of domestic subsidies, no mention of import subsidies is made in the GATT. These do occasionally occur, however, not directly but in the form of government purchases of essential commodities that are then resold to domestic consumers at lower prices than paid by the government. Again, the political power of domestic producers of substitute goods hold such subsidies to a minimum. Because of this and the fact that the income benefits to foreign producers from the subsidies minimizes any international tension-creating aspects of this trade distortion, the framers of the rules of GATT apparently believed any international political problems arising from the use of import subsidies would be de minimis.

Selective Domestic Taxes and Subsidies

The manner in which selective indirect taxes versus selective subsidies are handled in the GATT further illustrates the asymmetrical economic features of the existing code of 'good' international behavior. For indirect taxes such as an excise tax on a particular commodity, the destination principle of taxation is followed, namely, the product bears the tax in the country where it is destined for use. Therefore, the excise tax is levied on imports and rebated on exports. In contrast, for selective subsidies such as a production subsidy on a particular product, the origin principle of taxation is adopted. Since this means that the subsidy applies only to goods produced in the subsidizing country, imports do not receive the subsidy whereas exports do.

Under the simplifying assumption of fixed terms of trade, adopting the destination principle for indirect taxes has the effect of leaving domestic production unchanged but decreasing foreign purchases when the product is imported and increasing foreign sales when it is exported. The price domestic consumers pay for the product rises by the amount of the tax. On the other hand, following the origin principle when a production subsidy is introduced has the effect of increasing the production of the subsidized good and either increasing exports or reducing imports. The domestic price of the subsidized product remains unchanged from its free trade level. However, if the origin rather than destination principle is followed in the tax case, the domestic price of the good remains unchanged while domestic production declines. Similarly, in the subsidy case using the destination rather than origin principle results in a lower price for consumers but no change in the output of the subsidized product.

These various relationships are shown in Figure 1. Let the fixed terms of trade be indicated by the slope of the line d_sD_t, production by the point P (fixed factor supplies and competitive conditions are

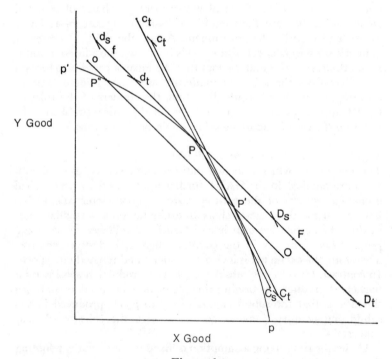

Y Good

X Good

Figure 1.

assumed), and free trade consumption by the points F and f depending upon whether the Y good is exported or imported, respectively. If a production tax is imposed on the Y good and the destination principle is followed, passing the tax on to consumers will reduce the domestic consumption of Y but this decline will be matched by either an equal increase in exports or decrease in imports. The points D_t and d_t indicate the consumption bundles in the export and import cases and the reciprocal of the slope of the line through these points the price of Y in terms of X. Under the origin principle where only domestically produced Y is taxed, production shifts to P′ and consumption to either O or o, depending upon whether Y is exported or imported. The price of Y remains unchanged.

The same figure can be used to depict the case where the domestic production of Y is subsidized and either the origin or destination principle is followed. If Y is subsidized without any rebate on exports or subsidy of imports (the origin principle) the domestic production of Y will shift to P″ and consumption change to O in the export case or o in the import case. On the other hand, if the subsidy is rebated at the border for exports and given to imports of the item (the destination principle), the production point would remain at P and the consumption points be D_s or d_s respectively.

It should be noted that the increase in exports (or reduction in imports) can be just as large when Y is taxed and the destination principle is followed as when Y is subsidized and the origin principle used. It should also be pointed out that from the viewpoint of the nation's total welfare nothing can be said about the superiority of the origin versus destination principle without detailed knowledge about the country's tastes and cost conditions. Adjustments at the border in both the selective indirect tax and subsidy cases merely convert a production inefficiency into a consumption inefficiency. In second-best terms such an international adjustment does not get at the basic domestic reason for the initial inefficiency.

The differential GATT treatment at the border of goods affected by taxes and by subsidies is simply a by-product of the producer bias that affects so many government interventions into domestic markets. The purpose of the excise tax is not to tax domestic production but to tax domestic consumption and the use of the destination principle makes it a consumption tax. Collecting the tax at the manufacturing stage is merely aimed at reducing the costs of collection. Similarly, the purpose of selective subsidies is usually to subsidize the domestic production of a product and not the domestic consumption of the good. Thus, the origin principle is adopted.

89

Countervailing Actions

As noted above, under present GATT border adjustment rules domestic subsidies increase exports or reduce imports compared to what they would be under free trade conditions. Should the increase in exports cause or threaten material injury to an established industry in the importing country, this country can impose a countervailing duty under Article VI of the GATT equal to the subsidy granted. Under conditions of an infinitely elastic foreign demand for the product the foreign duty will fall entirely upon the subsidizing country and the price its producers receive will fall by the duty. The situation is depicted in Figure 1 with the line $c_s C_s$. The cost of producing Y exclusive of the subsidy falls from the reciprocal of the slope of the production possibilities curve at P″ to the reciprocal of its slope at P with production shifting to the latter point and consumption to C_s. The price received by the country for Y (and paid by its consumers) will equal the reciprocal of the slope of the line $c_s C_s$. As is evident from the Figure, the countervailing duty restores exports to their free trade level only by chance; exports after the duty can be greater or less than their free trade level. If the subsidizing country's demand for the import good is inelastic, i.e., the supply curve of the export good is backward bending, the countervailing duty will have the effect of increasing the country's exports above their subsidized level.

There is no GATT provision for countervailing against domestic subsidies on imported products but injury to foreign exporters could be just as substantial in this situation as in the export-subsidy case. The counterpart of permitting a levy in the export case would be to allow the exporting country to introduce a countervailing subsidy on exports equal to the subsidy granted domestic producers abroad. The effect in Figure 1 would be to shift output in the country subsidizing production from P″ to P and consumption from o to c_s. The apparent rationale for not permitting this type of countervailing action is, as mentioned earlier, that the producer bias of GATT extends only to domestic markets. Actions are permitted to counter foreign measures that cause injury to domestic producers as a result of increased imports but are not allowed when the injury is the consequence of a loss of export markets.

For consistency similar countervailing actions to those in the subsidy case might also be permitted for indirect taxes. Since the use of the destination principle increase exports above (or imports below) their free trade level, countervailing action by foreigners might be allowed. Specifically, in the export case a duty equal to the rebated tax or in the import situation an export subsidy equal to the border

tax might be permitted. In Figure 1 the line c_tC_t would dep
case with P' being the production point and C_t and c_t the fin
sumption points in the export and import cases, respectively.

As in the case of the various border adjustments analysed earlier,
none of the countervailing actions discussed above entirely offset the
initial Pareto inefficiency. Again, this inefficiency is caused by a
domestic policy and cannot be completely eliminated by an international measure.

Conclusions

The preceding discussion of the GATT hopefully is sufficient to indicate the rather unsatisfactory nature of this Agreement in terms of
the behavior standards generally applied by economists. The objectives of those establishing the organization were mainly political, and
they were quite willing to slant the rules in favor of a particular
domestic pressure group, namely, producers, in order to help gain
acceptance of their broad trade-liberalizing recommendations.

The view that trade distorting measures can be an important source
of increased international tensions still seems to be valid today. However, levels of the main distortion that the founders of the GATT
focused upon, namely, tariffs, are currently low enough in the industrial nations on most imported items to no longer be a significant
source of irritation to exporting countries. Instead of tariffs, quantitative import controls now stand as the major type of import barrier,
especially against the exports of developing countries. Many of these
countries are rapidly increasing their industrial potential, and they
are becoming increasingly frustrated by the unwillingness of the established industrial nations to open up certain markets for simply produced manufactures. This leads to the very form of international
political tension that the founders of GATT wished to prevent. Similarly, the growing shortage of certain key raw materials coupled with
the greater ability and willingness by developing countries to restrict
exports of these items is increasing the degree of dissatisfaction on the
part of the older industrial economies towards the developing nations.
Disputes among industrial countries, especially with regard to the
trade implications of various domestic aids, will occasionally be important but the main area of concern in the foreseeable future for
trade policy and international political relations is North-South trade.

The implications of this are that the GATT should focus both
upon gradually dismantling existing quantitative restrictions in the
industrial countries on products of potential export interest to the
developing nations and upon establishing mechanisms for ensuring

the developed nations that their industrial activity cannot suddenly be disrupted seriously by export restricting actions on the part of raw material suppliers. Unfortunately, the recent Tokyo Round of trade negotiations made very little progress in either of these crucial areas.

Since producers (including workers) are more likely to incur significant reductions in real income as a result of changes in trade than are consumers, there is some justification for the producer bias of the GATT on income distribution grounds. However, assistance to producers should only be temporary and occur only when they are significantly injured. Moreover, ideally aid should be provided in a manner that does not distort optimum production and exchange relationships. However, given the apparent inability in most countries to provide aid of this sort on a rapid basis, temporary trade-distorting measures may be justifiable as a second-best way of furnishing producer assistance. The existing safeguard provisions of the GATT (Article XIX), which permit a temporary increase in duties to help counter serious injury due to increased imports arising from free-market forces, illustrate the use of this principle. Such duty increases should, however, be tied to substantive domestic adjustment measures, should be carefully monitored by the GATT, and should not be allowed when import increases are related to macro-economic factors and thus better handled by using macro-economic tools. Carrying this principle over to a country's export-competing industries would imply that, if serious injury occurred in one of these sectors as a result of sudden export losses related to free market, micro-economic factors abroad, temporary export subsidies might be also permitted. Thus, efforts would continue to eliminate all the various types of direct trade distortions, but temporary assistance in the form of counter trade-distorting measures would be allowed until more satisfactory domestic adjustment policies become generally accepted.

Temporary assistance to producers also seems to be the proper way to deal with domestic actions by governments that have unfavorable trade effects. Some progress in directly negotiating reductions in the distorting effects of the measures is sometimes possible but for the foreseeable future governments are likely to continue to insist they be given a free hand to deal with matters they consider to be mainly internal in nature. Selective indirect taxes and production subsidies fit into this category of policies. Under the approach just outlined and where existing border adjustment rules are being followed, an import-competing industry seriously injured by increased imports either diverted from the internal market of another country that increases its indirect taxes on the industry's product or resulting from the sub-

ROBERT E. BALDWIN

sidization of domestic production by the foreign country would be permitted to impose a temporary tax on the imported goods. Similarly, an export industry injured as a consequence of an increase abroad in indirect taxes on its product or in production subsidies might be allowed to introduce temporary countervailing export subsidies.

The principle could be applied in other international trading relationships as well as, for example, in dealings with state-owned or control enterprises or with private industries engaged in dumping. It is based on the notion that changes in a country's imports or exports of selective products (whether these are due to private micro-economic market forces or selective government policies that distort these forces) which are so rapid and extensive as to cause significant injury to foreign industries do not represent 'good' international behavior in terms of promoting harmonious international relations. Under careful international supervision a country with an injured industry would be permitted to introduce on a selective basis temporary trade measures to help offset the injury and permit smoother adjustments in their economic structures. A by-product of this approach is that GATT rules would be more balanced in their treatment of producers or consumers. For example, in cases where foreign countries are prepared to subsidize more or less indefinitely domestic production that is exported, consumers in other countries would not be prevented by permanent countervailing duties from benefiting from the lower price of the commodity. On the other hand, export industries that are injured through trade changes just as seriously as import-competing industries would qualify for possible assistance in the way import-competing sectors now do.

REFERENCES

Johnson, H. G., 'Optimum Tariffs and Retaliation' (1953–4), Review of Economic Studies, XXI (2), 142–153.
Johnson, H. G., 'The Cost of Protectionism and the Scientific Tariff (1960), Journal of Political Economy, LXVIII, 327–345.
Johnson, H. G., 'An Economic Theory of Protectionism, Tariff Bargaining, and the Formation of Customs Unions' (1965), Journal of Political Economy, LXXIII, 256–283.
Johnson, H. G. (ed.), Economic Nationalism in Old and New States (Chicago: University of Chicago, 1967).

Chapter Six

MOVEMENTS OF CAPITAL AND OF PERSONS
BETWEEN A COUNTRY WITH AN INCOME TAX AND
A COUNTRY WITH AN EXPENDITURE TAX REGIME*

J. E. Meade

MY PAPER is little more than a rearrangement and elaboration of some of the points made in Chapters 8 and 20 of the report on *The Structure and Reform of Direct Taxation* prepared by a committee of the Institute for Fiscal Studies of which I was chairman; but I hope that it may be of interest to have these ideas put together in a form designed for those who are specially interested in the theory of international factor movements.

I

IN THIS PAPER I wish to isolate for consideration one or two basic incentives which may arise for international movements of persons and of capital funds simply and solely as a result of differences in the tax base. For this purpose I make a series of outrageously simplifying assumptions.

The world is assumed to be made up of only two countries, namely ITland (the Income Tax country which has as its tax base the taxpayers' income) and ETland (the Expenditure Tax country which has as its tax base the taxpayers' expenditure on consumption). In order to abstract from all influences other than this difference in tax

* Harry Johnson was a most distinguished and indefatigable worker in the field of international economics and I greatly appreciate the opportunity to present a paper on an international topic in his honour. But how sorely we shall all miss his comments on our efforts. Harry did not admire the taxonomic approach to economic analysis and on one occasion expressed this view vigorously in respect to work of mine, though he made most generous amends in praise of the ideas which he found lurking beneath the taxonomic cover. My present paper is taxonomic. Would that Harry were with us, so that we could continue to debate the value of this method and to discuss the substance of the analysis.

structure, it is assumed that originally both ITland and ETland have Income Tax regimes with a single proportionate rate of Income Tax at a 50 per cent tax-inclusive rate on all incomes, and that in these circumstances the marginal product of labour and the real pre-tax wage rate and thus the post-tax wage is the same in both countries and the real rate of return on real capital investments and thus the real pre-tax and post-tax rate of return on savings is the same in both countries, because there is free and costless movement of factors between the two countries.

This does not imply that in this initial stage there will be no factor movements between ITland and ETland. Thus if population were growing faster in ITland than in ETland, there might be a net annual immigration from ITland to ETland which would serve to keep the real wage rate the same in both countries or if the proportion of income saved relatively to outlets for profitable investment were higher in ETland than in ITland there would be an annual flow of capital funds from ETland to ITland which would serve to keep the rate of yield on capital funds the same in both countries.

ETland then changes over from a proportionate Income Tax regime to a proportionate Expenditure Tax regime at an unchanged tax-inclusive rate of 50 per cent. I ignore any transitional difficulties; ETland taxpayers simply find that their current savings are now exempt from tax and that their current dissavings are liable to tax. Furthermore I am not concerned with the future dynamic effects of this change through any resulting change in the rate of capital accumulation in ETland. For this reason I assume that ETlanders spend the same amount on consumption as before. This means that if there were any net savings in ETland under the original Income Tax regime, ETlanders being now freed from tax on these savings would at the 50 per cent of tax have twice as large a gross sum of savings to place on the capital market. But the Government would have lost just as much tax revenue; and I assume that it borrows this amount instead of taxing this amount from savers in order to cover an unchanged level of government expenditure. Indeed so far this is the only significant change.

I make one final assumption, namely that ITland (which stands for the rest of the world) is much larger than ETland (which stands for a small island off the North West coast of continental Europe) with the result that the marginal products of labour and capital are unchanged in ITland whatever the effects of ETland's tax change may be on future international movements of people and capital funds.

I realise that I have moved from discussion a very great number of influences which in the real world would be of basic importance in considering the international effects of the difference between tax structures. I have assumed away (1) any change in tax rates which might result from a change in tax base, (2) any transitional difficulties, (3) the complications which might arise from the fact that tax schedules were progressive and not proportionate, (4) the existence of other taxes (such as customs and excise duties and in particular corporation tax) the interactions of which within an Income Tax or an Expenditure Tax may be very relevant, (5) the fact that there are more than two countries some of which may have Income Tax regimes, others Expenditure Tax regimes, and yet others (like the United Kingdom at present) a muddled mixture of the two regimes, and (6) finally the change in the dynamic growth paths of the economies concerned which may result from changed propensities to save and to invest or from tax-induced movements of labour and capital between the two countries. What I have left for consideration is the direct effect of the difference in tax base as such on certain incentives for international movements.

II

There are in fact at least five different ways in which ETland could operate a proportionate Expenditure Tax, and these are illustrated numerically in Table 1.

The most familiar method is that which is presented in Kaldor's classic book on the Expenditure Tax, whereby a taxpayer is taxed on his income plus his dissavings minus his savings. This is in fact the only feasible method of applying an Expenditure Tax which assesses each individual's expenditure separately and is, therefore, the only feasible method of applying an Expenditure Tax in which the rate of tax is related progressively to the individual taxpayer's level of consumption expenditure.

But in the case of a proportionate Expenditure Tax it is not necessary to assess each individual's expenditure separately. Arrangements can be made which directly or indirectly levy the single rate of tax on every purchase of consumption goods regardless of the identity of the particular individual who is making that particular purchase. This possibility is still relevant in the case of a progressive expenditure tax, since these indirect methods can be used for levying a basic or standard rate of tax on all taxpayers, other arrangements being superimposed in order to relieve those at the bottom end of the scale (e.g. by a tax credit or cash benefit) and to impose a progressive surcharge on an individual assessment basis on a limited number of taxpayers at the top end of the scale. Thus the consideration of these alternative impersonal ways of applying a proportionate expenditure tax is by no means irrelevant for real world purposes.

The essential difference between an Income Tax and an Expenditure Tax can be expressed in the following way. With an Income Tax at a 50 per cent rate a reduction of £100 in expenditure on consumption and its investment in real capital equipment which will produce, say, a 10 per cent yield of £10 a year which, after deduction of tax, leaves £5 a year to spend on consumption. The rate of yield to the saver is 5 per cent from a capital investment with a real yield of 10 per cent. With an Expenditure Tax at a 50 per cent tax inclusive rate a reduction of £100 in expenditure on consumption will, because of tax relief on savings, enable £200 to be saved and invested which at 10 per cent would yield £20 a year which, after Expenditure Tax, would finance £10 a year of consumption. The rate of yield to the saver on the £100 of consumption foregone is 10 per cent and is thus equal to the pre-tax real rate of yield on the real investment which is financed by the savings.

For this reason I include in the definition of Expenditure Tax regimes all arrangements which, given a single and unchanged rate of tax, would cause the rate of yield to a saver on any consumption foregone to be equal to the rate of yield on the real investment which the savings serve to finance.

The first column of Table 1 illustrates the effect of an Income Tax in reducing the yield to a saver below the rate of yield on the underlying real investment. The remaining five columns illustrate five different ways of taxing consumption while maintaining the yield to the saver at the same rate as the yield on the real investment financed by the savings. These methods, illustrated in the Table for a tax-inclusive rate of tax of 50 per cent are:-

(1) An Income Tax with remission of tax on savings and with imposition of tax on dissavings, the method discussed in Kaldor's book and applied to approved pension funds in the UK.
(2) An Income Tax with remission of tax on investment and with imposition of tax on disinvestment, the method implied in the U.K. regime of 100 per cent first year tax allowances for expenditures on certain forms of capital equipment.
(3) An Income Tax with remission of tax on the yield on investment, the method implied by the remission of tax in the U.K. on the annual value of owner-occupied houses.

Table 1

| | Income Tax | Methods of Expenditure Tax | | | Tax on Value Added | |
| | | (1) Income Tax with remission of tax on net savings | (2) Income Tax with remission of tax on net investment | (3) Income Tax with remission of tax on yield on investment | (4) Origin basis | (5) Destination basis |
	(a)	(b)	(c)	(d)	(e)	(f)
I. Earnings Spent						
1. Earnings (Factor Cost)	200	200	200	200	200	200
2. Less Income Tax	-100	-100	-100	-100	Nil	Nil
3. Consumption (Market Price)	100	100	100	100	200	200
4. Less Tax on Value Added	Nil	Nil	Nil	Nil	-100	-100
5. Consumption (Factor Cost)	100	100	100	100	100	100
II. Earnings Saved						
6. Earnings (Factor Cost)	200	200	200	200	200	200
7. Less Income Tax	-100	Nil	-100	-100	Nil	Nil
8. Savings	100	200	100	100	200	200
9. Remission of Income Tax	Nil	Nil	100	Nil	Nil	Nil
10. Investment in Capital Equipment (Factor Cost)	100	200	200	100	200	200
III. Return on Savings – Investment						
11. Annual Yield of Output (Factor Cost)	10	20	20	10	20	20
12. Less Income Tax	-5	-10	-10	Nil	Nil	Nil
13. Annual Consumption (Market Price)	5	10	10	10	20	20
14. Less Tax on Value Added	Nil	Nil	Nil	Nil	-10	-10
15. Annual Consumption (Factor Cost)	5	10	10	10	10	10
16. Rate of Return on Consumption Foregone line 15 ÷ line 5	5%	10%				

(4) and (5) A proportionate tax on all sales of consumption goods and services, which would be the effect of VAT at a tax-exclusive rate of 100 per cent, if there were no zero ratings or exemptions. I have called this tax a Tax on Value Added (or TVA), in order to distinguish it from the present VAT which is neither uniform nor universal. A TVA or VAT can be imposed on an origin basis (in which case imports are not taxed but exports are taxed) or on a destination basis (in which case imports are taxed but exports are exempt from tax). Table 1 illustrates only the closed-economy effects of the various taxes in which case, of course, origin is the same as destination. But in Table 1 I have stressed the difference of international application by expressing the TVA in both forms, because the difference will play an important role in my later analysis.

At this point the reader is advised to take time off to run his eye down each of the columns in Table 1 in order to make sure that he is familiar with the differences between the various regimes. The following distinctive features should be noted:-

(i) With a 50 per cent (tax-inclusive) rate of tax the Income Tax gives a yield to savers (the 5 per cent of line 16) which is only half the real rate of yield on the underlying investment (the 10 per cent shown in all cases by line 11 ÷ line 10). With all the five methods of Expenditure Tax the yield to savers (the 10 per cent of line 16) is equal to the real rate of yield on the underlying investment.

(ii) Method 1 gives tax relief to the saver of funds, whereas Method 2 gives tax relief to the investor of funds. The distinction can have an important effect on international flows of capital funds if the saver is in one country and the investor in another.

(iii) With all the Methods except 2 the pre-tax rate of yield to the saver (shown at 10 per cent by line 11 ÷ line 8) is equal to the real rate of yield on the investment which is financed by the savings (the 10 per cent of line 11 ÷ line 10). But in the case of Method 2, because the tax remission is given to the investor and not to the saver, the pre-tax market rate of return on savings (the 20 per cent shown by line 11 ÷ line 8) is twice as high as the 10 per cent real rate of yield on the underlying investment (line 11 ÷ line 10).

In this case the investor receives only £100 from the saver (line 8). But as a result he can finance £200 of investment (line 10), because he can set the whole of this £200 as a credit against his tax base, thereby at a 50 per cent tax-inclusive rate of tax, saving £100 in liability to Income Tax. Thus he finances the £200 of investment as to £100 from the saver's savings and as to £100 from his own saving of tax which would otherwise be payable. This causes the post-tax market rate of yield (line 13 ÷ line 8) instead of the pre-tax market rate (line 11 ÷ line 8) to correspond to the real rate of yield on the underlying investment. This feature which is peculiar to Method 2 can have an important effect on the international flow of capital funds.

(iv) For the operation of Methods (1), (2) and (3), (that is to say for all the Methods which start with a direct tax on income modified by a remission of tax on net savings, on net investment, or on the yield of investment) there is no distinction to be drawn between factor cost and market price. But for the operation of Methods (4) and (5) (that is to say for all the Methods which operate in the manner of an indirect tax on consumption expenditures) the distinction between factor cost and market price is at the root of the matter. With Methods (4) and (5) people receive their incomes, whether earnings or investment income, free of all tax. They are taxed only when they come to spend these incomes and find the cost of living raised by the Tax on Value Added. This distinction can have important international implications because it may well affect attitudes towards double taxation relief. Thus the question may arise under Methods (1), (2) or (3) whether ETland or ITland should give relief from Income Tax because of Income Tax charged in the other country; but it may appear quite unreasonable that ETland should in any circumstances give relief from Tax on Value Added because of ITland's Income Tax, or *vice versa*, regardless of the underlying logic of the situation.

(v) Finally there is an important distinction for international repercussions between a Tax on Value Added on an Origin Basis (Method (4)) and a similar tax on a Destination Basis (Method (5)). The distinction can best be illustrated by supposing that ETland starts with a Tax on Value Added at a tax-exclusive rate of 100 per cent on a Destination Basis. In this case at the equilibrium rate of exchange between ETland's currency and ITland's currency, the cost of living will be twice as high in ETland as in ITland. ITland's consumption goods on importation into ETland will be subject to a 100 per cent duty; ETland's consumption goods, subject to a 100 per cent rate of duty if consumed in ETland, will be supplied to ITland free of tax. If ETland then changed over to an Origin Basis, ITland's goods would be sold in ETland at the same market price as in ITland; and ETland's goods would be sold in ITland at the same market price as in ETland. This distinction can be of great importance in affecting the movement of consumers between ITland and ETland and is the reason for listing Methods (4) and (5) separately in Table 1.

III

In a country with a closed economy (i) a taxpayer would be liable to the tax regime of that country, (ii) his expenditure on consumption would be spent on goods and services in that country and his savings would be directly or indirectly spent on capital development in that country, and (iii) he would receive his income from a source in that country. In an open economy, however, there are three relevant localities which do not necessarily coincide. Thus a taxpayer who is liable to U.K. tax may spend his income on a holiday in France or invest his income in a company in France, and he may have received income from dividends paid by a company which operates in the U.S.A. or from incidental earnings from work done in the U.S.A. In order to consider the relations between ETland and ITland it is necessary to draw these three distinctions.

(i) By an ETlander, I will mean a person who is resident in ETland and is, therefore, liable to the tax regime of ETland; and similarly for an ITlander. I neglect all problems of defining residence, ordinary residence, domicile and so on, and assume that a person for tax purposes clearly and unmistakably is either an ETlander or an ITlander.

(ii) An ETlander may spend or invest some of his income or resources in ITland, or *vice versa*. By this I mean something other than that he purchases some imports from ITland; I mean that he is actually in ITland when he spends on consumption (e.g. as a tourist) or that he invests his money in a concern which is based in ITland.

(iii) An ETlander may receive investment income from an ITland source or may make some earnings in ITland though he remains an ETlander for tax purposes, and *vice versa*.

These considerations immediately raise the question of Double Taxation Relief. I assume that in the original position in which both countries operated an income tax at the single proportionate rate of 50 per cent Double Taxation Relief was given, so that it would be a matter of indifference to any ITlander or ETlander whether he derived his income from an ITland or an ETland source; in all cases he would be taxed only once at 50 per cent income.

To the individual it would be a matter of indifference whether it was the country of origin or the country of destination of the income which gave the tax relief. The only difference would be whether it was the latter or the former government which enjoyed the tax revenue on an income originating in one country but received by a resident of another country. Since in this paper I am concerned only with the effect of tax rates on individuals' incentives, it is a matter of secondary importance which government gives the relief; but I shall assume that in the original situation in which both countries operated an income tax regime it was the government of the country of destination of the income which gave the relief.

But when ETland is operating an Expenditure Tax and ITland an Income Tax it is an open question what arrangements should, and what arrangements will, be made about Double Taxation Relief.

With these preliminaries I am ready for an exercise in taxonomic classification. I ask what will be the tax incentives for (i) movements of capital funds and (ii) movements of persons between ITland and ETland on the various combinations of assumptions regarding the five possible methods of operating an Expenditure Tax in ETland and regarding the arrangements for Double Taxation Relief between the two countries.

IV

I start then with possible tax incentives on the movements of capital funds between ITland and ETland. With free and costless factor movements and in the absence of any exchange controls over remittance of funds, all savers in both countries will invest their savings in whatever way will yield the highest post-tax rate of return, regardless of country.

Case 1. ET Methods 3, 4 and 5 without Double Taxation Relief
Consider first the case in which ETland applies the Expenditure Tax either by remitting tax on the yield on Investment Income (Method 3) or else by a Tax on Value Added on all consumption expenditures (Methods 4 and 5). In all these cases ETland does not impose an income tax on investment income (line 12 of Table 1). The common-sensical arrangement would then seem to be that no Double Taxation Relief should be given. Since ETland does not impose tax on investment income earned in ETland, it would not appear sensible for the ITland government to remit its tax in favour of ITlanders receiving investment income from ETland. And since ETland does not raise tax on investment income in ETland it would not at first sight seem

102

sensible for the ETland government to give relief to ETlanders from some other source of tax simply because the investment income from ITland was taxed.

With a rate of yield of 10 per cent on real capital investment in ITland, this would mean that both ITlanders and ETlanders would obtain a net-of-tax yield of 5 per cent on savings invested in ITland. The yield of ITland savers would be as shown in column (a) of Table 1 and the yield to ETland savers would be as shown in columns (d), (e) and (f) of Table 1 with the insertion at line 12 of the ITland 50 per cent rate of tax as a deduction from the annual yield on the investment.

If the rate of yield on real investment in ETland were also 10 per cent, then the ETlander whose savings were invested in ETland would receive a post-tax yield of 10 per cent (as shown in columns (d), (e) and (f) of Table 1), but the ITlander whose savings are invested in ETland would receive a post-tax yield of only 5 per cent, represented in columns (d), (e) and (f) of Table 1 as the value of line 11 ÷ line 8 reduced by the 50 per cent rate of tax in ITland.

Thus up to this point the effect would be that the change in tax regime in ETland would have no effect on the ITlanders' choice of country for the investment of their capital funds; they would receive a 5 per cent post-tax yield on investment in both countries whether ETland operated an income tax or an expenditure tax. But the change of tax regime would have a marked effect on the ETlanders' incentives, since with an income tax in both countries the post-tax yield would be 5 per cent regardless of the country of investment, whereas with an expenditure tax in ETland the ETlander would get a 10 per cent yield on investments in ETland and only a 5 per cent yield on investments in ITland.

There would thus be a tax incentive for ETlanders to invest at home rather than abroad. ITland is assumed to be a big country and ETland a small one. It is possible, therefore, that if ETlanders under an Income Tax regime had been lending and investing abroad on a large scale relatively to their own economy, then after the shift to the expenditure tax regime the increased investment in ETland would bring down the rate of yield on real investment in ETland while it remained 10 per cent in ITland. The yield in ETland could not, however, fall below 5 per cent (at which point it would pay all ETlanders and all ITlanders to invest capital only in ITland) nor could it in any circumstances rise above 10 per cent (at which point it would pay all ETlanders and all ITlanders to invest only in ETland).

The final result on post-tax yields is shown in Table 2. The market rate of interest at which investors can afford to borrow will in this case be equal to the real yield on investment in both countries. But the market rate of interest could fall to 5 per cent in ETland while it remained at 10 per cent in ITland, before ETland savers would find it worthwhile investing in ITland.

Table 2: Rates of Yield with Methods 3, 4 and 5 for ET.
No Double Taxation Relief.

		ETland			*ITland*		
		s	i	m	s	i	m
Residence of Saver:							
ETland	Max.	10%	10%	10%	5%	10%	10%
	Min.	5%	5%	5%			
ITland	Max.	5%	10%	10%	5%	10%	10%
	Min.	(2½%)*	(5%)*	(5%)*			

Origin of Investment Income

s = post-tax yield to saver.
i = real yield on investment.
m = market rate of interest.

* In this and the following Tables figures in brackets refer to market situations in which it would not be profitable for any transactions to take place.

Case 2. *ET Methods 3, 4 and 5 with Double Taxation Relief*
As already explained, it may at first sight seem inappropriate in these circumstances for either country to give any tax relief on investment income since investment income is not subject to tax in ETland. But in the absence of Double Taxation Relief the rate of yield on real investment in ETland can be reduced by anything up to 50 per cent below the rate of yield in ITland because of the tax incentive for ETlanders to invest in ETland. This would represent an inefficient use of capital which could be avoided by granting relief from tax on the yield on ETland's investments in ITland.

Such relief could be given by some form of subsidy by the ETland government on ETlanders' investment income from ITland (in order to make up for the tax levied in ITland). Alternatively it could be given by the ITland government refraining from taxing ETland enterprises in ITland because they would not be taxed in ETland, a procedure which might not recommend itself to taxed ITland enterprise in ITland competing with a tax free ETland enterprise in ITland. However the arrangements are conceptually possible and would have the result shown in Table 3. With this arrangement ETland savers obtain the full pre-tax yield of 10 per cent on their savings wherever they are invested and ITland savers obtain the post-tax yield of 5 per cent wherever their savings may be invested.

Table 3: Rates of Yield with Method 3, 4 and 5 for ET. Taxation Relief on Investment Income Originating in ITland.

| | Origin of Investment Income | | | | | |
| | ETland | | | ITland | | |
	s	i	m	s	i	m
Residence of Saver: ETland	10%	10%	10%	10%	10%	10%
ITland	5%	10%	10%	5%	10%	10%

s = post-tax yield to saver.
i = real yield on investment.
m = market rate of interest.

Case 3.   ET Method 1 without Double Taxation Relief

Case 4.   Method 1 with Double Taxation Relief

Next consider the cases in which ETland chooses to operate the expenditure tax by means of Method 1, i.e. by adding dissavings to, and subtracting savings from, the income base for taxation. Tables 2 and 3 will once more show the results on post-tax yields on savings.

If Method 1 is adopted in ETland, then (as shown in line 12 of Table 1) both in ETland and ITland a 50 per cent rate of tax is deducted from the yield on investments. It may in this case appear common-sensical to continue the Double Taxation Relief arrangements which are assumed to be made when both countries operated an income tax. In this case the outcome is as indicated in Table 3. ITlanders will obtain a post-tax return of 5 per cent on their savings wherever they are invested and ETlanders will obtain a 10 per cent return wherever their savings are invested. This is what results from the fact that the only change on the introduction of the expenditure tax in ETland is that ETlanders obtain a remission of income tax on that part of their incomes which is saved, regardless of where it is invested.

105

But the choice between Method 1 on the one hand and Methods 3, 4 or 5 on the other for the operation of a proportionate expenditure tax is for a closed economy merely a matter of administrative convenience; the real effects are exactly the same. While commonsense may suggest that with Method 1 Double Taxation Relief should be given whereas with Method 3, 4 or 5 it should not, this is perhaps a case where commonsense is misleading. Method 1 combined with Double Taxation Relief means that the ETland government is giving remission of ETland tax both on any ETland savings which are invested in ITland and also on the yield on any such investment. It is quite reasonable to argue that not both of these reliefs should be given by the ETland government on foreign investments. Either the remission of tax on saved income should apply only to such income as is invested in ETland or else the yield on such income when it is invested abroad should not enjoy relief from ETland tax even though it is taxed in ITland. If either of these reliefs were denied, then ETland savings would enjoy expenditure tax treatment only if they were invested in ETland; ETlanders would have a tax incentive to invest in ETland; and the position would be as shown in Table 2.

An arrangement whereby ETland denied tax remission on foreign investment but gave Double Taxation Relief on the yield on foreign investment might perhaps appear to the ITland government as being justifiable and compatible with the ITland government continuing to give Double Taxation Relief on the yield on ITland's investments in ETland. But at the same time it might appear unreasonable to the ITland government to continue to give Double Taxation Relief on the yield on ITland's investments in ETland, if ETland refused to give Double Taxation Relief on the yield on ETland's investments in ITland, even though ETland gave relief from tax on ETland's savings as they were invested in ITland. Thus commonsense might suggest to the ITland government that it should draw a distinction between these two cases; but commonsense would be misleading.

Case 5.   ET Method 2 without Double Taxation Relief

Case 6.   ET Method 2 with Double Taxtion Relief

Method 2 amounts to a subsidy paid by the ETland government on net investment in real capital development.[1]

In an open economy the question arises whether the ETland government pays the subsidy (i) in respect of real capital invested in ETland whether the investor is an ETland or an ITland resident or (ii) in respect of real capital investment carried out by ETland enterprises (i.e. by persons liable to ETland tax), whether the investment is physically located in ETland or in ITland.

Let us consider first the case in which the ETland government introduces into its income tax regime a subsidy on investment physically located in ETland. Let us first assume that Double Taxation Relief continues to be given on investment income after the change of tax regime in ETland, since investment income continues to be liable to tax in both ETland and ITland. The post-tax return to savers, whether they be ITlanders or ETlanders, will now remain at 5 per cent (i.e. at 50 per cent of the 10 per cent yield on real investment) on all real investment carried out in ITland. But on investment carried out in ETland the post-tax return to all savers will be 100 per cent of the real yield on the investment, as is shown in column (c) of Table 1. In this case all ITlanders and ETlanders would have incentives to channel all their capital funds into investment in ETland until the rate of yield on real capital investment in ETland had been reduced to 5 per cent to correspond to the post-tax yield on savings used to finance investment in ITland. The position would be as indicated in Table 4a.

Table 4a: Rates of Yield with Method 2 for ETland. Remission of Tax on Investment in ETland.

| | | Location of Investment | | | | |
| | | ETland | | | ITland | | |
	s	i	m	s	i	m
Residence of Savers:						
ETland	5%	5%	10%	5%	10%	10%
ITland	5%	5%	10%	5%	10%	10%

s = post-tax yield to saver.
i = real yield on investment.
m = market rate of interest.

It is possible however that Double Taxation Relief might not survive the change of tax regime in ETland. The ITland government might complain that the new system was subsidising investment in ETland at the expense of investment in ITland and might decide to offset this subsidy by refusing Double Taxation Relief on investment income earned by ITland savers on their investments in ETland. ETland's government might then retaliate by refusing Double Taxation Relief on ETlanders investment income earned on investments in ITland. Table 4b shows the resulting situation.

Table 4b: Rates of Yield with Method 2 for ET.
Remission of Tax on Investment in ETland.
Without Double Taxation Relief.

			ETland			*ITland*	
		s	i	m	s	i	m
Residence of Savers:							
ETland	Max.	10	10	20	$2\frac{1}{2}$	10	10
	Min.	$2\frac{1}{2}$	$2\frac{1}{2}$	5			
ITland	Max.	5	10	20	5	10	10
	Min.	$(1\frac{1}{4})$*	$(2\frac{1}{2})$*	(5)*			

s = post-tax yield to saver.
i = real yield on investment.
m = market rate of interest.

* No transactions would ever take place in this market.

The yields for investment in ITland by ITland savers would remain unaffected by the abolition of Double Taxation Relief so that the figures in the bottom right-hand compartment of Table 4.b are the same as in Table 4.a. Since ETland savers investing in ITland would no longer enjoy Double Taxation Relief they would receive a post-tax yield of only $2\frac{1}{2}$ instead of 5 on their investments in ITland (top right-hand compartment of Table 4.b).

But the yields in respect of investment in ETland will depend upon the comparative shortage of savings relative to investment opportunities in the two countries. Suppose first that ETland is so short of capital funds that both before and after any changes of tax regimes some capital funds must flow from ITland to ETland. In this case the market rate of interest must rise to 20 per cent in ETland in order after double taxation to give ITland savers the necessary post-tax return of 5 per cent which they could obtain on their savings in ITland. We would be on the Maximum lines in the left-hand compartment of Table 4.b. If at the other extreme ETland was very rich in capital funds so that some savings must continue to flow from ETland to

ITland after the abolition of Double Taxation Relief, the market rate of interest in ETland must fall to 5 per cent in order that the post-tax yield to ETland savers in ETland should not be greater than the $2\frac{1}{2}$ per cent which they can get from investments in ITland. We would be on the Minimum lines in the left-hand compartments of Table 4.b. Equilibrium might be reached at some level between these Maximum and Minimum lines with no capital movements in either direction.

Let us turn to the case in which the ETland government gives its tax subsidy not on all investments physically located in ETland, but on all investments, wherever located, provided that the investment is undertaken by an ETland taxpayer (e.g. a company resident in ETland), and let us start with the case in which Double Taxation Relief on investment income is continued so that all such income is taxed only once. In this case the 10 per cent yield on real investment in ITland could be enjoyed in full on their savings by ITlanders and ETlanders provided only that the investment project was carried out by an ETlander. There would be no incentive to invest in ETland rather than in ITland, so that the rate of yield on real investment in ETland would also be maintained at 10 per cent. The result would be as shown in Table 5.a. No investments would in fact be undertaken by ITlanders. All savings would be channelled through ETland enterprises. The post tax-return to savers (s) would be equal to the original yield on investment in ITland (i = 10 per cent) which we assume to be unchanged, but the market rate of interest ruling in ETland where all investment projects would be financed would be driven up to twice the yield on investment (m = 20 per cent) because, as we have shown above (page 100), with Method 2 it is the market rate of interest after tax which in this case is linked to the real yield on investment. The subsidy on investments drives up the rate of interest at which an ETland investor is prepared to borrow funds above the real yield on the investment, whereas an ITland investor could afford to offer a market rate to lenders no higher than the yield on the investment which it served to finance.

Once again the ITland government might object to the investment subsidy given by the ETland government to ETland companies; and in order to offset this it might refuse to give Double Taxation Relief to any ITlander's investment income which was derived from ETland companies. The ETland government might retaliate by refusing Double Taxation Relief on ETlanders' investment income derived from ITland companies. The result would be as shown in Table 5.b.

The yields for ETland savers investing through ETland companies

109

and for ITland savers investing through ITland companies would remain as in Table 5.a. But the removal of Double Taxation Relief would reduce by 50 per cent the post-tax yields to ETland savings invested through ITland companies and to ITland savings invested through ETland companies. ETlanders would continue with even more determination than before to invest their savings only through ETland companies. But ITland savers would be indifferent between ITland and ETland companies. For an ITlander the advantage of investing through an ETland company due to the ETland tax subsidy

Table 5a: Rates of Yield with Method 2 for ET.
Remission of Tax on Investment by ETlanders.
With Double Taxation Relief.

| | *Residence of Investor* | | | | | |
| | *ETland* | | | *ITland* | | |
	s	i	m	s	i	m
Residence of Saver: ETland	10%	10%	20%	(5%)*	(10%)*	(10)*
ITland	10%	10%	20%	(5%)*	(10%)*	(10)*

s = post-tax yield to saver.
i = yield on real investment.
m = market rate of interest.
* No transactions would ever take place in these markets.

Table 5b: Rates of Yield with Method 2 for ET.
Remission of Tax on Investment by ETlanders.
Without Double Taxation Relief.

| | *Residence of Investor* | | | | | |
| | *ETland* | | | *ITland* | | |
	s	i	m	s	i	m
Residence of Saver: ETland	10	10	20	$(2\frac{1}{2})$*	(10)*	(10)*
ITland	5	10	20	5	10	10

s = post-tax yield to savers.
i = yield on real investment.
m = market rate of interest.
* No transactions would ever take place in this market.

110

on such investment would be offset by the disadvantage of double taxation of the investment income derived from such an investment.

In this Section we have dealt only with some simple cases. Real world situations may, alas, be much more complicated.

In the first place, the rules for the remission of tax on investments may be based on complex and mixed principles. For example, in the U.K. at present, such tax subsidies are given through 100 per cent first year capital allowances (a) only in respect of certain investments such as in industrial plant and equipment, but (b) on all such investments physically located in the U.K. whether undertaken by a U.K. or a foreign investor, and also (c) on all such investments undertaken by U.K. resident companies whether the investment is physically located at home or abroad.

In the second place, there are three relevant sets of country distinctions to be made for tax purposes, namely: (1) the residence of the saver, i.e. of the person or institution who finally receives the investment income; (2) the physical location of the real investment itself; and (3) the residence of the company or other body which actually undertakes the investment. In this Section we have considered combinations of (1) and (2) and of (1) and (3). But tax arrangements may depend simultaneously upon all three considerations. Consider, for example, an ETland saver investing through an ITland company in a project physically located in ETland. One has to consider the tax treatments by both governments of (i) the investment in ETland by an ITland investor, (ii) of the profit arising in ETland to an ITland company, and (iii) of a dividend paid by an ITland company to an ETland shareholder.

The possible combinations of tax treatments of savings and investment by the ETland government and of the different treatments of the different elements of Double Taxation Relief mean that a complete classification of all possible cases becomes unattractive even to the most enthusiastic taxonomist. At this point he must hand over to those who are interested in examining the special features of actual cases arising in the real world.

V

I turn now to the question of the tax effects on the international movements of persons between ETland and ITland. This set of problems needs to be discussed under three main headings.

First, will the difference in tax structure between ETland and ITland give any incentive for persons to migrate and change their residence in order to change the tax regime to which they are liable

111

so as to be able to earn and consume their earnings under one tax regime rather than another? This question can without more ado be answered with a clear negative. The first half of Table 1 makes it clear that under all IT and ET regimes with the same 50 per cent (tax-inclusive) rate of tax the same one half of a worker's real product will be available for him to consume.

A second question is whether the difference between the two tax structures will lead to an incentive for persons to migrate and thus change their tax regimes in order to be under an expenditure tax when they wish to save and under an income tax when they wish to dissave.

A third question concerns the treatment of Double Taxation Relief on earnings. Depending upon the treatment of Double Taxation Relief, will the difference in tax structure between ETland and ITland affect the incentive of ETlanders to seek incidental earnings in ITland without changing their residence and liability to ETland's tax regime, and *vice versa*?

These last two questions need further attention, and it is convenient to consider the third question before the second.

With both countries on an income tax basis Double Taxation Relief would mean that incidental earnings from abroad would receive the same tax treatment as home earnings. As can be seen from a comparison between column (a) of Table 1, on the one hand, and columns (b), (c) and (d), on the other hand, earnings which are spent receive the same treatment with Methods (1), (2) and (3) of an Expenditure Tax as they do with an Income Tax. These Methods are based on an Income Tax with certain remissions of tax; but none of these remissions affect earnings which are spent. In these cases, therefore, Double Taxation Relief on earnings from a foreign source should continue, if the structure of the tax regime is not to affect the incentive to earn abroad as compared with the incentive to earn at home.

The problem is more complicated if ETland operates the Expenditure Tax by Methods (4) or (5) with a Tax on Value Added. The relevant factors in the two countries are illustrated in Table 6. We consider a case in which a given amount of labour will produce 200 units of output worth $200 in ITland. The situation in ITland is then illustrated in the right-hand column of Table 6. Because of the 50 per cent rate of income tax, the worker after ITland tax will retain to consume only 100 units out of his 200 units of output. Let us assume that since ITland is a large country these figures are unaffected in ITland by anything that goes on in ETland and that there is a common currency (e.g. gold standard) in use in both countries.

If ETland shifts from an Income Tax to a Tax on Value Added on an Origin Basis (Method 4) the money cost of living will be the same in ETland as in ITland, since imports from ITland into ETland are not taxed and exports from ETland to ITland are not given any remission of tax. In this case an ETlander's nominal earnings must be reduced from $200 to $100 with the change of tax[2], since earnings are now paid free of tax instead of subject to a 50 per cent deduction of income before expenditure, but the cost of living has not been raised by the Tax on Value Added.

Table 6: Effect of choice between an Origin Basis and a Destination Basis for a Tax on Value Added in ETland.

ETland		ITland	
Method 4			
I. ETland's TVA on an Origin Basis			
Earnings	$100	Earnings	$200
		Less Income Tax	− $100
Cost of Living	$1	Cost of Living	$1
Real Consumption	100	Real Consumption	100
Method 5			
II. Etland's TVA on a Destination Basis			
Earnings	$200	Earnings	$200
		Less Income Tax	− $100
Cost of Living	$2	Cost of Living	$1
Real Consumption	100	Real Consumption	100

If, however, ETland operates the Tax on Value Added on a destination basis (Method 5), the result will be as shown in Section II of Table 6. The cost of living will now be twice as high in ETland as in ITland, but the old level of pre-tax money wages will now be paid free of tax.

As far as a resident in the one country earns income in the other and consumes it abroad, there should be no tax applied by the home government of the worker. As is clear from Table 6, in all cases to produce 200 units will then enable the earner to consume 100 units, whatever his country of residence. But if part of foreign earnings are remitted home for consumption at home, the position is not quite as simple.

113

Consider first the situation under Method 4 (Section I of Table 6). An ITland worker will earn only $100 in ETland. This sum if it is taxed and spent in ITland will purchase only 50 and not 100 units of consumption goods. The ITland government should apparently give Double Taxation Relief on earnings in ETland remitted to ITland. On the other hand, an ETland worker can earn $200 in ITland which, after ITland tax, will leave $100, which will purchase 100 units of goods in ETland. The ETland government should, therefore, give no remission of tax in respect of the expenditure in ETland of money earned in ITland.

The position is, however, reversed if Method 5 is adopted and ETland's TVA is on a Destination Basis. In this case an ITland worker can earn $200 in ETland which, after ITland income tax, will still purchase 100 units of goods if spent in ITland. No remission of ITland tax is needed. On the other hand, $200 earned by an ETlander in ITland will after ITland tax be reduced to $100 which at a $2 cost of living in ETland would purchase only 50 units of goods. An ETlander's earnings in ITland, if remitted of ETland, should therefore be relieved either of ITland's income tax or of ETland's tax on value added.

Thus *either* (Method 4) ITland should give tax relief on ETland earnings remitted to ITland while ETland should not give relief on ITland earnings remitted to ETland or *else* (Method 5) ITland should not give tax relief but ETland should do so. Whether or not there is any probability of governments agreeing to either of these apparently one sided arrangements is another matter. But the logic of the situation can perhaps be intuitively best grasped in the following way. When foreign earnings are remitted for expenditure at home, there must for equilibrium in the balance of payments be a net increase of exports from the country in which the income is produced and earned to the country in which the goods are consumed. With Method 4 exports from ETland to ITland are subject to ETland's tax, so that they must be relieved from ITland's tax. But exports from ITland to ETland are not subject to ETland's tax; they have, as it were, already enjoyed remission of tax in ETland and no further remission is needed. And conversely with Method 5.

We are now in a position to consider in what circumstances it will pay persons to reside in ETland and be subject to ETland tax while they are saving and then to reside in ITland and be subject to ITland tax when they are dissaving and spending their previously accumulated capital funds on consumption.

The results are illustrated in Table 7, which is constructed on the

Table 7.

| | Expenditure Tax Operated By[1] | | | | | |
	Method 1	Method[2] 2(a)	Method[2] 2(b)	Method 3	Method 4	Method 5
Section I						
Earned in ITland	$200	$200	$200	$200	$200	$200
Accumulated in ITland after One Year	$105	$105	$110[d]	$105	$105	$105
Expenditure in ITland	$105	$105	$110[d]	$105	$105	$105
Cost of Living in ITland	$1	$1	$1	$1	$1	$1
Real Consumption in ITland	105	105	110[d]	105	105	105
Expenditure in ETland	$52½	$105	$110[d]	$105	$105	$105
Cost of Living in ETland	$1	$1	$1	$1	$1	$2
Real Consumption in ETland	52½	105	110[d]	105	105	52½
Section II						
Earned in ETland	$200	$200	$200	$200	$100	$200
Accumulated in ETland after One Year	$220[a]	$105[c]	$110	$110[b]	$110[b]	$220[a]
Expenditure in ETland	$110[b]	$105[c]	$110	$110[b]	$110[b]	$220[a]
Cost of Living in ETland	$1	$1	$1	$1	$1	$2
Real Consumption in ETland	110[b]	105[c]	110	110[b]	110[b]	110[b]
Expenditure in ITland	$220[a]	$105[c]	$110	$110[b]	$110[b]	$220[a]
Cost of Living in ITland	$1	$1	$1	$1	$1	$1
Real Consumption in ITland	220[a]	105[c]	110	110[b]	110[b]	220[a]

1. The figures in this Table are based on Tables 3, 4a, and 5a, i.e. on the assumption that Double Taxation Relief or its equivalent is given in all cases. In the absence of such relief the figures marked [a] would be anything between 220 and 210 (see Table 2), those marked [b] would be anything between 110 and 105 (see Table 2), those marked [c] would be anything between 110 and 102½ (see Table 4b), and those marked [d] would be 105 (see Table 5b).

2. Method 2(a). Tax Remission on Investment located in ETland.
Method 2(b). Tax Remission to Investors resident in ETland.

following assumptions. There is a single currency for both countries. In both countries a worker can produce the same real output. Under all Methods except 5 the cost of living will be the same in both countries (namely $1); but, as already shown in Table 6, it will be twice as high in ETland (namely $2) as in ITland (namely $1). In both countries pre-tax earnings will be the same (namely $200) except with Method 4, in which case, as shown in Table 6, it will be only $100 in ETland but $200 in ITland. We consider in Table 7 the case in which a worker produces 200 units of goods, saves the whole of his post-tax earnings for one year, and then spends those savings together with a year's post-tax interest on his savings either in the same country under the same tax regime or else in the other country after emigration to that country so that he is under the alternative tax regime for the expenditure of his capital. The figures in Table 7 are based upon the description of the tax regimes and the analysis of the results on rates of post-tax yield to savers, as given in the earlier sections of this paper.[3]

The conclusions to be drawn from Table 7 may be summarised as follows:-

(1) With Method 2 there is no incentive for migration of savers or dissavers. This is to be expected since the ETland tax regime applies to the locality of investment or to the residence of investors. It has nothing to do with the residence of savers or of spenders.
(2) With Methods (3) and (4) there is some tax advantage to save under the ETland regime, but there is no tax advantage in dissaving under the ITland rather than the ETland tax regime.
(3) With Methods (1) and (5) there is a very marked advantage in saving under the ETland tax regime but dissaving under the ITland tax regime. The results with these two methods can be summarised thus:-

Tax Regime for Savings	Tax Regime for Dissavings	Real Consumption
ETland	ITland	220
ETland	ETland	110
ITland	ITland	105
ITland	ETland	$52\frac{1}{2}$

Thus with Methods (1) and (5) there is a strong case for ETland to levy tax on capital funds owned by persons who emigrate from ETland to ITland and to give remission of tax on the expenditure in ETland of capital funds brought into ETland by a taxpayer who

116

migrates from ITland to ETland. In this case the first figure in the above table would be reduced from 220 to 110 and the last figure raised from 52½ to 105. Methods (1), (3), (4) and (5) would all then lead to the same result, namely that the adoption of an Expenditure Tax regime in ETland would give some advantage to those who saved under the ETland tax regime, but it would then make no difference under which regime the savings were dissaved and consumed.

NOTES

1. It is assumed that the investor has sufficient taxable income to be able to enjoy the whole of the tax advantage due to setting the cost of any new capital expenditure as a deduction from his tax base.

2. In fact it may be more probable that nominal pre-tax earnings in ETland's currency would remain unchanged in which case ETland's currency would have to be depreciated in terms of ITland's currency to give the result shown in Section I of Table 6.

3. For the situations analysed in Table 2 it is assumed in Table 7 that the post-tax rate of return to the ETland saver remains at the maximum 10% rather than being reduced to the minimum 5%. The general picture given in Table 7 remains valid for this case so long as the rate of return in ETland is not reduced to the minimum.

TAXATION SCHEMES IN A WORLD WITH INTERNATIONALLY MOBILE LABOUR AND CAPITAL: A COMMENT

Ronald W. Jones

PROFESSOR MEADE's paper, based upon several chapters of the recent report on *The Structure and Reform of Direct Taxation*, illustrates the way in which expenditure and income tax regimes differ for open economies. This comparison is complicated both by the existence in his analysis of five different alternative methods of arranging an expenditure tax and by the question of Double Taxation Relief. It is no wonder that the taxanomic approach is so useful in distinguishing these possibilities.

As I understand it, Meade's paper focuses on the impact of these tax systems when there exists international mobility of people and capital funds. Two possible questions come to mind. On the one hand one can ask how a change from an income tax system to an expenditure tax system induces a change in people's behaviour, in particular in their decisions to save or dissave. This is a question appropriate either to a closed economy or an open economy. On the other hand one can ask how this change in the tax system affects the desired *location* of people with given attitudes towards saving and consumption. It is this latter question that I think is important in the paper.

In this set of remarks I wish to pursue one issue that goes beyond the framework provided by Professor Meade but is nonetheless of interest to the theory of international factor movements. I adopt Professor Meade's assumption that for tax purposes a person is 'clearly and unmistakably' either a resident of E.T.-land (Expenditure-Tax-Land) or of I.T.-land (Income-Tax-Land). By this I mean that individuals are 'tagged' as subject to one country's tax regime or the other, and without going into detail, that appropriate

118

RONALD W. JONES

Double Taxation Relief is provided. Thus a resident of I.T.-land pays a flat (say 50) per cent of his income to I.T.-land's government, regardless of the source of income, and a person tagged as a resident of E.T.-land pays 50 per cent tax on his expenditures to his government, regardless of where those expenditures are undertaken. But people are allowed to make decisions about which 'tag' to wear. That is, following Professor Meade's exercise, ask what happens to the locational choice of people when the small country switches from an Income-Tax Regime to an Expenditure-Tax Regime.

The primary impact of such a tax change is to encourage savers to move to E.T.-land and dissavers to alter their tag to I.T.-land. If, as seems reasonable, savers and dissavers roughly balance each other, such tax-induced migration might be expected not drastically to alter the population figures of either country. But it may alter the quantity of actively-employed labour in the two countries and, as a consequence, the international location of real capital resources.

A simple scenario can be sketched that serves to capture some of these possible factor flows. Suppose individuals are typically characterized by expenditure/income relationships that vary over the life-cycle such that early and later years display dis-saving behaviour and middle years, in which wage income is relatively large, are characterized by a positive level of savings. If such is the case the demographic characteristics of E.T.-land and I.T.-land will systematically differ. Although the total population of E.T.-land may stay roughly constant, the labour force might be expected to grow.

Initially real capital has been allocated between the two countries so as to equalize the rates of return. The net migration of manpower to the Expenditure-Tax land might or might not disrupt this equality of returns, depending upon the underlying structure of production. In a Heckscher–Ohlin world with all capital inter-sectorally mobile and each area producing positive amounts of two commodities (with homogeneous labour and capital the only two factors of production), factor returns are locked into the given commodity prices in the large country (I.T.-land). In such a case the increase in E.T.-land's labour force would be accommodated by an alteration in the composition of output (in favour of labour-intensive commodities) without requiring any international re-allocation of the world's stock of capital.

Suppose, by contrast, that in E.T.-land the number of productive factors exceeds the number of commodities produced. This ordering would follow naturally in the short run if in each industry some

119

factors are occupationally restricted. The presumed movement of labour into E.T.-land would then cause the wage rate there to be depressed and the return to capital to be raised. Given the assumptions of the model international equality in wages is not a condition of equilibrium if residents are mostly required to work in their chosen country of residence. Individuals currently engaged in net savings have a positive inducement to reside and work in E.T.-land, and would be willing to accept a somewhat lower wage in order to obtain the tax benefits. However, with capital not 'tagged' as are individuals, the return to capital in E.T.-land cannot remain above that in the rest of the world. Real capital is induced to move to E.T.-land until rates of return to capital are again equalized. In this indirect way wage rates are also brought closer together, although as shown in the formal treatment below, wages in E.T.-land would still be driven to a lower level than in I.T.-land so that workers in I.T.-land who are saving only relatively small amounts would be dissuaded from moving to E.T.-land.

In this scenario the major impact of the small country's switch from an income tax system to an expenditure tax system has been to attract individuals who are currently saving and drive out individuals who are dissaving. This is a kind of 'gains-from-trade' response. All individuals are potentially better off if *different* tax systems are created in a world in which individuals differ in their 'taste' patterns (some saving, some dissaving). Such a reallocation of the world's population entails further real effects to the extent that savings habits are linked to other characteristics. If, as I have assumed, net savers are more likely to be engaged in the labour force, the country switching to an expenditure tax system gains labour and, typically, capital as well.

Finally, note that the demographic switch to a country of net savers may have direct bearing on balance-of-payments issues, although in Professor Meade's analysis the government always matches private savings with budget deficits.

Appendix

A simple model dealing with these issues has the Expenditure-Tax land (E.T.-land) producing a single commodity with three productive factors: (i) Labour, which is internationally mobile and sensitive both to wage rate differentials between E.T.-land and the large country (Income Tax land) and to a change in the tax structure in E.T.-land away from income taxes to an expenditure tax regime; (ii) Capital, which is assumed to be homogeneous and to be located where its return is maximized; and (iii) A specific factor (land, natural resources) which is internationally immobile. A change in E.T.-land's tax structure is assumed not to alter prices in the large country, I.T.-land. In particular, the world rate of return to capital, I.T.-land's wage rate, and commodity prices remain constant.

The total quantity of labour available for employment in E.T.-land is presumed to depend on two key variables: the local wage rate, w (relative to the fixed wage rate in I.T.-land), and the tax structure. Let this be captured by the expression:

(1) $$L = L(w,t).$$

The symbol, t, is a proxy for E.T.-land's tax structure. Instead of considering a massive switch in tax-regimes from a 50 per cent proportional income tax to a 50 per cent proportional tax on expenditures, I assume that initially some combination of the two tax systems (adding to 50 per cent) prevails. An increase in t indicates a further switch away from income taxes to expenditure taxes. As argued in the text, at a given wage rate this change in tax structure simultaneously causes net dis-savers to leave E.T.-land and attracts net savers. By assumption that in total numbers these roughly balance but that net savers represent a larger fraction of labourers than do net dis-savers, an increase in t cause L to expand:

$$\alpha \equiv \frac{1}{L}\frac{\partial L}{\partial t} > 0.$$

An increase in the wage rate as of given tax structure would also serve to attract labour, so that with obvious notation (a '^' represents proportional changes),

(2) $$\hat{L} = e_L\hat{w} + \alpha dt,$$

with $e_L > 0$.

The demand for labour in producing the single (Hicksian composite) commodity depends both on the output level, x, and the array of factor prices: the wage rate, w, the return to internationally mobile capital, r, and the rental on the specific (and internationally immobile) factor, s. Let E_L^w and E_L^s represent, respectively, the relative change in the quantity of labour required per unit output when the wage rate and the return to the specific factor each rise separately by 1 per cent. With the return to capital fixed by conditions in the large country (I.T.-land), the demand for labour, $L = a_L x$, changes as:

(3) $$\hat{L} = E_L^w\hat{w} + E_L^s\hat{s} + \hat{x}.$$

121

The return to the specific factor is assumed to be flexible so that the fixed supply equals $a_s.x$. (a_s and a_L represent the quantities of specific factor and labour respectively, required per unit of output). Therefore $\hat{x} = -\hat{a}_s$, or, by analogy with previous notation,

(4) $$\hat{x} = -E_s^w \hat{w} - E_s^s \hat{s}.$$

Substitute this expression into (3), and equate demand and supply of labour to obtain:

(5) $$[(E_L^w - E_s^w) - e_L] e\hat{w} + [E_L^s - E_s^s] \hat{s} = \alpha dt.$$

I assume that all factors are net substitutes for each other. Thus an increase in the wage rate by itself would reduce the net demand for labour on three counts: less labour is used per unit output, output tends to be reduced as the specific factor is used more intensively, and more labour is attracted into the country. The coefficient of $\hat{s}$ is positive since an increase in s would lead to greater intensity in labour usage and greater output (since the specific factor is used less intensively).

Relationship (5) indicates that factor prices must adjust in order that the expansion in the labour force induced by the change in tax structure is fully employed. But if competition is assumed, the fact that the commodity price is fixed in world markets and that capital rentals are also fixed implies that the wage rate and the rental on the specific factor must move in opposite directions. That is, if unit costs are kept equated to constant price,

(6) $$\theta_L \hat{w} + \theta_s \hat{s} = 0,$$

where θ_L and θ_s represent the distributive share of labour and the specific factor respectively. Thus (5) and (6) together can be used to solve for the factor price changes induced by the tax change:

(7) $$\hat{w} = -\frac{1}{\Delta} \theta_s \alpha dt$$

(8) $$\hat{s} = \frac{1}{\Delta} \theta_L \alpha dt$$

where $\Delta \equiv \theta_L (E_L^s - E_s^s) - \theta_s[(E_L^w - E_s^w) - e_L] > 0$.

Thus the shift towards greater reliance on expenditure taxes, and the presumed net inflow of labour from I.T.-land, drives down the wage rate and increases the return to the specific factor. Each of these changes induces a less intensive use of the specific factor and,

122

since its total availability is fixed, allows an expansion of E.T.-land's output level.

Finally, consider the international movement of capital. Unlike labour, capital is not 'tagged' by the tax authorities and will move where its return is maximized. As argued in the text there is a presumption that to preserve equal returns capital will have to move from I.T.-land to E.T.-land to accompany the net migration of labour. The total quantity of capital employed in E.T.-land is $K = a_K \cdot x$. Output has been shown to expand, but it is possible that the reduction in wages (causing capital intensity, a_K, to fall) will more than outweigh the effect of the rise in specific factor return, s, in raising capital intensity. The formal expression for $\hat{K} = \hat{a}_K + \hat{x}$ is, by (4),

$$(9) \qquad \hat{K} = (E_K^w - E_s^w)\, \hat{w} + (E_K^s - E_s^s)\, \hat{s}.$$

The coefficient of $\hat{s}$ is positive. The sign of the coefficient of $\hat{w}$ reflects the comparison between the degree of substitutability between labour and capital, on the one hand, and labour and the specific factor, on the other. If labour is at least as good a substitute for the specific factor as it is for capital (so that the coefficient of $\hat{w}$ is non-positive), the reduction in wages must tend to increase total capital usage (output expands by more than capital-intensity falls). By contrast, the situation in which the net inflow of labour would cause a net outflow of capital is characterized by a relatively high degree of substitutability between capital and labour and a low degree of substitutability between the specific factor and the other two.

Chapter Seven

IDENTIFYING FUTURE COMPARATIVE ADVANTAGE

A. I. MacBean

Introduction

The question addressed in this paper is: how far can the existing theories of international trade give guidance to the optimal pattern of trade for a given country at some future date, in economic circumstances which differ greatly from its current situation? The problem can be highlighted by the particular case of Iran, but is common to Venezuela and several other states whose current prosperity depends on the export of a non-renewable natural resource such as oil. The issue has both practical importance, as potentially influencing the future welfare of millions of citizens of these countries, and some theoretical interest, testing as it does the relevance and explanatory power of economic theory. It must be made clear that this paper was written before the revolution in Iran.

The Iranian Position

For many years the government of Iran has sought to reduce its economy's dependence on oil exports. Since the mid-1960s diversification into manufactured exports has been one important objective of economic policy. The tremendous boost given to their economy by the rise of oil prices in 1973–74 temporarily solved their balance of payments problems, but triggered an immensely ambitious development programme. This had a basic aim of turning Iran into a major industrial power, capable of sustaining its prosperity by a diversified industry which would replace declining oil revenues with manufactured products.

The consensus in Iran has it that the oil reserves are equivalent to about 30 years production at current levels of extraction, but actual

124

production levels could soon fall as a result of the increased difficulty and rising real costs of extraction. Moreover, domestic use of oil both as energy and as an industrial raw material is also increasing fast. As a result most Iranian economists estimate that net revenues from oil exports will peak in the mid to late 1980s and decline thereafter. To sustain rising levels of imports, required for even sharply scaled down rates of growth would require a dramatic rate of increase in manufactured and traditional (non-oil) exports (Kavoussi, 1978). Oil and gas accounted for over 97 per cent of visible exports in 1976. This gives urgency to policies to promote non-traditional exports even when optimistic assumptions are made about import replacement and the growth of agricultural and services exports.

Of course the estimates for oil revenues may turn out to be pessimistic. Iran has huge reserves of gas and coal. There are possibilities for nuclear and solar energy. Between them Iran may have considerable potential for substitution of alternative energy sources for petroleum which would release the latter for other uses. New oil and gas reserves may be proved, new technology may enable higher percentage recovery rates and so on. Given the vast size of the oil and gas sector in Iran any projections about that economy's prospects are extremely sensitive to whatever happens in that sector. As proven reserves, future discoveries and extraction rates are all matters of such uncertainty any planning exercise should perhaps simply be regarded as contingency planning. Given some moderately pessimistic assumptions for the petroleum sector what can Iran do to mitigate the effects which declining petroleum exports would have on the economy? Put at its most crude, what can Iran do to increase exports to plug the gap between resources and the requirements for some acceptable rate of growth?

Criteria for Resource Allocation

But, of course, exporting is not an end in itself. Its only long term justification is if it enables goods or services to be imported from abroad more cheaply than they can be produced at home. If exports have to be subsidised more than can be justified in offsetting costs due to trade-policy-induced, or other, distortions, and/or sustained for longer than can be justified by an infant industry argument, such exports would involve the economy in net social loss. The resources used up in producing such exports would have been better used in producing non-tradables, import substitutes or even in overseas investment. The pragmatic argument for paying more attention to exports in the case of Iran is that, like many other developing countries,

125

high levels of effective protection have already given excessive inducements to import substituting industrialisation and discriminated seriously against both traditional and non-traditional exports. (Yeats, 1975; Tizhoosh, 1978)

But, *in principle* the question of what to export should be considered as part of the general resource allocation problem of trying to maximise the real social value of national product (leaving questions of distributional equity to be taken care of by other means). Also, we are concerned with a world of both exogenous and policy induced change. Accordingly some currently unprofitable activities may be worth undertaking because they will eventually become sufficiently profitable to recoup current losses and repay subsidies; or external benefits produced by these activities may justify current and continued subsidies.

Recently, Iran has found it exceedingly difficult to increase commercial sales of manufactured exports. The reasons are not too hard to find. The world economy is relatively stagnant while Iran's economy has been booming with a faster rate of inflation in Iran than abroad. The pressure of domestic demand made it easy for firms to sell in the internal market and difficult to sell overseas. High levels of protection enable high economic rents to be earned from local sales while competition overseas can involve sales of Iranian exports at prices below cost. High prices for non-traded goods like housing and office space attract resources at the expense of both exports and import substituting industries. Only when domestic inflation is down to average world levels and levels of protection have been reduced, or offset by other policies, will the incentives to use resources for export equal the incentives to produce for the home market. But reducing inflation and protection are both policies which should be adopted for their own sake. Success would enhance the efficiency of all manufacturing in Iran.

In seeking activities which can contribute to non-oil exports of manufactures we are assuming that Iran will eventually reach a situation where the flow of oil and gas revenues is insufficient to balance the required flow of imports. In these circumstances the rial should depreciate. This would in itself stimulate import substitution and exports. The point of looking ahead to anticipate such an eventuality is to try to ensure that Iran has the capacity to meet that challenge. But we have to bear in mind that planners cannot predict the course of events in their own and other countries over the 10–20 year span involved. Nor can central planners understand the detailed problems of specific firms and industries. Of course the nation could attempt physical planning, with nationalised industries given clear physical targets and instructions to achieve them, but this would run grave risks of enshrining for long periods any initial errors of judgement about the future course of events. More realistically planning should attempt little more than to indicate the main directions of development and suggest the kinds of stimuli and guidance which can be given to private and public sector managements. It is the managements of these individual entitities who have to choose which goods to produce and make the actual decisions which will economise on or waste resources.

In mixed economies, such as Iran's, experience and theory both suggest that this can best be achieved when the price system is an adequate guide to the opportunity costs of the resources used up in production and the social value of the outputs of industry and agriculture. Prices should not be distorted by large subsidies, taxes or high protection against competing imports. But to move from a system which currently gives high protection to import substituting industries and which consequently produces high costs for exports and an overvalued exchange rate which in turn reduces the incentive to export, takes time and involves structural change and adjustment costs. Rather than move directly to such a situation it may be expedient to adopt the second best policy of trying to offset the extra costs, imposed upon exporting, by a general *ad valorem* subsidy to all manufactured exports while gradually harmonising and reducing protection. But the government may also have to intervene still more directly to assist production of exportable goods in situations where the private sector is currently unwilling to undertake the necessary large investments.

Can research identify activities which seem likely to provide in the future viable manufactured exports for Iran? The criterion for identifying a promising field for exporting is that there should be a reasonable expectation that the marginal social rate of return to Iran on resources used there should be at least as high as could be obtained in other activities. In project evaluation terms: the rate of discount which makes the present value of the stream of annual benefits accruing to Iran equal to the present value of the stream of costs should be higher than the internal rate of return obtainable in alternative projects and should exceed the shadow or accounting rate of interest for Iran. The benefits to Iran would normally be the annual revenues from the exports minus any repatriated payments to foreigners plus any external benefits. The costs would have to be measured as social opportunity costs including any external disbenefits such as pollution. All should be measured at international values with appropriate adjustments for transport costs. Exports would be at expected F.O.B. prices minus transport costs from the factory to the port while the costs of inputs would be measured at expected C.I.F. or F.O.B. prices depending on whether they could have been exported or imported with the appropriate adjustments for transport costs to and from the border. Non-tradable inputs should as far as possible be broken down into their tradable inputs and valued at international prices. Labour would be valued at its marginal opportunity cost including extra consumption. (Little and Mirlees, 1974; Krueger, 1974).

This means that at the then existing exchange rate the unit social opportunity costs of producing the exports should be less than or equal to the price obtainable in foreign markets less the costs of delivering and marketing them. In general, this would only occur when either the costs of the resources used were lower than for foreigners, or the resources were used more efficiently than can foreign producers or a combination of these. It is not enough that the resource input, say copper ingots, should be much cheaper in Iran than abroad. The cost of the copper ingot in Iran plus the cost of producing, say copper pipes from it, plus the cost of transporting and marketing the pipes in the foreign market must be less than the cost for the foreigner in buying ingots in Iran, transporting them to his country, processing and marketing the copper pipes himself. Otherwise Iran would be unable to compete in copper pipes and on economic grounds should simply export the unprocessed copper. This conclusion assumes that there are no net external benefits to processing copper, and that there is no infant industry case to be made for it.

In other words the choice of an individual exporting activity ideally ought to depend on project evaluation à la 'Little–Mirlees'. But that approach is very demanding in terms of data and resort to it may only be appropriate when the range of possibilities has been narrowed, reasonable prospects sorted out and technical feasibility studies mounted. So there could be considerable gains if some general pointers to likely exports can be found. Can the theory of international trade provide any answers?

The General Problem

If we look at some of the most important economic problems of the recent past it is not at all clear that economic theory has attained much success in explaining any of them. We have competing theories on inflation, unemployment, economic growth, income distribution and patterns of international trade. Nor has empirical research proved very successful in sorting out which give the best explanation of the past, let alone give useful guidance to the future when many of the parameters which are usually assumed fixed may have changed.

Given that track record for theory it may seem exceptionally fool-hardy for economists to venture into such an intrinsically difficult task as to attempt to foresee what types of goods and services a par-ticular nation might expect to be capable of exporting profitably some 10 to 20 years hence. The task may well be impossible, but to establish its impossibility may require at least a serious attempt to do it. If it is impossible, the policy conclusion could well be that nations such as Iran should try to adjust their internal prices as quickly as possible to reflect current opportunity costs (adjusted border prices) and leave it all to the independent decisions of private businessmen and con-sumers, save for the traditional areas of government control such as defence, policing, fire services, education and health.

While such a policy recommendation would have much appeal to many economists it is somewhat impractical, in the context of an economy like Iran, to advocate a completely laissez-faire solution. Quite apart from the politics of the matter it has to be recognised that the past and present system of protection through high duties, quantitative restrictions, licensing, price controls and subsidies has produced serious distortions which probably cannot be eliminated quickly without high transitional costs. While they persist, further interventions by government would be required to offset or allow for these distortions. Secondly, there may be benefits to be reaped from some investments which private investors cannot capture through the market. Thirdly, there may be distributional reasons for some direct intervention by government. Fourthly, there may be imperfections in the capital market or political risks which make it unrealistic to expect the private sector to undertake some large, long-term investments. Finally, much Iranian industry is at present in the public sector and it seems to be government policy for that to continue.

If some intervention is inevitable and some is likely to be justified for various of these reasons, criteria to guide these interventions will be required. Perhaps that provides at least a minimal justification for proceeding with research to see if rational analysis can be done on the issue of detecting future comparative advantage.

Insights from International Trade Theory

What insights, then can be gained from the theory of international trade? It is one of the most highly developed branches of economics; one which has a long history and has in the past made strong claims to influence the judgements of governments and men of affairs. But the strong normative propositions advanced by trade theorists in the past were seriously undermined by advances in welfare economics which raised the thorny issues of income distribution, interpersonal comparisons, externalities and 'second best' situations. While on the positive side of trade theory the strong conclusions for the pattern of trade which emerged from the more rigorous versions of the Hecksher–Ohlin theory were weakened by empirical evidence, much of which was inconsistent with either its main predictions or some of its key assumptions.

It is true that the most basic propositions of trade theory remain intact: (1) that the potential gain from trade stems from differences in the relative opportunity costs of producing goods in different countries; (2) that in the absence of barriers countries will export those goods in which their relative opportunity costs of production are lowest and import those where they are highest. But when it comes to explaining why the differences in costs arise there is an embarrassment of riches.

The pure simplicity of the Samuelson–Hecksher–Ohlin model has not survived confrontation with the statistical evidence. The relative capital to labour endowment of nations has turned out to be a rather poor explanation of which goods most countries export and which they import. When broadened to include other factors, such as natural resources endowment and human capital embodied in a trained and educated workforce, its explanatory power is greatly improved. But there still remain a number of worries. The assumption of identical production functions for example is too strong and could mislead. Two countries with very different factor endowments may be able to export the same product to world markets because they use quite different combinations of the factors in producing the good. Typically, technologies may be sufficiently similar in most industries, in most countries, for this assumption to be useful in general explanations of the pattern of trade, but it would be dangerous either to select or to rule out a particular class of exports for a given country on the basis of an assumption that there was only one way of producing them economically.

The spread of technology in synthetics, plastics and new ways of handling traditional materials have greatly increased the possibility of satisfying the same need in a great variety of ways, e.g. a boat hull can be made of timber, steel, aluminium, several types of plastic or ferro-concrete; and each of these materials demands different techniques from the others and can itself be handled in a variety of ways. For plastics these range from injection moulding to hand laid up fibre glass and resin.

The assumption of constant returns to scale may also be unhelpful in a number of specific industries. If this assumption were not to produce any bias in predictions of trade patterns then either economies of scale should seldom occur, or trade barriers, including international transport costs, transfers of knowledge, and differences in national tastes as well as tariffs and quotas should be negligible. But for most durable consumer goods and many capital goods, economies of scale in research and development, in production and in distribution are thought to be rather important. Given the great importance which most manufacturers attribute to a large domestic market the concept of a minimum optimum size, limited by the size of a readily accessible domestic market must carry weight. The problem is also tangled up with the effects of learning by doing so that the costs of producing fall with increased volume. The static nature of traditional trade theory ignores such factors, but quite clearly any country which is considering setting up a specific industry where internal economies of scale are important must consider limits imposed by the size of its domestic market.

Here, again the very fact of economies of scale, along with the likelihood of significant variations in patterns of demand between countries, has become a key element in yet another plausible hypothesis about trade patterns in the work of Linder. There, similarity in demand patterns based on similar living standards becomes a cause of a high volume of trade between two nations. Trade follows a sequence of events in which production to satisfy the home market grows to achieve economies of scale and leads to the export of goods to countries which produce similar but not identical products.

This in turn merges with the work of Grubel and Lloyd, with their stress on trade in differentiated products together with various types of economies of scale, as a major explanation of the fact that a great deal of trade is intra-industry and between the rather similar economies of the industrialised nations of the OECD.

Finally, the product cycle hypothesis of Vernon and associates, brings in time and innovation as yet one more strand in the tangled web of explanations of the pattern of international trade. Countries such as U.S.A. with high per capita incomes, consumers with a taste for novelty and firms which invest heavily in research will tend to export new goods or old goods produced with new technologies. But when production processes are simplified the parent company sets up subsidiaries in countries with lower labour costs which will produce

131

such goods first for their domestic markets and then may export them back to the U.S. This theory too helps to explain intra-industry trade in terms of such examples as the export of coloured TVs from U.S.A. while black and white sets were imported from Japan at a particular stage in that product cycle process.

One element, not touched on above, and indeed not much discussed in trade theory, with the honourable exceptions of Grubel and Lloyd in one of their explanations of intra-industry trade and in a recent paper by R. E. Falvey (1978) is the influence of transport costs. Yet for many developing countries this is likely to be a very important determinant of what goods can be exported and where. It could well be important for Iran.

The upshot of this rather cavalier summary of modern theory in the field of international trade is surely the recognition that there is no simple mono-casual explanation of trade patterns. There are a great many possible reasons why a nation should export a particular category of goods and import rather similar or very different ones. Some reasons may have greater universality, wider applicability than others, but when one examines a particular country, specific, quite idiosyncratic factors could be much more important.

Economics is still very much in the position described by Keynes in the foreword to the Cambridge Economics Handbooks:

'The Theory of Economics does not furnish a body of settled conclusions immediately applicable to policy. It is a method rather than a doctrine, an apparatus of the mind, a technique of thinking, which helps its possessor draw correct conclusions;'

What we have is some relevant questions to ask and a way of approaching the issue but not a set of rules which will give us a direct answer to the question of which types of goods a particular country such as Iran should export. Even the questions suggested by trade theories need to be supplemented by others when we turn to look at the *prima facie* exportables of Iran.

Determinants of Comparative Advantage in Iran

What follows is not based upon research. The Iran Planning Institute with U.N. Assistance intends to do this research. The present stage of that project is very preliminary and these remarks are based merely on some reading of mainly secondary sources and conversations with some well-informed Iranian economists. But it would be tedious to simply list the series of questions which form the basis of the planned research. It should help to provoke discussion if some guesses about future export prospects are hazarded here.

The final objective would be some ranking of fields of activity or individual activities in order of their comparative advantage. If there were substantial differences in the import content of the activities, assumptions about the future exchange rate of the Rial would affect private rates of return but should not affect ranking if the cost-benefit analysis has already allowed for exchange rate distortions. Assumptions about the appropriate rate of discount and accounting wage rates for unskilled and skilled labour would also be important. Frankly, I have little idea of what would be the most reasonable values to choose for these various rates. Their actual choice would surely be influenced by discussions with the Ministry of Planning and the Budget of Iran (PBI).

Turning to the more fundamental issues of the determinants of supply and demand which will form the main influences upon relative costs, the following seem to be key general factors which trade theory would suggest. They should be regarded merely as hypotheses to be tested by research.

(1) Relatively abundant natural resources should tend to give Iran an advantage in natural resource intensive exports. Even apart from oil Iran appears to be very rich in natural resources. She has the second largest reserves of natural gas in the world, a great deal of coal and high quality copper, and probably commercially viable quantities of phosphates, gold, nickel, lead and uranium.

(2) Compared with most countries Iran should have access to relatively cheap energy for a long time to come. She possesses within her borders oil, natural gas and coal. The last of these is still uncertain but appears likely to be enormous. Solar energy is available in abundance and Iran is close to the world's largest oil surpluses in Saudi Arabia and other Gulf States. On the basis of such readily available energy Iran might be expected to have a relative advantage in energy intensive activities.

(3) Iran has a population of about 35 million, growing at about 3 per cent per annum. Per capita income is over $2,000. Even allowing for the fact that much of the new wealth is concentrated in the hands of a few there is a substantial class of citizens with relatively high incomes. By most standards Iran should have a relatively large domestic market for many types of goods and services. This should give some advantage in setting up industries where the minimum optimum scale is substantial. It should also help in attracting foreign investment and technology for such industries.

(4) Iran has a large geographic area and low population density in most areas. Overall she has 634,000 square miles for a population of 35 million compared with the U.K.'s 94,000 square miles for 56 million, an average of 55 people per square mile compared with 595 in the U.K. This may be relevant to one cost which has not yet figured in trade theory, pollution. For those industries which are air polluting Iran may have some advantage from the possibility of locating them away from areas of high population density. Air pollution is, however, already a problem in the environs of Tehran.

(5) On the other hand, Iran is very short of fresh water and at least in one of the seas on which she borders, the Caspian, water pollution from human and industrial wastes is already a problem. The Gulf, as a long narrow sea, may also be at risk from pollution and certainly care ought to be exercised over disposal of wastes there. The shortage of water could prove an obstacle to industries with high water demands, unless waste energy or cheap energy can be used for recycling fresh water or desalinating salt water.

(6) The shortage of water is a serious obstacle to expansion of agriculture. Damage has already been inflicted on some traditional irrigation systems by excessive extraction rates on underground water which has started to lower the water table in some areas of Iran. Agriculture employs around 40 per cent of the labour force but accounts for under 10 per cent of GDP. Despite substantial investment agricultural growth is far below the Fifth Plan targets. Iran has moved from near self-sufficiency in food production in the late 1960s to become a large net importer of food in the mid-1970s. Poor soil, low rainfall, backward technology, and a lack of skilled farming labour are said to be serious obstacles to rapid growth in this sector, but lack of incentives due to past policies may also be a significant factor. Certain traditional exports such as nuts and vegetable oils may continue and grow somewhat, but it seems unlikely that Iranian agriculture will produce much increase in either direct exports or inputs to new industry. But it could probably release labour for other activities with some substitution of work for leisure if farm incomes were allowed to rise.

(7) In recent years Iran's economy has been short of labour. This is evidenced in high wages for construction workers, service workers and drivers. Rather large numbers of immigrant workers have been brought in from Pakistan, India, Afghanistan and, surprisingly, South Korea. Precise estimates of their numbers are impossible, but informed guesses put their numbers at 2 to 3 per cent of the labour

134

force. The recent and continuing civil disturbances have brought a halt to a great deal of construction work and led to unemployment.

In general, wages are fairly high in the formal sector. Skilled labour of the plumber, electrician, mechanic type is scarce. At the professional level of accountants, engineers, business managers, doctors, lawyers, computer programmers, there appears to be serious shortages; incomes are very high and there are large numbers of foreigners.

These manpower shortages would suggest that Iran is extremely unlikely in the near future (5 to 10 years) to be able to follow the labour intensive industrialisation path to exports pioneered so successfully by the newly industrialised countries (NICs) such as South Korea, Hong Kong, India, Pakistan, Brazil and Mexico. High wages combined with relatively low productivity of labour in Iran combine to rule this out for some time. But a 3 per cent population growth combined with the effects of the literacy programmes of the government may change this situation drastically in 10 to 20 years. Improving the quality of labour through investment in training ought to be a high priority for Iran, provided ways of doing this successfully can be found. The graduates of the present schools designed to produce skilled workers are not looked upon with any favour by employers in Iran. Success in the future seems likely to depend even more than in the past on the ability to absorb technology and managerial skills. Study of the methods of Germany in industrial apprenticeships and the training of skilled workers could pay dividends to Iranian industry.

(8) The other major resource stressed in both trade and development theory is capital. In terms of fixed capital, social overhead, transport equipment and machinery Iran must be very poor for an economy with such a relatively high per capita income. In terms of financial capital, reserves of foreign exchange and ownership of foreign assets Iran is probably rather well off. The amount of investment which has been attempted in recent years has been very high but because of bottlenecks at the ports, poor implementation of schemes, delays, manpower shortages and failures of management its productivity has been low. A great deal has gone into military hardware and defence technology. Given the international mobility of capital and its low marginal social productivity in Iran, it is difficult to see Iran as possessing a comparative advantage in capital intensive exports, based upon cheap capital, vis-à-vis OECD nations, but there might be some scope for such exports to other LDCs.

Most of the foregoing points suggest that Iran may have or may develop a comparative advantage in certain natural resource and energy intensive industries. Air pollution and labour shortage may force some of these industries out of the developed countries. The metallurgical industries in Europe have in fact been the largest employers of immigrant labour. For social reasons such labour is unlikely to be accepted back into Western Europe in the same numbers as before the recent recession. If Iran is able to offer metallic ores, relatively cheap energy, sites, labour and a stable political environment she stands a good chance of attracting such metal processing industries. Joint ventures with overseas companies, including for example Krupps, in which Iran already has substantial investment, could prove a highly successful way of moving into this field.

Demand and Marketing Problems

Linder's theory of representative demand is at least suggestive of other possible lines of export development in Iran. A numerous, reasonably affluent population in an extremely hot climate has given rise to a large internal market for air-cooling equipment. One variety of this operates simply on fanned air driven through straw matting kept moist by pumped water. In the extremely dry air of Iran the rapid evaporation produces a significant cooling of the air temperature and increase in comfort. Such equipment is much cheaper and less costly in energy consumption than normal air conditioners. There should be a market for such equipment in many hot arid countries. Such an industry should provide stimulus and perhaps external economies for the production of electric motors, fans, water pumps, compressors, refrigerators, freezers, etc.

Given the high transport costs from Iran to Western Europe, U.S.A. and Japan, Iran may well have to look elsewhere for markets for manufactures. It is unfortunate that under the Shipping Conferences cargo liner freight rates escalate according to value added, producing yet another obstacle to trade in manufactures. (Yeats, 1977)

The obvious first market for Iran for many products seems to be the fellow Islamic states of the Gulf. Their proximity, similarities in climate and culture and their affluence make them very attractive and surely worth detailed investigation. Iran may also be able to move into services such as tourism, shipping and insurance in relation to these and other Arab states. Other possibilities may be in some development of its trading area with Afghanistan, Pakistan and Turkey. But one could speculate endlessly on the possibilities. Only detailed research could show which can be moved from possible to probable.

In the end, as was said early in this paper most of the decisions have to be taken in a decentralised fashion by managers in the private

136

or public sector. The task of government should be mainly to get the signals correct so that these decisions are taken on a consistent and hopefully optimal basis. But government should also try to avoid taking decisions which cut off possible lines of advance. Some lines of investment are almost certain to pay off. Better internal transport is essential to industrial advance and investment in systems of education and training which will produce technically competent, but versatile skilled labour would be another essential area for development.

Many might wish government to stop there, but as was argued earlier this would probably be impossible and may well not be desirable. For quite some time prices will not reflect social opportunity costs and government intervention will be required. There may be other tasks even in industry which government, perhaps in collaboration with foreign enterprise, can undertake which would not be undertaken by private entrepreneurs in Iran.

ACKNOWLEDGEMENTS

I am grateful to participants at a Seminar in the Iran Planning Institute in July 1978 for comments on some thoughts of mine on this topic, to participants in the Oxford Seminar in memory of Professor Harry Johnson for their comments on this paper and to Jan Tumlir of the GATT and Alexander Yeats of UNCTAD for discussions on this subject in Geneva in August 1978. I am also grateful to the United Nations for financing a one month visit to Iran as a consultant to the Iran Planning Institute. Responsibility for any remaining errors of fact or judgement in the paper is mine alone.

REFERENCES

Falvey, R. E. (1976), 'Transport Costs in the Pure Theory of International Trade', *Econ. Journal*, 343 (September 1976), pp. 536–550.

Kavoussi, R. (1978), 'The Industrial Exports of Iran', Iran Planning Institute Working Paper (April 1978).

Little, I. M. D. and Mirlees, J. A. (1974), *Project Appraisal and Planning for Developing Countries* (London: Heinemann).

Tizhoosh-Taban, M. H. (1978), 'Effective tariffs and industrial development in Iran', draft Ph.D. thesis, University of Lancaster.

Yeats, A. J. (1976), 'A Sensitivity Analysis of the Effective Protection Estimate', *J. of Dev. Economics*, 3, pp. 367–376.

Yeats, A. J. (1977), 'Do International Transport Costs Increase with Fabrication? Some Empirical Evidence', *Oxford Econ. Papers* 29 (November 1977), pp. 458–471.

Chapter Eight

THREE SIMPLE TESTS OF THE STOLPER–SAMUELSON THEOREM

Stephen P. Magee

1. Introduction

Second only in political appeal to the argument that tariffs increase employment is the popular notion that the standard of living of the American worker must be protected against the ruinous competition of cheap foreign labor.

Stolper and Samuelson (1941, p. 333).

HARRY JOHNSON made important contributions to many fields, particularly to the pure theory of international trade. His influence was especially significant on the theory of tariffs: witness the collection of classic papers in his *Aspects of The Theory of Tariffs* (1972). An important question in tariff theory is the effect of a tariff on the distribution of income. The Stolper and Samuelson (1941) theorem asserts that in a two-factor world with complete mobility of factors within a country, liberalization of international trade will lower the real income of one factor of production and increase the real income of the other. It is one of the four central propositions in the 2×2 theory of international trade, along with the factor price equalization, Heckscher–Ohlin and Rybczynski theorems.

The most extreme theoretical alternative to the Stolper–Samuelson theorem is the theory of noncompeting groups advanced by Cairnes (1874). It suggests that factors of production are industry-specific even in the long run so that trade liberalization would benefit all factors in the export industry (which enjoy increased demand) but hurt all factors in the import-competing industry (which faces increased import competition). Studies by Mayer (1974) and Mussa (1974) combine short-run immobility with long-run factor mobility to yield intermediate results: one factor will, say, unambiguously, gain both in the short and in the long run while the other will gain in the short run but lose in the long run from trade liberalization. This intertemporal conflict could be resolved by present-value calculations, if the factors have sufficient information about the adjustment path. While these present-value calculations would be tedious, they could be done.

The intertemporal consideration highlights the difficulty of constructing direct statistical tests which would establish the empirical relevance of the Stolper–Samuelson vs. Cairnes models. The researcher would have to determine factor intensities, factor elasticities of substitution, all variables affecting inter-industry movements in the factors of production (moving costs and geographical dispersion of plants), discount rates, expectations of the likelihood of government adjustment assistance, etc. The enormity of this task explains the shortage of direct empirical tests of the two models.

The original Stolper–Samuelson article itself suggests an indirect approach. Tariffs are set by politicians. Recent work on the economics of special-interest politics indicates that tariffs can be thought of as prices which clear political markets (see Brock and Magee; 1978 and 1979). An important question, using this approach, is the manner in which coalitions form. Any theorem regarding the redistributional effect of a tariff also implies the way in which coalitions are likely to form for and against tariffs: Stolper–Samuelson suggests that lobbying activity will occur along factor lines (capital vs. labor) while Cairnes suggests that they will occur along industry lines (import-competing vs. export). This paper provides three tests of these contrasting forms of lobbying behavior. We assume that the factors of production base their lobbying on rational present-value calculations of their self interest. If the present value of their income streams (inclusive of non-pecuniary considerations and taking lobbying costs into account) would be increased by free trade, we can expect them to lobby for freer trade (and vice versa). This 'revealed-preference' approach to testing for the redistributive effects of tariffs shifts the voluminous amount of information required for an empirical test from the researcher to the representatives of the factors of production.

Three revealed-preference tests of the competing theorems are described and performed on 1973 United States data in Section 2. Section 3 discusses limitations, alternative interpretations and some implications of the tests. The results generally reject Stolper–

139

Samuelson and accept the Cairnes approach. This is consistent with the view that factors are less mobile between industries in advanced industrial societies because of sector-specific human capital and high-technology physical capital.[1] Another interpretation is that lobbying costs and free-rider problems are lower for industry lobbies than for factor lobbies.

2. The Empirical Results

> In other words, whatever will happen to wages in the wage good (labor intensive) industry will happen to labor as a whole. And this answer is independent of whether the wage good will be imported or exported . . .
>
> Stolper and Samuelson (1941, p. 344).

Simplicity, statistical methodology and data availability dictated that the tests be limited to two factors of production, capital and labor. The cost of this limitation is that we may be testing other relationships (e.g., substitutability or complementarity between two out of many factors) rather than the two competing theories.

Capital and production labor in the U.S. were chosen to illustrate the tests. The American labor movement has been actively engaged in lobbying on trade policy in the last decade. Most of the headlines have placed labor on the side of greater protection, although we shall see shortly that this position is far from unanimous. Similarly, management in many industries has lobbied actively. Since management is chosen by stockholders, I assume that management's interests coincide with the owners of the firm's physical capital. Regardless of the positions of the factors not considered here (land, skilled labor, etc.), it is of some interest whether production labor and capital are protagonists or antagonists on the question of freer United States trade.

The empirical evidence used in this paper is taken from the Summary of Testimony for the Hearings before the Committee on Ways and Means in the U.S. House of Representatives on the Trade Reform Act of 1973, May–June of 1973. These summaries revealed the preference of 29 trade associations (representing management) and 23 unions for either freer trade or greater protection. A summary of the results together with the related Standard Industrial Classification (SIC) codes are shown in Table 1. In cases where the information was ambiguous or where no information was given, the staff of the Ways and Means Committee and other experts in Washington were consulted. Table 1

Table 1: Positions of Groups on U.S. Trade Policy by Industry.

SIC	Industry	Trade Balance	Trade Associations Name	Capital's Position[†]	Labor's Position[†]	Labor Unions Name
2015	Poultry	41	Poul. and Egg Instit. of Am.	F		
2026	Dairy	-1	Nat'l Milk Prod. Fed.	P		
2085	Distilling	-416	Dist. Spirits Counc.	P	P	Dist., Rect., Wine and Allied Wkrs
2092	Soybeans	320	Nat. Soyb. Processors	F		
21	Tobacco	130	Tobacco Institute	F	F	Tab. Int'l Workers Union
22	Textiles	-418	Am. Txt. Man. Inst.	P	F	Text. Wkrs Union of America
23	Apparel	-486	*	P	P	Amalg. Clothing Wkrs
26	Paper	-632	Am. Paper Inst.	F	F	United Papers Wkrs Int'l.
2815	Chemicals	81	Syn. Org. Chem. Man.	P	P-M	Int'l Chem. Wkrs Union
2821	Plastics	527	Society of the Plast.	P	P	United R.C.L. and Plast. Wkrs
2911	Petroleum	-505	Amer. Petrol. Inst.	F	P	Petroleum Wkrs Union
30	Rubber	92	Rubber Man. Assoc.	M	P-M	United Rubber Wkrs
3021	Rubber Shoes	-82	Rub. Man. Ass. – Footwear D.	P	P	United Rubber, C, L and P
31	Leather	-364	Tanners Coun. of Am.	P	P	Int'l Leath. Goods Wkrs
3141	Shoes	-471	Am. Footwear Assn.	P	P	United Shoewkr of America
32	Stone, etc.	12	Stone Glass & Clay C. Com.	P	P	Un. Glass and Ceramic Wkrs
331-2	Iron/Steel	-1923	Am. Iron and Steel Inst.	P	P	IAIW and Un. Steelw. of America
3732-3	Lead/Zinc	-137	Lead/Zinc Prod. Com.	M		
3334	Aluminum	-95	Alum. Assn.	F	M	Alum. Wkrs Int'l Union
3421	Cutlery	-16	Nat. Ass. of Scissors M.	P	P?	*
3423	Hardware	38	Bldrs Hardw. Manuf.	P	P	Int'l Assn of Tool Craftsmen
35	Machinery	4029	Mach. and Allied Prod. Inst.	F	F?	Int'l Assn of Machinists
3522	Tractors	146	Caterpillar Tractor	F	*	
3541	Mach. Tools	25	Nat'l Mach. Tool Bldrs	M	P	Int'l Assn of Tool Craftsmen
3562	Bearings	23	Anti Fr. Bearing Man.	P	P?	*
3572	Bus. Eq.	-21	Comp. and BE Man. Assn	P	M?	
36	Electrical	701	Nat'l Electr. Man. Assn	M	P	Int'l Broth. of Eelct. Wkr
3711	Cars	-1730		F	P	United Auto Wkrs
3713	Trucks	1203	Hvy Duty Truck Man.	F	F	Transport Wkrs U. of America
3720	Aviation	1695	Gen. Aero Man. Assoc.	F	F	Int. Assn of Mach. and Aerospace
3751	Bicycles	-296	Cycle Parts and Acc. Ass.	P	P	Am. Watch Wkrs Union
3871	Watches	-126	Am. Watch Ass.	P	F	Int. U. of Dolls, Toys
3941	Toys	-51			F	

Source: U.S. Ways and Means (1973).   † P = protectionist;   F = free trade;   M = intermediate (ambiguous).
* Position determined from other sources.   Trade balance given in millions of dollars (1967).

should not be read in terms of each group's position on specific items in the 1973 trade bill but rather its general position on freer vs. more restricted trade. This position is presumed to reflect its preference both for itself and other industries since trade bills are seldom industry specific. 'P' stands for a protectionist position, 'F' for freer trade and 'M' for mixed positions (powerful subgroups within the organization on both sides).

The quotation from Stolper and Samuelson (1941) at the beginning of this section suggests three empirical implications of their theorem in a simple two-factor world.

1. *Capital and labor in a given industry will oppose each other on the issue of protection (or free trade) for that industry.*
2. *For the country as a whole, each factor will favor either free trade or protection but not both.*
3. *The position taken by capital or labor in an industry on the issue of protection will be independent of whether the industry is export or import-competing.*

These implications form the basis of the three tests.

TEST 1

The first implication suggests that we could test the competing hypotheses for two factors of production with a 2×2 contingency table, as shown in Table 2. Each industry can be placed in one of the four mutually exclusive and exhaustive cells, depending on the position of its capital and labor on trade policy.

Table 2: Contingency Table for the Probable Positions of Capital and Labor on Protection vs. Free Trade.

		Position of Labor	
		1. Protectionist	2. Free Trade
Position of Capital:	1. Protectionist	P_{11}	P_{12}
	2. Free Trade	P_{21}	P_{22}

The number of industries in each cell, when divided by the total number of industries, yield the probabilities shown. The first item, P_{11}, for example, is the probability that a randomly chosen industry will have both capital and labor lobby for protection. The sum of the four cell probabilities equals one.

The Stolper–Samuelson theorem asserts that capital and labor will oppose each other on trade policy: thus, the diagonal elements should equal zero. Furthermore, all labor will support one policy while capital will do the reverse. Thus, one of the off-diagonal elements will equal 1 while the other will equal 0. In short, Stolper–Samuelson asserts that 3 of the 4 cells in Table 2 will contain zeros.

The Cairnes factor-specific model predicts sharply contrasting results. With immobility of both factors, the prices of capital and labor move with the price of industry output. Thus, capital and labor in an industry will work together on trade policy, implying that the only nonzero elements in the matrix will be in one of the two diagonal boxes: $p_{11} + p_{22} = 1$.

The results of this test for 21 of the industries in Table 1 are shown in Table 3. The term n_{ij} represents the number of industries falling into each cell. It is apparent from observation that the data are strongly supportive of the Cairnes factor specific model and

Table 3: A Classification of n = 21 Industries According to the Political Preferences of Capital and Labor.

	Position of Labor		
	1. Protectionist	2. Free Trade	
Position of Capital: 1. Protectionist	$n_{11} = 14$ ($p_{11} = 0.66$)	$n_{12} = 1$ ($p_{12} = 0.05$)	$P_1 = 0.71$
2. Free Trade	$n_{21} = 1$ ($p_{21} = 0.05$)	$n_{22} = 5$ ($p_{22} = 0.24$)	$P_2 = 0.29$
	($p_1 = 0.71$)	($p_2 = 0.29$)	

reject the Stolper–Samuelson hypothesis. In only 2 industries do labor and management oppose each other: management is for free trade in petroleum and protectionist in tobacco, with labor being the reverse.[2] *In 19 out of 21 industries, labor and management work together on the question of protection.* To perform a test of statistical significance would belabor the obvious.

TEST 2

The second implication of the Stolper–Samuelson theorem is that all of labor will favor either free trade or protection (similarly for capital). Test 2 provides a test of the degree of unanimity of each factor on one position or the other. Table 4 summarizes the data from Table 1 for capital and labor. (More observations are possible for capital here since its position does not have to be paired with knowledge of labor's position.)

Table 4.

	Number of Industries (1)	Proportion of Cases (2)	Value of z in a Normal Approximation of the Binomial (the hypothesis is rejected at this level of significance)	
			Hypothesis Tested	
			Stolper Samuelson (3)	Factor Specific (4)
Capital's Position:				
Protectionism	15	$p_1 = 0.63$	4.49	0.50
Free Trade	9	$p_2 = 0.37$	(0.000003)*	(0.31)
Labor's Position:				
Protectionism	16	$p_1 = 0.76$	2.10	4.01
Free Trade	5	$p_2 = 0.24$	(0.018)*	(0.000003)*

* Hypothesis rejected.

Notice that only 63 per cent of the industries selected show capital supporting the preferred alternative (protectionism). Stolper–Samuelson predicts that all capital would choose one alternative or the other (100 per cent vs. 0) and should not split this way (63 per cent vs. 37 per cent).

Since it is impossible to test the sample observations in Table 4 against the hypothesis that $p_1 = 1.0$ and $p_2 = 0$, we must set some arbitrary value of p_1 which is less than 1.0. I arbitrarily set $p_1 = 0.9$ and $0.2 = 0.1$ as the hypothesized Stolper–Samuelsons values. Thus, a sample which showed 90 per cent of capital supporting the preferred alternative (say, protection) and only 10 per cent supporting the other (free trade) would be consistent with the factor mobility assumption implicit in Stolper–Samuelson. Similarly, I arbitrarily set $p_1 = p_2 = 0.5$ as the hypothesized population values associated with the factor-specific model. Notice that we bias against acceptance of Stolper-Samuelson if p_1 is set too close to 1 and the test of factor specificity is influenced by the random breakdown of the sample between protectionists and free traders. If there is a tendency for only one group to lobby, there is also a tendency to reject the Cairnes model of factor specificity.

The test is conducted as follows. What is the probability that the sample proportions in column (2) of Table 4 would have been obtained if the true population proportions were those hypothesized ($p_1 = 0.9$ for Stolper–Samuelson and $p_1 = p_2 = 0.5$ for Cairnes?). We use the binomial distribution for the test. Since the number of trials exceeds 20 ($n = 24$ for capital and $n = 21$ for labor) an

144

approximation must be used. The Poisson distribution could be used but is recommended only when $p_1 = 0.05$. Thus, we must use the normal approximation. We transform the number of cases ($x = 15$ for capital and $x = 16$ for labor) apparently satisfying the hypothesis into the standardized normal random variable, z (see Freund; 1971, pp. 75 and 175):

$$(1) \qquad z = \frac{x - np_1}{\sqrt{np_1 (1 - p_1)}}.$$

The tabulated values of z are shown in columns (3) and (4) of Table 4, along with their significance levels.

Consider capital. If the true population proportion is 0.9 (Stolper–Samuelson) the chances of obtaining a proportion of $p_1 = 0.63$ are only 0.0003 per cent, whereas the chances of getting $p_1 = 0.63$ are 31 per cent when the hypothesized value is 0.5 (Cairnes). Thus, for capital the results reject the factor mobility hypothesis implicit in Stolper–Samuelson and cannot reject the factor-specific Cairnes hypothesis. The sample proportion of labor favoring protection is 0.76: both Stolper–Samuelson and Cairnes are rejected, with the latter rejected more decisively. The results for labor are thus inconclusive. Notice that we biased the test in favor of Stolper–Samuelson by choosing the larger of the two sample proportions to compare with the hypothesized value of 0.9.

As an aside, the data in Table 4 permits a test of the Burgess (1976) result that American labor would gain at the expense of American capital with greater protection. If they were true, we should observe that labor would support protection in a larger proportion of the industries than capital. Using the test described in equation (1), we find that $p_1 = 0.76$ is significantly greater than 0.63 at the 0.11 level ($z = 1.25$) while 0.63 is significantly less than 0.76 at the 0.06 level ($z = 1.58$). Thus, the data here is not inconsistent with the Burgess results; it supports him using one test and almost confirms his result when the order of the test is reversed. I view these results as mixed, however, and turn instead to a third and stronger test of the factor mobility assumption than is provided by either Test 1 or 2.

TEST 3

Test 2 merely indicated the degree of unanimity (or lack thereof) which a factor has for a specific trade policy. Here we test whether or not a factor prefers a policy which is beneficial to the industry in which it is currently employed. If it does, factor specificity is

145

implied; if not, factor mobility (among other things) is more likely. Two versions of this test are presented: the first is a proportion test while the second allows continuous variation in the industry's trade balance.

Consider the data in Tables 5a and 5b. There are the same industries which were used in test 2^3. However, the rows in Table 5 classify the industries according to whether they are export or import-competing. A tendency for dominant diagonality indicates Cairnes factor specificity while independence of the sectors and the trade positions is consistent with Stolper–Samuelson factor mobility. The usual test of association in these tables is a straightforward application of the Chi-square test, χ^2. While χ^2 is a good measure of the significance of the association, it is not useful as a measure of the degree of association between sectoral location and the factor's preferred trade policy (Fleiss (1973, p. 41)). The odds ratio does provide such a test (Fleiss (1973, pp. 43–46)). The sample odds ratio, 0, equals

$$(2) \qquad 0 = \frac{p_{11}/p_{12}}{p_{21}/p_{22}} = \frac{p_{11}\,p_{22}}{p_{12}\,p_{21}}.$$

Notice that the odds of a factor favoring protection relative to free trade are p_{11}/p_{12} if the factor is in the import-competing sector and p_{21}/p_{22} if it is in the export sector. If these odds are the same, then knowledge of the factor's sectoral location gives us no information about the factor's most likely policy preference. In this case, the numerator and denominator in (2) are equal and the odds ratio equals 1. Stolper – Samuelson predicts $0 = 1$ while factor specificity implies $0 > 1$. Let us test these hypotheses.

The standard error of 0, s.e. (0), is approximately:

$$(3) \qquad \text{s.e. } (0) = \frac{0}{\sqrt{n}}\sqrt{\frac{1}{p_{11}} + \frac{1}{p_{12}} + \frac{1}{p_{21}} + \frac{1}{p_{22}}}.$$

[Fleiss (1973, p. 45)). The values of 0 and s.e. (0) from (2) and (3) are reported in Tables 5a and 5b. The calculations indicate that the odds of capital in the import competing sector favoring protection are 4 times those of capital in the export sector; for labor, the same odds ratio is 8·8. The standard errors are 3·6 and 10·9, respectively. The significance tests should not be performed using just these standard errors. Rather, calculate the variable Y,

$$(4) \qquad Y = \left[\frac{0 - 0^h}{\text{s.e. } (0)/\sqrt{n}}\right]^2$$

146

Table 5a: Industries with Capital's Position on Free Trade Related to the Trade Sector (n = 24)

		Position of Capital		Odds Ratio *(stand. error)*	χ^2 *(sig. level)*
		1. Protectionist	*2. Free Trade*		
Sector of Industry	1. Import-Competing	$n_{11} = 10$ $(p_{11} = 0.42)$	$n_{12} = 3$ $(p_{12} = 0.12)$	4.0 (3.6)	4.1 (0.05)
	2. Export	$n_{21} = 5$ $(p_{21} = 0.21)$	$n_{22} = 6$ $(p_{22} = 0.25)$		

Table 5b: Number of Industries with Labor's Position on Free Trade Related to the Trade Sector (n = 21)

		Position of Labor		Odds Ratio *(stand. error)*	χ^2 *(sig. level)*
		1. Protectionist	*2. Free Trade*		
Sector of Industry	1. Import-Competing	$n_{11} = 11$ $(p_{11} = 0.53)$	$n_{12} = 1$ $(p_{12} = 0.04)$	8.8 (10.9)	3.3 (0.10)
	2. Export	$n_{21} = 5$ $(p_{21} = 0.24)$	$n_{22} = 4$ $(p_{22} = 0.19)$		

See Appendix Table 1 for the SIC codes of the numbers in each cell.

which has a Chi-square distribution with 1 degree of freedom (Freund (1971, p. 214)). 0^h is the hypothesized value of the odds ratio against which we are testing the obtained sample value, 0.

The values of χ^2 computed from (4) for Y and their significance levels are shown in the last column of Tables 5a and 5b. Both capital and labor differ significantly from the hypothesized Stolper–Samuelson independence of lobbying positions and sectoral location: Stolper–Samuelson is refuted for capital at the 5 per cent level and labor at the 10 per cent level.

A limitation of the qualitative test just completed is that it does not consider the association between a factor's position on trade policy and the extent to which each industry is export or import-competing. We can remedy this problem partially by testing, for each factor, whether there are significant differences between the trade balances in industries containing free traders vs. industries containing protectionists. If more positive trade balances are associated with the free trade position, we can reject the Stolper–Samuelson theorem. If there is no significant difference in the trade balances, then the positions are independent of sectoral location and we can reject the Cairnes model. The results are shown in Table 6.

Notice that the average trade balance in industries in which capital supports free trade is $689 million while it is − $254 million if capital is protectionist. The difference is statistically significant using three different tests for equality of the trade balances of the two groups. The average trade balance in industries in which labor supports free trade is $985 million while it is − $321 million in labor-protectionist industries. These differences are significant for two out of three of the tests.

I conclude from both versions of test 3 that both capital and labor lobby for protection in ways consistent with the Cairnes model of factor immobility and inconsistent with the Stolper–Samuelson model of factor mobility.

3. Caveats and Conclusions

Tests 1 and 3 provide refutation of Stolper–Samuelson relative to Cairnes. In test 2, Stolper–Samuelson was rejected for capital while labor was impossible to classify as mobile or specific; this is not inconsistent with the *a priori* assumptions made in theoretical discussions by Mayer (1974) and Mussa (1974) that capital is *quasi*-fixed in the short run relative to labor. What conclusions

148

are we to derive from these results? We deal first with the possibility that they might have been obtained spuriously.

For the thirty-three industries in Table 1, there is no significant relationship between the trade balance and capital per man. However, this fact does not explain our failure to confirm the Stolper–Samuelson results. In fact, exactly the reverse is true. We know from the pure theory of international trade that with two products and two factors, the closer the factor intensities of the two sectors, the greater the magnification affect of product prices on factor prices. Hence, the closer the factor intensities in production, the greater the potential benefit to either factor from affecting relative product prices through legislation.

It is possible that the likelihood of foreign retaliation against greater protection in the United States might bias the results away from Stolper–Samuelson? No, foreign retaliation will help the scarce factor and hurt the abundant factor.[4] In the Stolper–Samuelson framework, if the scarce factor succeeds in raising its returns by increasing the home price of importables relative to exportables, then foreign retaliation will simply cause the product price ratio to increase further as foreign demand drops for United States exports. Again, this consideration would bias the results in favor of Stolper–Samuelson.

One clear empirical violation of the simple two factor Stolper–Samuelson assumption is the presence of other factors of production (land, skilled labor, etc.). If labor and capital are complementary, relative to these other factors, do we have an alternative explanation of the results presented here? This point seems reasonable but applies only to test 1: it cannot explain the results of test 3 in which each factor's lobbying position was significantly related to its sectoral location.

One explanation of the Leontief paradox which seemed consistent with the Stolper–Samuelson approach, was that the U.S. is skilled labor abundant and unskilled labor scarce. It is possible that the labor unions, in the tests above, represent unskilled labor in the industries favoring protection and skilled labor in the industries favoring free trade. If so, the approach would improperly aggregate two diverse groups of labor and spuriously reject Stolper–Samuelson. However, tests showed no significant difference in production wage rates between the two labor groups (those for and against freer trade). Thus, the labor groupings here appear to be homogeneous and avoid this pitfall.

Could the degree of unionization bias the tests, since unions largely spoke for labor? A test of the average proportion of labor unionized between the two labor groups also found no significant difference (for those for and against freer trade). Thus, the position on free trade is independent of the degree of unionization. However, one could argue that labor leaders will not represent the 'true interests' of their constituency. The truth of this proposition is questionable in light of many voting models; the rational elected union official will take the position favored by the median union member. Thus, there should not be a tendency for him to work against the 'best interests' of union members.

However, the problem of how well union leaders represent their own constituency is probably less important than the question of wage differentials and the question of whether the interests of union labor also coincide with those of the nonunion labor. Wage differentials do not pose serious problems for the Stolper–Samuelson theorem: the theorem holds at all points in the Edgeworth–Bowley box so long as product factor intensities are defined in 'value rather than physical' terms (see the discussion in Magee (1976 pp. 25–32)). However, unionization is more likely to generate low labor turnover than a smoothly operating wage differential. (The average per cent of unionization is over 60 per cent in the industries in Table 1). Because of seniority systems coupled with positive union/nonunion wage differentials, union labor should be more industry-specific than nonunion labor. Since many unions are organized along industry lines because of organizational efficiency, one might think that the presence of union lobbying groups generate data favorable to labor specificity. However, their lobbying positions need not favor their industry if Stolper–Samuelson accurately describe labor's interests.

In comments on an earlier draft of this paper Harry Johnson suggested a reconciliation of these results with the Stolper–Samuelson theorem. Protection can benefit both factors in the short run in import-competing industries with short-run immobility. But if both factors are mobile in the long run, the position of one of the factors must ultimately deteriorate. Since many import-competing (standardized goods) industries in the U.S. are 'traditional industries', they use older labor. If standardized goods industries are also more capital intensive because of assembly-line type production (à la Leontief and Vernon), then labor would ultimately be hurt by their expansion through higher tariffs. But, if the long run is far enough away, this long-run deterioration is economically irrelevant. If all workers in the shoe industry were

150

old and the present value of the long-run Stolper–Samuelson effects did not dominate the (reverse) factor specific effects before their retirement, then these workers would lobby as if they were sector specific. Thus, even if the Stolper–Samuelson theorem were empirically valid, it might not be detectable in the presence of older workers for whom the long run never comes.

NOTES

* The author wishes to thank Robert Baldwin, William Brock, Franz Gehrels, Peter Gray, Ronald Jones, Rachel McCulloch, Tracy Murray, Carlos Rodriguez and especially Harry Johnson for comments on an earlier draft of this paper, which was first presented at the Eastern Economic Association Meetings in Bloomsburg, Pa., April 17, 1976; Harry Eisenstein, Stephen Thompson and Doug Van Ness for research assistance; and the Center for the Management of Public and Nonprofit Enterprise, Graduate School of Business, University of Chicago and the National Science Foundation for financial support.

1. Franz Gehrels suggested this point.

2. The petroleum case is weakened by the split between the major oil companies and the independents; the latter are opposed to free trade.

3. The composition of industries in Tables 5a and 5b also differs from those in Table 3. Table 3 was restricted to industries in which the position of both management and labor were known. Tables 5a and 5b require only that the position of one side be known. Also, two industries included in Table 3 were dropped from 5a and 5b because of inability to allocate them to one of the two trade sectors because of small trade balances (SIC 32 and 3421).

4. Ronald Jones suggested this point.

REFERENCES

Brock, William A. and Magee, Stephen P. 'The Economics of Special-Interest Politics: The Case of the Tariff,' *American Economic Review*, 68 (May 1978), pp. 246–250.

Brock, William A and Magee, Stephen P. 'Tariff Setting in a Democracy,' John Black and Brian Hindley, eds., *Current Issues in International Commercial Policy and Economic Diplomacy*. London: Macmillan Press, 1980.

Burgess, David F. 'Tariffs and Income Distribution: Some Empirical Evidence for the United States'. *Journal of Political Economy*, 84 (February 1976), pp. 17–46.

Cairnes, J. E. *Some Leading Principles of Political Economy*. London: Macmillan, 1874.

Fleiss, Joseph L. *Statistical Methods for Rates and Proportions*. New York: John Wiley, 1973.

Freund, John E. *Mathematical Statistics*, 2nd ed., Englewood Cliffs: Prentice-Hall, 1971.

Hays, William L. and Winkler, Robert L. *Statistics*. New York: Holt, Rinehart and Winston, 1971.

Johnson, Harry G. *Aspects of the Theory of Tariffs*. London: George Allen & Unwin, 1971.

Magee, Stephen. *International Trade and Distortions in Factor Markets*. New York: Marcel Dekker, 1976.

Mayer, Wolfgang. 'Short-Run and Long-Run Equilibrium for a Small Open Economy. *Journal of Political Economy*, *82* (October 1974), pp. 955–968.

Mussa, Michael. 'Tariffs and the Distribution of Income: The Importance of Factor Specificity, Substitutability, and Intensity in the Short and Long Run'. *Journal of Political Economy*, *82* (December 1974), pp. 1191–1203.

Stolper, Wolfgang and Samuelson, Paul A. 'Protection and Real Wages'. *Review of Economic Studies*, *9* (November 1941), pp. 58–73. Reprinted in AEA *Readings in the Theory of International Trade*. Homewood, Illinois: Richard D. Irwin, 1950, pp. 333–357.

United States Congress, Committee on Ways and Means, Hearings on HR: 6767, The Trade Reform Act of 1973 (15 Parts), May 9–June 15, 1973; Part 15, pp. 5171–5317, Washington: U.S. Government Printing Office, 1973.

Appendix

SIC Codes for the Industries in Tables 3, 5a and 5b in the Text.

Table 3.
Labor

		Protectionist	Free Trade
Management	Protectionist	2085, 22, 23, 2815, 2821, 3021, 31, 3141, 32, 331–2, 3421, 3423, 3562, 3871	21
	Free Trade	2911	26, 35, 3522, 2713, 3720

Table 5a
Management

	Protectionist	Free Trade
Import Competing	2085, 22, 23, 3021, 31, 3141, 3572, 3751, 3871, 331–2	26, 2911, 3334
Export	21, 2815, 2821, 3423, 3562	2015, 2092, 35, 3522, 3715, 3720

Table 5b
Labor

	Protectionist	Free Trade
Import Competing	2085, 22, 23, 3021, 3141, 2911, 31, 331–2, 3711, 3871, 3941	26
Export	2815, 2821, 30, 3423, 36	21, 35, 3713, 3720

153

A COMMENT ON MAGEE'S THREE SIMPLE TESTS

Christopher Bliss

STEPHEN MAGEE has undertaken a fascinating study and his results stand as a challenge to all those who have felt that simple trade models cannot say anything definite enough to be tested about the world, and particularly to those who have been rather grateful for that conclusion. After Leontief's elaborate attempt to test the Hecksher–Ohlin theory, this approach is marvellously simple and its clearly robust result is all the more impressive.

The main point that I want to mention is one which is not discussed in the paper and which provides a possible third model to add to the Stolper–Samuelson and Cairnes models which the author makes his main alternatives. The case that I have in mind is one in which there is a deficiency of overall effective demand. One would then usually assume that the imposition of tariffs or other protective measures would help to raise the level of home activity and would be likely to benefit both capital and labour, at least in the short run. This requires that factors be willing to accept a cut in their real rate of remuneration per unit after tariffs are imposed, where they would not have effected the same outcome directly by cuts in the money price of factor services, and hence be dismissed as 'irrational'. It also requires that the government be willing to impose tariffs to increase activity where fiscal and monetary policy of an appropriate kind would be a superior policy. Nevertheless the, no doubt irrational, view that imports cause unemployment and that they should be curtailed when unemployment is high, commands a lot of support and it may be behind some of the lobbying that the author has observed. If so, it would bias his findings towards what he has interpreted as the Cairnes outcome.

There is no point in detailing the many problems that arise because the Stolper–Samuelson model is extremely simple where reality is complicated. Most of these will have been remarked by Professor Magee's readers and his approach gains from going for the direct strong result rather than setting up alibis for the theory in various complications. One point however deserves mention.[1] The Stolper–Samuelson theory deals most naturally with perfectly-vertically integrated industries which use original factors to produce final output. The actual industries and trade unions whose spokesmen lobby the U.S. Congress typically use intermediate goods as inputs including some importable intermediates. One can extend the theorem to cover this case, but the results change somewhat. For example, both capital and labour may favour the lowering of the tariff on intermediates used by their industry. Ideally one would like to have to hand the results of an input-output study showing the direct factor-demand components of various imports and their substitutes. It might well emerge that the resultant factor interests were not organized as lobbies and the practical difficulty or expense of organizing real-world lobbies to approximate to Stolper–Samuelson factor groups may explain some of the author's findings.

NOTES

1 Emphasised in discussion by Professor Ann Krueger.

Chapter Nine

THE INCOME-LEVEL OF EXPORTS AND TARIFF DISCRIMINATION*

Michael Michaely

I

THE ISSUE of trade policy of the highly-developed countries in relation to their less-developed partners has gathered momentum in
recent years, probably mainly because of two developments. One is
the general clamour for a 'new international economic order', an
important part of which would presumably be more favourable terms
of trade for the LDC's in their transactions with the developed part
of the world – the improvement being achieved, to a large extent, by
more favourable tariff treatment on the part of the developed
countries.[1] The other factor is the astonishing growth over the last
decade in the exports of many LDC's to the DC's – particularly exports of manufactures. With this growth came an increasing resentment in at least some DC's or some sectors to imports from LDC's;
and a mounting suspicion that a further rapid rise of exports from
LDC's to DC's is likely to meet an increased level of barriers to this
trade.

The tariff-level issue – or, more generally, the issue of the level of
trade barriers – may be separated into two parts: the 'positive' and
the 'normative' aspects. First, it is often argued that the existing
structure of trade barriers discriminates against the trade of LDC's,
this discrimination being one of the causes of the unfavourable, or
'unfair', terms of trade of these countries. The normative aspect of the
issue has been the argument that discrimination in favour of this trade
of LDC's should be explicitly introduced into tariff treaties and into
the network of tariffs and non-tariff barriers to trade. This argument

* For research assistance I am indebted to Matti Gutraich and Eva Jondal.

has, in fact, been accepted in principle by the highly-developed countries, an acceptance that has led, *inter alia*, to the introduction into the GATT scheme of the 'generalized system of preferences', by which developed countries are entitled to grant special tariff concessions to the LDC's.

The present study is confined to the first aspect, overlooking entirely the second. It does not ask whether tariff discrimination in favour of LDC export should take place, or what are the pros and cons of such policy. It is, rather, an empirical study which tries to establish whether the existing system of tariffs and non-tariff barriers discriminates in favour, or against, the trade of LDC's. It will also inquire whether the nature of this trade would lead to the anticipation of future discrimination, in one direction or another.

In trying to establish whether any discrimination is involved in the trade-barriers system, it is assumed in this study that *no discrimination*, either way, is applied to the trade of specific *countries*. This assumption determines, indeed, the nature of the present study; and should it grossly violate the facts, the findings of this study would lose much of their meaning. It is assumed, thus, that any non-uniformity in the level of tariffs and other trade barriers is expressed in varying levels of barriers to the flows of different *goods*. Discrimination against or in favour of a country is due only to its pattern of specialization: if it specializes in goods which face high barriers in international trade, it is confronted with a high level of barriers in general, and may thus be said to be discriminated against – although not by design specifically aimed at this country. And, in contrast, a country whose exports happen to be primarily concentrated in goods which face low trade barriers, enjoys discrimination in its favour.

The study, moreover, does not apply to the trade of specific countries, but to the trade of LDC's in general.[2] Its subject matter may thus be defined as follows: Does the system of the tariffs and non-tariff barriers, in the highly-developed part of the world, discriminate against, or in favour, of goods in which low-income countries tend to specialize?

II

Two sets of data will be used. One consists of a measure of the income-level of the trade in each good; the other, of data on tariffs and NTB (non-tariff barriers) in the highly-developed countries.

The income level of a trade flow is a measure designed to indicate whether the flow originates in (for exports) or is destined to (for imports) high or low income countries; and it is simply the weighted average of the income levels of the countries involved in the trade flow.[3] For the exports of a given good i, the index of the income level, y^x, is defined as follows:

$$y_i^x = \sum_j y_j \frac{x_{ij}}{x_{i\cdot}} \text{ where:}$$

x_{ij} = exports of good i by country j

$x_{i\cdot}$ = world exports of good i

y_j = index of income of country j.

The term y_j is defined as $100\ Y_j/Y_u$, where Y_j is country j's level of per-capita income, and Y_u is per-capita income of the U.S. It is thus a measure of *relative* richness or poorness (the degree of 'richness', or of 'development' being indicated by the level of per-capita income); with 100 as the index of the U.S., the richest country in 1973, the point of time to which this set of data refers. The index of income level of the exports of a good is thus a synthetic expression of the level of income of the countries which export this good. The highest possible level of the index is 100 – in the hypothetical case of a good exported solely by the United States. Similarly, the lowest boundary is the income level of the poorest country: in this case this would be 1, the income index of Laos (with a per-capita income, that is, just 1 per cent that of the U.S.). In a similar way, the income level of the import of a good would be the weighted average of the income levels of the importing countries, with the import shares serving as weights.

Goods are classified by the 3-digit level of the SITC, containing 174 items, and the index refers to export flows in 1973. The data of the income-level of exports are presented in Table A–1.

The other set of data contains 6 series of indicators of barriers to trade: nominal tariffs, effective rates of protection, and indexes of the level of NTB's, each for the United States and, separately, for a group of countries consisting of the six original members of the E.E.C., the U.K., Japan, and Canada (to be referred to henceforth as 'other' developed countries). It is based on estimates carried out by the U.S. International Trade Commission, which refer to the post Kennedy–Round situation (that is, roughly, the late 1960's).[4] The data are presented in Table A–2.[5]

III

A good exported mostly by less-developed low-income countries, will have a low income-level index of exports; the more the export of such a good is concentrated in these countries, and the lower the countries' incomes, the lower the index. Hence, if in general exports originating in low-income countries face relatively high barriers to trade, a negative correlation of the indexes of income level of exports and of the levels of barriers should be found. If, on the contrary, imports originating in low-income countries are admitted relatively more freely than other goods, the correlation of the two indexes should be positive. Such correlation provides, therefore, a test of the relationship of the levels of trade barriers to the levels of income of the countries from which the goods originate.

Table 1: Income Level and Trade Barriers: Correlation Coefficients (r).

| | Index of Income Level (y_i^x) | |
Trade Barrier	All Goods (1)	Categories (5)–(8) (2)
(1) Nominal tariff, U.S.	0.038	−0.036
(2) Nominal tariff, others	0.078	0.047
(3) Effective tariff, U.S.	0.022	−0.109
(4) Effective tariff, others	−0.074	−0.222
(5) Index of NTB, U.S.	−0.036	−0.149
(6) Index of NTB, others	−0.086	−0.104

None of the coefficients is significant at the 5% level.

The correlation coefficients are shown in column (1) of Table 1, for all (168) goods. It appears immediately that no relationship exists between the variables under consideration: all correlation coefficients are very low, with R^2 in the vicinity of zero (and are, of course, insignificant at any reasonable requirement of level of significance). The conclusion which must be drawn is that the existing structure of barriers to trade in the highly-developed countries – the levels of nominal tariffs, of effective tariffs, and of non-tariff barriers – does not discriminate either in favour of or against the exports which originate primarily in LDC's.

It might be argued that this apparent absence of discrimination in the system implies, in effect, some measure of discrimination *against* exports originating in LDC's in the *relevant range* of goods. Exports of LDC's, the argument would run, consist largely of primary goods – foodstuffs and raw materials. These goods, primarily the latter group, usually face little competition from domestic production in the highly-developed countries, and are thus unlikely to raise much demand for import barriers in the latter. Moreover, low tariff levels on intermediate goods are commonly used, in the universally prevalent system of escalated tariffs, to provide high effective protection for later stages of production. Hence, a low level of trade barriers on imports of primary goods may be anticipated. Had such goods been excluded, leaving only categories of goods in which substitution between imports and local production is likely to be meaningfully high, the system of barriers would then show discrimination against the goods exported relatively heavily by low-income countries.

Table 2: Levels of Trade Barriers, by Major SITC Categories.

Trade Barrier	SITC Category								
	(0)	*(1)*	*(2)*	*(3)*	*(4)*	*(5)*	*(6)*	*(7)*	*(8)*
				a. Average (Unweighted)					
(1) Nominal tariff, U.S. (%)	6.0	16.9	4.3	2.2	4.5	6.1	8.2	6.0	11.6
(2) Nominal tariff, others (%)	9.1	53.2	4.4	4.7	7.7	7.8	9.2	8.7	10.9
(3) Effective tariff, U.S. (%)	23.4	26.1	7.5	4.1	6.7	9.5	14.2	7.6	20.5
(4) Effective tariff, others (%)	21.6	60.4	5.9	10.4	14.5	12.6	20.2	11.3	16.7
(5) Index of NTB, U.S.	3.3	0.6	0.4	1.7	0.2	0.1	0.3	0.2	0.7
(6) Index of NTB, others	5.1	7.8	1.2	1.3	3.1	0.4	0.6	0.2	0.6
				b. Median					
(1) Nominal tariff, U.S. (%)	5.3	19.4	3.2	2.8	3.3	5.3	6.5	5.5	11.3
(2) Nominal tariff, others (%)	9.4	51.7	4.9	6.0	7.9	7.8	8.7	8.9	10.6
(3) Effective tariff, U.S. (%)	7.4	25.5	3.1	5.8	4.3	8.9	11.0	6.2	18.5
(4) Effective tariff, others (%)	20.6	58.2	5.8	13.6	13.6	11.1	14.5	11.0	18.0
(5) Index of NTB, U.S.	1.9	1.2	0.9	2.0	0.2	0.1	0.3	0.4	0.6
(6) Index of NTB, others	4.7	8.5	0.3	0.8	3.0	0.2	0.3	0.3	0.3

To test this presumption, correlation coefficients have been calculated between the respective measures of trade barriers and the index of income level of exports not of all goods, but only of the (99) goods which are classified in the SITC major categories (5) to (8) – excluding categories (0) to (4) which clearly constitute primary goods. These correlation coefficients are presented in column (2) of Table 1 – and the result which emerges from them is once more unmistakably clear. All correlation coefficients are close enough to zero (and insignificant) to justify an inference that the structure of the systems of barriers to trade is, on the whole, indifferent to the income level of the exporting countries – even when only categories of goods which include mostly manufactures are investigated.

The reason for this apparent absence of an impact of exclusion of primary goods on the outcome is that both components of the foregoing hypothesis seem to be invalid. One was a presumption that primary goods face, on average, relatively low trade barriers. In Table 2 the (unweighted) means and the medians of the levels of trade barriers are presented by major SITC categories. It appears that while average levels of barriers (whether represented by the mean or by the median) do differ substantially among categories, no consistent difference appears between the categories of mainly primary goods ((0) to (4)) and the other categories. The second component was the presumption that low-income countries tend to concentrate their exports relatively heavily in the categories of primary goods.

Table 3: Income Level of Exports, by Major SITC Categories (unweighted averages, 1973).

SITC Category	Income Level (y_i^x)
0 Food and live animals	55.4
1 Beverages and tobacco	61.7
2 Crude materials, inedible	53.2
3 Mineral fuels, lubricants	53.2
4 Animal and vegetable oils	56.3
Average (0)–(4)	56.0
5 Chemicals	64.4
6 Manufactured goods, by material	61.4
7 Machinery and transport equipment	73.8
8 Miscellaneous manufactured articles	63.2
Average (5)–(8)	65.7

Although this presumption is usually taken as only too obvious, it seems to be refuted by the facts. This is shown in Table 3 (which draws on Table 1 in my (1978)). It may be seen that the income-level

161

of exports is, in general, quite close in the categories (0) to (4) to its level in the other categories. Indeed, it appears that only category (7) – machinery and transport equipment – deviates materially from the rest, and could be classified as a high-income group; whereas all other categories do not differ much, on average, from each other. Thus, even if there were a relatively low level of trade barriers on flows of primary goods, it could not be expected to act – in general and *on average* – as a source of discrimination in favour of the exports of low-income countries.

IV

By the assumption of uniform treatment of countries, applied here, any discrimination in the structure of trade barriers in favour of or against low-income countries could arise only from the *nature of* the *goods* these countries are exporting. And, although no overall discrimination in either direction has been found, it is worth exploring the relationships of the tariff structure to the attributes of goods – relationships which, if they do indeed exist, may have worked to offset each other in their overall impact on the degree of discrimination in the system. Indications of such relationships might possibly help to forecast the *future* course of discrimination, assuming an expected pattern of development of the trade structure of the LDC's.

One such relationship – the most obvious, perhaps – has just been explored: the distinction between primary goods and manufactures. We have seen that such a distinction would not lead to discrimination between the major classes of countries. A few other attributes suggest themselves as potential sources of discrimination.

One is the labour content, or labour ratio, in the production of goods. It is often suggested that high-income countries tend to establish particularly high trade barriers to the entry of goods whose labour content is high and, hence, whose import would lead to the displacement of relatively large amounts of labour in the importing country. It is presumed that the less-developed, low-income countries tend to export in relatively high degree goods whose labour content is high and capital content low. If this presumption holds, barriers on the trade of labour-intensive goods would have a particularly strong impact on the exports of low-income countries.

Another hypothesis worth testing is that it is the component of unskilled labour, rather than labour in general, which is the subject of protection. High-income countries may be expected to have a comparative advantage in industries in which relatively high skills are required, and a comparative disadvantage in goods which are intensive in unskilled labour. These countries may presumably be reluctant to admit freely imports of the latter goods. To the extent that high barriers are indeed erected against such goods, this would be a factor discriminating against the low-income countries, which presumably export only little of the high-skill goods.

Still another possible hypothesis is that countries tend to establish high barriers to trade in goods destined directly for final consumption; whereas they tend to admit relatively freely imports of goods which would need some transformation before being turned into consumer goods. Raw materials are an obvious case in point – and have already been discussed. But final investment goods are another group of this nature.

The possible existence of such relationships is examined, again, by correlation analyses. Table 4 presents the correlation coefficients of each of these possible explanatory variables – the capital/labour ratio involved in production of a good, the skilled labour ratio (to total labour input), and the ratio of sales for final consumption – with the six sets of indicators of trade barriers.[6]

It appears, from column (1) of Table 4, that the capital/labour ratio variable has no explanatory power at all as a determinant of the pattern of trade barriers: the correlation coefficients involved are all very low (R^2's around zero), and all but two are insignificant. It should

Table 4: Attributes of Goods and Trade-Barriers Levels: Correlation Coefficients (r).

Trade Barrier	Capital/Labor Ratio (1)	Skilled Labor Ratio (2)	Proportion of Sales for final Consumption (3)
(1) Nominal tariff, U.S.	−0.217	−0.171	0.278
(2) Nominal tariff, others	−0.146	−0.213	0.365
(3) Effective tariff, U.S.	−0.256	−0.290	0.270
(4) Effective tariff, others	−0.177	−0.318	0.502
(5) Index of NTB, U.S.	−0.114	−0.365	0.487
(6) Index of NTB, others	−0.114	−0.420	0.628

Italicised figures are significant at the 5% level.

163

be pointed out that the testing of this variable has been carried out here because it is probably of interest in itself. Even, however, had a correlation (positive or negative) been found between the variable under consideration and the tariff structure, it would have been of no consequence to the immediate issue on hand, which is the possible reason for *a-priori* expectation of tariff discrimination among goods by income level of exporters. The reason for this is that the widely-held presumption stated before, that low-income countries concentrate their exports on goods with a high labour/capital ratio, is apparently incorrect: no general relationship is found between labour intensity in production of goods and the income level of exports of these goods.[7]

The skill ratio, represented in column (2), appears to have some explanatory power; but it is a weak one. All but one of the indicators of trade barriers – the level of nominal tariffs in the U.S. – appear to be significantly and negatively correlated with the variable at hand. And this variable is itself positively correlated with the income level of exports of goods.[8] Hence, this would be a factor working against the low-income countries, leading to a relatively higher level of barriers on their exports. But the size of the correlation coefficients would indicate that this factor is of only minor importance.

Of the variables tested, that of the proportion of sales for final consumption, represented in column (3), appears to be most relevant. All correlation coefficients of this explanatory variable with levels of trade barriers are significant, all are positive, and some seem to be high enough to indicate a substantial impact. This is true particularly with regard to the levels of non-tariff barriers, in both the U.S. and in the 'other' countries, and for the level of effective tariffs in the latter. In general, whatever the indicator of trade barrier tested (nominal tariffs, effective tariffs, and NTB's), the relationship to the explanatory variables appears to be stronger in the group of 'other' countries than it is in the U.S.: the coefficients in rows (2), (4) and (6) are higher than those in rows (1), (3) and (5) respectively (this is true also for the skill-ratio variable, but is of lesser consequence there).

What inference does this finding indicate for the issue at hand? Contrary, again, to some popularly-held notions, it appears that low-income countries tend to specialize, relative to high-income countries, in goods which are primarily destined directly for final consumption.[9] Hence, the finding points to the operation of a factor which tends to establish a degree of discrimination *against* the low-income countries in the structure of trade barriers, particularly in the system of non-

164

tariff barriers, and more noticeably in the highly-developed countries other than the U.S.

While this factor may have been of only little consequence hitherto – hence the roughly neutral findings about discrimination in the present structure of trade barriers – it may be expected to assume much more significance in the future. Looking at the range of goods of which LDC's have tended recently to expand production and exports, particularly among manufactured goods, one would get the impression that these tend to be goods destined to a relatively large extent for final consumption. This impression, to be sure, is not sufficient evidence, and a more rigorous empirical verification would be desirable; even if found true, moreover, a projection of this tendency into the future would be still in the nature of conjecture. If this conjecture, however, is borne out, the present findings indicate that in the future the structure of trade barriers would tend increasingly to discriminate against the exports of the low-income countries. Put differently, while it seems that on average the present system is rather neutral, it is one which *at the margin* – that is, when related to trade *expansions* – tends to entail a degree of discrimination against exports of low-income countries. Thus, to come back to a hypothesis tested earlier (in Section III), it seems likely that some discrimination against exports of LDC's does indeed exist in the *relevant* range of goods – although relevance is determined by criteria different from those presumed in the earlier test.

V

The main conclusions of this study are:

i. The existing structure of trade barriers does not imply, on the whole, any degree of discrimination either in favour or against exports of low-income countries. This is true for barriers both in the United States and in the group of other major highly-developed countries – the original EEC members, the United Kingdom, Canada, and Japan; and it holds for the scales of nominal tariffs, of effective protection rates, and of non-tariff barriers.

ii. The structure of trade barriers does not reveal any distinction between major categories of goods; likewise no overall tendency is found towards either high or low barriers on imports of labour-intensive goods. A slight tendency appears to increase the level of barriers with the increase in intensity of unskilled labour in the production of goods.

iii. A clear tendency is revealed, on the other hand, for the level of trade barriers to increase with the extent to which a good is destined directly for final consumption. This implies the existence of a factor which works to raise the level of barriers on low-income exports (relative to other goods) – a factor which at present has probably only a minor effect on the average structure but which may have a more substantial impact on the future expansion of exports by LDC's.

Two policy implications, primarily, are suggested by these findings.

a. Inasmuch as the highly-developed countries wish to lower the trade barriers faced by the exports of low-income countries (relative to the barriers to other trade flows) on a most-favoured-nation basis, namely, by lowering barriers on imports of goods rather than on imports from specific countries, this could not be achieved by a favourable treatment of any *major category* of goods. Specifically, the lowering of barriers on exports of primary goods as a whole would not work in favour of the low-income countries.[10] A favourable treatment would have to involve a much more specific, narrowly defined range of goods.[11]

b. The expansion of exports of LDC's seems likely to be concentrated in manufactures largely destined for final consumption. With the *existing* structure of trade barriers, this would imply that exports of LDC's would face an increasingly higher level of barriers, and would be increasingly discriminated against in relation to barriers on exports from other countries. For this to be avoided – that is, for the present absence of discrimination at least to remain intact – a relative lowering of barriers on trade in these particular goods would be called for.

NOTES

1. Such a change in tariff policies – unlike, perhaps, other possible components of a 'new international economic order' – is likely to be approved by economic analysts. Thus, for instance, a notable observer of development and trade suggests as one of the major conclusions of his recent study that '[highly-developed countries] should make more space for the LDC's in world trade, by reducing their barriers to LDC exports of manufactures and agriculture products. This is the best and most effective way of helping the LDC's' (Lewis 1978, 76–77).

2. For estimates of the positions of individual countries, see the recent study by Yeats (1978).

3. This measure is expounded, and various characteristics of the findings based on it are analysed, in Michaely (1978). The data of the income-level of trade used in the present study are drawn from that source.

4. United States International Trade Commission (1975). The source provides data classified by the SIC (Standard Industrial Classification). I have transformed these into SITC data. For the method of transformation, as well as several other notes on concepts and methods, see the Appendix to this paper.

5. Whereas Table A–1 provides data for 174 goods, Table A–2 includes only 168. For six items – 041, 212, 244, 267, 863, and 896 – data on trade barriers could not

be compiled. The present study is confined, therefore, to the 168 goods of Table A-2.

6. Data of the three explanatory variables are drawn from Hufbauer (1970, Table A-2, 212-220). These data are available not for all (168) goods covered in the present study but to only 118, including all the goods in the SITC major categories (5) to (8) and 19 selected goods in the categories (0) to (4). The present part of the study is hence confined to this group of 118 goods. See Hufbauer for explanation of the methods of constructing the data.

7. See Michaely (1978).

8. *Ibid.*

9. See, again, *ibid.*

10. This statement is concerned, of course, with *relative* levels. The lowering of barriers on exports of primary goods without a compensating change in the barriers imposed on other goods (assuming that *effective* rates as well as nominal rates are not increased anywhere in the system) would constitute a lowering of the overall level of trade barriers and would presumably benefit low-income countries just as it would their high-income partners.

11. It is certainly no accident that the main concrete result of the 'generalized system of preferences' until now has been the specially favourable treatment granted to trade in tropical products. This segment of primary goods – mainly tea, coffee, cocoa, spices, sugar, and tropical fruits – is distinctly the sector of exports with the lowest income levels. It would be much more difficult to define any similar *group* of goods with a markedly low income level (as opposed to *individual* goods – such as, for instance, jute).

REFERENCES

Hufbauer, G. C. (1970), 'The Impact of National Characteristics and Technology on the Commodity Composition of Trade in Manufactured Goods', in R. Vernon (ed.), *The Technology Factor in International Trade*. New York: Columbia University Press for the National Bureau of Economic Research, 154-231.

Lary, H. B. (1968), *Imports of Manufactures from Less Developed Countries*. New York: Columbia University Press for the National Bureau of Economic Research.

Lewis, W. A. (1978), *The Evolution of the International Economic Order*. Princeton: Princeton University Press.

Michaely, M. (1978), 'Income Levels and the Structure of Trade', Stockholm: Institute for International Economic Studies, Seminar Paper No. 110.

United States International Trade Commission (1975), *Protection in Major Trading Countries*. Washington, D.C.: USITC Publication 737.

Yeats, A. J. (1978), *Trade Barriers Facing Developing Countries*, Stockholm: Institute for International Economic Studies Monograph Series, 9 (mimeo).

Appendix

SOURCES AND METHODS FOR DATA ON TRADE BARRIERS

As indicated in the text, the source of the raw data on tariffs and NTB's is the U.S. International Trade Commission publication (1975). Nominal tariff rates and indexes of NTB's are drawn from Table 3 (pp. 44–49), as follows: U.S. nominal tariff – column (4); 'other' countries nominal tariff – column (9); U.S. index of NTB's – column (11); and 'other' countries index of NTB's – column (16). Effective tariff rates are drawn from Table 10 (pp. 91–96): The U.S. – column (7); and 'other' countries – column (12).

The original data used in the U.S.I.T.C. publication were partly compiled by it and partly taken from GATT compilations. It was originally drawn up by various forms of classification, and converted, using concordance schedules, into the classification of IO–SIC (Input-Output Standard Industrial Classification). Averaging of individual items into the IO–SIC commodities was carried out, in the U.S.I.T.C. work, in alternative ways: using import shares (those of the U.S., or of the 'others', as the case may be) for weighting; or calculating simple (unweighted) averages. I have selected the simple-average calculation, which seems preferable for the present purpose. The problems involved in the interpretation of averages of tariff levels weighted by import shares are well known, and are compounded in comparisons of tariff scales of various countries. Simple unweighted averages too have a problem of interpretation, and could at worst be of little meaning; but they are free of biases. It should be noted, though, that the rank correlations of the alternative schedules of barriers (import-shares-weighted vs. simple averages), are given in the source and indicate a strong similarity. Overall results and generalizations would thus not be much affected by use of the alternative schedules.

168

The index of NTB is explained on pp. 16–17 of the source. It is designed to measure the frequency of appearances of various forms of NTB in the imports of each good. The *absolute* level of the index is devoid of meaning: at best, it is an ordinal measure, not a cardinal one. Even then, it is probably less reliable than the measures of tariff levels.

In the present study, all data are classified by the (3-digit) SITC (Standard International Trade Classification). To convert the data from the IO–SIC, as they appear in the source, to the SITC, I have constructed a concordance list (this may be obtained from the author upon request). This is based partly on a concordance list in Lary (1978), but mostly on Appendix A (pp. A–1 – A–8) in the U.S.I.T.C. publication, which presents the concordance relating the 5-digit SITC items to the IO–SIC. I have not adopted the latter fully, but made a selective list, according to the apparent content of each IO–SIC and SITC item – omitting SITC items which seem of little relevance to the IO–SIC item. Any such (remaining) SITC item was assumed to have the level of trade barrier of the IO–SIC item a component of which it constitutes. The 5-digit SITC items were then aggregated into 3-digit SITC items by the use of simple, unweighted averages of the levels of trade barriers.

Table A–1: Indexes of Income Levels of Exports and Imports, by Commodity.

SITC Code	Commodity	Income level of Exports (y_j^x)	Income level of Imports (y_j^m)
0	*Food and live animals*		
001	Live animals	60.85	49.58
011	Meat – fresh, chilled, frozen	58.56	63.64
012	Meat – dried, salted, smoked	74.86	49.58
013	Meat – canned or prepared	58.29	70.88
022	Milk and cream	70.05	34.91
023	Butter	69.11	51.39
024	Cheese and curd	71.69	64.75
025	Eggs	69.43	60.98
031	Fresh fish	46.80	67.73
032	Canned or prepared fish	52.04	62.17
041	Unmilled wheat	88.30	29.95
042	Rice	53.20	16.80
043	Unmilled barley	78.37	56.37
044	Unmilled maize	81.70	51.32
045	Unmilled Cereals, n.e.s.	76.04	54.90
046	Wheat meal or flour	72.24	12.12
047	Non-wheat meal or flour	70.50	39.74

SITC Code	Commodity	Income level of Exports (y_j^x)	Income level of Imports (y_j^m)
	Food and live animals—continued		
048	Cereal preparations	71.08	49.33
051	Fresh fruit and nuts	30.79	66.65
052	Dried fruit	40.13	54.41
053	Preserved or prepared fruit	43.92	67.74
054	Fresh vegetables	47.50	63.26
055	Preserved or prepared vegetables	44.52	68.10
061	Sugar and honey	24.74	52.16
062	Sugar preparations	61.23	62.10
071	Coffee	11.39	76.82
072	Cocoa	16.80	69.25
073	Chocolate	66.69	67.27
074	Tea	10.12	40.31
075	Spices	13.45	45.60
081	Animal feeding stuff	58.51	59.22
091	Margarine, shortening	68.14	44.51
099	Food preparations, n.e.s.	67.28	47.20
1	*Beverages and Tobacco*		
111	Non-alcoholic beverages, n.e.s.	65.98	55.86
112	Alcoholic beverages	54.30	68.21
121	Tobacco, unmanufactured	54.85	59.73
122	Tobacco manufactures	71.69	43.19
2	*Crude materials, inedible, except fuel*		
211	Hides and skins	60.74	52.07
212	Fur skins	69.28	70.88
221	Oil seeds, nuts, kernels	73.92	60.52
231	Crude synthetic rubber	29.89	52.99
241	Fuel wood and charcoal	55.73	56.75
242	Rough wood	37.43	53.35
243	Shape wood	69.56	65.63
244	Raw cork and waste	22.14	53.02
251	Pulp and waste paper	80.83	61.90
261	Silk	19.10	57.45
262	Wool and animal hair	58.31	55.61
263	Cotton	33.64	43.88
264	Jute	9.67	42.84
265	Vegetable fibers, excluding cotton and jute	31.83	55.31
266	Synthetic, regenerated fiber	68.02	46.34
267	Waste of textile fabrics	79.70	38.63
271	Crude fertilizers	32.08	51.65
273	Stone, sand and gravel	63.63	64.61
274	Sulphur	64.36	49.47
275	Natural abrasives	56.60	69.46
276	Other crude minerals	60.18	58.71
281	Iron ore, concentrates	51.46	67.64
282	Iron and steel scrap	84.14	45.62

SITC Code	Commodity	Income level of Exports (y_i^x)	Income level of Imports (y_i^m)
	Crude materials, inedible, except fuel—continued		
283	Nonferrous base metal ore, concentrates	39.55	64.76
284	Nonferrous metal scrap	75.33	64.77
285	Silver and platinum ores	59.46	71.94
291	Crude animal materials, n.e.s.	50.57	65.49
292	Crude vegetable materials, n.e.s.	53.42	64.66
3	*Mineral fuels, lubricants, related materials*		
321	Coal, coke, briquettes	85.12	60.39
331	Crude petroleum	23.45	55.48
332	Petroleum products	38.49	67.71
341	Natural gas and manufactures	65.66	72.98
4	*Animal and vegetable oils and fats*		
411	Animal oils and fats	80.46	44.56
421	Fixed vegetable oils, soft	50.53	41.06
422	Fixed vegetable oils, non-soft	24.91	57.92
431	Processed animal and vegetable oils	69.41	53.62
5	*Chemicals*		
512	Organic chemicals	75.00	53.49
513	Inorganic elements, oxides, etc.	69.20	56.18
514	Other inorganic elements	71.81	47.81
515	Radioactive and associated elements	86.44	76.90
521	Coal, petroleum etc. chemicals	56.24	57.47
531	Synthetic organic dyestuffs, etc.	81.06	45.20
532	Dyes n.e.s., tanning products	49.51	32.54
533	Pigments, prints, etc.	71.04	48.22
541	Medical and pharmaceutical products	71.34	41.90
551	Essential oil, perfumes, etc.	61.97	54.13
553	Cosmetics, etc.	66.36	49.97
554	Soaps and cleaning preparations	70.94	48.20
561	Manufactured fertilizers	68.26	37.41
571	Explosive and pyrotechnic products	63.86	46.18
581	Plastic materials, etc.	73.50	54.58
599	Chemicals n.e.s.	72.78	46.31
6	*Manufactured goods classified by material*		
611	Leather	44.72	62.20
612	Leather manufactures	55.53	65.66
613	Fur skins, tanned or dressed	64.30	65.78
621	Rubber materials	71.81	52.54
629	Rubber articales, n.e.s.	65.61	62.14
631	Veneers, plywood, etc.	50.91	67.40
632	Wood manufactures, n.e.s.	64.23	72.76
633	Cork manufactures	30.70	65.67
641	Paper and paperboard	76.57	60.40
642	Paper articles	68.92	53.78

SITC Code	Commodity	Income level of Exports (y_j^x)	Income level of Imports (y_j^m)
	Manufactured goods classified by material— continued		
651	Textile yarn and thread	56.54	49.46
652	Woven cotton fabrics	47.08	53.48
653	Woven non-cotton fabrics	56.91	55.22
654	Lace, ribbons, tulle, etc.	65.33	53.07
655	Special textile products	68.49	57.23
656	Textile products, n.e.s.	40.45	50.04
657	Floor coverings, tapestry, etc.	56.16	72.04
661	Cement building products	46.50	51.40
662	Clay building products	62.20	59.88
663	Other non-metal mineral manufactures	71.41	59.99
664	Glass	70.74	61.78
665	Glassware	66.12	55.66
666	Pottery	61.51	68.48
667	Pearls, precious and semi-precious stones	50.52	62.62
671	Pig iron	56.53	68.06
672	Ingots of iron and steel	66.74	40.39
673	Iron and steel shapes	71.23	58.01
674	Universals, plates and sheets of iron and steel	68.05	55.32
675	Hoop and strip of iron and steel	75.18	55.66
676	Rails and other track materials of steel	65.12	28.63
677	Iron and steel wire, excluding rod	71.80	55.61
678	Iron and steel tubes, pipes, etc.	70.18	56.08
679	Iron and steel castings, unworked	75.24	48.89
681	Silver, platinum, etc.	62.29	72.03
682	Copper	42.96	63.26
683	Nickel	74.22	80.08
684	Aluminium	69.93	60.51
685	Lead	57.62	55.64
686	Zinc	64.47	62.86
687	Tin	19.07	66.89
689	Non-ferrous base metals, n.e.s.	62.79	71.71
691	Structures and parts, n.e.s.	68.79	47.52
692	Metal containers	64.40	45.32
693	Non-electric wire products	65.49	60.81
694	Nails, screws, etc. of iron, steel or copper	71.06	67.75
695	Tools	74.81	54.01
696	Cutlery	61.71	62.28
697	Base-metal household equipment	58.27	57.25
698	Metal manufactures, n.e.s.	69.82	58.60
7	*Machinery and transport equipment*		
711	Non-electric power machinery	76.86	59.32
712	Agriculture machinery	75.94	50.87
714	Office machines	75.53	64.25
715	Metal-working machinery	77.35	49.71
717	Textile and leather machinery	74.53	41.07

SITC Code	Commodity	Income level of Exports (y_j^x)	Income level of Imports (y_j^m)
	Machinery and transport equipment—continued		
718	Machines for special industries	77.71	42.14
719	Non-electric machines, n.e.s.	75.99	49.50
722	Electric-power machinery, switches	74.64	50.00
723	Equipment for distributing electricity	66.38	46.72
724	Telecommunications equipment	67.54	60.72
725	Domestic electric equipment	67.26	61.56
726	Electro-medical, X-ray equipment	80.13	58.89
729	Electric machinery, n.e.s.	72.54	57.71
731	Railway vehicles	69.76	29.60
732	Road motor vehicles	76.21	67.81
733	Road non-motor vehicles	66.81	68.86
734	Aircraft	87.17	55.47
735	Ships and boats	66.84	57.38
8	*Miscellaneous manufactured articles*		
812	Plumbing, heating and lighting fixtures	67.83	58.25
821	Furniture	67.94	72.64
831	Travel goods, handbags	46.24	73.96
841	Clothing, except fur	45.33	73.15
842	Fur clothing	57.41	79.05
851	Footwear	41.12	78.84
861	Scientific instruments and apparatus	75.12	60.03
862	Photographic and cinematographic supplies	76.79	57.73
863	Developed cinema film	55.67	43.67
864	Watches and clocks	79.68	54.69
891	Musical instruments, recorders, etc.	66.76	68.18
892	Printed matter	67.62	61.26
893	Plastic articles, n.e.s.	68.72	67.50
894	Toys, sporting goods, etc.	58.40	71.16
895	Office supplies, n.e.s.	72.63	49.43
896	Works of art, etc.	73.21	71.49
897	Gold and silver ware, jewelry	60.71	67.36
899	Other manufactured goods	56.46	62.06

Table A–2: Levels of Trade Barriers

SITC Code	Nominal Tariffs (%)		Effective Tariffs (%)		Non-tariff Barriers (index)	
	U.S. (1)	EEC, Canada, Japan, U.K. (2)	U.S. (3)	EEC, Canada, Japan, U.K. (4)	U.S. (5)	EEC, Canada, Japan, U.K. (6)
001	5.4	4.5	16.7	10.1	1.6	2.3
011	5.2	9.4	5.5	36.3	1.9	5.3
012	5.2	9.4	5.5	36.3	1.9	5.3

SITC Code	Nominal Tariffs (%) U.S. (1)	Nominal Tariffs (%) EEC, Canada, Japan, U.K. (2)	Effective Tariffs (%) U.S. (3)	Effective Tariffs (%) EEC, Canada, Japan, U.K. (4)	Non-tariff Barriers (index) U.S. (5)	Non-tariff Barriers (index) EEC, Canada, Japan, U.K. (6)
013	5.2	9.4	5.5	36.3	1.9	5.3
022	6.6	11.9	93.9	25.6	7.7	11.1
023	12.6	11.1	271.7	15.1	13.3	12.1
024	14.3	15.5	65.0	37.8	20.0	10.8
025	5.9	7.5	15.7	26.8	1.5	4.9
031	1.4	9.5	0.6	18.4	0.9	2.4
032	2.9	10.6	4.5	22.8	0.6	2.9
042	4.5	5.6	8.0	17.9	2.6	6.3
043	4.6	4.7	7.4	6.6	1.9	5.9
044	4.6	4.7	7.4	6.6	1.9	5.9
045	4.6	4.7	7.4	6.6	1.9	5.9
046	6.1	7.3	14.7	20 5	4.1	6.2
047	6.1	7.3	14.7	20.5	4.1	6.2
048	3.3	10.4	3.3	27.1	1.7	5.4
051	5.7	8.8	8.0	—	0.8	4.6
052	10.7	10.8	24.4	21.4	0.2	3.9
053	9.2	10.3	19.7	21.5	0 4	4.6
054	8.0	7.7	13.5	13.3	0·8	4.6
055	10.5	10.3	23.1	20.1	0.6	4.0
061	4.6	20.2	4.0	51.6	6.7	3.9
062	6.1	9.5	13.5	15.2	5.5	3.6
071	2.8	10.2	1.1	44.7	1.2	3.7
072	3.7	8.0	3.3	6.7	1.4	3.1
073	1.8	7.3	−1.3	6.7	2.1	1.7
074	7.9	4.9	11.9	5.8	0.9	2.4
075	5.2	6.0	7.3	7.1	0.7	3.0
081	3.2	9.7	−1.7	18.0	2.5	3.2
091	22.9	12.0	—	61.7	3.3	4.0
099	8.0	11.6	14.0	34.4	1.1	2.6
111	0.5	6.5	−3.9	8.3	0.0	4.4
112	16.3	23.5	24.7	35.9	2.4	9.8
121	28.3	102.9	57.2	80.4	0.0	8.8
122	22.4	79.8	26.3	117.0	0.0	8.2
211	4.7	5.0	5.4	17.6	1.2	2.6
221	2.6	6.7	4.6	7.0	1.0	4.1
231	1.8	6.2	−0.5	7.2	0.0	0.2
241	0.0	3.1	−0.9	4.0	0.0	0.0
242	0.5	2.5	−1.6	−3.8	0.0	0.0
243	1.7	5.9	2.7	9.8	0.1	0.1
251	0.0	1.8	−3.1	−0.6	0.0	0.0
261	13.9	9.8	30.9	22.8	1.0	0.7
262	14.0	3.7	52.8	4.1	0.0	0.1

SITC Code	Nominal Tariffs (%)		Effective Tariffs (%)		Non-tariff Barriers (index)	
	U.S. (1)	EEC, Canada, Japan, U.K. (2)	U.S. (3)	EEC, Canada, Japan, U.K. (4)	U.S. (5)	EEC, Canada, Japan, U.K. (6)
263	4.8	1.7	9.3	1.4	1.7	2.9
264	7.9	4.9	11.9	5.8	0.9	2.4
265	7.9	4.9	11.9	5.8	0.9	2.4
266	13.5	8.3	30.7	13.9	0.4	0.2
271	1.0	2.3	−5.1	−2.4	0.0	0.1
273	2.0	5.7	1.6	6.2	0.0	0.1
274	3.2	2.8	3.1	2.3	0.0	0.5
275	2.3	5.7	1.8	6.4	0.0	0.1
276	3.2	4.7	3.6	3.8	0.0	0.3
281	2.4	1.0	2.5	−0.1	0.0	0.0
282	2.4	1.0	2.5	−0.1	0.0	0.0
283	3.4	1.8	3.8	0.6	0.0	0.0
284	6.1	5.5	12.7	11.1	0.0	0.2
285	1.5	2.3	0.7	1.0	0.0	0.2
291	3.4	6.1	3.5	14.6	1.3	2.8
292	1.9	7.8	1.2	9.8	0.3	2.1
321	0.0	0.6	−1.5	−0.9	0.0	3.8
331	3.1	6.2	6.4	15.4	2.8	0.7
332	2.5	5.8	5.0	11.7	1.2	0.0
341	3.1	6.2	6.4	15.4	2.8	0.7
411	2.2	6.8	1.7	8.7	0.1	1.6
421	9.1	8.0	16.4	22.2	0.0	4.8
422	3.0	8.3	4.3	17.2	0.2	4.4
431	3.6	7.7	4.2	9.9	0.2	1.5
512	5.0	8.9	7.5	15.5	0.3	0.1
513	3.0	5.2	2.4	6.2	0.0	0.1
514	5.3	7.5	6.8	10.9	0.0	0.1
515	4.3	4.9	5.5	5.6	0.0	0.2
521	5.8	7.8	8.9	12.8	0.2	0.4
531	7.2	7.5	10.4	10.2	0.1	0.3
532	5.3	6.2	9.9	8.5	0.3	0.1
533	4.1	7.6	3.0	10.7	0.0	0.1
541	7.0	8.6	10.1	12.0	0.1	0.1
551	11.0	9.4	19.5	11.1	0.3	1.7
553	8.6	13.0	27.6	44.1	0.0	0.0
554	5.3	9.3	8.8	16.7	0.1	0.0
561	2.6	3.6	−1.2	0.7	0.0	0.2
571	8.8	9.7	11.9	12.9	0.0	0.0
581	8.3	7.8	12.3	10.4	0.1	0.1
599	5.0	7.7	7.8	13.3	0.3	0.5
611	5.0	10.4	5.5	23.5	0.0	0.0

THE INCOME-LEVEL OF EXPORTS AND TARIFF DISCRIMINATION

SITC Code	Nominal Tariffs (%)		Effective Tariffs (%)		Non-tariff Barriers (index)	
	U.S. (1)	EEC, Canada, Japan, U.K. (2)	U.S. (3)	EEC, Canada, Japan, U.K. (4)	U.S. (5)	EEC, Canada, Japan, U.K. (6)
612	4.5	12.4	4.3	19.7	0.0	0.0
613	24.6	15.0	43.1	20.5	3.0	2.0
621	5.3	6.2	7.9	8.1	0.1	0.0
629	5.2	9.4	5.0	13.2	0.2	0.0
631	4.3	7.6	9.2	14.7	0.1	0.2
632	5.3	7.9	11.2	15.1	0.0	0.3
633	5.3	7.9	11.2	15.1	0.0	0.3
641	6.0	11.1	9.0	19.7	0.0	0.0
642	6.9	11.6	12.2	18.5	0.0	0.2
651	12.2	8.6	24.1	15.4	0.9	0.4
652	12.2	9.2	27.9	20.7	2.0	1.6
653	15.1	11.0	38.4	25.7	1.8	1.4
654	14.0	11.5	27.2	25.8	1.7	2.2
655	13.9	11.5	30.8	27.5	2.1	2.0
656	14.3	13.3	24.6	33.1	2.3	2.7
657	8.6	13.7	8.9	40.6	1.1	0.7
661	4.8	5.4	8.5	7.4	0.0	0.0
662	8.0	8.4	12.9	12.0	0.1	0.3
663	5.1	8.1	8.3	11.2	0.0	0.0
664	10.9	9.7	16.7	13.2	0.0	0.4
665	13.2	11.5	22.1	16.1	0.0	2.5
666	13.2	11.5	22.1	16.1	0.0	2.5
667	11.3	9.4	26.7	16.1	0.0	0.7
671	5.0	7.3	7.7	12.1	0.1	0.2
672	5.8	7.8	8.9	12.8	0.2	0.4
673	7.0	8.1	10.7	11.4	0.0	0.4
674	7.1	7.8	11.6	10.2	0.0	0.5
675	7.1	8.0	11.0	11.4	0.0	0.5
676	5.8	7.8	8.9	12.8	0.2	0.4
677	7.1	8.0	11.0	11.4	0.0	0.5
678	6.5	9.0	9.8	13.6	0.0	0.1
679	5.0	9.5	5.7	13.9	0.0	0.0
681	6.4	6.1	11.7	10.3	0.0	0.1
682	5.6	8.3	9.4	18.5	0.0	0.0
683	6.1	7.5	8.2	10.5	0.0	0.2
684	6.2	7.3	11.5	14.5	0.0	0.0
685	4.8	6.4	4.8	10.6	0.0	0.2
686	7.4	6.5	16.0	11.2	0.0	0.3
687	6.3	6.5	10.8	10.4	0.0	0.1
689	6.4	5.6	11.1	7.1	0.0	0.1
691	6.3	8.4	8.5	10.8	0.0	0.1
692	6.5	9.9	11.3	16.0	0.3	0.0
693	6.6	10.4	9.4	18.1	0.0	0.1
694	5.2	10.0	5.5	14.4	0.0	0.0

SITC Code	Nominal Tariffs (%)		Effective Tariffs (%)		Non-tariff Barriers (index)	
	U.S. (1)	EEC, Canada, Japan, U.K. (2)	U.S. (3)	EEC, Canada, Japan, U.K. (4)	U.S. (5)	EEC, Canada, Japan, U.K. (6)
695	6.4	8.5	7.6	10.2	0.0	0.1
696	17.6	12.3	43.6	23.9	0.0	0.4
697	7.3	10.1	12.3	17.8	0.0	0.3
698	7.1	10.0	10.2	15.8	0.0	0.1
711	4.6	8.9	5.0	10.6	0.3	0.3
712	3.1	8.4	0.3	10.9	0.0	0.4
714	4.6	8.7	5.0	10.5	0.0	0.2
715	7.3	9.4	9.3	12.4	0.0	0.0
717	6.3	8.1	8.6	10.1	0.0	0.8
718	5.1	7.3	5.3	8.2	0.0	0.0
719	5.2	8.0	5.6	9.5	0.0	0.1
722	8.8	9.8	12.7	12.4	0.0	0.2
723	9.2	9.7	13.5	12.7	0.0	0.3
724	5.4	9.0	5.7	11.1	0.0	0.4
725	6.0	8.8	7.7	11.8	0.0	0.0
726	2.7	8.9	1.3	10.7	0.0	0.0
729	6.4	9.3	7.6	11.7	0.0	0.5
731	9.7	8.6	17.1	11.2	0.0	0.2
732	4.2	11.3	5.3	20.9	0.0	1.4
733	7.3	10.5	13.5	18.3	0.0	0.6
734	4.9	8.6	5.6	10.4	0.5	0.2
735	5.6	3.4	6.7	−0.6	3.3	0.3
812	9.4	9.0	18.6	10.3	0.7	0.4
821	8.6	11.8	16.0	23.0	0.7	0.9
831	13.2	12.8	24.2	19.7	0.0	0.2
841	21.7	15.5	35.3	28.6	2.4	2.3
842	24.6	15.0	43.1	20.5	3.0	2.0
851	11.5	13.8	16.8	20.2	0.0	0.1
861	11.4	9.6	18.2	13.0	0.1	0.2
862	7.9	10.3	10.0	13.1	0.2	0.3
864	13.6	10.9	27.7	17.3	0.0	0.3
891	5.3	8.7	5.2	12.3	0.0	0.2
892	2.0	4.4	1.3	4.0	2.0	0.4
893	7.1	9.1	7.9	12.2	0.5	0.0
894	11.2	11.7	19.7	18.5	0.6	0.6
895	11.4	10.0	18.2	13.8	0.1	0.1
897	16.6	12.0	37.4	21.1	0.0	0.9
899	9.8	9.8	24.8	91.6	0.2	0.2

Chapter Ten

THE ECONOMIC WORLD ORDER AND NORTH-SOUTH TRADE RELATIONS*

Juergen B. Donges

THE PURPOSE of this paper is to discuss some trade aspects of the demands for a New International Economic Order (NIEO), vigorously made by the less developed countries (LDCs) since 1974. One is the proposal to establish producer-consumer agreements for primary commodities of which LDCs are major exporters. A second issue relates to the proposal for freer access of LDC manufactured exports to the markets of the industrial nations (DCs). As the demands for a NIEO rest upon the view that the prevailing international trading system inherently discriminates against LDCs, it may be worthwhile first to put the discussion of the two trade issues into historical perspective by reappraising, very briefly, world trade trends since 1950 as perceived by the LDCs.

Some Thoughts on LDCs' Exports

World trade (measured by exports at constant dollar prices) has expanded at a rapid rate in the post-war period; roughly 6 per cent per annum between 1950 and 1960 and nearly 8 per cent a year from 1960 to 1973, the year of the quadrupling of the oil price. Only the subsequent recession in the DCs reduced the speed of world trade growth. As trade expanded faster (by a factor of 1.5) than production, the world economy increased its degree of integration, after the previous phase of disintegration during the years from the Great Depression (1929–31) until the end of World War II.

It is well-known that the share of LDCs as a group in world trade

* I wish to thank Ulrich Hiemenz, Hans R. Krämer, Rolf Langhammer, Klaus-Werner Schatz and Bernd Stecher for many helpful comments on an earlier draft. I am also grateful for the criticism at the Symposium.

Table 1: Changing Shares of World Merchandise Exports (per cent)*

| | SITC | Developed countries | | | Developing countries | | | | | |
| | | | | | Total | | | Excluding OPEC | | |
		1955	1970	1975	1955	1970	1975	1955	1970	1975
Food and related products	0+1+22+4	48.7	59.0	63.3	42.6	31.8	28.7	41.0	29.3	27.5
Agricultural raw materials	2 less 22, 27, 28	49.4	58.4	61.3	40.4	30.3	26.2	38.5	25.6	24.3
Crude fertilizers and minerals	27+28	52.6	58.0	54.3	33.0	31.4	32.8	31.5	28.0	29.7
Mineral fuels	3	31.7	26.5	17.4	57.5	63.1	73.9	9.0	10.1	11.0
Chemical products	5	88.1	88.9	87.3	5.1	3.9	5.4	5.0	3.7	4.6
Machinery and transport equipment	7	86.6	87.6	87.1	0.7	1.6	2.8	0.6	1.5	2.7
Iron and steel	67	86.6	82.5	86.5	0.9	3.3	2.7	0.9	3.1	2.5
Non-ferrous metals and products	68	59.2	63.6	67.9	33.9	29.0	22.0	33.5	28.6	21.2
Other manufactures	6+8 less 67, 68	82.6	79.9	78.1	8.8	11.2	13.4	8.7	10.9	13.0
Total export	0–9	64.7	71.9	66.2	25.4	17.6	24.1	22.5	11.8	11.4

* The percentages do not add to 100 because centrally-planned economies are excluded.

Source: UNCTAD, *Handbook of International Trade and Development Statistics*, 1976 – UN, *Monthly Bulletin of Statistics*, May 1977.

has been declining. In 1955 (the first year for which world trade data by commodity categories are available) the LDCs had a share in world exports of 25.4 per cent. Twenty years later, this share was only slightly lower, at 22.5 per cent. The big oil price increase of 1973/74 played a large part, however, in sustaining the figure. If OPEC is excluded, the export share of LDCs in 1975 was only 11.4 per cent (Table 1). Moreover, the LDCs lost ground even in fields where their resource endowment should have given them a comparative advantage: in food products, agricultural raw materials, and non-ferrous metals. On the other hand, the LDCs were able, contrary to earlier forecasts, to increase their share in various groups of manufactures, which globally experienced a faster expansion than total world exports.

From this lagging of LDCs behind world trade expansion advocates of the NIEO draw the conclusion that the prevailing international trading system is unjust to LDCs. It is argued that, contrary to what happened to the DCs and to what is stated by the pure theory of foreign trade, the LDCs did not gain from international trade; according to the neo-Marxian interpretation of the world economy, they found themselves in a position of 'unequal exchange'. This argument involves two distinct aspects. The first one suggests absence in principle of any trade gains. To this one may retort that the simple fact that LDCs have concluded trade contracts with DCs, and have done so not just once but again and again, is an indication that they may also have gained. Otherwise they would not have participated in trade. Gains arise from the possibility of extending in various ways each country's frontiers of investment and consumption. Trade enables countries to make better use of domestic resources for which there is insufficient internal demand, to realize economies of scale in spite of the narrowness of the domestic market, and to exploit the dissemination of knowledge and international competition so as to strengthen economic initiative, raise efficiency and thereby increase real national income. These gains need not necessarily be reflected in a tendency to 'equal remuneration for equal work' throughout the world, as the theories of unequal exchange axiomatically claim. Incomes per capita will vary, both within a country and among nations, in accordance with the possession of working skills and attitudes, the ownership of physical capital, and the ability to take risk. To the extent that such differences between central and peripheral areas persist, they could be overcome by income-support for backward regions; this is one of the purposes of official development assistance given by DCs to LDCs. Second, the gains from trade may appear larger *ex ante* than *ex post*. When a developing country embarks upon some specific export activity, it will try to bring the expected gains as close as possible to quantitative goals established in advance. Even if the original target is attained, it may be found inadequate if the trading partner has fared even better. Resentment arising from the (greater) success of others is the likely consequence.

Advocates of the NIEO tend to attribute the secular fall in the LDCs' share of total world exports solely to unfavourable external demand conditions. They overlook the simple though fundamental truth that DCs enjoying growing incomes will, with given trade policies and with positive marginal propensities to import, raise their demand also for exports of LDCs. In spite of this, the unfavourable-demand-factors argument retains some validity. It refers essentially to low and declining income elasticities of world demand for staple foods, to raw-material-saving technological progress, and to competition from synthetic substitutes. It is undeniable that certain primary commodities which face such an unfavourable trade environment make up a much larger proportion of LDC exports than of DC exports. However, this is only one side of the coin. Many LDCs have promoted economic development through policies of industrialization based on import substitution behind high trade barriers (Little, Scitovsky and Scott, 1970). In many cases, overemphasis on import substitution has turned the internal terms of trade between agriculture and industry against the former and has thus held back the development of a strong, diversified agricultural export capacity. Although world demand for a great number of primary products exported by LDCs has not increased as fast as the world demand for manufactured products, LDCs failed in many cases to keep pace even with this somewhat weak growth of world demand.

As far as manufactured exports are concerned, there is also much emphasis on unfavourable external demand conditions and little consideration of supply-side factors. Again, heavily protectionist import substitution policies led to a great number of inefficiencies in domestic production, distorted cost structures throughout the manufacturing sector, and penalized domestic industries in the world market (Balassa and Associates, 1971). Industrial firms which might have sold either in the home market or abroad found that value added in export activities appeared substantially lower than value added in import-substituting production. A frequently unjustified inferiority complex and illusion of inefficiency emerged, which may be considered the most powerful obstacle to manufactured export expansion by LDCs. As a matter of fact, the exceptional expansion of world trade in the sixties and early seventies was particularly beneficial to those LDCs whose industrialization policies had most clearly shifted away from excessive emphasis on import substitution, and become more aggressively outward-looking. South Korea and Taiwan (since 1961), Israel (since 1962), Brazil (since 1966), and Colombia (since 1967) are cases in point (Donges and Riedel, 1977; Balassa, 1978a; Krueger, 1978; Donges and Müller–Ohlsen, 1978). The change of policy did not mean that further import substitution was stopped. It meant only that export industries were given equal, or at least improved, chances of development along with import substituting activities.

If LDCs are willing and able to seize the opportunities which integration into the world economy – as opposed to its abandonment through excessive import substitution – offers them, they need not worry much about their terms of trade. The critics of the prevailing order are nevertheless concerned about it, alleging in accordance with the famous Prebisch–Singer thesis a secular movement in the terms of trade against LDCs. Apart from the fact that empirical evidence is far from conclusively confirming the critics, the attempt to blame an actual deterioration in the terms of trade upon the international order involves a fundamental misconception. The point is that the terms of trade (however defined) are not independent of a country's adaptability to changing market situations. In a growing world economy where the income elasticities of demand differ between goods, the terms of trade are bound to worsen for those countries which fail to adjust their supply structure and thereby to raise the weighted average of the income elasticity of world demand for their products. One may argue that LDCs lack such supply adaptability by definition; but experience so far does not support this view – in reality various LDCs have exhibited a considerable amount of adaptability. This means that the efforts of LDCs should be concentrated on further diversification of their export structures. However, the main thrust of LDCs, at least at the diplomatic level, has underlined reforms of the commodity sector of world trade as an area of vital interest for LDCs.

Commodity Schemes
Under UNCTAD's guidance, a vigorous effort has been mounted in recent years to establish producer-consumer schemes for between 10 ('core') and 18 ('Nairobi') primary commodities,[2] linked together by a common financing mechanism. This 'Integrated Programme for Commodities' (IPC), as it is officially labelled, is at the centre of the debate on the NIEO. While the official documents of UNCTAD state a great variety of objectives, the main economic purposes of the IPC

are to stabilize commodity prices at levels remunerative to producers in real terms (while not unfair to consumers) and to improve the secular trend of these prices, so that earnings from commodity exports are increased. These two objectives are to be met respectively through internationally operated buffer stocks and through price indexation and other price-rising measures. Extensive theoretical and empirical analyses, critically surveyed by Harris, Salmon and Smith (1977), indicate that, contrary to the view of the UNCTAD Secretariat and the 'Group of 77', the economic effects of the IPC, if it can be implemented, are not entirely clear and that the assumption of major benefits to the LDCs is open to serious question. Attempts so far made to quantify the prospective costs and benefits of the IPC show that under certain conditions LDCs could be among the loosers and DCs among the winners (Behrman, 1977; Baron, Glismann and Stecher, 1977).

With regard to the objective of price stabilization, the key problem is the difficulty of forecasting supply and demand shifts and thereby predicting the future path of market-clearing commodity prices – an indispensable condition for obtaining the desired results. If market-clearing prices are above the target price, then buffer stocks and production capacities may not be large enough to satisfy demand at the target price, so that the producing countries will feel themselves disadvantaged, and therefore press for an increase in the target price. If, on the other hand, market-clearing prices remain below the projected ones (a story well-known from the experience of EEC agricultural policy), the central buffer stock agency has constantly to withdraw production from the market. This is expensive, and aside from probably implying the deliberate destruction sooner or later of production surpluses or their use for purpose other than those originally intended, may even induce producing countries to commit a breach of the arrangement. In any case, deviations between policy-determined and market-clearing prices will lead to unpredictable transfers of income either from producing to consuming countries or vice versa. I do not see how this forecasting problem can be satisfactorily solved in an uncertain world, with the help of either national governments, the UNCTAD Secretariat or a central buffer stock management, however well-staffed. These bodies are not more knowledgeable than the market. In fact, experience with international commodity agreements has on the whole been disappointing; they have either failed, or not even come into operation (cocoa), because of unanticipated gluts or shortages.

Another problem arises from the widely accepted view that resource-rich LDCs might be interested not so much in more stable commodity prices as in more stable foreign exchange earnings from the export of those commodities. It cannot be taken for granted that price stabilization via buffer stocks, even if feasible, will also smooth fluctuations in export earnings. If shifts in demand are the major source of price instability, commodity schemes may indeed stabilize both variables. If fluctuations in output are the major source, a reduction of price instability may imply greater volatility of export earnings. Similar considerations apply to resource-poor LDCs (and DCs) as far as import expenditures are concerned.[3]

Turning now to the goal of raising prices, this issue may pose even worse difficulties. This holds, to begin with, for the 'indexation proposal'. The case for linking prices of LDC primary commodity exports with the price which these countries have to pay for their imports and manufactures from DCs derives, as we are told by UNCTAD and representatives of the Group of 77, from the strong inflationary movements which have afflicted the world economy in recent years. This inflation, besides being unsettling in itself, has allegedly caused an adverse shift in the terms of trade of developing countries and an erosion of their capacity to import. If the objective of indexation is protection against inflation, Johnson (1976, pp. 13–14) has argued persuasively that nominal commodity prices will lag, if at all, only temporarily behind world inflation rates. A different question may arise from unexpected inflation. To deal with this, contracts involving long-term sale and purchase commitments should be provided with an index clause so that they are formulated in real rather than nominal terms. Unanticipated acceleration of deceleration of inflation would then not affect the expected value of payments. In practice, the market generates such contracts to some extent, particularly in the field of minerals. But producers from LDCs are not always in a position to obtain all contracts they want, because commodity processing firms in DCs, especially the vertically integrated multinational corporations, can accomplish their desire for stability in prices and flows through international stockpiling.

If the objective of indexation is to preserve for LDCs some purchasing-parity relationship between the prices of commodity exports and manufactured imports, then different economic considerations arise, of which three seem particularly worth mentioning. First, whenever the price elasticity of supply is high (which can be assumed to be the case in the medium and long run), indexation will stimulate expansion of production which might then exceed the increase in demand. The resulting excess supply in the world market will exert downward pressure on commodity prices. Attempts to keep prices artificially high will inhibit the diversification of production, both horizontal and vertical, in the resource-rich LDCs themselves. Second, the resource-poor LDCs will suffer the most. They will have to pay higher prices not only for manufactured imports, but also for the raw materials subject to indexation. Other things equal, their economic development process will come up against balance-of-payment constraints sooner than would otherwise be the case. Third, as a number of DCs account for a significant share of world production of primary commodities (almost two fifths, excluding oil), indexation will also transfer income to them. If they are excluded from the price-support arrangement, they will increase their market shares at the expense of the costlier suppliers from the Third World. If they are not excluded, but neutralize the price increases due to indexation by taxing their own producers, they will create an artificial encouragement to expand capacities for processing raw materials, at the expense of developing countries which might have a comparative advantage in this field. All this means that the fixing of relative prices between two types of goods (primary commodities and manufactures) and the maintenance of primary commodity prices above market equilibrium levels tend to be self-defeating and, by giving wrong signals to economic agents, encourage misallocation of resources both nationally and worldwide. This in turn generates a need for additional governmental intervention either to support the price-fixing mechanism or to correct its negative side effects.[4]

Apart from indexation, many producers are anxious actually to lift commodity prices to, as the IPC puts it, 'remunerative' levels. In other words, commodity trade is envisaged as a suitable vehicle for redistributing world income in a North-South direction. Assuming the LDCs (as producers) to have realized that OPEC-like price-raising agreements among them are difficult to implement and then to hold for long in present and foreseeable circumstances,[5] the IPC can be interpreted as an approach which, in addition to its price stabilization objective, aims at cartelization with active support from the consumer countries. This has implications for export earnings (import expenditures) which may differ from those discussed earlier in connection with price stabilization attempts.[6]

LDCs as exporters would benefit from artificially 'remunerative' (higher) prices in terms of foreign exchange in every case. Although demand by consumers may decrease as prices are raised, it is always profitable for producers to expand output even if running into excess production. While successful cartelization requires output and export

185

restrictions to support the higher price, price-raising producer-consumer agreements may not. Any excess production can be sold to the IPC-management or to governments, and can be used for inferior purposes or even destroyed. The obvious model here is the EEC's Common Agricultural Policy, although in the case of the IPC exporting LDCs would probably have to share the costs of disposal of excess supplies. According to estimates made by Baron, Glismann and Stecher (1977, p. 38), the increase in export earnings from 'core' commodities would be particularly sizeable in the case of sugar, copper, coffee, and cotton (in that order), in addition to beef and soy-beans. The study also shows that the increase in export earnings is in most cases significantly higher than that which would be achieved through producer cartels. This may explain why several LDCs insist so strongly that the IPC has to guarantee 'remunerative' prices.

All this is not to say that specific international commodity policies make no economic sense at all. There is evidence that protective agricultural policies by DCs, bilateral commodity trade agreements, and trade within horizontally and vertically integrated multinational corporations tend to narrow the size of the competitive world market in such a way as to make commodity prices fluctuate more than they would otherwise do (Harris, Salmon and Smith, 1977, pp. 24–31). In the interest of those who have to rely heavily upon the marginal, highly competitive world market, it is right to acknowledge the potential benefits of an effective price stabilization, even if one recognizes that not all price fluctuations are necessarily bad. But does this acknowledgement require an IPC?

One aspect rarely discussed in this connection is that greater stability may benefit not only the LDCs as such, but also their indigeneous producers and particularly the smallholders. The IPC does not assure assistance to them. A nationally operated tax-cum-subsidy scheme, which imposes progressive export taxes when world market prices are high and provides for subsidies when they are low, could be an appropriate device. It would channel the money where it is really needed inside the country. The DCs could effectively contribute to the operation of such a scheme by providing both finance and administrative advice (if required).

International commodity agreements, if agreed upon, will undoubtedly require financing, in order to have any prospects of success. Financing the various agreements through a common fund may be cheaper than financing them individually, if the price movements of the individual commodities are negatively correlated. Indeed, Behrman (1977, pp. 40–42) and Baron, Glismann and Stecher (1977, pp. 15–18), using different approaches, have identified some potential saving of initial cash requirements. However, in order to realize the pooling effect of a Common Fund, this needs only to be organized as a clearing agency. A right to interfere in the policy of the buffer stock management of individual commodity agreements is not necessary to attain the objective at issue. If the UNCTAD Secretariat and some spokesmen of the Group of 77 insist so vehemently on establishing a Common Fund with policy-making capabilities, one is inclined to presume that the ultimate objective is to raise real commodity prices in a cartel-type manner with the support of the major consumer countries. This is quite rational behaviour on the part of LDCs, once it is realized that OPEC cannot be easily emulated in other commodity fields. But it is also understandable that those who would have to bear the higher prices feel little sympathy with such plans.

A more important negotiating objective in a strictly limited economic context would be to improve on international schemes of compensatory financing. These provide loans automatically, if foreign exchange receipts from primary commodity exports decline below a target level for cyclical reasons, and ensure that the loans are paid back by the exporting country when export earnings recover and eventually, perhaps helped by price increases, exceed the target revenue level. Such a scheme might be attractive to LDC governments because of its built-in automaticity. It is appealing from an economic point of view because it does not interfere too much with the price mechanism, and because its operationality does not depend crucially on reliable prediction of equilibrium prices.

The IPC includes a compensatory financing scheme in addition to, but not as a substitute for, commodity agreements with a Common Fund. The proposal envisages compensation of fluctuations in total (rather than only commodity) export earnings of LDCs, without placing limitations on the amount of drawings and the timing of repayments. While this scheme still awaits concrete negotiations, there are two mechanisms already in operation. One is the compensatory financing facility of the IMF (introduced in 1963 and revised in 1966 and 1975). The other is the so-called STABEX-system within the Lomé Convention between the EEC and (now) 58 African, Caribbean and Pacific (ACP) countries, established in 1975 and to expire in 1985, if not extended. The two schemes differ from each other with respect to the funds available, the mechanism of operation, the terms of transfer, and the country and product coverage.[7] Although these schemes are primarily intended to stabilize export earnings over time, the STABEX facility involves a real resource transfer in so far as finance is provided interest-free or in the form of grants to the least developed, land-locked or island ACP countries; loans which are not repaid during the period that the Lomé Convention is in force can be waived by the EEC.

Since the inception of these schemes, many LDCs have made use of compensatory financing, some of them frequently. ACP countries drew on both the STABEX and the IMF facility. Their contribution to stabilization of export earnings has been constrained mainly by country quota ceilings on the outstanding compensatory drawing (IMF), the small product coverage and limited resources available (STABEX), the requirement of having balance-of-payments difficulties and of pursuing appropriate policies for solving them before a country can obtain compensatory finance (IMF), and the somewhat arbitrary criteria which a borrowing country may have to meet (STABEX). From this experience it follows that improvements in the system of compensatory finance, which might be considered in future negotiations, could aim at enlarging the resources made available to LDCs, at providing a broad product and country coverage, at making access to the facility as easy as possible, at granting special treatment with concessional terms to the poorest LDCs, and at providing finance as quickly as is necessary to achieve an anti-cyclical rather than a pro-cyclical effect. It should also be worthwhile to avoid an overlapping of various schemes. The choice then is between reforming the IMF drawing facility or globalizing the STABEX system. The former may be easier than the latter (Donges, 1979).

However, the inherent weakness of the scheme, a possible tendency towards over-production, remains, since economic incentives for reducing production when prices go down are weakened. The fact is that compensatory financing schemes, like international commodity agreements, are at best semi-efficient means of attacking the symptoms of the commodity problem. In the medium and long run they may even be counterproductive, since the 'foreign exchange illusion' they create could unduly reduce the economic pressure to diversify away from commodity production into the more downstream activities of processing and manufacturing. First-best policies would concentrate mainly on diversifying the export structure of LDCs, particularly into manufactured products. This brings me to the second trade issue of the NIEO.

The Market Access Proposal

Notwithstanding UNCTAD's efforts to institute an international regulation of world trade in primary commodities, many LDCs regard accelerated growth and diversification of manufacturing output as the main driving force of their economic development. At UNIDO's Second General Conference on Industrial Development held at Lima in March 1975 the LDCs as a whole expressed their intention to increase their share of world industrial production to 25 per cent by the end of the century as compared to roughly 8 per cent in the mid-1970's. While the speed thus envisaged for industrialization may not seem readily attainable, experience shows that LDCs may be capable of unexpectedly accelerating their industrialization efforts. To make this possible, they will be eager to import whatever investment goods and technology is necessary to complement domestic factors of production. To finance these imports, the LDCs must expand their manufactured exports rapidly. Export expansion not only helps to pay for imports directly, but also critically determines the LDCs' capacity to borrow and to service debt. Export growth could, and should, involve more trade among the LDCs themselves. But presumably it must (continue to) rely heavily on access to DC markets.

The international trading system will therefore have to provide for competition and open markets, in DCs as well as in LDCs. Generally speaking, DCs must refrain from introducing new or additional non-tariff import barriers as a counter-measure to reduced tariffs, as they did in the case of textiles, clothing, shoes, steel, electrical appliances, ships and others; they should further gradually liberalize on an MFN basis those imports still subject to restriction; and they should encourage a shift of resources away from lines of production liable to come under increasing competitive pressure from LDCs – essentially labour-intensive, raw-material-intensive, and standardized capital-intensive goods. By the same token, this means that they should concentrate more on sophisticated capital-, skill-, and research-intensive goods. The LDCs, which on the whole maintain substantially higher levels of import protection, should also reduce tariffs and soften quantitative restrictions; they should avoid currency overvaluation; and they should pursue overall domestic economic policies which reduce the labour-saving bias in manufacturing investment, thereby bringing their structure of production more into line with comparative advantages which they have at present and may develop in the future. So much for the basic principles.

Sceptics will rightly object to this. The limited economic management capabilities of LDCs may make it difficult for them to implement such a programme. As regards DCs, it seems politically difficult for them to be responsive to the export needs of LDCs (or even to their mutual export interests), particularly since the severe recession of 1974–75. Both trade unions and entrepreneurial associations in trade-impacted industries have actively sought government assistance or protection. The weak economic outlook in many DCs in the later 1970s has made it harder for governments to resist protectionist demands (Blackhurst, Marian and Tumlir, 1977). Surprisingly, even though the DCs fared well from the liberalization of trade in the fifties and sixties and owed part of their rapid economic growth to the advantages of growing international specialization, international trade is now regarded by many as a source of serious market disruption, a view strengthened by the mounting volume of manufactured exports from low-wage countries. In other words, the capacity or willingness to adapt of producers and workers in DCs has fallen behind the speed of changing comparative advantage in the world economy.

The fundamental point here is that the GATT is being circumvented. In the fifties and sixties, protectionist measures applied by DCs were generally compatible with the principle of non-discrimination, which is the keystone of the GATT. The major departure from the principle was the Long-term Cotton Textiles Arrangement of 1962. Recently, however, DCs have increasingly resorted to selective protectionism and non-tariff barriers (Balassa, 1978b, pp. 9sqq.). Apart from subsidies, bilaterally negotiated voluntary export restraints and 'orderly marketing' agreements have become the most frequent devices. Some governments have been tempted to encourage cartelization of industries with a view to defending market shares against foreign competition; the EEC particularly finds this idea appealing, steel production and shipbuilding being cases in point (Tumlir, 1979). Governments of DCs are thereby by-passing the GATT and infringing the agreed international rules on which the world trade order has been built. This seems politically convenient at present for LDCs as well as for DCs. The former tend to attach high value to the fact that their terms of trade may improve, since compliance with the negotiated arrangements often requires the establishment of an export cartel for supplying the product in question. The DCs will enjoy political comfort at least in the short-run; and as they are 'organizing free trade' (to use the French term), they may even believe that they are following an effective prescription for integrating the newcomers from the South step by step into the world economy, in line with a predicted import absorption capacity of the DCs.

The violation of the principle of non-discrimination by some DCs reflects a view that North-South trade relations have to be adapted to domestic problems. This is wrong, not only because there are domestic changes to which the international system cannot adapt itself and remain an order, but also because import barriers cannot transform underlying comparative cost disadvantages into advantages. It is, moreover, an illusion to think that DCs can reap benefits from quasi-free trade among themselves and confine their protectionist measures to low-cost suppliers from LDCs. Equity considerations will exert irresistible pressure on national governments to grant equal treatment to any domestic industry, irrespective of whether the import competition it faces comes from South Korea, Taiwan and Brazil or from Japan, Italy and Spain.

What arises in such circumstances is an unnecessary and uncalculable uncertainty for LDC exporters, DC importers and DC import-competing industries alike. LDCs may be induced to redirect investment into areas where they do not have, and cannot easily develop, a comparative advantage in the medium run. In the DCs, investments may be directed into socially less productive areas and lead to less process-, product- and locational innovation than is required if international competitiveness is to be regained. While the basic function of the GATT is to create confidence in agreed rules both by showing what behaviour can avoid international conflicts and by facilitating solutions should conflicts arise, today's DC governments have established a *de facto* principle of revocability of previous import concessions, if sought by domestic producers on grounds of 'market disruption'. Moreover, protective devices such as voluntary export restraints, orderly marketing arrangements or cartelization of manufacturers carry the danger of creating export diversion to third countries. If exporters from South Korea or Brazil find their sales to the EEC curtailed, they will try to expand them into other markets, for instance, the USA. The US may also restrict these imports. The process of export diversion then continues in other directions with similar consequences, so that in the last analysis it will be virtually impossible for any producer in DCs and LDCs to make sound investment decisions at the domestic level for dealing with the demands of change in an open, market-oriented world economy. This uncertainty poses a particularly serious problem for actual or would-be exporters in LDCs, since these are generally too small in size (not merely in comparison to multinational corporations) to collect information on the various trade measures in operation at any given time in DCs and then to manage the procedures without incurring substantial expense. And in general, the mere threat of protectionist measures based on market disruption considerations may impose a welfare loss on the exporting country, as Bhagwati (1978) has pointed out.

Another part of the problem is that any attempt by governments

191

(or by the EEC Commission) to 'organize' import growth implies that they are able to predict accurately the future capacity of DCs for imports from LDCs. If they had perfect knowledge of the country's optimal (or approximately optimal) production structure in the medium and long run, it would be possible to gear trade policy and other domestic economic policies in such a way that the optimum is attained. But in this case market forces would act in the same direction. The government may still have an information advantage over the market in so far as its own policies are concerned. First-best policy would be for the government to feed the private sector this information. In the real world, however, knowledge of future expansion of domestic and foreign demand and of future changes in comparative advantage is far from perfect. Why then should policy-makers, who normally will not personally have to meet capital losses resulting from wrong forecasts, do a better job than private investors, who may go bankrupt if they take unsound investment decisions and who therefore will try to examine as carefully as possible the profit prospects of a particular project? There is no empirical evidence to support faith in the government's superior wisdom. But government bodies themselves may have a quite different perception of their capabilities. They may not even be aware of the fact that their periodic interventions in trade and in the domestic industrial structure could sooner or later amount to central investment planning, which would reduce the scope for individual choice, for rewarding initiative and risk-taking, and for productivity growth. Judging by the frequency with which they invoke import protection, businessmen and trade-unionists do not always appear to understand this ultimate danger; or they may, probably mistakenly, think that the danger is too remote to worry about at present.

The LDCs would suffer most. They could try to retaliate within the GATT framework. But due to their relative weakness in world trade the retaliation method is not really viable. Either it is not effective or it causes more harm to the retaliating LDCs themselves than to the DCs. Awareness of this fact among LDCs must lead them increasingly to mistrust a trading system which, at best, is liberal only if they can be kept at bay. It will reinforce claims for a NIEO based on politically determined worldwide decision-making. It should not pass unnoticed that, in Germany for example, both entrepreneurial associations and trade unions representing manufacturing branches most heavily exposed to import competition from LDCs take a rather sympathetic view of the NIEO on the grounds that this would lead to more ex ante co-ordination in international trade. Furthermore, they readily identify themselves with the currently fashionable concepts of 'delinking' LDCs from the present international economic system (as discussed by Díaz–Alejandro, 1978), since this obviously would make LDCs more inward – and less outward-looking. Extrapolating these trends, one can see a disintegration of the world economy and a return to economic isolationism, perhaps followed by a proliferation of political conflicts among countries. as a not unlikely result.

In order to halt and reverse these tendencies, it would be probably helpful if the economies of DCs were to recover more strongly from their recessionary state. Trade liberalization has always been more attainable in periods of sustained growth and full employment. But we must remember that the present difficulties of so many industries in DCs can hardly be ascribed to great inroads by LDC suppliers into DC markets. This holds even for the textile industry, which did not obtain the expected relief from international competition either through the discriminatory Long-term Cotton Textiles Arrangement nor through its successor, the Multi-Fibre Arrangement (of 1973, renewed in 1977). Since it happens that in many European DCs the real wage structure has, on equity grounds, become rather rigid, the average level of real wages in manufacturing has become too high in relation to productivity, and profit margins have been significantly narrowed, a considerable proportion of actual unemployment is structural rather than cyclical. The recent experience of West Germany is a case in point (Fels and Weiss, 1978). In such circumstances, a job gap will remain even after overall effective demand and thus average capacity utilization have increased again. The closing of this job gap requires investments in new products, processes and locations, i.e. growth-oriented changes in the production and employment structure. The extent to which these investments, particularly those embodying R & D efforts and leading to the creation of new firms, take place will depend on the expected return on capital. Import protection would not be the appropriate policy. It does not by itself promote the growth of potential output, but rather maintains the utilization of given capacities in structurally weak activities at a certain level[8] – which amounts to saying that the efficient producers in the country, including the export industries, are discriminated against.

The case for free (or freer) trade between North and South (and among DCs) must be built upon its own merits, irrespective of the business cycle phase in which the economy finds itself at a given point of time. What governments in DCs have to explain to their con-

193

stituency is that economic growth has always entailed structural changes of production and employment and will continue to do so. Structural change includes adjustment to international competition, which emerges when foreign suppliers produce more cheaply than domestic ones. Jobs and industrial capacity will be lost, or their expansion will slow down, but the counterpart of this pressure to adjust is the creation of new jobs and physical capacities in higher productivity lines including the manufacture of exports to LDCs. Admittedly, this is easier said than done; the pervasiveness of protectionist sentiment in present-day DCs can be overcome only if policy is forward-looking, i.e. is such as to encourage rather than inhibit structural change. This condition is not fulfilled in all cases. But there is really no possibility of evading the issue, if the DCs want to continue as guardians and advocates of a liberal economic world order.

Taking this as given, trade liberalization, as mentioned earlier, does not mean abrupt implementation of freer trade, either by DCs nor by LDCs. It means progressive reduction of trade barriers, announced in advance and made irreversible. The Tokyo Round of multilateral trade negotiations, concluded in 1979, achieved a further cut in industrial tariffs of about 35 per cent, the implementation to be spread over eight years. Codes of conduct on certain non-tariff barriers were also agreed. One study had previously estimated that with tariff cuts of 40 per cent, effected on a most-favoured-nation (MFN) basis, LDCs' merchandise exports to DCs could rise by an extra 2.1 per cent or $1.8 billion annually at 1974 values if textiles were excluded and by 4.5 per cent or $4 billion if there were an equivalent liberalization of textile imports by DCs (Cline et al., 1978, pp. 207–227). So LDCs have a clear interest in further across-the-board MFN tariff reductions.

This holds even if one takes into account the Generalized Systems of Preferences (GSP) now in operation in the major DCs, the value of which would be automatically eroded. The non-reciprocal tariff preferences in their existing form are limited, and will continue so, in both scope and product coverage. Once preferential tariff quotas are being fully utilized, further expansion of LDC exports to DCs has to overcome the same tariffs as DC exports. Moreover, special trade arrangements such as those embodied in the Lomé Convention and in the EEC's Global Mediterranean Policy, have already reduced the potential benefits of preferential advantages to other LDCs, and so will the probable enlargement of the EEC through Greece, Portugal and Spain. Comparisons of the increase in LDC export earnings under

MFN tariff cuts and under the GSP show that, on certain plausible assumptions, the trade-creating effect of MFN tariff cuts may well outweigh the simultaneous erosion of the trade-diversion effect contained in the GSP (Baldwin and Murray, 1977). Needless to say, however, improvements in the GSP, particularly to assist the industrially less advanced countries within the LDC group in their effort to build up some export capacities, have not been rendered superfluous by the tariff reductions agreed in the Tokyo Round.

As to non-tariff barriers, a breakthrough towards their removal may be more difficult to accomplish. Much will depend on whether adequate safeguard provisions (against market disruption) can be agreed (which has not been the case in the Tokyo Round). They must be neither too liberal or too rigid, they should be applicable only in a non-discriminatory manner, they should be subject to strict criteria as regards time limitations, the definition of 'market disruption' and international approval and surveillance, as well as domestic policies to ease the process of structural adjustment.

In view of their strength in the world economy, the major DCs (USA, EEC, Japan) have taken the lead in strengthening rules capable of abating the protectionist trend of the 1970s and initiating a new phase of relatively unobstructed liberal trade. Whether LDCs should make reciprocal trade-barriers reductions in their own economies is debatable. As for most of them the small country assumption holds (at least as far as trade in manufactures is concerned), reciprocity is not necessarily required on balance-of-payments grounds, particularly if flexible exchange rates are going to prevail. More complicated is the issue of 'special and differential treatment' of LDCs, which has been recognized in the Tokyo Round. The heart of the problem is that less obligations and more rights for LDCs in the GATT could reduce the adaptability of the trading framework when conditions change (Golt, 1978). This is particularly evident in connection with the eligibility of individual countries for special and differential treatment as LDCs. If they are allowed from the outset to decide for themselves whether or not they are eligible, there is no mechanism which assures that they will elect themselves out at a later stage when they have developed a strong trade sector. A 'graduation' formula, which automatically strips successful LDCs of their special privileges, could help, provided it is evolutionary in nature. This, however, requires consensus on a definition of 'success' both now and for the future. The debate on the NIEO has shown how the perception of success may vary among governments.

195

Concluding Remarks

This paper has taken as its point of departure the proposition that the external trade relations of a LDC, as of any country, depend crucially on domestic policies and social factors. With a given international trading environment, LDCs can do a great deal themselves to diversify exports, increase their total amount and reduce their volatility.

Yet, outward-looking policies and attitudes of LDCs will be more successful, the better the international market mechanism works. It is difficult to see how the IPC could contribute significantly to well-functioning commodity markets. Liberalization of trade within a multilateral framework could, however, contribute. Foreign-exchange receipts of LDCs would rise sharply as a result of freer trade. Price stabilizing commodity agreements would probably yield a smaller increase, if any. On the other hand, expanded compensatory credit facilities may be advisable and even necessary in the context of freer trade, particularly to help stabilize the import capacity of those LDCs whose exports consist mainly of primary products.

Intensification of North-South trade need not, of course, benefit all LDCs. The gains may be greater for the more developed LDCs. There will at all times be some least developed countries, which may be unable to share in a newly expanding world trade. They will continue to need development aid from the DCs and other wealthier countries in the form of direct grants and concessionary loans, and certainly a larger volume of assistance than they have been granted hitherto. But international commodity agreements designed to raise relative prices of raw materials above their long-term market trend in order to transfer more resources to the producer countries will either not work or will induce DCs to cut their public aid.

.

NOTES

1. This section summarizes the analysis in Donges (1979).

2. The 'core' commodities are: coffee, cocoa, tea, sugar, cotton, sisal, jute, rubber, copper, and tin. At UNCTAD IV in Nairobi (May/June 1976) it was agreed that beef, bananas, vegetable oils (palm oil and soybeans), tropical timber, phosphate, iron ore, manganese, and bauxite should also be included in the arrangement at a later stage.

3. The discussion so far was based on a standard partial equilibrium market model. The conclusion may change, if demand and supply curves are not linear over the relevant range, if their shifts are multiplicative rather than additive, if the price instability is both supply and demand determined, and if producers have less than perfect foresight. While the studies cited above provide some

JUERGEN B. DONGES

information in this regard, the major part of the empirical analysis remains to be done, whether by UNCTAD in Geneva or elsewhere.

4. Whether or not indexation, if implemented, would improve the terms of trade of LDCs is an empirical question. Evidence is scarce in this field, but Baron, Glismann and Stecher (1977, pp. 72 sqq.) have provided some quantitative estimates for the 'core' commodities. Had indexation been applied during the period 1954–76, the study concludes that the prices of sugar, sisal, rubber and tin would have increased, on average, more than they actually did, whereas for the remaining six commodities the hypothetical prices would have lagged behind the actual ones.

5. The prospects for effective cartel arrangements improve according as resource-rich LDCs enjoy a large share in world exports, have a significant price advantage over substitute products, face no important exchange shortages, and are not vulnerable to economic retaliation by consuming countries. Furthermore, the price elasticities both of world demand for the commodity in question and of supply from third countries have to be low. Most primary commodity markets do not combine these characteristics required for successful cartel pricing.

6. There are also different welfare implications. Price stabilization (if feasible) will normally lead to an increase in total world welfare. Gains tend to exceed losses, so that the gainers can compensate the losers. Multilateral price-raising agreements, however, might lead to a reduction of world welfare. This is due to the costs of disposal of production surpluses, which are higher than the differences between gains and losses. For quantitative estimates see Baron, Glisman and Stecher (1977, pp. 18 sqq. + 34).

7. Originally, the STABEX scheme was applied to twelve primary commodities, including a few by-products, exported by ACP countries to the EEC: bananas, groundnuts, coconut products, palm oil and palm kernel products, cocoa, coffee, tea, cotton, sisal, hides and skins, wood, and iron ore. In 1977, the product coverage was extended to cloves, gum arabic, wool, mohair, pyrethrum, vanilla, and ilang-ilang. The 1979 negotiations on a further five-years extention have provided for the inclusion of rubber and a few other agriculture products.

8. This may also be true of cartels which are concluded to withstand import competition. As defensive cartelization generally involves arrangements to reduce production capacities, it easily could inhibit investments which increase efficiency, speed up technological progress and create sufficient new viable jobs. For an analysis of this issue, see Tumlir (1978).

REFERENCES

Balassa, B. (1978a), 'Export Incentives and Export Performance in Developing Countries: A Comparative Analysis'. *Weltwirtschaftliches Archiv*, Vol. 114, pp. 24–60.
Balassa, B. (1978b), 'World Trade and the International Economy: Trends, Prospects and Policies', *World Bank Staff Working Paper*, No. 282, May.
Balassa, B. and Associates (1971), *The Structure of Protection in Developing Countries*. Baltimore/Md., The Johns Hopkins Press.
Baldwin, R. E. and Murray, T. (1977), 'MFN Tariff Reduction and LDC Benefits under the GSP'. *The Economic Journal*, Vol 87, pp. 30–46.
Baron, S., Glismann, H. H. and Stecher, B. (1977), *Internationale Rohstoffpolitik: Ziele, Mittel, Kosten*. Tübingen: J. C. B. Mohr.

Bhagwati, J. N. (1978), 'Market Disruption, Export Market Disruption, Compensation, and GATT Reform', in *The New International Economic Order: The North–South Debate*, pp. 159–191, ed. Bhagwati, J. N., Cambridge/Mass., London: MIT Press.

Behrman, J. R. (1977), *International Commodity Agreements: An Evaluation of the UNCTAD Integrated Commodity Programme*. Washington/D.C.: Overseas Development Council.

Blackhurst, R., Nicolas, M. and Tumlir, J. (1977), *Trade Liberalization, Protectionism and Interdependence*. Geneva: GATT.

Cline, W. R. et al. (1978), *Trade Negotiations in the Tokyo Round – A Quantitative Assessment*, Washington/D.C.: The Brookings Institution.

Díaz-Alejandro, C. F. (1978), 'Delinking North and South: Unshackled or Unhinged?', in *Rich and Poor Nations in the World Economy*, pp. 87–162, by Fishlow, R. et al., New York: MacGraw-Hill Book Co.

Donges, J. B. (1979), 'UNCTAD's Integrated Programme for Commodities: Economic Implications and Europe's Response', in *The Role of Europe in the New International Economic Order*, pp. 129–150, ed. M. V. Abeele, Bruxelles: Institut d'Etudes Européennes.

Donges, J. B. and Müller-Ohlsen, L. (1978), *Außenwirtschaftsstrategien und Industrialisierung in Entwicklungsländern*. Tübingen: J. C. B. Mohr. (Kieler Studien No. 157.)

Donges, J. B. and Riedel, J. (1977), 'The Expansion of Manufactured Exports in Developing Countries: An Empircal Assessment of Supply and Demand Issues'. *Weltwirtschaftliches Archiv*, Vol. 113, pp. 58–87.

Fels, G. and Weiss, F. (1978), 'Structural Changes and Employment: A Lesson of West Germany', in *Unemployment and Capital Shortage in the World Economy*, pp. 31–53, ed. Giersch, H., Tübingen: J. C. B. Mohr.

Golt, S. (1978), 'Developing Countries in the GATT System'. *Thames Essays*, no. 13, London: Trade Policy Research Centre.

Harris, S., Salmon, M. and Smith, B. (1977), 'The Analysis of Commodity Markets for Policy Purposes', November, *mimeographed* (for the Trade Policy Research Centre).

Johnson, H. G. (1976), 'World Inflation, the Developing Countries, and an Integrated Programme for Commodities'. *Banca Nazionale del Lavoro Quarterly Review*, pp. 309–335.

Krueger, A. O. (1978), *Foreign Trade Regimes and Economic Development–Liberalization Attempts and Consequences*. New York: National Bureau of Economic Research.

Little, I., Scitovsky, T. and Scott, M. (1970), *Industry and Trade in Some Developing Countries – A Comparative Study*. London, New York, Toronto: Oxford University Press.

MacBean, A. I. and Balasubramanyam, V. N. (1976), *Meeting the Third World Challenge*. London: Macmillan.

Tumlir, J. (1978), 'Salvation Through Cartels? On the Revival of a Myth', *The World Economy*, Vol. 1, pp. 385–395.

Tumlir, J. (1978), The 'New Protectionism, Cartels and the International Order', in *Challenges to a Liberal International Economic Order*, pp. 239–258, ed. Ammacher, R. C., et al, Washington/D.C.: American Enterprise Institute.

Chapter Eleven

THE COMMODITIES PROBLEM AND THE
INTERNATIONAL ECONOMIC ORDER: WHAT RULES
OF WHAT GAME?

*Stuart Harris**

1. Introduction

HARRY JOHNSON, in one of his last comments on our subject said it
was important for professional economists 'to be very wary of discussing proposals of the kind embodied in the demand for a new international economic order purely in terms of their economic aspects'.
(Johnson, 1978, p. 360–361). Starting from that perspective the aim
of this paper is to discuss some economic issues involved in the North-
South debate on commodities and the policy prescriptions that follow.

While the specific proposals of the New International Economic
Order (NIEO), and especially those dealing with commodities under
the Integrated Programme on Commodities (IPC), have attracted
most professional attention, an important and relatively neglected
issue is whether their emergence reflects a major policy problem for
the North. The South has charged that the existing commodity
trading system is inefficient and discriminates against the South; and
that in consequence, a new international economic order is required
which will among other things, resolve the problems of the existing
commodity market mechanisms and the trading rules under which
they work.

The North has been generally unwilling to accept that any existing
problems are sufficient to warrant major institutional change; and
reluctant to accept the market intervention implied in the IPC proposals. Reliance on the market, it is argued, is in the best interests of
developing and developed countries alike. Existing trading arrange-

* With the normal disclaimers, I am grateful to Brian Hindley for helpful
discussion and comment in the preparation of this paper; and to Alasdair MacBean
and John Black for comments on an earlier draft.

ments have worked particularly well (Jackson, 1978), and any limitations are seen as failures to adhere to the 'rules of the game' for international commodity trade; the developing countries should stick to the existing rules seeking to improve them if they find them lacking, rather than attempting to establish new ones.

The present paper raises four questions. The first two concern the evidence for the claims by the developing countries of inefficiency or discrimination in commodity marketing arrangements and in the rules of the international trading game for commodities; the remaining two consider the nature of the game for which rules exist or are sought, and the criteria for judging the existing system and the proposed solutions.

2. *Existing Commodity Market Arrangements*

(i) Market Efficiency

Specific interest in the efficiency of the commodity marketing system – the range of private, corporate and governmental agencies involved in the purchase, sale and transfer of commodities – tends to reflect one's point of departure. Economists in exporting countries have been concerned with price and market instability, price levels, and the failure of the system to promote the appropriate international division of labour in commodity production. For those in importing countries, the main concerns are possible interferences with markets, supply security, and a renewed interest – not unequivocally accepted by all – in the consequences of commodity price instability for macro-economic policies.

The empirical evidence on commodity market efficiency is limited. Unlike those on financial markets, the relatively few studies of commodity futures markets raise some doubts about the efficiency of markets (Harris, Salmon and Smith, 1978; Gordon Smith, 1978); in any case this evidence is concerned with short-term markets which may meet certain criteria of efficiency in a market clearing sense but have distorting longer term effects. Since, in many respects, empirical evidence is virtually impossible to obtain either to support or to deny the propositions involved, we have to address the problem indirectly. Testing of assumptions is one way of testing propositions – and indeed is inevitable when welfare propositions are involved. (Graaff, 1967).

In competitive markets, inefficiencies can be looked for where there are externalities: significant scale economies; restrictive practices, in factor as well as product markets; uncertainty; less than universal full employment; and any departures from economic behaviour of a consistent kind.

(ii) Externalities

Externalities in commodity production or processing are not uncommon. In the production of lead and zinc, mercury, uranium and feed lot beef, for example, and in the processing of commodities such as alumina and wool, social and private costs differ because of the environmental costs involved. An example of a consumption externality could arise from the use of uranium, where resultant pollution could spread well beyond the consumption area with adverse effects on the domestic welfare of non-consumers including exporters. Again, private and social costs and benefits may diverge substantially where depletion of exhaustible resources is significant. Overall, however, commodity externalities may be of only moderate quantitative significance.

(iii) Indivisibilities

Indivisibilities in minerals markets are extensive. Some 1050 mines, each with a capacity of over 150,000 tonnes of ore per year, account for over 90 per cent of all mining output (excluding coal) in the western world (Mining Magazine, 1978).[1] Fewer significant indivisibilities exist for agricultural products, but they are growing in importance, particularly where capital intensive processing, handling or distribution facilities – as for sugar, bananas and meats – are required. How much these factors affect long term resource allocation is difficult to determine, but they are important for the possibilities of restrictive trade practices.

(iv) Restrictive Trade Practices

For many commodities, prices received on world markets bear little relationship to marginal costs of production for well known reasons: non-competitive industry or market organisation, sometimes with government supporting action; government barriers to trade at the frontier; and subsidies. Barriers to entry – scale economies in production, information systems and marketing, technology secrecy and established brand names – make it difficult to enter the market and to break up existing market concentration.

In a systematic examination of restrictive practices, difficulties of specification and classification are substantial. A recent classification by Rangarajan (1978),[2] according to the type of market control existing for major traded commodities, divided markets into five groups ranging from a 'closed market', defined as one where there is an inte-

201

gral relationship between buyer and seller – either a technical tie-up, or a common ownership link – to a 'generally free' market where there is not. This classification is set out in Table 1. Too much reliance cannot be placed on such a classification, nor is it always clear what factors have gone into subjective decisions for individual commodities. A number of minerals for which competition is very limited, such as molybdenum, chrome, zirconium, platinum, cobalt and diamonds, are not included at all. Yet, the table probably offers a reasonably balanced guide.

A complication is that economics gives little guidance in making judgements on restrictive practices at the industry level, with empirical evidence difficult both to obtain and to interpret. Institutional mechanisms are an insufficient pointer. On the London Metal Exchange (LME), often regarded as a competitive market, efforts to influence LME prices by copper producers have not generally been very successful. For lead and particularly zinc, however, the thin markets have enabled producers in the past to influence the market to support the producer price. Nor is market structure always helpful; for example, to classify markets for tea and bananas as oligopsonistic, or closed, because four companies blend some 85 per cent of tea sold in Britain, the largest consumer, and three multinational companies control nearly seventy per cent of the world banana market, does not indicate the extent of competition in the production or sale of these commodities. Our domestic competition policies reflect this ambiguity. It is frequently assumed in domestic restrictive practices legislation that limits to competition may be beneficial;[3] internationally this is more difficult to argue because the distribution of benefits is uncertain, and because national policies can frequently rely on international competition to prevent serious non-competitive outcomes.

That the general incidence of restrictive practices in commodity markets is quite widespread is well known. The assumption is often made, however, that fiercely competitive conditions in a market clearing sense are equivalent to competitive conditions in a resource allocation sense; and that even if price competition is absent, other forms of non-price competition are generally equivalent (and benign) in an efficiency-of-resource-allocation sense. This assumption is not self evidently valid. Possibly in many of these markets, the end result differs little from that of a competitive market, but this is a matter of judgement rather than proof, on which genuine differences of opinion are to be expected. It is, moreover, a weaker analytical conclusion in its predictive implications than that the markets are the orthodox competitive markets of economic theory.

Table 1: Exports of Major Primary Commodities Classified by Nature of Market (U.S. $ billion, 1972).

Generally free		Controlled/distorted		Closed		Oligopolistic buyers		Partly open and partly closed	
1. Oilcake	2.4	1. Wheat	9.8	1. Phosphate	1.5	1. Coffee	4.3	1. Wood and products	7.1
2. Cotton	3.7	2. Sugar	8.0	2. Iron ore	3.8	2. Oilseeds	5.2	2. Copper	7.0
3. Wool	2.5	3. Beef	3.7	3. Bananas	0.7	3. Vegetable oils	3.6	3. Aluminium	2.0
4. Hides/Leather	2.8	4. Maize	5.7	4. Bauxite	1.5	4. Tobacco	2.1	4. Nickel	0.9
5. Natural rubber	2.6	5. Rice	2.0			5. Cocoa	1.4	5. Lead	0.6
6. Tin	1.2	6. Wine	1.9			6. Tea	0.8	6. Zinc	1.3
7. Jute	0.2	7. Butter	1.3						
8. Hard fibres	0.2	8. Citrus fruit	1.2						
9. Pepper	0.2								
TOTAL	15.9	TOTAL	33.5	TOTAL	7.4	TOTAL	17.4	TOTAL	19.0
Percentage of grand total	17.1		36.0		7.9		18.6		20.4

Source: L. N. Rangarajan, *Commodity Conflict: The Political Economy of International Commodity Negotiations*, Croom Helm, London, 1978.

These private restrictive practices are less important than those resulting from government actions. Some of the markets classified as 'generally free' by Rangarajan have been affected substantially by trade restrictions. For example, oil cake is affected by high EEC and Japanese effective protection; world cotton prices were set for much of the 1960s by United States support prices; and even world wool price levels are affected by United States protection to domestic wool producers (Houck, 1966).

Many agricultural commodities are so protected that the international markets are largely marginal markets, with prices which are highly unstable, bearing little relationship to economic prices except in a market-clearing sense. While the products affected most in this way are temperate agricultural products of less immediate interest to the developing countries than tropical products, many such items, such as sugar, vegetable oils and oilseeds, meats, grains, tobacco, cotton and tropical fruits, are competitive with developing country production. The marginal nature of the market can be seen from the proportions of total production sold on 'world' markets for cotton (32 per cent), rice (4 per cent), wheat (20 per cent) and beef (17 per cent). Even for sugar, where the proportion is much larger (51 per cent), there are a number of distinct markets, with various price levels, and the relationship of the 'world' market price to an economic price other than in a market clearing sense is questionable.

A number of raw materials face no major government trade restrictions, but these are often commodities – such as bauxite or manganese – where factors other than price influence trade flows (Tilton, 1966). For a number of processed products, moreover, tariff and non-tariff restrictions remain important trade barriers.

(v) Uncertainty

Uncertainty has implications where insufficient markets exist for risk bearing. While futures markets, long term contracts and other mechanisms (such as vertical integration) are used to transfer the risk burden, the extent of the gap in risk transfer markets is a matter for debate. Some see the observed lack of organised risk markets as sufficient evidence of market imperfections. Others, reacting to the relaxation of our traditional assumptions that information is a free good and transactions costless, see virtually any lack of such markets as a measure of transactions costs. In the middle are those who see moral hazard, myopia, information market imperfections through inappropriability and through the competitive incentive to subsidise

204

incomplete or incorrect information, as leading to incomplete markets for risk and uncertainty without knowing how large the gaps are.

(vi) Full Employment
In practical terms, less than universal full employment of resources, specifically labour, is characteristic of much of the world even if unemployment levels in developed countries in the later 1970s are atypical. Yet to a considerable degree, the arguments for adherence to an open world economy are predicated upon sustained global prosperity and full employment.

(vii) Non-Market Motivations
Finally, markets for commodities are affected by other than profit maximising behaviour by producers. In particular, government agencies in one form or another are major influences in many markets. The centrally planned economies of Eastern Europe, USSR and China normally account for about 10 per cent of world non-fuel commodity exports. For commodities such as wheat, sugar, diamonds, chrome, crude oil, coal, cobalt, potash, manganese, sulphur, zinc, meat, wool, timber and tungsten they are important, though not always regular or stabilising influences, and their influence seems likely to grow.

Governmental market influences are also important outside the Eastern bloc. Government stockpile activities, as with the US strategic stocks, have been important market influences. Many countries outside Eastern Europe, USSR and China have substantially centrally planned economies; and in many market economies state enterprise is significant – such as Canadian potash, Swedish iron ore, British coal and Norwegian oil. The importance of state equity holdings in a number of important minerals is shown in Table 2. Over half the Western World's iron ore production comes from mines state owned, controlled or with significant state equity; and nearly half the capacity for primary copper. State involvement is also substantial in the tin, bauxite, manganese and phosphates industries. State involvement through equity participation in aggregate is likely to grow in developing countries, despite some movement in the opposite direction, and political developments such as in Namibia and Rhodesia could lead in the same direction.

State equity ownership is not necessarily related to state influence. We have taken 'significant state equity interest' to cover 10–50 per cent of equity held by the state. This is not control, though what that term means is ambiguous; effective control can be achieved with less than 10 per cent holding, while a majority holding may not provide

205

effective control. In many countries, the freedom of the foreign – or local – investor to behave as a profit maximising private trader is often severely limited or influenced by governments in other ways where no government equity holding exists.

Moreover, in most countries – with the United States the major exception – mineral resources are state property. Even where mineral resource exploitation is normally in private hands government permission is required for exploitation, and conditions of various kinds can be, and often are, imposed at that stage.

Governments participate much less in agricultural production, but frequently government or semi-governmental agencies are directly involved in trade, as with Canadian wine imports, Brazil's coffee exports, Japanese meat or grain purchasing and French tobacco procurement. The Australian Wheat Board or Nigerian cocoa marketing authorities may not behave differently from a private company in the same monopoly position; a difference would exist, however, were a number of private enterprises to be competitively marketing the same commodities.

(viii)   An Assessment

The point of this summary exploration of commodity markets is to consider whether, from the analysis of competitive economic markets, it is possible to argue with confidence that international commodity markets are efficient. Given the extensive 'management' – in various forms – of commodity markets, the case appears on those criteria far from proven. This is not to argue that any other system is necessarily more efficient; but nor can we conclude that no action is the optimal strategy. We simply do not know how close to an economic optimum we are and we need to be cautious in judging the efficiency of the existing commodity trading system. Demsetz has argued that 'modern analysis has yet to describe efficiency in a world where indivisibilities are present and knowledge is costly to predict', (Demsetz, 1969), and this seems even more true of commodity markets where other assumptions of the analysis also are open to question. Even if distributional problems do not enter the issue, there can be genuine differences about the facts of market efficiency, and the consequences of particular imperfections.

The second part of our first question concerned discrimination. Outside agriculture perhaps, whether discrimination results is difficult to determine, since barriers to the markets' competitive operation, apart from externalities, arise from the activities of actors in all parts of the market. The South argues that the inefficiency of existing markets is discriminatory, depressing the prices of its commodity exports and its terms of trade.

The empirical evidence on terms-of-trade movements is itself inconclusive – though it was never clear what was being measured, or whether it could answer our questions either way. A better measure has been put forward by Spraos (1980), which relates the terms of trade to the more general issue of the international division of labour. The terms-of-trade argument raises the issue of diversification which may have significant public good aspects. Collective diversification action by producers may, through its price effects, yield gains which exceed adjustment costs; rationalisation of commodity production may thus require international policy intervention.

3. The Rules of the Game

The South's complaint against the commodity trading system concerns not merely the market mechanisms but also the institutional arrangements and customary practices at the multilateral, regional and bilateral level – the rules of the game – that determine the conditions under which trade takes place. We have looked at the commodity markets in terms of the South's claim that they are both inefficient and discriminatory; we now look at the 'rules of the game' in the same light.

The basic principles of the postwar trading system are largely described by three characteristics:

(a) a generally liberalising approach to trade;
(b) a non-discriminatory multilateral approach to international issues; and
(c) freedom of the market.[4]

These three characteristics are seen as the basis for the existing 'rules of the game' of the international economic system. The South's call for an NIEO, therefore, is seen as rejecting these basic principles.

The developing countries – and a few others – are concerned principally with what happens in commodity trade and for this trade, it is at least open to question whether the call for an NIEO/IPC is a rejection of a system based on the three principles set out above. For commodities it can be argued that the rules of the game

(a) were not fully aimed at those objectives;
(b) to the extent that they were, would achieve the objective imperfectly;
(c) have, in any case, been widely breached from the start; and

(d) do not effectively cover many important influences on international commodity trade.

(1) The Existing Rules

The intergovernmental rules of the game for commodities are set largely by GATT, through the OECD, UNCTAD, FAO, regional arrangements such as the EEC, and market systems such as the rules of trading, bilateral contracts, arbitration procedures, provisions for financial transfers and the like have grown in relative importance. We limit our attention here largely to the rules and operation of the GATT, established primarily to maintain world peace by avoiding competitive, i.e. conflict creating, solutions to world trading problems.[5] At the same time, since free trade is the normal basis on which economists judge the efficiency of trade matters, it is useful to see how effectively the GATT and related rules foster economic efficiency.

The main GATT principles affecting the achievement of free trade are non-discrimination and tariff reduction. Non-discrimination was

Table 2

State Ownership or Significant Equity Interest in World Mine Capacity[1]

Commodity	Approximate Percentage of Total World Capacity[2]	
	Excluding C.P.E.'s	*Including C.P.E.'s*
Copper	40.0–45.0	50.0–55.0
Uranium[3]	22.5–27.5	n.a.
Phosphates[3]	37.5–42.5	55.0–60.0
Bauxite[3]	40.0–45.0	50.0–55.0
Coal	25.0–30.0	65.0–70.0
Lead	17.5–22.5	37.5–42.5
Zinc	22.5–27.5	37.5–42.5
Nickel	25.0–30.0	40.0–45.0
Iron Ore[3]	40.0–45.0	60.0–65.0
Tin[3]	42.5–47.5	55.0–60.0
Manganese[3]	52.5–57.5	67.5–72.5
Crude Oil	72.5–77.5	77.5–82.5

1. 'State Ownership or Significant Equity Interest' has been taken as consisting of an equity holding of 10% or more.

2. The capacity figures for centrally planned economies (CPE's) have been excluded from the denominator as well as the numerator in column 2 and correspondingly added to both numerator and denominator in column 3.

3. In the absence of satisfactory capacity figures, adjusted production figures have been used as the basis for the estimates.

Source: Stuart Harris (1980).

the 'cornerstone' of the agreement (Curzon, 1965), both for its contribution to economic efficiency and in a wider sense. While absolute non-discrimination is impossible – imposing a tariff discriminates against those with a trade interest in that item and in favour of those without – tariffs can otherwise be imposed non-discriminatorily. Although originally tariffs were expected to be the sole or main form of trade restriction, this failed to eventuate for commodities; quantitative restrictions were widely and increasingly used, and non-discrimination is more difficult both to achieve and to monitor with quantitative controls. A similar problem applies with respect to state trading – important also for commodities. Thus the principal of non-discrimination in the GATT was less effective for commodities. Although a limited number of exceptions were permitted in the original agreement, the non-discrimination principle has been watered down since the GATT came into effect; and a major exception has since been provided for in the textiles arrangements. Perhaps more important are the outcome of the Multilateral Trade Negotiation (MTN) safeguards discussions; the indirect effects of GATT waivers; and non-compliance in the case of agricultural commodities either with waiver requirements or with the GATT itself.

Although the general objective of the GATT rules is trade liberalisation, they provide only a qualified mechanism for this purpose. This is because the provision made in the GATT for reciprocity limits the extent to which the process of negotiation can proceed. Gains from reciprocity depend initially upon the starting point – those starting with no tariff restrictions have no bargaining power. A country must also be in a position to gain from any concessions through its competitive strength; while others must be equally responsive and prepared to negotiate.

The non-discrimination and reciprocity principles together tend to put the emphasis on products of special interest to the major trading nations, particularly when bilateral negotiation is dominant as the negotiating technique. (Johnson, 1967). While the linear tariff-cutting procedure of the Kennedy and Tokyo Rounds reduced this bias for manufactured goods, the exceptions – agriculture being excluded and tariffs on processing substantially excluded in practice – maintained the discrimination against commodities.

The economic theory underlying the GATT has since required qualification. Dam has pointed out that the theory at the time the Agreement was drafted saw customs unions (or 'complete' preference areas) – in the context of which protective barriers to agricultural trade have been maintained and intensified – as promoting economic efficiency, and 'partial' preferences as undermining it in a basically unqualified way now seen as inappropriate (Dam, 1970; also Johnson, 1965). The assumptions that reductions in trade barriers were always beneficial was also fundamental to the GATT, as was the view that subsidies were always inimical.[6] The GATT rules are less liberalising for commodities partly because negotiation of reciprocal trade concessions on commodities, under quantitative restrictions, is more difficult than for manufactures under tariffs. More exceptions are also permitted for agriculture and fisheries than for manufactures;[7] and subsidy provisions are quite permissive for all forms of primary product in contrast to the provisions for manufactures.

In addition to the granting of major waivers from the rules, an important early one being that on United States agriculture, even the more limited rules have been extensively breached or ignored for commodities. There has been little practical interest in the GATT in determining the full scope of such breaches. Besides the extensive use of variable levies, on the legality of which the GATT has not ruled, but which appear opposed to the spirit of the GATT at least, breaches of the GATT rules on commodities through use of quantitative restrictions, other non-tariff barriers and subsidies are substantial. Even where, as with the processing of primary commodities, tariffs remain a common trade restriction instrument, slow progress has been made on liberalisation.

Finally, it is difficult to argue that the failure of the GATT rules has been offset by specific international provisions for commodity agreements. A simple generalisation is that initially the GATT provisions for international commodity arrangements tended to be permissive, with exemptions from the rules provided where accepted international agreements operated. Early attitudes were influenced by the agricultural protection and trading issues of the postwar food shortages, European recovery adjustments and Korean war boom. In this context, before Part IV of the GATT dealing with developing countries was adopted in 1964, the '... passivity of the GATT secretariat coincided with the view of certain contracting parties, notably the United States, that some kinds of commodity agreements were hardly consistent with the GATT system.' (Dam, 1970, p. 245).

The difficulty of achieving commodity agreements is well known. For those already negotiated, special – and pre-existing – political factors appear to have been important: as for example, the historic United Kingdom/Malaya links in the case of tin; the United States Alliance For Progress with Latin America in 1961 in the case of coffee; the need in the Kennedy Round trade negotiations to appear to achieve something tangible on agriculture for the International Grains Arrangement (IGA) of 1968; and United States domestic political needs for the 1978 sugar agreement. Present developed-country attitudes to international commodity arrangements are not entirely consistent: a more explicit approach to management of an international market is welcomed where developed countries have related domestic policy interests – grains in the IGA and the 1978–79 MTN negotiations; the 1978 informal understandings on steel; and the 1978 sugar agreement – but is otherwise generally opposed; and selective support is forthcoming in the North-South dialogue and IPC context where uncertainties exist about future supplies – as with tin and rubber.

A few specific offsets have occurred, though of a limited and special nature. The generous price provisions in the 1961 coffee arrangements for example, were of significance to coffee producers at the time; in considering food aid conventions in grains arrangements, however, account would have to be taken of the price raising effects of the export provisions in the arrangements on the import bills of developing countries.

Despite a presumption that fuller observance of existing GATT rules would contribute little to efficiency, it is difficult to make such a judgement. Apart from the absence of adequate empirical data, there is frequently no agreement on the costs or benefits of market features such as instability, or of industry characteristics such as concentration or of particular techniques such as stabilisation arrangements within commodity agreements.

For discrimination the answer is clearer. The Haberler Report concluded that for primary producers, the '. . . rules and conventions which are at present applied to commercial policy and international trade show a lack of balance unfavourable to their interest'. (*Trends in International Trade*, 1958, p. 125). There has been some limited compensation subsequently through non-reciprocity in tariff negotiations[8] and generalised preference arrangements, but there seems little basis for revising Harry Johnson's conclusion of a decade or so ago that the rules of the game discriminate against developing countries. (Johnson, 1967; 1969).

(ii) Influences outside the Rules

Many important influences on the direction and profitability of trade are covered little if at all by the existing international machinery or rules. The GATT has tried to adapt to state trading for example, but with great difficulty. For commodities, state trading – offering, in addition to discrimination, less predictable and at times perverse market responses – is increasing in importance. The major gaps in the international trading rules for commodities, however, probably concern restrictive trade practices and investment.

Although rules on restrictive practices were originally seen as essential, with a chapter on the subject in the Havana Charter, this aspect was lost with the ITO. Since then, multilateral efforts to achieve understandings on restrictive trade practices internationally have been unsuccessful. The subject came before the GATT on several occasions but no agreement was reached on required action, either there or in the UNCTAD where moves have been made more recently toward establishing such a code. Some action has been taken in the OECD and in the EEC which either limit restrictive practices for particular industries or for member countries at a more general level.

The issue has also come up in the context of the United States' attempt (after 1975) to extend its domestic anti-trust law internationally for potash, uranium and zinc. This action has wide ramifications, though even with agreement on the general objectives of the action, the philosophies of individual countries – such as the United States and Britain – on the subject of industrial concentration and collective action do not always coincide. Moreover, for various reasons a country may apply its policies less than fully, as with the United States policies towards its oil companies; or apply different policies domestically and internationally, as with the United States maintenance of export cartels for such commodities as phosphates and phosphoric acid.

Even if countries agree with the objective of limiting restrictive trade practices internationally, differences of view can arise as to how these may best be overcome, and the extent to which particular derogations from national sovereignty are required to achieve these ends. Frequently, as with uranium for example, the issue is a difference less of philosophy about restrictive practices than about the causes of the problem and about the form and likely consequences of the response. (Harris, 1978).

Investment patterns are also important in determining the flow and benefits of commodity trade; as a means by which many trade rules can be circumvented; and in their integral relationship to the coincidence of restrictive practices. Yet there is little international agreement on the regulation of investment. With governmental controls, particularly in resource industries, almost universal and with multinational corporations important for many traded commodities, the lack of codes of conduct for international investment – including

212

agreed investor and host country rights, problems of technology transfer, transfer pricing or export franchises – creates uncertainty and facilitates distortions.

The possibilities of indirect subsidies to exports through investment aids (such as depreciation schedules, investment tax credits, subsidised credit finance, government loan guarantees or direct provision of finance, infrastructure, land, transport or exploration marketing or other services) are almost limitless. Investment subsidies through export-import banks and export credits guarantee corporations or their equivalents in countries such as Japan, France, Germany, US or Britain influence the levels as well as the direction of investment as do the investment policies of international institutions such as the World Bank. They are also liable to affect, therefore, the terms of trade of commodity exporters. A terms-of-trade effect, and for commodities with less than unitary elasticity of demand a loss of revenue, would also result from proposals such as the International Resources Bank proposed by the United States at the UNCTAD Conference in Nairobi in 1976, designed to increase investment in minerals development in developing countries.

Clearly, for commodities, the trade rules have major gaps, and GATT's success in liberalising trade on commodities has been very limited. Of course, comparisons with situations as they would have been in the absence of the GATT may be less adverse; but the commodity exporters' argument that they still await their part of the bargain GATT was supposed to represent is not easily controverted.

4. Criteria For Judging The System

Before considering the implications of these conclusions about the rules of the game and the gaps in them, we need to look at what the 'game' itself is about. The normal criterion, also used to evaluate the IPC proposals, is economic efficiency.

The different treatment of commodities under the trade rules arises not because commodities are seen as part of a different game but for non-economic reasons. For economists, the general trade rules based on efficiency objectives apply particularly to commodities because of their assumed lack of product differentiation. We have to look at the efficiency criterion for commodity trade therefore in the general trade context.

(i) Efficiency

The usual assumption is that the more liberal the trading system, the more efficient the use of the world's resources. That conclusion

213

requires a zero divergence between social values and costs and prices at the world level; yet economists 'have long known that the assumptions needed for favouring free trade are not fully met in the actual world, but they generally have minimised the practical significance of this fact' (Baldwin and Kay, 1975, p. 118).

In questioning the validity of that approach, two additional problems arise. First, even accepting that 'free trade is best', free trade does not come about of its own accord. It is a collective good and given our expectations that participants in cartels will cheat, and of free riders in collective goods analysis, it should be unsurprising that the normal inclination is not to play a non-zero sum game. Free trade needs to be imposed and enforced (Scitovsky, 1942). Adherence to the necessary collective rules requires that countries put global efficiency ahead of national gains. With competition, the issue for individual countries, as distinct from the global society, is the level of the optimum trade restraint. This is usually assumed to be small, though whether seen as such by the countries involved is less clear. Johnson suggested that even with full and total tariff retaliation it is still possible in the final equilibrium for one country to be better off than in the free trade position, though taken together both countries would be worse off – and he judged it more likely that they would both separately be worse off (Johnson, 1967). The extent of retaliation is important but, as with any policy measure, much would depend upon the way that any measures were introduced.

Second, we have the second-best argument that with significant existing divergences and distortions, a movement towards free trade does not necessarily improve efficiency. The conditions under which this will not be true have been discussed in detail in the literature (Meade, 1957; Corden, 1974). Their importance here lies in the empirical nature of the issue and in the fact that they do not provide unique guides to policy but many possible guides depending upon the circumstances.

Trade expansion, while promoting international efficiency, lays countries open to risks which they often see as threatening economic efficiency. Governments' concerns to reduce risks and uncertainty in commodity markets relate to their perceptions of problems of excessive market instability; excessive or disruptive competition, i.e. where adjustment costs are regarded as too high; inadequate security of supply; the loss of autonomy of decision making; and inadequate use of their bargaining power.

The effectiveness with which the rules of the game ensure that governmental reactions in those situations are mutually consistent, i.e. are co-operative rather than competitive, will influence the efficiency of the global commodity trading system. Yet no unanimity exists about which measures are consistent with liberalising or efficiency-improving actions. Price instability, for example, may itself indicate inefficiency; economic costs are involved when prices fail to reflect long-term supply and demand relationships and market participants act upon them, a not uncommon situation. (Harris, Salmon and Smith, 1978). Yet, traditional economic analysis is dubious about the efficiency of stabilising actions for commodities; consequently the North has seen stabilisation primarily as a concession to the South, and not as improving efficiency, and as a result the position is taken that producers should meet any costs of stockholding.

In the traditional analysis, stabilisation involves two separate problems, depending on whether instability results from shifts in demand or in supply – with different solutions needed for each (Johnson, 1978). Empirical analysis of the causes of instability indicates that the results are sensitive to methods of analysis and that distinguishing between them in a way that yields meaningful generalisations is difficult (Harris, Salmon and Smith, 1978). This is less of a problem given that traditional analysis has been shown to have limited general applicability and that its results depend heavily upon very restrictive assumptions: linear demand and supply curves; perfect information; and parallel supply and demand curve shifts. With these assumptions relaxed, the likelihood of a welfare gain from commodity price stabilisation is significantly increased, though its distribution remains unclear. When the assumption of no risk aversion is removed, the results become sensitive to assumptions about expectations (Turnovsky, 1978; Just et al., 1977).

The dynamic effects of instability are similarly in dispute. Arguments about the 'ratchet effect', concentrating on the micro-economic price impact, are inconclusive; and long-term costs and benefits of instability through its impact on investment do not enter the calculus. The belief that economic management can overcome problems of large fluctuations in GNP in developing countries when much smaller oil price rises (2 per cent or so in GNP terms) gave rise to critical management problems for the North may now have diminished.

Other examples on which legitimate differences exist regarding what is consistent with a move to liberal trading and the achievement of efficiency are: customs unions; preferences or, more recently, discrimination within GATT; and safeguard arrangements against market disruption.

The potential for policy conflicts is wide. Agreement may be diffi-

215

cult even with clear understanding of each country's objectives – or agreement on the objectives and their weighting – since little consensus may exist on the technical means of achieving those objectives. For example, the relative weights given by France and Germany to efficiency and security could be similar, but French 'organised free trade' concepts and German interests in competitive markets for non-agricultural raw material imports probably reflect, in addition to national interests, different philosophies and technical understandings.

Moreover, technical agreement itself is not enough, given uncertainty. Governments react adversely to uncertainty; reliance on the market itself requires faith in the outcome of an uncertain and largely unpredictable mechanism; those convinced of the result (for whatever reason), and so willing to gamble, will differ from those whose experience and ability to adjust or cope – or whose inclination to prepare for the worst – leads to different conclusions. (Graaff, 1967). Efficiency, however, is not the only motivation of governments; so far in discussing efficiency separately from income distribution we have followed the convention which equates welfare with real income and assumes distributional problems to be dealt with independently – made easier by the greater total welfare that efficiency provides. To the extent that this approach is open to question, then efficiency is not a sufficient criterion for judging the commodity trading system.

The distributional assumptions of the analysis are open to question for a number of reasons. For example, a welfare gain is assumed to exist if gainers could overcompensate losers and still be better off themselves. Policy conclusions drawn from this often ignore the potential nature of the welfare gain; a country such as Tanzania may not gain from some international policy move, but if it could potentially be compensated by lump-sum transfers, it is counted as though it did gain.[9]

The analysis also assumes that the welfare of a Tanzanian or an American is determined exclusively by his own material well-being. Yet it has been recognised since Veblen that consumption choices may be influenced by past or present consumption patterns of others; and the literature is increasingly accepting that the individual's welfare may also be a function of the stability of his income and of the level of his income relative to others.

My final difficulty is that moving from individual welfare to social welfare, or judging particular distributive outcomes, tends to require some form of societal value judgement. This may be problematic even when measuring changes over time of priced output or consumption within a single economy. When non-price aspects of social welfare are taken into account, in practice hardly separable from price aspects, and when we look at a world system, potential difficulties multiply. What Graaff calls a 'sufficient consilience of opinion' (Graaff, 1967, p. 168) or Mishan refers to as 'what men of goodwill regard as reasonable' (Mishan, 1975, p. 388) should perhaps be capable of determination in a reasonably homogenous group, such as contemporary Western society, but may be impossible to identify in the face of the vast differences of beliefs and value systems between countries such as Tanzania and the United States.

In answer to our final question then, efficiency is not a sufficient criterion for defining the rules of the game; if it were, we would not always know how to achieve it; and if we did know, different perceptions would exist as to what it means, how to achieve it, and how to share the gains. Thus the concept of co-operation on which it is based does not provide a clear policy guideline and would still be accompanied by extensive opportunities for conflict.

(ii) Conflict Resolution

Conflict over distribution seems especially likely. Countries may accept the constraints of collective rules if they can see a gain to themselves; they are more likely, however, to want a reasonable share of that gain. In disputes over sharing gains, a willingness to trade-off a smaller cake for an acceptable distribution is probably widespread. Moreover, countries frequently do not trust one another, and this uncertainty leads to a standard form of the prisoner's dilemma; indeed, in principle, the issues lend themselves to analysis by game theory methods.[10] In practice, the information needs for a formal game theory model are too great to enable an appropriate pay-off matrix to be constructed, especially when we consider who the players in the game are. Analyses usually assume individuals, but in reality the players include governments, national and international bureaucracies and corporations, whose various objectives are frequently inconsistent with collective international action. Together with the many policy options, often seeking goals such as status and prestige with immeasurable pay-offs, this makes a game theory approach infeasible.

Motives other than efficiency and income distribution are also important. Johnson noted that '. . . it is arguable that the social welfare function should be deduced from the revealed preferences of the community, as expressed in governmental decisions rather than imposed (or denied existence) by the observing economist'. (Johnson,

1971, p. 21). His opinion was that governments prefer trade over no trade, but not free trade over trade subject to government interference. Others argue more strongly that government decision makers have multiple rather than single policy targets, as an inevitable end product of a system of variable domestic power relationships. (Cohen, 1977). Indeed revealed, as opposed to stated, preferences normally include not only security, stability and national – as distinct from international – efficiency, but such things as national autonomy, equity, status, prestige and involvement in decision making. These objectives frequently conflict with global efficiency objectives and with one another.

Criteria other than efficiency by which the system could be judged therefore include the effectiveness by which conflicts are avoided or minimised, as was the primary aim of the postwar rules of the game.[11] In these terms the postwar trade rules appear to have kept serious conflict within narrow limits and in this sense have succeeded. But the emergence of UNCTAD commodity pressures reflects something, if only a changed bargaining position; its added potential for conflict had arisen already with some ownership transfers taking place in developing countries, attempts to increase commodity prices and more strident bilateral bargaining.

In addition, the reduced effectiveness of the trading rules has been recognised by the North and changes in them have been sought, through the MTN and subsequently. These are unlikely to remedy the imbalance of coverage of commodity trade, however, or to be offset by improvements elsewhere – the contrary seems more likely.

5. Conclusion

In terms of the initial question in this paper, given that the international commodity trading system will not remain free from a variety of pressures for change, and given the doubts that we have cast on the conventional policy responses to commodity issues, a significant policy problem does exist for the North. We have not looked specifically at the IPC proposals which, together with some additional demands such as indexation, have been extensively criticised in the literature (Johnson, 1978, 1978a; Donges, 1977; Kreinin and Finger, 1976). Much of this criticism may be well founded, given the normal simplifying assumptions and analytical framework of micro-economics; and if the IPC propositions are seen as pronouncements about real-product-optimising policies. Yet economic policy objectives are seldom those of maximising real product, as economists have long acknowledged (Johnson, 1960, 1965; Cooper and Massell, 1965), though the analysis still provides limited policy guidance without substantial further elaboration.

The orthodox responses to the South's policy proposals in terms of market efficiency and the effectiveness of the international rules of the trading game are open to question in at least three respects. First, even if we could argue that we are concerned only with efficiency and not with distributional aspects, and that, for example, neither status nor risk avoidance are consumption goods, we cannot be unambiguously sure of our welfare conclusions or about the efficiency of particular policy instruments.

Second, however, we cannot assume efficiency to be independent of objectives such as status or uncertainty, nor can distributional factors be ignored or kept separate. A complex issue for economists in policy discussion is when to accept existing distortions as parameters and when to treat them as capable of variation. Economists cannot avoid making such judgements; for example, Curzon seems to suggest that exporters were slow to recognise the 'facts of life' – the parameters – in the GATT treatment of agriculture (Curzon, Chap. VII). Yet such judgements are not value free; to urge a first-best policy has distributional implications for those who bear the cost burden and who might otherwise benefit from compensatory intervention.

Third, the IPC proposals are normally analysed largely in terms of static gains and losses, from which we can say little about the long-term efficiency consequences. Such analyses, which largely overlook information problems, dynamic effects and uncertainty, tend generally to confirm the non-interventionist status quo. Yet many interventions in the market which economists support, such as management of the foreign exchange market, or perhaps tariff reductions, might fail a similar test. For tariffs, reliance on dynamic arguments – the stimulus to competitive entrepreneurship – often replaces inconclusive static arguments; but the dissatisfaction with static analysis that this reflects is seldom extended to commodity issues.

The status quo is also favoured by the existing institutional arrangements, which emphasise due deliberation based upon detailed and objective research. The voting procedures for commodity negotiations have similar effects, (Harris, 1978); and so do the somewhat agnostic conclusions of this paper! Does this bias towards inaction matter? Commodities perhaps receive undue attention in relation to their significance for world economic efficiency and development. The practical scope for making substantial improvements in the commodity marketing system may also be limited, even though important to the countries involved, for whom they still represent nearly 80 per cent of export earnings.

The more important issues for the North is the wider one of the international economic order, given the problems we have highlighted regarding conventional policy responses on the 'rules of the game'. The point of departure for the postwar economic institutions was that potentially threatening international conflicts arise more easily in the absence of a set of effective rules. Without rules conflicting policies are harder to avoid and disputes tend to be settled largely by economic power.[12] Moreover, the process is cumulative, as countries increasingly take inward looking actions as a defence against the actions of other countries and global economic efficiency suffers from competitive actions inconsistent with collective gain.

Given the practical limits to multilateral bargaining, a collective international solution has to be imposed. Domestically, governments impose collective rules; internationally the trend appears to be to accept less international sovereignty rather than more. A sufficiently powerful country could impose rules, as the United States did in the post-war period. Increased EEC economic and political power and reduced US internationalism have been among the factors lessening the sense of order, with global leadership now a joint, weakened and much more ad hoc management process by the US/EEC.

To achieve the best result in a non-zero sum game – however managed – some collective bargaining is inevitable. If participation by commodity exporters in the collective rules is considered worthwhile, therefore, those exporters will need to share appropriately in the global gains. At present they may reasonably doubt whether they are doing so.

In the sphere of tariffs the non-zero sum game argument provides the traditional justification for recommending policies from general principles rather than from a detailed analysis of benefits and costs. For commodity price stabilisation, there are no similar general principles available, unless some requirement is accepted to offset any presumed imbalance of existing policies, or some compensation or bribery is seen as warranted to ensure adherence to collective rules. The dilemma arises that even were stabilisation accepted, like free trade, as a 'good thing' having collective or external benefits, such social benefits would be difficult to internalise for specific policy measures.

More effective rules of the game are needed both to avoid international conflict and because the opportunity for collective gain can be exploited only if economic analysis is accepted as a 'rough guide' to

efficiency.[13] To achieve this acceptance, however, we must be readier
to acknowledge the limitations of our analysis, and the fact that the
rules of the game may be unbalanced. The market mechanism may
not work very well for commodities, but, like democracy, it is the best
that we have if applied flexibly within acknowledged constraints; in
democracy, moreover, we accept short-run inefficiency to achieve
long-run efficiency.

It is sometimes argued that international issues are determined
essentially by power relationships. Many fear that the changes currently envisaged in the rules of the game will move the system further
towards increased management by, and perhaps primarily in the
interests of, the larger countries, based more on a dispute settlement
basis than on collective rules. In that case, bargaining or compensation remains relevant, depending upon the perceived bargaining
power of the participants – on which, however, economics has little
to say. We need then to be careful that we do not let our property
rights as economists in particular forms and methods of analysis relevant to part of the world economic system, and our policy conclusions drawn from that analysis, give to the exercise of such power
a specious intellectual respectability.

NOTES

1. The commodities covered are: gold, copper, bauxite, nickel, silver, lead,
zinc, molybdenum, tin, iron ore, titanium, asbestos, potash, phosphates, uranium,
manganese, diamonds, platinum, chrome, mercury, boron and tungsten.

2. Details of the market structures for particular commodities are obtainable
from a variety of sources. A range of commodities is covered in Rangarajan (1978)
and Harris, Salmon and Smith (1978); for minerals good general references
are Clarfield *et al.* (1975), Bossan and Varon (1977) and Tilton (1977). For
agricultural commodities, various FAO and UNCTAD studies provide extensive
detail. UNCTAD also has done a number of mineral market studies.

3. The assumption in the British legislation that mergers are a good thing has
been questioned (Secretary of State for Prices, 1978); this should itself perhaps be
seen as a bargaining outcome (not an economic judgement) made in the context
that recognised that international competition was the ultimate safeguard.

4. At times this is qualified by the use instead of such terms as 'open market
mechanism'. Such terms tend to beg the question as to the criteria applicable, or
on whose judgement the market is judged to be open.

5. A more comprehensive study is being undertaken for the Trade Policy
Research Centre.

6. The second-best argument for tariffs, under which this assumption may not
hold, is discussed below. The validity of the GATT prohibition on subsidies when
compensatory subsidies are warranted on second-best grounds has been discussed

221

COMMODITIES PROBLEM: INTERNATIONAL ECONOMIC ORDER

in Harris (1975). See also Sjaastad (1978). The general principles are discussed in Corden (1974).

7. The material on agricultural restrictions is voluminous and difficult to consolidate. The Haberler report is still broadly relevant and more up to date detail is available from various FAO documents. See for example FAO (1975).

8. A point commonly overlooked by those arguing that this concession to the developing countries should be removed.

9. Theoretically, of course, there is no automatic presumption that lump sum transfers would need to be made by the rest of the world to Tanzania; it could be that Tanzania would need to make lump sum transfers to the rest of the world.

10. Hamada has spelled out examples in the field of money, although he takes them no further than illustrative cases (Hamada, 1975); see also Cooper (1975) and Cohen (1977) who follow the same approach.

11. Bergsten et al. suggested seven economic criteria by which to judge an international economic system: efficiency, growth, full employment, income distribution, price stability, quality of life and economic security (Bergsten, Keohane and Nye, 1975.) See also Baldwin and Kay (1975).

12. In the monetary context, Richard Cooper concluded that a free-for-all system '. . . would allow large nations to try to exploit their power at the expense of smaller nations. It would give rise to attempts to pursue objectives that were not consistent with one another . . . with the resulting disorganisation of markets'. (Cooper, 1975).

13. The term is used by Little in his examination of the assumptions underlying welfare economics and, especially relevant here, international trade theory. See Little (1957), especially Chapter XIII.

REFERENCES

Robert E. Baldwin and David A. Kay (1975), 'International Trade and International Relations' in C. Fred Bergsten and Lawrence Krause (eds.), *World Politics and International Economics*, Brookings Institution, Washington, pp. 99–131.

C. Fred Bergsten, Robert O. Keohane and Joseph S. Nye (1975), 'International Economies and International Politics: a Framework for Analysis', in C. Fred Bergsten and Lawrence Krause (eds.), *World Politics and International Economies*, Brookings Institution, Washington, pp. 3–36.

Rex Bosson and Bension Varon (1977), *The Mining Industry and the Developing Countries*, Oxford University Press for the World Bank, Washington.

K. W. Clarfield, et al. (1975), *Eight Mineral Cartels: The New Challenge to Industrialised Nations*, McGraw-Hill for Metals Week.

Benjamin J. Cohen (1977), *Organising the World's Money: The Political Economy of World Monetary Relations*, Macmillan, London.

C. A. Cooper and B. F. Massell (1965), 'A New Look at Customs Union Theory', *Economic Journal*, Vol. 75, December, pp. 742–747.

Richard N. Cooper (1975), 'Prolegomena to the Choice of an International Monetary System', *International Organisation*, Vol. 29, No. 1, reprinted in Bergsten and Krause, *op. cit.*, pp. 63–97.

W. M. Corden (1974), *Trade Policy and Economic Welfare*, Clarendon Press, Oxford.

Gerard Curzon (1965), *Multilateral Commercial Diplomacy*, Michael Joseph, London.

STUART HARRIS

Kenneth W. Dam (1970), *The GATT: Law and International Economic Organisation*, University of Chicago Press, Chicago.

Harold Demsetz (1969), 'Information and Efficiency: Another Viewpoint', *Journal of Law and Economics*, Vol. 12, pp. 1–22, reprinted in D. M. Lamberton (ed.), *Economics of Information and Knowledge*, Penguin Books, Middlesex, 1971, pp. 160–186.

Jurgen Donges (1977), 'The Third World Demand for a New International Economic Order: Government Surveillance versus Market Decision-Taking in Trade and Investment', *Kyklos*, Vol. 30, pp. 235–258.

FAO (1975), *Agricultural Protection and Stabilisation Policies: A Framework of Measurement in the Context of Agricultural Adjustment*, Doc. No. C75/Lim/2, Rome, October.

J. De V. Graaff (1967), *Theoretical Welfare Economics*, Cambridge University Press, London.

Koichi Hamada (1975), 'Alternative Exchange Rate Systems and the Interdependence of Monetary Policies', in Robert L. Aliber (ed.), *National Monetary Policies and the International Financial System*, University of Chicago Press, Chicago, pp. 13–33.

Stuart Harris (1975), 'Tariff Compensation: Sufficient Justification for Assistance to Agriculture?', *Australian Journal of Agricultural Economics*, Vol. 19, No. 3 (December).

Stuart Harris (1978), 'The Case for a New Commodity Regime: Confused Arguments and Unresolved Issues', in G. Goodwin and J. Mayall (eds.), *A New International Commodity Regime?*, Croom Helm, London.

Stuart Harris (1980), 'State Ownership in the World Mineral Industry', *CRES Working Paper*, Australian National University, Canberra (forthcoming).

Stuart Harris, Mark Salmon and Ben Smith (1978), *Analysis of Commodity Markets for Policy Purposes*, Thames Essay, Trade Policy Research Centre, London.

James P. Houck (1968), 'Wool Policy in the United States: its Direct Impact on Australian Exports', *Australian Journal of Agricultural Economics*, Vol. 12 (June), pp. 16–23.

John H. Jackson (1978), 'The Crumbling Institutions of the Liberal Trade System', *Journal of World Trade Law*, Vol. 12, No. 2 (March–April) pp. 93–106.

Harry Johnson (1965), 'An Economic Theory of Protectionism, Tariff Bargaining and the Formation of Customs Unions', *Journal of Political Economy*, Vol. 73, June, pp. 256–283.

Harry Johnson (1967), *Economic Policies Towards Less Developed Countries*, Brookings Institution, Washington.

Harry Johnson (1967a), 'Optimum Tariffs and Retaliation', in *International Trade and Economic Growth: Studies in Pure Theory*, Harvard University Press, Cambridge.

Harry Johnson (1969), 'The North–South Problem in the World Economy and the Implications of UNCTAD 1968', Chapter 1 in Kyoshi Kojima (ed.), *Pacific Trade and Development II*, Japan Economic Research Centre, Tokyo.

Harry Johnson (1971), *Aspects of the Theory of Tariffs*, Allen and Unwin, London.

Harry Johnson (1978), 'Commodities: Less Developed Countries' Demands and Developed Countries Responses', Chapter 9, Jagdish Bhagwati (ed.), *The New International Economic Order: The North South Debate*, M.I.T. Press, Cambridge, Mass., pp. 240–251.

Harry Johnson (1978a), Contribution to Panel Discussion in Bhagwati (ed.), *op. cit.*, pp. 359–361.

223

Richard E. Just, Ernst Lutz, Andrew Schmitz and Stephen Turnovsky (1977), 'The Distribution of Welfare Gains from International Price Stabilisation under Distortions', *American Journal of Agricultural Economics*, Vol. 59, No. 4, pp. 652–61.

Mordechai Kreinin and J. M. Finger (1976), 'A Critical Survey of the New International Economic Order', *Journal of World Trade Law*, Vol. 10, pp. 493–512.

I. M. D. Little (1957), *A Critique of Welfare Economics*, 2nd edn., Clarendon Press, Oxford.

James Meade (1955), *Trade and Welfare*, Oxford University Press, London.

Mining Magazine (1978), Vol. 138 (March), p. 227.

E. J. Mishan (1975), *Cost Benefit Analysis*, 2nd edn., Allen and Unwin, London.

L. N. Rangarajan (1978), *Commodity Conflict: The Political Economy of International Commodity Negotiations*, Croom Helm, London.

Tibor Scitovsky (1942), 'A Reconsideration of the Theory of Tariffs', *Review of Economic Studies*, Vol. IX, pp. 89–110.

Secretary of State for Prices and Economic Protection (1978), *A Review of Monopolies and Mergers Policy: A Consultative Document*, HMSO (Cmnd 7198), London.

Larry A. Sjaasted (1979), 'Commercial Policy, "True Tariffs", and Relative Prices', in Brian Hindley (ed.), *Current Issues in Commercial Policy*, Macmillan, London (forthcoming).

Gordon W. Smith (1978), 'Commodity Instability and Market Failure: A Survey of Issues', in F. Gerard Adams and Sonia A. Klein (eds.), *Stabilising World Commodity Markets*, D. C. Heath, Lexington Books, Lexington, Mass., pp. 161–188.

John Spraos (1980), 'The Terms of Trade of Primary Commodities of Developing Countries', in Stuart Harris (ed.), *Commodity Policy Issues in the North–South Dialogue*, Macmillan for the Trade Policy Research Centre, London (forthcoming).

Stephen Turnovsky (1978), 'The Distribution of Welfare Gains from Price Stabilisation: A Survey of Some Theoretical Issues', in F. Gerard Adams and Sonia A. Klein (eds.), *Stabilising World Commodity Markets*, D. C. Heath, Lexington Books, Lexington, Mass., pp. 119–148.

Trends in International Trade: A Report by a Panel of Experts (1958), GATT, Geneva.

John Tilton (1966), 'The Choice of Trading Partners: An Analysis of International Trade in Aluminium, Bauxite, Copper, Lead, Manganese, Tin and Zinc', *Yale Economic Essays*, Vol. 6, No. 2 (Fall).

John Tilton (1977), *The Future of Non-Fuel Minerals*, Brookings Institution, Washington.

PART 3

Chapter Twelve

EXCHANGE-RATE INSTABILITY, TRADE IMBALANCES,
AND MONETARY POLICIES IN JAPAN AND
THE UNITED STATES

Ronald I. McKinnon

UNDER FLOATING exchange rates, how serious are policy makers responding to new theoretical and empirical developments in international trade and finance? Following Harry Johnson in taking a consistent monetary or portfolio approach to explaining exchange-rate fluctuations,[1] I shall argue that a wide gap exists between theory and practice.

First, the monetary approach implies that a country's exchange rate neither can nor should be determined by the ebb and flow of commodity trade. In particular, the United States government was mistaken in 1977 to encourage the dollar to depreciate in response to the American trade deficit. The traditional elasticities approach, which would have the exchange rate respond to the state of the trade balance, has become inappropriate.

How then is the exchange rate to be determined if not by the international flow of goods and services? The emerging theoretical and empirical consensus among academic economists emphasizes financial and money-market conditions between nations in the short run, and the theory of purchasing power parity in the long run. My second major theme is, therefore, that central banks in Japan, America and Europe are unduly insulating themselves from events in the foreign exchange market, and this is at the root of the extreme short-run fluctuations in exchange rates among major convertible currencies since 1973. Whether one speaks pejoratively of monetary nationalism, or more self righteously of national monetary autonomy or sovereignty, the underlying concept is inconsistent with a stable world financial system.

But having central banks adjust better to each other requires

225

rather subtle institutional changes in the operation of the world dollar standard on the one hand, *and* changed official perceptions of the usefulness of short-term rates of interest as intermediate target variables on the other. Regarding the dollar standard, the traditional American monetary policy of benign neglect – where all foreign official purchases or sales of dollars are liberally tolerated but also fully sterilized in their impact on the American monetary base – has to be carefully re-examined. Regarding short-term rates of interest, expected movements in exchange rates are now sufficiently large to have strong 'Fisher Effects' in national money-markets – even in the United States. That is, nominal interest rates at short term may well be dominated by anticipated exchange-rate movements. In turn, this deceives monetary authorities, who had become accustomed to using short-term interest rates as indicators of whether to expend or contract the domestic money supply, into behaving perversely.

Thirdly, if the exchange rate is determined by money-market conditions, how then is an equilibrium balance of trade established? Again eschewing the elasticities approach, I appeal to the balance between national income and expenditures: the absorption approach. By looking at investment-savings propensities on the part of the private sector, and fiscal offsets in the form of government saving or dissaving, trade deficits and surpluses can be more or less fully explained. For example, I argue that Japan may now be a natural international creditor, just as individual European countries and the United States were in earlier periods. The only major anomaly with the current Japanese trade surplus is that the private Tokyo capital market is insufficiently open to foreigners.

These three propositions are quite general. In the main, however, I shall confine the empirical examples to Japanese–American trading relationships over the years 1977–78. The large Japanese trade surplus and American deficit, and the sharp fall in the yen/dollar exchange rate, illustrate the above propositions in a conveniently extreme form.

The 'J' Curve and the Demise of the Elasticities Approach
Why has commodity trade responded so little to exchange-rate changes?

With the advent of floating, the future direction of exchange-rate movements has proved highly uncertain. Although unbiased predictors, forward rates of exchange contain little information on actual movements of spot rates into the future.[2] Unexpected cyclical movements of 1 per cent in one day, 5 per cent in a week or 25 per cent in a year are now not unusual.

This uncertainty weakens the incentives of merchants to engage in short-run commodity arbitage internationally, and thus results in sharp departures from purchasing power parity in markets for individual goods apart from homogeneous primary commodities. Output, trading and pricing decisions for industrial goods are made for finite time intervals and do not continually respond to exchange-rate fluctuations – unlike the foreseeable discrete devaluations that are still common in less developed countries. Indeed, most industrial products can be treated as Hicksian 'fixprice' goods whose prices are sticky in the short run, and which are invoiced in the home currency of the producer.[3] Thus, when country A's currency unexpectedly appreciates, the foreign-currency prices of A's industrial products on world markets rise more or less in proportion. The law of one price need not hold for weeks, months or even years (Aliber 1976, Isard 1977). And it may not be in the interests of merchants to engage in active arbitage in industrial commodities if tomorrow's exchange rate is unknown. Hence, the quantities of goods traded respond sluggishly to exchange-rate fluctuations giving rise to a modern version of 'elasticity pessimism'[4] – although I do not believe that this is a useful way of formulating the problem.

One can be more negative regarding the elasticities approach to exchange-rate stability and the trade balance. In response to an *unanticipated* change in an exchange rate, the short-run behavior of 'non-speculative' merchants is bound to be perverse: the celebrated 'J' curve effect (Magee 1973). Within the period for which industrial goods are contracted – say, to be paid for within 90 days – an appreciation of the domestic currency will *increase* foreign-exchange earnings from exports. The convention that exporters of industrial goods invoice in their home currency makes the foreign-exchange costs of these goods higher within the contract period where quantities – by definition – cannot change. This proposition still holds even when non-speculative importers hedge optimally (McKinnon 1979, Chapter 7). Thus, in the goods market, appreciation increases – rather than reduces – the excess demand for the home currency in terms of the foreign so that pressure for further appreciation inevitably develops. This proposition remains true even beyond the immediate contract period.

Indeed, one can show that a foreign-exchange market without speculators – without holders of interchangeable foreign- and domestic currency-assets – is necessarily unstable in the short run.

If the market consists only of non-speculative merchants and manu-factures who hedge as best they can, no determinate (floating) exchange rate is possible (McKinnon, 1979, Chapter 7). Hence, the old debate on whether private speculation is stabilizing or de-stabilizing is somewhat beside the main point once central banks have withdrawn from the market. Rather the question should be rephrased, 'Is private speculation on net balance sufficiently strongly stabilizing?' And the answer depends heavily on private assessments of future monetary policies of participating central banks.

As a corollary to this proposition, suppose central banks impose substantial restrictions on asset adjustments – short-term capital flows – by potential private speculators in an exchange market without official parities. (The Bank of Japan and the Bank of France, among others, are well known for imposing such regulations from time to time.) Then, willy-nilly, the central bank will be drawn back in as the principal speculator or market maker, without which the flow of commercial payments between non-speculative merchants would become completely disorganized. And the uneasy coexistence of intensive official intervention, coupled with restraints on private short-term capital flows, has been observed many times since 1973.

Multinational Investment and the Real Exchange Rate
Many readers will grant our argument that the exchange rate cannot be determined by commodity flows within the short run of days or weeks. But in the intermediate or long run – say months or years – shouldn't the balance of trade respond positively to a depreciation if the exchange market can hang on that long? In particular, suppose the 'real' exchange rate depreciates: the external value of a currency falls proportionately more than its relative internal rate of price inflation thus causing a prolonged departure from purchasing power parity. Shouldn't quantities of exports now flexibly adjust upwards, and quantities of imports adjust downwards, enough to overcome their higher invoice prices?

I shall argue that such longer run 'stabilizing' adjustments in the goods market are unlikely to occur. When capital is mobile internationally, investment and output can be sufficiently buoyed in response to a real depreciation that the balance of trade need not improve at all. Instead, the likely result is the mercantilist effect of having domestic output artificially stimulated at the expense of one's trading partners. The underlying problem of exchange-rate nstability remains unresolved.

228

To illustrate this general proposition, let us focus on bilateral trade between Japan and the United States over the past two years or so. The monthly *real* exchange rates in Table 1 are calculated on the principle of relative purchasing power parity using 1953 as the (arbitrary) base year. Movements in the nominal yen/dollar exchange rate are deflated either by relative wholesale price indices (WPIs) or by relative consumer price indices (CPIs) in order to give alternative estimates of movements in the real exchange rate. Because wholesale prices cover a more or less representative basket of tradable goods, whereas the CPI includes non-tradable services, I shall use only the WPI in the subsequent analysis.[5]

Table 1: The Yen/Dollar Exchange Rate for 1977–78 (monthly averages).

	Nominal Exchange Rates		Price Indices (1953 = 100)		Real Exchange Rate	
	(1)	(2)	(3)	(4)	(5)	(6)
			WPI Japan	CPI (Japan)	(2)/(3)	(2)/(4)
	Current (Yen/$)	1953 = 100	WPI(U.S.)	CPI (U.S.)		
1977						
Jan	291.1	80.7	88.9	179.6	0.908	0.449
Feb	285.1	79.0	88.2	178.6	0.896	0.442
Mar	280.6	77.8	87.3	178.7	0.890	0.435
April	275.1	76.2	86.2	180.1	0.884	0.423
May	277.6	76.9	86.0	180.8	0.895	0.425
June	273.0	75.7	86.1	178.7	0.879	0.423
July	264.8	73.4	85.4	177.4	0.859	0.414
Aug	266.6	73.9	85.7	176.8	0.863	0.418
Sept	267.0	74.0	85.5	179.3	0.866	0.413
Oct	255.1	70.7	84.8	179.6	0.833	0.394
Nov	244.8	67.9	84.0	176.7	0.808	0.384
Dec	241.3	66.9	83.1	175.7	0.804	0.381
1978						
Jan	241.1	66.8	82.3	175.3	0.811	0.381
Feb	240.3	66.6	81.6	174.9	0.816	0.380
Mar	231.5	64.2	80.8	175.3	0.794	0.366
April	221.7	61.4	79.5	175.7	0.773	0.350
May	226.4	62.7	79.1	174.9	0.793	0.358
June	214.3	59.3	78.3	172.0	0.757	0.345
July	199.9	55.3	77.1	171.6	0.717	0.322
Aug	188.5	52.2	76.5	170.8	0.682	0.306

Source: *International Financial Statistics*, IMF (various issues), compiled by Masahiro Kawai.

Despite the monetary turmoil of the early 1970s, the real yen/ dollar exchange rate was still about 91 per cent of its 1953 'parity' as of January 1977. And this real exchange-rate had not moved significantly further from unity during the previous 24 years. From January 1977 to August 1978, however, a substantial real depreciation of the dollar of 25 per cent was accompanied by a nominal depreciation against the yen of 35 per cent. I hypothesize that this real depreciation could not of itself have been expected to reduce the Japanese trade surplus or American trade deficit in 1979.

In contrast, the traditional analytical response is to distinguish between tradable and non-tradable goods (Salter 1958, Dornbusch 1974), and to consider the appreciation of the yen to depress the production of tradable goods in Japan while raising the demand for them – and vice versa in the United States. Unfortunately, this traditional analysis depends heavily on the law of one price holding in the market for tradable goods. In reality, deviations from purchasing power parity are particularly pronounced under floating exchange rates as Table 1 makes abundantly clear. Because of sticky invoice prices, the appreciation of the yen forces the prices of Japanese goods – both tradable and non-tradable – to rise above their American equivalent. Moreover, this traditional Salter analysis is static in the sense that the ongoing flow of investment and saving is not formally modelled, although Salter stresses the need to increase domestic absorption if the trade surplus is to be reduced.

Instead, consider modelling just the Japanese side of the adjustment process (on the understanding that the American response to the exchange rate is approximately the inverse) on a 'fixed price' basis. Note that the internal yen prices of Japanese goods are indeed sticky: Japanese wholesale prices in June of 1978 were the same as in 1976 and were stable within a margin of one or two percentage points in the interim. Consumer prices were also remarkably stable, perhaps because the Japanese economy was depressed. Thus the yen value of output in Japan in 1976–78 provides a stable real numeraire on which to build a Keynesian-type income-expenditure model, where real and nominal values are virtually the same.

Then, in yen per dollar, movements in the nominal exchange rate e are equivalent to real changes because of the constancy of the Japanese price level. Dollar prices inflation in the United States would be equivalent to a rise in e, but otherwise foreign repercussions to income-expenditure changes in Japan are ignored in the algebraic model.[6] What is essential about this model, however, is that e is initially given from 'outside' by financial considerations not yet formally considered. One can then test whether the flow of commodity trade eventually responds in a stabilizing fashion to, say, a fall in e: an appreciation of the yen like that portrayed in Table 1.

The four basic behavioral equations are:

(1) $\quad X = X(e)$ where $X'(e) > 0$ $\qquad$ Exports

(2) $\quad eM = mY$ where $0 < m < 1$ $\qquad$ Imports

(3) $\quad I = I(e, i; \alpha)$ where $\dfrac{\partial I}{\partial e} > 0$ and $\dfrac{\partial I}{\partial i} < 0$ $\quad$ Investment

(4) $\quad S = sY$ where $0 < s < 1$ $\qquad$ Saving

To these we add the accounting identities:

(5) $Y = C + I + X - eM$ $\qquad$ Gross National Product

(6) $S = Y - C$ $\qquad$ Saving-Consumption

(7) $T_d = X - eM$ $\qquad$ Trade Balance in Domestic Currency

(8) $T_f = \dfrac{X}{e} - M$ $\qquad$ Trade Balance in Foreign Currency

Within these eight equations, we have eight endogenous flow variables: Y, C, S, I, X, M, T_d and T_f. The exchange rate e and the interest rate i are given by financial considerations outside the model.

The yen export function – equation (1) – is straightforward for a Keynesian 'fix price' world. Japanese goods are invoiced in yen, and important costs of production like money wages are fixed in yen, so that the yen prices of manufactures are quite rigid even beyond the period of currency contract. Thus, when e declines in the 'intermediate run', Japanese goods are seen to be more expensive so that world demand for them falls.

M is the dollar value of imports (fix price) so that their yen value, eM, declines with e unless M increases. For simplicity, I have assumed in equation (2) that the demand for imports is proportional to income with a unit (yen) price elasticity of demand.

The investment function – equation (3) – is the more novel part of the model, and is basically responsible for the unconventional results that are obtained. Investment I is strongly and positively influenced by the real exchange rate e. (The usual rate of interest also appears but it is not manipulated.) That is, a change in e lasting a few months or a year or two is perceived to be permanent by 'non-speculative' investors with stationary expectations. Thus

231

Japanese costs of production – wages and locally produced intermediate materials – are raised above world levels by the general
appreciation of the yen. Japan is perceived to be a high cost country
for producing internationally tradable goods in the *future*, so that
multinational firms reduce *current* investment there or set up
subsidiaries in low wage countries like the United States. Within
the world economy, I am hypothesizing that the real exchange rate
has a first-order effect on where new private physical investment is
located. e is an index of profitability of producing (cost of production)
of internationally tradable goods.

Finally, in equation (4), the yen value of saving is proportional
to national income. Because the government is not represented
explicitly, S and I in the model have both private and public
components.

Solving equations (1) through (6), the equilibrium level of
national income Y* is simply

$$(9) \qquad Y^* = \frac{I(e) + X(e)}{m + s}$$

where

$$(10) \qquad \frac{dY^*}{de} = \frac{1}{m+s} \left[\underset{+}{\frac{\partial I}{\partial e}} + \underset{+}{\frac{\partial X}{\partial e}} \right] > 0.$$

Because both the yen value of exports and investment fall as e
declines, one expects the real appreciation of the yen exhibited in
Table 1 to depress national income in Japan (and contribute to a
business boom in the United States). And, as of September 1978,
this is indeed the case. *Private* investment in Japan is depressed, and
industrial output has barely returned to what it was at the end of
1973. Unemployment has become a significant problem for the
first time in the postwar period.

However, the main rationale for this 'intermediate term' model
is to examine the impact on the trade balance of a real change in
the exchange rate. In terms of the domestic currency (yen) we have

$$(11) \qquad T_d = X - eM$$

and

$$(12) \qquad \frac{dT_d}{de} = \underset{+}{\frac{s}{m+s} \frac{\partial X}{\partial e}} - \underset{+}{\frac{m}{m+s} \frac{\partial I}{\partial e}} \gtrless 0.$$

From equation (12), the indeterminant response of the yen trade
balance to a change in e is a weighted sum of the export and invest-

ment responses. In the case of an appreciation where e falls, exports decrease but if investment falls sufficiently, imports (in yen) could decrease even more. Whence the indeterminant sign in equation (12):

But we simplify further in assessing the relative importance of the export and investment responses. Suppose trade is approximately balanced, and hence domestic saving approximately equals domestic investment, such that

(13) $$X \approx mY \text{ and } I \approx sY.$$

Further, define the *elasticities* of both the export and investment responses to be:

(14) $$E_X = \frac{dX}{de} \cdot \frac{e}{X} \text{ and } E_I = \frac{dI}{de} \cdot \frac{e}{I}$$

Then substituting equations (13) and (14) into (12), we obtain a remarkably simple expression for the sensitivity of trade balance in domestic currency to the real exchange rate:

(15) $$\frac{dT_d}{de} = \frac{sm}{m+s} \cdot \frac{Y}{e}(E_X - E_I).$$

Thus $dT_d/de > 0$ only if $E_X > E_I$. In the case of balanced trade, only if the elasticity of the export response exceeds that of investment do we get the 'normal' effect of a devaluation (rise in e) improving the balance of trade.

The upshot is that an appreciation of the yen relative to the dollar *could* depress income and investment in Japan so that the trade surplus does not fall, Similarly, investment and income could be stimulated in the United States so that the American trade deficit widens. The goods market may remain incapable of determining an equilibrium rate,[7] even for a time horizon of months or years beyond that ordinarily associated with the 'J' curve effect.

The Absorption Approach to the Trade Balance and Financial Dissaving by The Government
How then is an 'equilibrium' flow of imports and exports to be established among countries with floating convertible currencies and no detailed exchange controls or pervasive tariffs on commodity trade? Again we can appeal to the integration of the world capital market and simply consider the balance between saving and investment in individual countries – that necessarily spills out into the balance of trade as the difference between exports and imports.

To fix ideas, consider the familiar identities from the national income accounts:

(16) $$S - I = X - eM$$

(17) $$S = S_p + S_g \text{ where } S_g = R - G$$

where

I is private investment

S_p is private saving

S_g is government financial saving

R is government tax revenue

G is government expenditures.

Leaving the export, import, and investment functions as defined in equations (1), (2), and (3), let us modify the saving function – equation (4). Suppose only *private* saving is a constant fraction of national income:

(4)′ $$S_p = s_p Y \text{ where } 0 < s_p < 1.$$

Further, let us depart from the usual practice of treating the government surplus S_g as if it were endogenous. Rather suppose S_g is exogenously given a policy variable. (I realize that government revenue is dependent on the level of national income. Nevertheless, a government can adjust expenditures and tax rates in important ways so as to dominate S_g.) By this means we bring fiscal policy explicitly into the analysis. In looking at the recent Japanese experience, it proves very convenient to think of government financial saving S_g (or financial dissaving if $S_g < 0$) to be an important policy parameter, without worrying about the precise mix of expenditures and taxes.[8]

Now making use of the functional equations (1), (2), (3) and (4)′ – and substituting these into the identities (16) and (17) – the equilibrium level of income is

(18) $$Y^* = \cdot \frac{X(e) + I(e) - S_g}{m + s_p}.$$

Not only does the real exchange rate e influence Y through the export and investment functions, but the level of government financial saving is negatively related to Y with a multiplier effect of $1/m + s_p$. Within our very simple Keyensian income-expenditure framework with fixed prices, only private saving and imports

234

are endogenous leakages in the process of income generation. Some readers may find it more familiar to think of $-S_g$ as the vertical intercept of a consumption function that includes government consumption. So an increase in government 'dissaving' (through reduced taxes or increased expenditures) shifts upwards the whole flow of spending in the economy. Notice that the asset structure – including the money supply – has not been specified so that neither the interest rate nor the exchange rate can be determined within the model.

However, the state of the trade balance is determinate. In domestic currency we have

$$(19) \qquad T_d = X - eM = \frac{s_p X(e) - mI(e) + mS_g}{m + s_p}.$$

Not only private saving, investment and exports, but now the level of government saving S_g influences the trade surplus. Note, however, that T_d and S_g are not related on a one to one basis. The multiplier effect of S_g on T_d is simply $\frac{m}{m + s_p} < 1$. That is, an increase in public saving reduces income and private saving so that the trade surplus does not rise as much as the public finances improve. Nevertheless, they are positively related. Indeed, as the private propensity to save, s_p, becomes 'small' as in the United States, deficits or surpluses in the government budget at the margin could dominate changes in the trade balance. And this idea is important in interpreting the current Japanese-American trade imbalance.

In recent experience, private saving propensities for each country have been fairly stable. Japanese household saving as a proportion of household disposable income has been about three times that prevailing in the United States. Discrepancies in gross savings rates – including retained earnings, capital consumption allowances, and government – are less pronounced but still striking. From 1960 to 1975, Japanese gross domestic saving averaged about 36 per cent of GNP; whereas in the United States gross saving from all domestic sources averaged about 18 per cent, or half as much. [9] And, with some cyclical variation, gross investment matched gross saving in both countries so there was no need to run trade surpluses or deficits on a sustained basis, i.e. no need for sustained *net* capital inflows or outflows.

However, beginning with the energy crisis in 1974 and the world recession in 1975, private investment in Japan slumped and has

235

not recovered. The gross figures that are available in the IMF statistics, as displayed in Table 2, fail to show the full extent of fall in private investment because they include publically financed fixed capital formation. Even so, by 1977 the fall is impressive: investment is 6 to 7 per cent of GNP less than in 1970. If private saving were a constant proportion of GNP, one would have expected the trade balance to go into surplus by the amount investment falls if there were no other offsets in the Japanese economy.

The emergence of a trade surplus is quite definite by 1977 and the beginning of 1978 – but it is still only of an order of magnitude of abour 2 per cent of GNP. Somewhat surprisingly, Japanese fiscal offsets are large and growing. The government financial deficit was over 6 per cent of GNP in 1977. Otherwise the Japanese trade surplus would be even larger. (In so far as the gross investment series includes new publically financed capital accumulation that has been increasing strongly in Japan, one cannot exactly offset the fall of investment in the first row with the rise in the public sector deficit in the second in netting out the effect on the trade balance.) So the trade surplus is not 'large'; measured as a proportion of the yen value of GNP, it is back to where it was in the early 1970s. Nevertheless, the trade surplus might seem formidable to foreigners because the Japanese economy is bigger than in the early 1970s, and the yen has appreciated so much.

If one believes with the American government that the Japanese trade surplus is in need of 'correction', one response is for the Japanese government to increase the volume of financial dissaving as represented by $S_g < 0$. And in 1978 the Japanese government's fiscal deficit is even larger than the 6.2 per cent of GNP recorded in Table 2 for 1977. On the other hand, we have established that further real appreciation of the yen would be worse than useless – private investment in Japan would slump even further. Indeed, the sharp appreciation in 1977–78 seems to have contributed significantly to the depressed condition (and trade surplus) of the Japanese economy.

On the other side of the coin, just the inverse of this analysis applies to the United States. America is experiencing a business cycle boom where, unlike Japan, private investment [10] as a proportion of GNP is now substantially greater than in 1975 as indicated in Table 3. Government financial dissaving, however, has been reduced only slightly in response to the upsurge in investment in 1977 and 1978 (see Table 3). Combined with the fact that private

Table 2: Gross Investment and Government Financial Saving
in Japan (as a proportion of GNP).

	1971	1972	1973	1974	1975	1976	1977	1978
Gross Investment[1]	0.367	0.366	0.399	0.381	0.323	0.315	0.308	0.308
Government Surplus	−0.002	−0.016	0.016	−0.016	−0.048	−0.020	−0.062	−0.065
Current Account Trade Surplus[3]	+0.026	+0.023	0.000	−0.010	−0.001	+0.007	+0.016	+0.018

Source; *International Financial Statistics* of the International Monetary Fund.
1. Lines 93e and 93i.
2. Line 80.
3. Line 90e–line 98e.
Note: All entries have been standardized for the level of GNP appearing on line 99a.

saving (not shown) in the United States is a percentage point less than its historical norm, this government deficit leaves a savings gap that is covered by drawing on foreign saving. And indeed the government deficit of 50 or so billion dollars per year in 1977 and 1978 is large relative to the current account deficit of about 30 billion dollars per year. This deficiency of saving in the United States is being made good, in part, by the transfer of surplus saving from Japan.

One could even say that this transfer of saving from abroad has helped to sustain the current business boom in the United States. Without foreign central banks buying U.S. Treasury securities (they now hold about 20 per cent of total U.S. government debt) a crunch in the American capital market could already have occurred. Therefore, the American trade deficit has probably been a benign influence during 1977–78 in preventing more inflationary pressure from developing in the United States.

Two further aspects of this income-expenditure approach to the Japanese-American trade balance are important to note. First, 'unfair' Japanese trade practices are not responsible. For example, removing high barriers on agricultural imports into Japan would simply alter the composition of Japanese imports without much affecting the net surplus. A similar rationalization of American energy policy would probably reduce imports of fossil fuels into the United States, but would be offset elsewhere as long as America is deficient in saving. The microeconomic details of trade in this or that commodity are dominated by broad investment-saving considerations – unlike current heated political discussions of these issues would suggest.

Table 3: Gross Investment and Government Financial Saving in the United States (as a proportion of GNP).

	1971	*1972*	*1973*	*1974*	*1975*	*1976*	*1977*	*1978*
Private Gross Investment[1]	0.150	0.161	0.168	0.152	0.124	0.143	0.156	0.165
Government Surplus[2]	−0.023	−0.015	−0.007	−0.009	−0.049	−0.033	−0.027	−0.021
Current Account Trade Surplus[3]	−0.005	−0.009	−0.001	−0.006	+0.006	−0.003	−0.015	−0.015

Source; *International Financial Satistics.*
1. Line 93ee and 93i.
2. Line 80.
3. Line 90e–line 98e.

Japan, a Natural International Creditor?

In order to understand the 'unbalanced' economic relationship between the two countries one must look at *financial* considerations rather than commodity trade. Apart from monetary policy that is treated below, the principal anomaly about the present situation is that the Tokyo capital market remains too inaccessible to foreigners. The national counterpart of the surplus of saving in Japan, displayed in Table 2, is that foreigners be able to issue bonds and stocks freely in Tokyo. Restraints on their doing so have been recently relaxed but not yet removed. Even more importantly, exchange controls on Japanese firms and households that inhibit them from buying financial assets abroad are still considerable.[11] The commercial banks play a dominant role in domestic financial intermediation between investors and savers, and the rather tight restraints by the Bank of Japan on their acquisition of foreign (dollar) assets could well be eliminated.

With such controls on private capital outflows, how then is Japan's large trade surplus 'financed'? If the current-account surplus exists, there must be a counterpart build-up of financial claims on foreigners if only from the principle of double entry bookkeeping. Because private capital outflows are less than the trade surplus, there is chronic incipient upward pressure on the yen (in terms of dollars). To prevent the yen from rising as much as it would otherwise, the Japanese government enters the foreign-exchange market to buy dollars and sell yen. The dollars so purchased are then invested in U.S. Treasury bonds or bills, whose recent build-up in Japanese official exchange reserves has been quite rapid – see Table 4. The Japanese government is thus forced into being a (unwilling) financial intermediary for the trade surplus, and by international convention is trapped into acquiring U.S. government debt whose yield is not particularly attractive. But, with much unnecessary upward pressure on the yen, there is (must be) a capital outflow that exactly matches the Japanese trade surplus.

With the important caveat that this serious imperfection in the private Japanese capital market be removed, I see nothing wrong with Japan becoming a major international creditor like the U.S. was from the 1940s to the early 1960s, or like Britain prior to 1914. Personal saving in Japan is very high relative to other industrial countries. Because Japan is now at the frontier of new technology along with other OECD countries, it may be difficult to sustain the profitability of the high levels of domestic investment that occurred in the 1950s and 1960s. Hence, investment abroad could be socially useful given the needs of less developed countries and the fact that the net surplus of the OPEC countries are coming to an end in the foreseeable future. Alternatively, a less satisfactory adjustment mechanism is to reduce the Japanese trade surplus by having the Japanese government increase its already large fiscal deficit so that government dissaving offsets private saving.

Intervention by Central Banks and Domestic Monetary Adjustment

If not by the trade balance, how then is the equilibrium exchange rate to be determined? For any pair of countries, the monetary approach would emphasize money-market conditions in the short and 'intermediate' run, and purchasing power parity in the long run.[12] To take a specific example of the former, I hypothesize that the Japanese and American central banks have not co-ordinated their monetary policies to prevent the dollar from falling sharply against the yen in 1977 and the first half of 1978 (Table 1).

At this point the reader might well boggle, and note the huge recent accumulation of dollar reserves by the Bank of Japan. From December 1976 to May 1978, dollar reserves held by the Bank of Japan rose from $13.8 billion to $25.1 billion (see Table 4) – about 81 per cent! From the ordinary working of the world dollar standard, the U.S. Federal reserve system was passive but certainly gave its approval to the massive interventions by the Bank of Japan to buy dollars and sell yen. In stopping the appreciation of the yen, however, the interventions were largely a failure. Why?

Again taking a purely monetary approach, the chronic upward pressure on the yen reflected an incipient excess supply of dollars and excess demand for yen, both of which could be expressed in terms of the reserve money base of the two banking systems –

239

column (1) in Table 4 and in Table 5. In the interbank trading that is the heart of the foreign exchange market, these excess demands and supplies are claims on the two central banks – the ultimate means of payment within each country. Hence, for the intervention in the foreign exchange market to be 'equilibrating' it must succeed in eliminating the excess demand for high-powered yen in terms of high-powered dollars. The straight forward solution

Table 4: Japanese Monetary Indicators
(end of period, billions of yen).

	(1) Central Bank Reserve Money	(2) M_1: Currency and Demand Deposits	(3) M_2: (2) + Time Deposits	(4) Exchange Reserves (millions of $.U.S)	(5) Money Market Rates of Interest (period average)
1976 (Dec)	16,132	56,179	142,248	13,883	7.11
1977 Jan	14,186	52,295	139,132	13,792	7·00
Feb	14,492	52,138	139,423	14,137	7.00
Mar	15,016	54,584	142,349	14,313	6·69
April	14,495	53,452	143,039	14,614	5.87
May	14,177	53,291	143,959	14,509	5.18
June	14,905	54,973	147,143	14,652	5.48
July	15,070	55,407	148,675	14,953	4.66
Aug	14,562	53,147	147,123	15,128	5.57
Sept	14,564	53,192	148,910	15,243	4.98
Oct	14,403	53,534	148,854	16,914	4.92
Nov	14,699	56,406	151,903	19,475	4.62
Dec	17,481	60,786	158,032	20,126	5.01
% Change 1977	8.4%	8.2%	11.1%	50.0%	
1978 Jan	15,006	56,122	154,040	20,654	4.79
Feb	15,378	56,179	154,040	21,435	4.80
Mar	16,086	58,814	157,331	26,431	4.62
April	15,685	59,411	161,166	24,919	4.14
May	15,629	59,632	161,040	25,140	4.06
% Change from May 1977 to May 1978	10.2%	11.9%	11.9%	73.3%	
June	16,499	61,462	165,075	24,747	4.11
July	16,348	60,434	165,488	26,762	4.44
Aug					4.39

Source: IMF *International Financial Statistics* (various issues).

240

is to have the reserve money base in yen in Japan expanding relative to its dollar equivalent in the United States.

Ambiguity is difficult to avoid in making statistical comparison between the two countries. However, the American monetary base expanded somewhat faster: from May 1977 to May 1978 the American reserve base expanded 13.0 per cent where the Japanese base increased by 10.2 per cent.[13] Because American *money* GNP was expanding slightly more slowly than the Japanese, taken at

Table 5: United States Monetary Indicators
(end of period, billions of dollars).

	(1) Central Bank Reserve Money	*(2)* M_1: Currency + Demand Deposits	*(3)* M_2: *(2)* + Time Deposits	*(4)* Money Market Rates of Interest[1] (*period average*)
1976 (Dec.)	118.9	319.2	796.6	4.65
1977 Jan	120.7	294.3	772.7	4.61
Feb	120.7	203.3	775.7	4.68
Mar	120.4	297.7	788.4	4 69
April	122.7	301.9	789.0	4.73
May	119.6	298.0	791.1	5.35
June	121.3	312.1	808.9	5.39
July	124.3	307.4	806.2	5.42
Aug	126.1	313.4	816.3	5.90
Sept	127.9	305.8	812.5	6.14
Oct	127.2	317.3	832.8	6.47
Nov	128.2	325.9	846.7	6.51
Dec	130.7	345.5	875.3	6.56
% *Change 1977*	*9.9%*	*8.2%*	*9.9%*	
1978 Jan	128.1	318.3	849.1	6.70
Feb	134.2	315.6	851.2	6.78
Mar	133.0	319.8	867.0	6.79
April	131.8	329.7	876.7	6.89
May	135.1	333.0	888.5	7.36
% *Change from May 1977 to May 1978*	*13.0%*	*11.7%*	*12.3%*	
June	134.2	335.6	895.1	7.60
July	130.6	331.9	893.3	7.81
Aug	137.2	331.6	897.2	8.04

[1]. Federal Funds Rate.

Source: *International Financial Statistics* (various issues).

face value these figures indicate that American monetary policy was slightly more expansive than that of the Bank of Japan. However, mutual adjustment requires that American monetary policy be *actively* more contradictory if one starts 1977 from a position of an incipient excess supply of dollars.

But why didn't the massive interventions in the foreign exchanges by the Bank of Japan cause both domestic monetary bases to adjust more appropriately? After all, yen were injected into the system and dollars removed.

Consider the Japanese side first. The foreign exchange component of the monetary base (assets of the central bank) has historically been about one third of the total base. Why wasn't such a massive injection of yen through this one component enough to increase the total base more sharply? If dollar reserves increased by 50 per cent in 1977, this alone should increase the monetary base in Japan by 16 or 17 per cent. However, the actual increase in the Japanese monetary base during 1977 was only 8.4 per cent. This acquisition of foreign exchange by the Bank of Japan was largely sterilized by a sharp fall in an important domestic component of the base: central bank claims on commercial banks. Unlike the United States, in the past the Japanese monetary base has expanded by the commercial banks borrowing reserves from the Bank of Japan rather heavily. However, in the depressed business environment in Japan in 1977–78 with limited domestic demand for loans and low rates of interest, the Japanese commercial banks found themselves with excess reserves. Hence, as even more reserves were injected into the system through the foreign exchange market, the commercial banks simply repaid their old borrowing. Thus, sterilization of much of the impact of foreign exchange intervention on the yen monetary base was largely *automatic*, although some could be due to discretionary policy by the Bank of Japan. But the sterilization was nonetheless real if non-discretionary.

On the American side, we have the normal workings of the dollar standard. Foreign central banks are responsible for foreign-exchange stabilization by intervening in terms of the common intervention or 'Nth' currency – the U.S. dollar. And passivity on the part of the United States is necessary to avoid conflict if the other N-1 countries have independent foreign exchange policies. But the acquisition of 'dollars' by foreign central banks is not American base money, rather all dollar bank accounts are quickly switched into U.S. Treasury bonds or bills.[14] Therefore no symmetrical contraction occurs in the U.S. banking system even if

242

monetary expansion is occuring abroad as a result of foreign-exchange interventions – as it did in a massive way in 1971 and again in 1973. All that happens is that the issue of non-monetary debt by the U.S. Treasury becomes much easier.

Should we be worried about this difference in domestic monetary adjustment in Japan (and other countries) in comparison to the United States? For the most part, no. This monetary asymmetry reflects the workings of the informal dollar standard where a hundred or more central banks throughout the world buy or sell dollars for their own national currencies. The United States would be foolish to allow its monetary base to be affected by what the Chilean, Indian, Kuwaiti and most other governments might do in their day-to-day foreign exchange operations. If American monetary policy itself is quite stable – as it was during the 1950s and early 1960s – the asymmetry places no substantial burden of adjustment on other countries.

However, if American monetary (and fiscal) policy is unstable as has been the case in recent years, more American responsiveness to certain kinds of foreign-exchange transactions would seem warranted. Indeed, the foreign exchanges may contain valuable information that would enable the American authorities to do a better job of short-run monetary control – as we shall see.

The Demise of Short-Term Interest Rates as Suitable Intermediate Targets for Monetary Policy

Emphasizing the automatic character of the domestic sterilization of foreign-exchange interventions helps us to understand the institutional framework in both Japan and the United States within which such destabilizing monetary policies could occur. But surely both the Federal Reserve System and the Bank of Japan are capable of offsetting discretionary action. The Fed could have adjusted its ongoing open-market operations to restrict the growth in the monetary base in the United States. The Bank of Japan could have been more resolute in offsetting the repayment of 'borrowed' reserves by the commercial banks. Nevertheless both central banks were apparently content – indeed convinced they were behaving responsibly – to allow the domestic monetary growth that was inconsistent with a stable foreign-exchange market on the one hand, and consistent with recession in Japan and inflation in the United States on the other.

I submit that an important part of the explanation is the 'unusual' behavior of short-term rates of interest in both countries. From

243

column (5) in Table 4, the Japanese interbank call-money rate fell from 7.1 per cent to about 4.1 per cent during December 1976 to June 1978. In the United States, the federal funds rate increased from about 4.6 to 7.6 per cent – column 4 in Table 5. Not only are these interest-rate movements large in absolute terms from the point of view of either country, but the change of 6 percentage points in the spread is striking. And, of course from the interest-rate parity theorem, the forward premium on the yen has shifted to reflect the new spread: it was about 4 per cent in June of 1978 and by September 1978 had shifted upwards to about $5\frac{1}{2}$ per cent per year. This differential between short-term rates of interest is consistent with the view that the 'market' firmly expected the yen to continue to appreciate for a year or so into 1979. (The differential between long-term rates of interest in both countries is much less.)

Monetary authorities in each country often treat short-term rates of interest as intermediate target variables – virtually policy instruments in of themselves. When short-term interest rates are high or rising, this indicates that money is tight or tightening. Similarly, a sharp fall in short-term rates to unusually low levels indicates excess liquidity in the domestic money market. This is the traditional *modus operandi* for monetary authorities throughout recent history. While predating Keynes, it is fully consistent with the Keynesian theory of liquidity preference. No wonder American officials believed they have been following a tight money policy or one of restraint, and Japanese monetary authorities have felt that they were doing their best to be expansionary!

Unfortunately, the underlying model the authorities were implicitly using requires one of the following:

(i) that the economy is completely closed to international flows of private financial capital including trade credit,

(ii) or that the economy is so large that foreign monetary conditions – including exchange-rate movements – can be ignored,

(iii) or that there exists a stable exchange rate bracketed by at most a modest band, within which the market continually expects the exchange rate to regress toward the middle of the band.[15]

While conditions (i) or (iii) were approximately true for Japan in some parts of the postwar period, and conditions (ii) or (iii) applied to the United States, none of the three apply to either country at the present time. Instead, we have open economies with floating exchange rates, about which expectations are in state of flux.

In 1978 the market's projection of a continued decline of the dollar against the yen (and against many European countries) imparted a strong Fisher effect into short-term rates of interest in both countries and some in Western Europe. Expected dollar depreciation has, through outflows of private capital into interest-bearing assets abroad, forced American short-term rates upwards. These higher interest rates in the U.S. money market, coupled with the expected dollar depreciation, reduce the demand for money – particularly non-interest bearing base money – in the United States. This excess dollar liquidity is what causes the dollar to actually fall against the yen. However, instead of taking this fall in the dollar as a signal that there is excess liquidity in the American money market, the authorities look at the higher short-term rates of interest and decide that money is 'tight'! Because the authorities take the wrong signal, they fail to move resolutely to remove the excess liquidity – which of course perpetuates the dollar's decline. A wild swing in the exchange rate becomes self-sustaining.

The same scenario can be portrayed in terms of the institutional mechanism in the United States for actually determining monetary policy – the supply of base money – in the very short run of days or weeks. Although nominally committed to a Friedman rule that limits the growth in the money supply – say to between 6 and 8 per cent per year for M_1 – the authorities cannot accurately calculate what M_1 is at any point in time until many weeks after the event. Thus the accepted operating procedure of the Federal Open Market Committee (FOMC) is to choose a very short-run rate of interest – currently that on federal funds – as the proximate target.

Suppose that the target is 8 per cent for any reason, and initially the American money market is in equilibrium at that rate. Now suppose there is a scare in the foreign exchange market: a flight from the dollar. The resulting incipient upward pressure on money market rates of interest will then induce the FOMC to *buy* U.S. Treasury bills, and thus expand reserve money in the system, in order to prevent short-run rates from rising above 8 per cent! The money supply then expands faster than that warranted by a Friedman rule – putting more pressure on the foreign exchange market. In a few weeks authorities become nervous about the excessive monetary expansion and raise the interest target slightly to, say, $8\frac{1}{4}$ per cent. This is insufficient to forestall upward pressure on interest rates from expected exchange depreciation, and monetary expansion again occurs with another upward ratchet in short-run interest rates.

Probably the inverse of this story can be told for the Japanese money market for 1977–78, with interest rates moving downward.

Clearly, it becomes necessary to abandon monetary policy based on short-term rates of interest when Fisher effects, incorporating expected exchange-rate changes, dominate. But what should replace it? Getting the correct signals for the execution of short-run monetary policy is not a trivial matter. And the problem is particularly acute now that American monetary policy is unstable, and the confidence of the general public in the Federal Reserve's commitment to stable money has been eroded.

Clearly exchange rates themselves are potential indicators for short-run policy. A country could seek out trading partners whose price levels are known to be more stable, and then make an effort to stabilize their exchange rates through appropriately adjusting the domestic monetary base to foreign-exchange intervention. In particular, suppose the dollar drops sharply in the foreign exchange markets against major trading partners such as Germany and Japan which have stable monetary systems. This drop reflects an excess supply of dollars in the United States, or an excess demand for yen or Deutsche marks in Japan or Germany. If central banks intervene to prevent the dollar from falling, then *mutual adjustment* in the domestic bases of the two countries involved is indicated.

The foreign exchange markets have also provided useful information for the American authorities in other historical periods – information they have chosen to ignore. Prior to the breakdown in August of 1971 of the Bretton Woods fixed parities, and the further breakdown in March 1973 of the Smithsonian Agreements, large deficits occurred in the American balance of payments. Foreign central banks bought dollars in vast quantities and converted them into U.S. Treasury securities early in 1971 and late in 1972. In neither period, did the American Federal Reserve allow the U.S. monetary base to contract, although in retrospect it appears as if the United States monetary policy was too expansive in early 1971 and again in 1972. Although care must be taken, the state of the foreign-exchange markets may well be a better short-run indicator of ease or tightness in the American money market than is the interest rate on federal funds.

Clearly, the American monetary base should be adjusted in the short run to better accommodate foreign exchange interventions by one or two major trading partners. And the economic importance of Japan and Germany, with governments that are stable and friendly, makes them candidates for closer monetary co-operation with the United States.[16]

In the long run, however, the United States, Japan or Germany are probably better off following consistent Friedman rules delimiting their rates of monetary expansion. Because the United States is now on a higher inflation path than either of her two major trading partners, American monetary expansion from one year to the next is likely to be somewhat higher, thus necessitating some net depreciation of the dollar of a few percentage points per year against the yen and Deutsche mark. However, the authorities can still make a rough calculation in any one month of that exchange rate consistent with purchasing power parity. Then the wild swings in the dollar/yen or dollar/DM exchange rates, experienced since 1973, could easily be dampened provided that short-run interventions by central banks are accompanied by symmetrical adjustments in their respective monetary bases. No longer would we have the spectacle of central banks intervening 'unsuccessfully', and so further demoralizing the exchange markets. And domestic monetary stability would be enhanced, particularly in the United States where monetary policy in the short run seems to be without an effective guiding principle.

Postscript

This paper was completed before President Carter's dramatic announcement on November 1, 1978 of a major new program to stabilize the foreign exchange value of the dollar. If sustained, such a program is obviously consistent with the policies advocated above, and represents a sharp departure from American monetary policies that had been followed hitherto.

Besides massive intervention in the foreign exchange market, however, it remains to be seen whether the American government will make the necessary supporting adjustments in domestic monetary policy:

(1) to allow the U.S. monetary base to change *pari passu* with any interventions that occur. If dollars are purchased with, say, yen, the American monetary base should contract commensurately. Equally important, if yen are repurchased for dollars as the exchange market stabilizes, the American monetary base should expand freely by the amount of the repurchases.

(2) The federal funds rate of interest should now be allowed to 'float' without any official or unofficial target for pegging it. This

means that the day-to-day rule for *domestic* credit expansion by the FOMC should be a small percentage increase in the monetary base, which is directly controllable – unlike M_1 or M_2.

Although in the long run a pure Friedman rule for steady proportional expansion in the American monetary base should be established, the demand for base money in dollars is now (late 1978) too unstable for such a rule to be rigidly imposed. In particular, as foreign exchange dealers and multinational corporations regain their confidence in the dollar (because of the stabilization program), it is important to avoid excessive deflation. The monetary base should expand to satisfy the newly increased demand. But this increased supply of base money need not (should not) come through domestic credit expansion by conventional open market operations. Rather, when an incipient upward pressure on the dollar develops in the foreign exchanges, the Fed can simply repurchase yen, Deutsche marks, Swiss francs etc., and in so doing allow the American monetary base to expand naturally.

NOTES

1. Rather than citing all of Harry Johnson's own voluminous work on the subject, I simply note that his four contributions reprinted in *The Monetary Approach to the Balance of Payments*, edited by Jacob Frenkel and Harry Johnson (1976), were enormously influential.

2. For one of many studies on this point, see Bradford Cornell (1977).

3. As extensively documented by Sven Grassman (1973) and (1976). This is true provided that the home currency is convertible, and changes in exchange rates are not unidirectional or otherwise easily anticipated.

4. Perhaps arising out of experiences with fluctuating exchange rates in the 1920s and 1930s, economists were quite pessimistic about quantity responses to exchange rate changes in the 1940s and early 1950s as reviewed by Arnold Harberger (1957).

5. Economists have disputed the circumstances under which one or another price index is appropriate. (McKinnon 1979, Chapter 6 and Dornbusch and Jaffee *et al.* 1978) Fortunately, in the Japanese–American case for 1977–78, it makes little difference which deflator is used.

6. Non-technical readers can skip the algebra without losing the main thread of the argument.

7. The conditions for the 'normal' effect of an appreciation reducing the trade balance in foreign currency are less stringent if there is a trade deficit

$$\frac{dT_f}{de} = \frac{d\frac{1}{e}T_d}{de} = -\frac{T_d}{e^2} + \frac{dT_d}{de}$$

Clearly if the trade balance deficit is sufficiently large, we get the 'normal' effect of a decrease in $_e$ reducing T_f and vice versa. This asymmetry in the algebra

RONALD I. MCKINNON

between trade deficit and surplus situations arises because the model is incomplete:
the response of trading partners has not been explicitly taken into account. A full
analysis of the conditions for stability in the foreign exchange market leads to
look at the export and import responses from both sides. Even with a more
complex two-country model, however, our qualitative results remain the same.

8. Notice that S_g is not a measure of total government saving. Real capital
accumulation could be tax financed and not appear in S_g. Rather, $-S_g$ is simply
the amount that expenditures for goods and services exceed tax collections.

9. These figures are computed from the *United Nations Statistical Yearbook* (1976).

10. Unlike Japan, a separate series on private investment does appear in the
International Financial Statistics for the United States.

11. See pages 296 to 273 in the *28th Annual Report on Exchange Restrictions*,
International Monetary Fund, Washington, D.C. 1977.

12. We have seen that investment is influenced (distorted) by changes in the
real exchange rate from long-run equilibrium – i.e. by deviations from purchasing
power parity. Establishing 'parity' in the purchasing powers of national monies
eliminates the mercantilistic advantage of producing in country A as opposed
to country B. Thus, parity is important for economic harmony among nations:
to prevent some from unduly inflating and others from being unduly depressed.
The mechanism of inflation and depression, itself, pushes nations toward PPP
in the long run – but in an uncertain and unsteady fashion.

13. It should be noted that such a comparison can be strongly influenced by
seasonal adjustment. If we use December 1976 as the base month (the Christmas
bonus season) it appears as if the Japanese monetary base is 3.2% *lower* whereas
the American monetary base is 13.6% higher as of May 1978.

14. The details of this foreign-exchange intervention under the dollar standard
are nicely laid out in Anatol B. Balbach (1978).

15. In a fully open economy, such regressive expectations are necessary for the
Keynesian theory of liquidity preference to be valid: where high interest rates
indicate tight money and low rates accurately indicate that 'excess' liquidity is
being supplied. For a justification of this view, see McKinnon (1971).

16. A more complete discussion of the issues involved can be found in Ronald
I. McKinnon, 'A New Tripartite Monetary Agreement or a Limping Dollar
Standard?' *Princeton Essays in International Finance*, No. 106, October 1974.

BIBLIOGRAPHY

Aliber, Robert, 'The Firm under Pegged and Floating Exchange Rates', *The
Scandinavian Journal of Economics*, Vol. 78, No. 2, 1976.
Balbach, Anatol B., 'The Mechanics of Intervention in Exchange Markets',
Federal Reserve Bank of St. Louis, *Review*, February 1978.
Cornell, Bradford, 'Spot Rates, Forward rates and Exchange Market Efficiency',
Journal of Financial Economics 5, 1977.
Dornbusch, Rudiger, 'Real and Monetary Aspects of the Effects of Exchange-
Rate Changes', pp. 64–81 in *National Monetary Policies and the International
Financial System*, edited by Robert Z. Aliber, University of Chicago Press, 1974.
Dornbusch, R. and Jaffee, D. *et al.*, 'Purchasing Power Parity: A Symposium',
Journal of International Economics, Vol. 8, May 1978.
Frenkel, Jacob A. and Henry G. Johnson, *The Monetary Approach to the Balance
of Payments*, George Allen and Unwin, 1976.

EXCHANGE-RATE INSTABILITY, ETC. IN JAPAN AND THE U.S.A.

Grassman, Sven, 'A Fundamental Symmetry in International Payments Patterns', *Journal of International Economics*, May 1973.
Grassman, Sven, 'Currency Distribution and Forward Cover in Foreign Trade: Sweden Revisited', *Journal of International Economics*, May 1976.
Harberger, A. C., 'Some Evidence on the International Price Mechanism', *Journal of Political Economy*, Vol. 65, 1957.
IMF, International Financial Statistics (various issues).
IMF, *28th Annual Report on Exchange Restrictions*, 1977.
Isard, P., 'How Far Can We Push the Law of One Price?', *American Economic Review*, December 1977.
Magee, S. P., 'Currency Contracts, Pass Through, and Devaluation', *Brookings Papers on Economic Activity*, 1, 1973.
McKinnon, Ronald I., 'Monetary Theory and Controlled Flexibility in the Foreign Exchanges', Princeton *Essay in International Finance*, No. 84, April 1971.
McKinnon, Ronald I., 'A New Tripartite Agreement or a Limping Dollar Standard?', Princeton *Essays in International Finance*, No. 106, October 1974.
McKinnon, Ronald I., *Money in International Exchange: The Convertible Currency System*, Oxford University Press, 1979.
Salter, W. E., 'Internal and External Balance: The Role of Price and Expenditure Effects', *Economic Record* 36, March 1960.
United Nations Statistical Yearbook 1976, 1977.

APPRECIATION AND THE TRADE BALANCE: A COMMENT

W. M. Corden

McKinnon has an interesting and novel argument suggesting that an appreciation of the yen tends to *improve*, rather than worsen, the Japanese trade balance. This is additional to any possible J-curve effect. It may help to put this new argument into the broader perspective of standard devaluation (or upvaluation) theory. I shall be taxonomic.

(1) One might assume that fiscal and monetary policies keep Japanese absorption (expenditures in real terms on domestic and foreign goods and services combined) constant. An exchange rate appreciation will tend to switch expenditure away from Japanese goods, and hence worsen the current account as well as decrease demand for Japanese goods, the extent of this effect depending on the relevant elasticities. Of course, if the terms of trade improve the current account may improve, the J-curve effect being a special case of this.

(2) One might assume that fiscal and monetary policies in Japan are so manipulated as to maintain a constant level of demand for Japanese goods and services. In this case the appreciation of the exchange rate would be associated with an expansion of absorption, which would reinforce the adverse direct effect of the appreciation on the current account.

(3) Finally, one might assume that absorption is endogenous, being neither kept constant (as in the first case) nor manipulated to maintain a constant level of demand for Japanese goods (as in the second case) but rather varying endogenously in response to the appreciation. Here one can have various sub-cases, McKinnon's being one of them.

(i) Policy might keep the nominal money supply constant. Appreciation lowers the average domestic price level, hence raises the real money supply, and will thus lead to some increase in absorption and deterioration in the current account additional to the direct switching effect of the appreciation. This effect would be temporary if the balance-of-payments deficit were allowed to reduce the nominal money supply (as in models of the monetary approach to balance-of-payments theory).

(ii) Another sub-case can be derived from a model which, I think, originated with Diaz–Alejandro. Appreciation raises real wages and reduces profits (assuming that non-tradeables are labour-intensive relative to tradeables, or some similar assumption). Supposing that the marginal propensity to save out of profits is higher than out of wages, that these propensities are not affected by the change in the average price-level, and that investment remains unchanged, absorption will then rise owing to the shift in income distribution towards wages. This will have an adverse effect on the current account, as in the earlier cases I have described.

(iii) Finally, there is the McKinnon sub-case which is a mirror image of the Diaz–Alejandro case. Appreciation causes profits in tradeables to fall – in the Japanese case, the relevant effect being the adverse effect on expected profits in export industries. This will reduce investment, which *reduces* absorption and improves the current account, possibly offsetting the direct effect of appreciation in worsening the current account. In this manner McKinnon's paradoxical result is obtained. The income distribution effect lowers absorption, rather than raising it, as in the Diaz–Alejandro case.

The special features of this part of the McKinnon story appear to involve the following aspects. (a) The adverse effect on investment of the fall in profits of industries producing tradeables is not offset by a rise in investment in non-tradeables owing to an increase in profits there. This might be regarded as plausible if one bears in mind that a substantial part of non-tradeables would be publicly produced or would be labour-intensive (services). (b) The rise in real wages due to the appreciation does not lead to an offsetting or more than offsetting increase in spending out of wage income. One would have to allow for lagged effects here and would have to provide explanations for the high Japanese household savings ratio. Is the negative effect on investment spending really greater than the positive effect on consumption spending, allowing time for adjustment? (c) Finally, Japan-

252

ese fiscal and monetary policies are passive, allowing absorption to be endogenous rather than manipulating absorption so as to obtain desired levels of demand for Japanese goods and services.

McKinnon has clearly drawn attention to an interesting possible relationship, though he would agree that it only represents part of the story.

McKinnon's paper suggests that, to some extent, yen appreciation has determined the Japanese current account surplus, rather than the other way round. I would not rule out some role for the J-curve effect and for the adverse effect of appreciation on investment outlined above, but it seems to me that the main story has to go the other way: the surplus has determined the appreciation. For various, essentially domestic, reasons, the United States has had a higher rate of real demand (absorption) expansion than Japan, or there have been certain structural factors, all of which have yielded a Japanese surplus and dollar deficit at a constant real exchange rate. In addition, American prices have lately risen faster than Japanese prices, so that nominal appreciation of the yen relative to the dollar has been required to maintain even a constant real yen-dollar rate. Anyway, various underlying factors, domestic in origin, have produced the current account imbalances, not compensated by private capital movements, and have given rise to the yen appreciation not just in nominal but in real terms. Relatively slow absorption growth in Japan (combined with structural changes) caused the yen appreciation – clearly a desirable adjustment – even though the appreciation itself may possibly have had some effects on absorption along one of the lines discussed above.

Finally, let me turn to one of the central themes of the paper, with which I wholly agree. In all the OECD countries the private sector is in financial surplus and the public sector in financial deficit. In some countries the private surplus exceeds the public deficit, notably in Japan, while there are others – notably the United States – where the private surplus is less than the public deficit. Is there anything wrong with this situation? Some countries are net financial borrowers and some net lenders, and these relationships change over time. One can take the view that private savers and investors in each country, and governments, can and should make their own decisions, taking into account a variety of domestic considerations as well as the interest rates prevalent on world markets (which ought to influence domestic interest rates). Governments can be intermediaries in this process, as in the case of Japan : net private hoarding in Japan partly finances the huge Japanese fiscal deficit and partly ends up as additional

253

claims on non-residents, mainly in the form of additions to official reserves – i.e. lending abroad by the Japanese government. Whether this situation is the norm, as McKinnon suggests, depends on whether the exceptionally high household savings ratio in Japan is here to stay, or is a transitional phenomenon, and whether an even bigger fiscal deficit is not possible and likely.

Chapter Thirteen

PURCHASING-POWER PARITY UNDER FLEXIBLE RATES

Jürg Niehans

THE DOCTRINE of purchasing-power parity postulates an intimate relationship between the rate of exchange between any two currencies and their purchasing power in terms of goods and services. Its basic idea goes back at least to the Ricardian period.[1] It was fully articulated as an economic doctrine by Gustav Cassel (1916, 1918, 1921, 1925) more than half a century ago. With the advent of generally floating exchange rates it has found renewed interest, reflected in critical surveys.[2] Nevertheless, current literature gives the impression that its economic meaning is not much clearer than it was fifty years ago. The present paper tries to give a concise, non-technical, but comprehensive survey of the doctrine, its economic meaning, its limitations and its possible policy applications, under floating exchange rates.

1. The Common Sense of Purchasing-Power Parity

The PPP-doctrine postulates that the exchange rate between two countries is proportionate (but not necessarily equal) to their relative commodity prices. This can be formalized by writing

$$
(1) \qquad\qquad e = k \frac{P_1}{P_2},
$$

where e is the price of currency 2 in terms of currency 1, P_1 and P_2 are the local-currency values of a given market basket in, respectively, country 1 and country 2, and k is a constant.[3] Cassel (for example, 1925, p. 104) emphasized that k, reflecting transport costs, tariffs and other non-monetary factors, will generally differ from 1. He regarded it as impossible for economic theory to determine k. Today we would say that k depends on all the 'real' factors behind the international division of labor.

In terms of percentage changes, the PPP-doctrine becomes

(2)
$$\frac{de}{e} = \frac{dP_1}{P_1} - \frac{dP_2}{P_2},$$

where on the right there appears the difference between two price index numbers. However, the PPP-relationship is not claimed to hold, and k is not claimed to be constant, under all circumstances. In fact, it is only claimed to hold, and k is only claimed to be constant, with respect to one particular set of underlying causes, namely changes in the money supplies. Suppose the quantity theory of money (or, more exactly, of prices) is valid in each country. With respect to commodity prices this means that

(3)
$$\frac{dP_1}{P_1} = \frac{dM_1}{M_1} \text{ and } \frac{dP_2}{P_2} = \frac{dM_2}{M_2}.$$

With respect to exchange rates it means that the price of currency 2 in country 1 also moves in proportion to M_1, while the price of currency 1 in country 2 moves in proportion to M_2, whence

(4)
$$\frac{de}{e} = \frac{dM_1}{M_1} - \frac{dM_2}{M_2}.$$

The PPP-proposition is thus established as a simple corollary of the quantity theory. It essentially says that the money supply affects the price of foreign exchange in the same way as other prices.

Not surprisingly, the PPP-principle is subject to the same qualifications as the quantity theory. There are, in particular, four such qualifications. (1) The principle is valid *ceteris paribus* in the sense that changes in tastes and technology are abstracted from. In reality, of course, such 'real' changes are usually present. In general, therefore, PPP does not provide a total explanation of exchange rate fluctuations, but only an explanation of the partial effects of money supply changes. (2) The PPP-principle applies to fiat money exogenously supplied by the government. It would not be strictly valid, for example, under a gold standard, where the purchasing power of money, in the last analysis, depends on the production costs in gold mining relative to other industries, while the quantity of money is endogenous.[4] (3) The principle presupposes that money is the only asset exogenously supplied by the government. In the presence of government debt it requires that the latter be expanded or contracted in proportion with the money supply. (4) The proposition applies to prices and exchange rates in full stock/flow equilibrium after all temporary adjustments have run their course.

This is what may be called the common sense of PPP. It is clearly a meaningful proposition in the sense that it is not tautological and may conceivably be false. It is also a proposition whose validity seems to be beyond serious doubt. At the same time, because of its very straightforwardness and simplicity, it is not very exciting. However, economists have little reason to disdain true propositions just because they are simple. Despite its simplicity, the PPP-proposition was exposed to many misunderstandings, and most of these, though often exploded, leave their traces even in recent contributions.

The most common misunderstanding interprets PPP as an international implication of the 'law of one price' according to which goods, traded internationally without transportation costs and trade impediments, have the same price in different countries. This arbitrage argument leads to what became known as the 'absolute' PPP-doctrine according to which $k = 1$, so that a given currency, if converted at the current exchange rate, buys the same basket of goods in different countries.[5] About this interpretation of PPP Samuelson (1964) seems to have said whatever there is to say. It is either trivial (to the extent it is applied to costlessly-traded goods) or wrong (to the extent it is applied to other goods) and in any case irrelevant (inasmuch as PPP in the quantity theory sense does not depend on it).[6]

A second misunderstanding shows up in the ongoing discussion about the appropriate choice of price indices. From the underlying theory it is clear that, in principle, this choice does not matter, provided the index number is not restricted to costlessly-traded goods. It must not be thus restricted because for such goods PPP would appear to be valid even if the underlying monetary theory were false; a test of mere arbitrage would be misinterpreted as a test of PPP. With respect to non-traded or not-costlessly-traded goods the choice of an index number does not matter because, according to the quantity theory, *each individual price* varies in proportion to the money supply, leaving relative prices unchanged.[7]

A third source of confusion has to do with the causal interpretation of PPP. The latter is often alleged to maintain that the effect of prices on the exchange rate is stronger than the reverse effect of the exchange rate on prices. In fact, PPP does not imply a causal relationship in either direction, but an association between endogenous variables jointly influenced by a common cause, namely monetary changes. Since exchange rates will usually react more promptly to monetary changes than domestic commodity prices, a casual '*post hoc ergo propter hoc*' argument may easily lead to the erroneous conclusion that exchange rate changes are the cause of price changes rather than the other way around (see Frenkel, 1978).

Fourth, the PPP-doctrine does not imply that in the course of economic history exchange rates are expected to move parallel to relative commodity prices. As a matter of historical fact, tastes and technology, and thus k, are constantly changing, and these real changes influence exchange rates just as well as the monetary factors. Just as a divergence between national price levels and the money supply in the course of time does not, in itself, invalidate the quantity theory, so a divergence between time series of an exchange rate and the respective price ratios does not necessarily invalidate PPP.[8] Much of the so-called testing of PPP is thus besides the point.[9]

A fifth, and final, misunderstanding is the notion that PPP is supposed to apply to short-run changes in exchange rates. This is clearly not so; just like the underlying quantity theory PPP is a long-run relationship, claimed to be valid in full equilibrium. That commodity prices react to changes in monetary policy with a considerable lag is the basic proposition of monetary dynamics. It is the fundamental reason why monetary policy has real, if temporary, effects on the economy. During the adjustment period, which may last for years, exchange rates would be expected to deviate from PPP, perhaps strongly. The following sections will trace this adjustment process through its successive stages.

2. Instantaneous Overshooting

Cassel (1921) realized that static PPP may take a long time to be attained and that, in the meantime, the exchange rate would 'overshoot' with powerful effects on the economies concerned (see also Haberler, 1933, p. 48f.). His analysis reads strikingly modern today and it was not improved upon before 1975. The present section concentrates on the instantaneous aspects of overshooting which manifest themselves so-to-say overnight, before commodity prices, output and trade flows have had time to react. A pure asset approach is thus appropriate, showing how asset prices (and thus interest yields and exchange rates) have to adjust so that the given stocks of assets are willingly held despite the change in monetary policy. This problem has been extensively analysed by Girton and Henderson (1977) and the following account is largely a summary of their contribution. The exposition in the present section is based on the case of a once-over

258

change in the exogenous supply of financial assets in a stationary economy. As a consequence, expected inflation is zero throughout.

We may assume that the private sector, including both domestic and foreign individuals and firms, holds four assets, namely domestic cash balances, foreign cash balances, domestic bonds, and foreign bonds, where the last two are assumed to be imperfect substitutes. By virtue of the wealth constraint the demand for foreign cash balances may be regarded as implied in the demand functions for the remaining assets. The demand for each asset depends on the domestic interest rate, the foreign interest rate and the exchange rate. The domestic interest rate has a positive effect on the demand for domestic bonds, but a negative effect on the demand for domestic cash balances and foreign bonds. The foreign interest rate has a positive effect on foreign bonds, but a negative effect on domestic bonds and money.

While the interest effects are clear enough, the influence of the exchange rate requires perhaps a word of explanation. In particular, it must be realized that the *level* of the exchange rate exerts its instantaneous influence on the asset demands through its effect on the expected *change* in the exchange rate. Specifically, for given exchange rate expectations a higher current level of the exchange rate is associated with an expected future decline (or a reduced increase) and thus an expected capital loss on foreign money and bonds. A lower level of the exchange rate, on the other hand, is associated with an expected capital gain (or a reduced capital loss) on foreign assets. As a consequence, the level of the exchange rate has a positive effect on domestic money and bonds, but a negative effect on foreign assets.

At each instant, the two interest rates and the exchange rate move in such a way that the demand for each asset is equal to the respective supply as determined by the central bank. At the expense of an additional simplification this mechanism can be visualized graphically. The simplification consists in the assumption that the foreign central bank keeps the foreign interest rate constant by suitable open-market operations in foreign currency. We are thus left with the interplay of supply and demand for domestic money and domestic bonds jointly determining the domestic interest rate and the exchange rate. In figure 1, the M-curve connects all those combinations of an interest rate and an exchange rate that keep the demand for money equal to the supply; in view of the opposite influences of the two determinants it is upward-sloping. The B-curve, on the other hand, connects those points that provide equilibrium between the supply and demand for bonds; since both arguments have a positive effect, it is downward-sloping. Equilibrium will be attained where the two curves intersect.

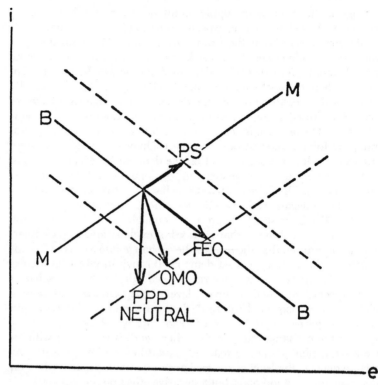

Figure 1. Instantaneous Effects of Monetary Policy.

The effects of different monetary policies can now be determined by considering the corresponding shifts in the two curves as indicated by the arrows in figure 1. Since commodity prices cannot change overnight, each change in the exchange rate indicates a corresponding deviation from PPP. Foreign exchange operations (FEO) and open market operations (OMO) affect the exchange rate and the rate of interest in the same direction, but the first has a stronger effect on the exchange rate, while the second has a stronger effect on the rate of interest. This means that a mere portfolio shift (PS), defined as a shift between foreign and domestic securities of the central bank at an unchanged money supply, can also be used to affect both the exchange rate and the rate of interest. By combining operations in foreign and domestic securities at appropriate levels, a desired effect on the exchange rate can be combined with various desired interest effects. In

260

particular, it would be possible, in principle, for the central bank to lower the domestic interest rate without any instantaneous effect on the exchange rate, as indicated by the vertical arrow, and thus without an instantaneous deviation from PPP.

From the point of view of minimizing the foreign disturbances resulting from domestic monetary policy it may thus be important for the central bank to have at its disposal two monetary instruments with different comparative advantages. A mathematical check would show that all of these conclusions remain valid even if the foreign central bank does not fix the level of foreign interest rates.

3. Short-Term Output and Trade Effects

While the instantaneous effects of monetary policy are restricted to asset prices, these, in term, will rapidly begin to affect the flows of trade, production and consumption. Actually, since the instantaneous adjustment depends crucially on the expected future course of the exchange rate, these flow effects are important, if indirect, determinants even of the instantaneous asset adjustment. Ideally, the instantaneous stock adjustment and the short-term output and trade effects should thus be described by the same model.

For the purpose of the present section it is instructive to change the assumption about the underlying monetary policy in two respects. First, it will now be assumed that there is no government debt, so that monetary policy is neutral (and PPP holds) in full equilibrium. Second, the initial disturbance is assumed to be a shift from a stationary money supply to a positive rate of monetary expansion. As a consequence, there is no instantaneous change in the quantity of assets. The question is, how the economy will react to such a change in policy.

The answer can be given in terms of figure 2. Suppose at a certain moment T the central bank switches from a non-inflationary policy to a course of steady monetary expansion as expressed by the M-curve (note that the upper part of the graph is in logarithmic terms). The instantaneous effect, most lucidly analysed by Dornbusch (1976c), will be a pronounced, if temporary, undervaluation of the currency relative to PPP as reflected in the instantaneous rise of the e-curve above the p-curve. This is due to three reasons. First, domestic prices typically lag behind the expansion of the money supply, as expressed by the deviation of the p-curve from the M-curve. Even if the exchange rate just followed the money supply, the temporary rigidity of nontraded-goods prices would thus result in the overshooting relative to PPP. Second, the equilibrium price path $\bar{p}$ shifts upward relative

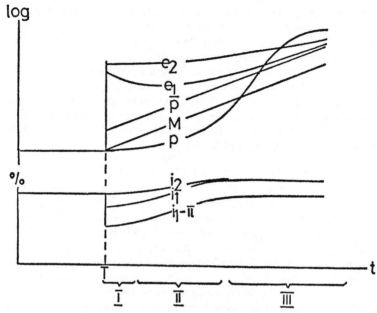

Figure 2. The Short-Run Adjustment Path.

to the money supply because with expected inflation the demand for real balances is reduced; this reduction in the demand for real balances will be reflected in an additional increase in the price of foreign exchange.[10] Third, the decline in the real rate of interest, due to a marked initial decline in the nominal rate (i) relative to expected inflation (π) as pictured in the lower part of figure 2, can only be reconciled with the given asset supplies if the real exchange rate is expected to decline. This, in turn, requires an initial rise of the nominal exchange rate beyond the $\bar{p}$-curve, to which it will eventually gravitate.

The instantaneous undervaluation of the currency relative to PPP involves overshooting of the exchange rate in at least one sense and possibly two. Since the domestic real interest rate declines instantaneously relative to the foreign real rate, asset market equilibrium certainly requires an instantaneous overshooting of the exchange rate relative to its equilibrium path $\bar{p}$. A relative decline in the *real* rate of interest thus results in an overshooting, and thus an expected decline, in the *real* exchange rate.[11] In addition, the *nominal* exchange rate may (see the e_1-curve) or may not (see the e_2-curve) overshoot depend-

262

ing on whether the *nominal* interest rate exhibits an initial decline. If there is no initial decline in the nominal interest rate, a real undervaluation of the currency will be associated with nominal overvaluation. Of course, with continuing inflation the future exchange rate will, sooner or later, inevitably catch up with the present exchange rate, no matter how much the latter may overshoot.

When this instantaneous overshooting occurs, the violent fluctuations of the exchange rate, far exceeding anything that seems to be justified by the underlying 'real' factors, may appear to have lost any 'rational' basis, being at the mercy of 'irrational' speculators. It may thus be worth pointing out that, once an unexpected change in monetary policy has taken place, such overshooting is compatible with perfectly rational portfolio adjustments under correct expectations about the future course of yields and exchange rates. There are no unexploited profit opportunities, as the expected changes in exchange rates simply compensate for the interest differential. Capital flows, furthermore, will be stabilizing at the margin in the sense that any further increase in the current exchange rate would trigger a capital inflow.

The instantaneous asset effects are followed by output effects. The basic reason for these output effects is the slow adjustment of the prices of current output, represented in figure 2 by the p-curve, with the associated fluctuations in real interest rates. For a closed economy, the sequence of events is now fairly well understood. In the beginning, real interest rates are low. After a while, output begins to rise beyond its normal level while prices still remain fairly stable. Later, however, nominal interest rates will catch up with the expected rate of inflation, output declines in apparent 'stagflation', while prices begin to rise more rapidly. The question is how this sequence of events is modified in an open economy through floating rates.

At the present time, this question can only be answered in a tentative, conjectural and incomplete way.[12] It seems that the likely sequence of events can be divided into three phases (see figure 2). In each phase, and indeed for any period, the exchange rate must be such that the net capital outflow (inflow), called forth as the net effect of a relatively low rate of real interest and the expected appreciation of the real exchange rate, is just matched by the trade surplus (deficit), called forth as the combined effect of prices and domestic income. The stages differ in the way this equality is achieved.

At first, there is likely to be a *perverse phase*, essentially due to the familiar J-effect, where the quantities of traded goods seem impervious to the depreciation of the currency, so that the trade balance in

263

value terms may actually deteriorate. As a consequence, the over-shooting of the exchange rate will have to be strong enough to attract a net capital inflow despite the decline in the real interest rate. This capital inflow will help to finance domestic investment stimulated by the monetary expansion, but the domestic expansion will also be somewhat weakened compared to a closed economy.[13]

In the second phase, the higher price of foreign currency will gradually attract additional resources into the production of traded goods, producing a trade surplus. The overshooting of the exchange rate will thereby be attenuated to such an extent that the low level of real interest rates can now call forth a matching outflow of capital; foreign assets will thus build up. This is the expansionary phase, where the effects of monetary policy are strengthened by the flexibility of the exchange rate. Clearly, this phase cannot last forever. While the exchange rate, and thus the price of traded goods, decline from their peak levels or continue to rise at a retarded pace, the increase in the demand relative to the supply of nontraded goods will drive up their price. This, together with the increase in domestic demand, will eventually reach a point where the export surplus disappears. This also means that the real rate of interest has caught up with the expected decline in the real exchange rate, thus stopping the capital outflow. The accumulation of foreign assets comes to a halt.

This will often not be the end, however. If the perverse phase was short and weak while the expansionary phase was long and pronounced, the stock of foreign assets, at the end of the second phase, will still be above its long-run equilibrium level. In this case, there must be a third phase, which is again contractionary (see Niehans, 1977). The continuing decline in the real exchange rate will begin to dominate the vanishing interest differential, calling forth renewed capital inflows, while the rise in domestic prices and income will now dominate the rise in the exchange rate, calling forth a matching import surplus. Either monotonically or in continued oscillations, the economy will gradually approach the long-run equilibrium in which PPP is satisfied and foreign assets have returned to their initial level.

As indicated above, the exact profile of this adjustment process is still subject to much uncertainty. By and large it seems that the flexibility of the exchange rate tends to accentuate, rather than to dampen, the fluctuations in output during the adjustment process: At first, before the stimulating effects of monetary expansion appear, international repercussions are likely to be contractionary; when output gradually rises above its normal level, international repercussions reinforce the expansion; when 'stagflation' finally sets in, it will often be aggravated by the reappearance of import surpluses. International monetary theory learnt from Mundell (1961, 1963), Krueger (1965) and Sohmen (1967) that flexible exchange rates enhance the efficacy of monetary policy. If the above conjectures about the adjustment process are valid, this familiar argument reappears with a new twist: Instead of a static proposition about under-employment equilibrium it is now a proposition about fluctuations along a dynamic adjustment path. Even now it is clear, however, that the specific features of this adjustment path will be very sensitive to variations in the behavior of the economy.

4. Long-Run Deviations from Purchasing-Power Parity

As pointed out in section 1, the PPP-proposition relates to the case where fiat money is the only exogenous asset. If the government and/or the central bank can also determine the amounts of domestic and foreign securities held by the private sector, there may be deviations from PPP – an international counterpart to Metzler's finding (Metzler, 1951). In contrast to the deviations from PPP commonly discussed in the literature, deviations of this sort occur even in full equilibrium and with constant tastes and technology. The following discussion is based on the case of a small economy in balanced growth with a foreign interest rate no lower than the rate of growth.[14]

Suppose such an economy produces a traded good, x, and a non-traded good, y, according to the solid production possibility curve in figure 3. For the traded good, PPP is trivially satisfied through arbitrage. If the relevant price level is measured by some positively-weighted mean of the two prices, the currency will thus appear to be overvalued relative to PPP whenever the traded-goods price declines relative to the nontraded-goods price. With traded-goods arbitrage providing, so-to-say, an anchor, PPP can thus be reduced to a problem of relative prices.

The consumption possibilities are obtained by adding to the production possibilities the imports of traded goods that can be financed from the net return on foreign assets. For increasing amounts of foreign assets, this results in the family of broken curves, derived from the production possibility curve by horizontal shifts. For given foreign assets, equilibrium is reached where the corresponding consumption possibility curve is tangent to an indifference curve. With an increasing amount of foreign assets this equilibrium moves along the expansion path EE. If both goods are superior, this move is associated with a declining relative price of the traded good and thus an increasing overvaluation of the currency relative to PPP. The problem of

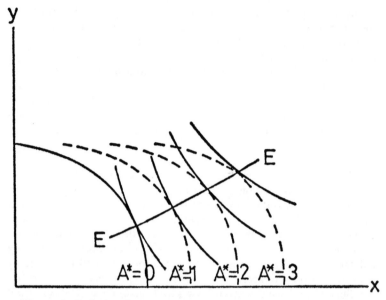

Figure 3. Relative Prices and Foreign Assets in the Long Run.

PPP has thus been converted into a particularly simple case of the transfer problem with foreign asset returns appearing as the 'transfer'.

The question is how different policies affect total foreign assets. The answer can be given in terms of a diagram that looks qualitatively identical to figure 1, though the slopes of the two curves may, of course, be different.[15] The meaning of exchange rate variations, however, is now different. Specifically, expected exchange rate changes are now zero, and the level of the exchange rate exerts its influence on asset demand through its effect on the real value of assets in terms of traded goods.[16]

If the government increases its domestic debt, the system, in effect, moves along the PS arrow. The resulting increase in interest rates reduces the demand for foreign assets and thus produces an undervaluation of the currency relative to PPP. If the central bank creates money through purchases of foreign securities along the FEO arrow, foreign assets will increase, an increase in private demand, induced by a falling interest rate, being added to the foreign-security purchases of the central bank. The consequence will be an overvaluation of the currency relative to PPP. The effect of open-market purchases of domestic securities is qualitatively similar;[17] while there are no central bank purchases of foreign securities in this case, the increase in private demand, resulting from a marked fall in domestic interest rates, is all the stronger. A mathematical analysis would reveal, however, that the overvaluation resulting from foreign-exchange purchases is likely to be larger, dollar by dollar, than the overvaluation resulting from open-market purchases.

Isn't there a neutral monetary policy for which the PPP-principle strictly holds? In fact, there is more than one, for any monetary policy that keeps the amount of foreign assets constant would do the trick. A particularly simple case of a neutral policy is obtained if the increase in government debt as a percentage of total domestic assets is equal to the percentage increase in the money supply. In this case, the private sector does not buy foreign assets because the rate of interest is constant and the central bank does not buy foreign assets by assumption. This seems to be the special case for which PPP was originally constructed. It is interesting to note that in the long run PPP is maintained by a horizontal move in the system, while the avoidance of instantaneous deviations requires a vertical shift.

Some of these long-run results may, at first sight, look paradoxical. Wouldn't one expect foreign-exchange purchases to result in an undervaluation of the currency rather than in an overvaluation? The apparent paradox is easily resolved once it is recognized that the intuitive expectation relates to short-term reactions to *changes* in foreign assets, while the PPP-principle, and thus the present discussion, relates to long-run equilibrium where foreign assets are fully adjusted to their desired level. Once the eye has adjusted to the long-run perspective, the argument is intuitively plausible and, indeed, almost self-evident: The larger the imports which can be financed by the net receipts from foreign assets, the larger is the fraction of resources allocated to the production of nontraded goods and the higher is their relative price. A policy which, in the short run, seems to favor the export industries by large central-bank purchases of foreign exchange thus turns out, in the long run, to encourage the expansion of the domestic sector.[18]

5. *Purchasing-Power Parity as a Monetary Rule*

During the half-decade after the final breakdown of the Bretton Woods system, short-run lapses from PPP, with their consequences for output and trade, emerged as one of the vicious aspects of floating rates. Perhaps inevitably, it was proposed, therefore, that monetary policy should be used to keep exchange rates close to PPP (see Optica Report, 1976). On the surface, such schemes may look plausible, but on closer inspection it turns out that they are unlikely to achieve their purpose and may actually make matters worse. Specifically, a monetary policy based on PPP can be shown to involve the following problems.[19]

1. The PPP-rule would tend to transform random disturbances in the monetary system into permanent inflation or deflation. The reason is that present monetary policy, through the exchange rate, becomes dynamically dependent on past monetary policy. Whenever past monetary policy, for some reason or another, was particularly expansionary, the PPP-rule will automatically transmit this bias to present and future monetary policy. In many cases, the PPP-rule will also produce oscillations, and in exceptional cases, particularly if the overshooting is weak, the inflation (or deflation) rates will become increasingly large. As a matter of principle, present monetary policy should not be mechanically linked to past monetary policy.[20]

2. It is not certain that the PPP-rule would reduce the fluctuations in domestic output caused by foreign influences. It is true that it would eliminate the disturbances caused by the temporary deviations from PPP. However, in doing so it would create disturbances of its own, caused by the required changes in the domestic money supply. It is clear that the disturbances thus created under the PPP-rule would go in the opposite direction from those that would appear otherwise: While foreign monetary expansion, in the absence of a domestic PPP-policy, would impose on the domestic economy a temporary recession, in the presence of a domestic PPP-policy the disturbance would have the form of a temporary expansion. It is not clear, however, in which case the disturbance would be larger, and it could well be larger under the PPP-rule. If the objective were the perfect stabilization of output, the required policy would be a partial application of the PPP-rule in such a way that the contractive disturbances caused by the remaining deviations from PPP are just neutralized by the expansionary disturbances caused by domestic monetary policy.

3. Under the PPP-rule a country would lose the monetary autonomy which is commonly regarded as the basic justification of flexible exchange rates. This is because the transition of a foreign country to a higher long-term rate of inflation would automatically be translated into long-term inflation at home, though not necessarily at the same rate. Inflation rates would again become internationally interdependent, though in a different, and perhaps more complex, way than under the gold/exchange standard.

In view of these difficulties, I am inclined to conclude that the PPP-rule, interpreted as requiring close correspondence of the exchange rate to PPP, does not offer a viable rule for monetary policy. This does not necessarily mean that the dynamic lapses from PPP should be passively accepted, but it means that the monetary response should not follow the simple PPP-rule. In particular, the following considerations might help to reduce the lapses from PPP.

1. The most violent disturbances seem to be created by changes in expectations concerning the long-run trend of monetary policy, while short-run fluctuations in stabilization policies along a given trend give relatively little trouble. The basic requirement, therefore, seems to be a steady long-run course of monetary policy.

2. Major (net) interventions into the foreign-exchange market should be restricted to periods where the temporary deviation from PPP seems to be beyond reasonable doubt and very large. In such cases, intervention may, however, be essential if serious repercussions on output and employment at a later date are to be prevented.

3. Intervention should only be partial in the sense that the apparent (or suspected) gap between the exchange rate and PPP should not be completely closed.

4. Successful intervention may require that more than one policy instrument be used simultaneously. For example, it may be possible to counteract an apparent overvaluation of the currency, if deemed necessary, by a temporary shift in central bank assets from domestic securities to foreign securities without changing the money supply.

It is evident, however, that a significant improvement in the practice of managed floating would require a much better understanding of the dynamics of the adjustment process. In the present state of the art, the PPP-doctrine, as the international counterpart of the quantity theory, continues to be significant mainly as a reminder that given monetary disturbances, however large, cannot affect output and employment forever. This insight may not be profound, but on the battlefield of policy-making it often helps.

NOTES

1. See the references in Frenkel (1976, 1978) and Officer (1976).

2. See, in particular, Officer (1976) and the symposium on purchasing-power parity in the Journal of International Economics, May 1978.

3. The interpretation of the PPP-doctrine in this section is essentially identical to the one given by Haberler in 1933 (p. 34 f.).

4. On this time-honored point see Niehans (1978a), p. 142 f.

5. It has often been alleged that Cassel entertained this, as Samuelson called it, 'bizarre' notion (Samuelson, 1964, p. 147/148; Officer, 1976, p. 6). This criticism

is based on superficial reading of sometimes careless writing; in fact, Cassel was explicit about the deviations of k from unity and he clearly championed the 'relative' interpretation of PPP.

6. It may be worth pointing out that the formulation of 'absolute' PPP given in Frenkel (1978) is actually a version of relative PPP.

7. In empirical applications there is, however, the problem that the full adjustment of prices, down to the last piece of real estate, may take a long time. One might thus try to find particular prices, or index-numbers of prices, which promise to be leading indicators of what *every* price will eventually do.

8. Thus Samuelson (1964) and Balassa (1964) argued that traded-goods prices are likely to decline relatively to nontraded-goods prices in the course of economic development, resulting in an overvaluation of the currencies of highly developed countries relative to PPP. While important as a proposition about the trend of the 'real' factors, this argument cannot really be regarded as a criticism of PPP.

9. A valid test might be provided by a dynamic model in which both prices and exchange rates are explained by the present and past values of exogenous variables, including the money supplies. It could then be checked whether the lag coefficients of the relative money supplies with respect to prices and exchange rates each add up to unity. (For such an approach see Driskill, 1978). Valid tests could also be provided by inflation periods during which the changes in the money supplies were clearly very large compared to any possible real changes. Such tests are reported in Frenkel (1976).

10. It may also result, despite the neutral character of the monetary expansion, in an increase in foreign assets in the steady state. This permanent effect, noted by Calvo and Rodriguez (1977), will here be disregarded, though it would produce a lasting deviation from PPP.

11. Expressing this proposition in real terms has the advantage that its wording is valid both for changes in nominal interest rates and for changes in expected inflation rates.

12. Partial answers are provided in Dornbusch (1976a, 1976b), Kouri (1976), Calvo and Rodriguez (1977) and Genberg and Kierzkowski (1978). See also the following references. Stanley Black drew my attention to the fact that the reference to Kouri's excellent paper in Niehans (1977) is in error inasmuch as trade flows adjust passively, not to the required stock adjustment, but to the exchange rate as determined by instantaneous asset equilibrium. Trade flows, in turn, determine capital flows and thus the change in asset stocks. I welcome this opportunity to correct the error.

13. These perverse effects were emphasized in Niehans (1975).

14. The discussion draws on Niehans (1978c), where the full analysis is given.

15. This simple exposition is possible on the assumption that the demand for assets is independent of relative prices.

16. Measuring real assets in terms of traded goods is again a simplifying device.

17. The same result was reached by Genberg and Kierzkowski (1978).

18. This difference between short-run effects and long-run effects was also noted by Genberg and Kierzkowski (1978).

19. The following discussion is based on Niehans (1978b). On the dynamics of the PPP-rule see also DeGrauwe, Steinherr and Basevi (1978).

20. This is also a weakness of the proposal, made by the German Sachverständigenrat in its 1976/1977 annual report, to determine target exchange rates on the basis of the relative rates of monetary expansion and then to use monetary policy to keep actual exchange rates on target.

270

JÜRG NIEHANS

REFERENCES

Balassa, B. (1964), 'The Purchasing-Power Parity Doctrine: A Reappraisal', *J. of Pol. Ec.*, 72 (*1964*), 584–596.

Calvo, G. A. and Rodriguez, C. A., 'A Model of Exchange Rate Determination under Currency Substitution and Rational Expectations', *J. of Pol. Ec.*, 85 (*1977*), 617–625.

Cassel, G., 'The Present Situation of the Foreign Exchanges', *Ec. J.* 26 (*1916*), 62–65.

Cassel, G., 'Abnormal Deviations in International Exchanges,' *Ec. J.*, 28 (*1918*), 413–415.

Cassel, G., *Das Geldproblem der Welt*, München (Drei Masken), 1921.

Cassel, G., *Das Geldwesen nach 1914*, transl. by Briemer, W., Leipzig (Gloeckner), 1925.

De Grauwe, P., Steinherr, A., and Basevi, G., 'The Dynamics of Intervention Rules in Foreign Exchange Markets,' 1978 (unpublished).

Dornbusch, R., 'The Theory of Flexible Exchange Rate Regimes and Macroeconomic Policy', *Scandinavian J. of Ecs*, 78 (*1976a*), 255–275.

Dornbusch, R., 'Exchange Rate Expectations and Monetary Policy', *J. of Int. Ecs*, 6 (*1976b*), 231–244.

Dornbusch, R., 'Expectations and Exchange Rate Dynamics', *J. of Pol. Ec.*, 84 (*1976c*), 1161–1176.

Driskill, R., 'Monetary Policy and Exchange Rate Dynamics', Ph.D. Dissertation, Johns Hopkins University, 1978 (unpublished).

Frenkel, J. A., 'A Monetary Approach to the Exchange Rate: Doctrinal Aspects and Empirical Evidence', *Scandinavian J. of Ecs*, 78 (*1976*), 200–224.

Frenkel, J. A., 'Purchasing-Power Parity – Doctrinal Perspective and Evidence from the 1920s', *J. of Int. Ecs*, 8 (*1978*), 169–191.

Genberg, H. and Kierzkowski, H., 'Real and Nominal Effects of Economic Policies in a Dynamic Model of Exchange Rate Determination,' 1978 (unpublished).

Girton, L. and Henderson, D. W., 'Central Bank Operations in Foreign and Domestic Assets under Fixed and Flexible Exchange Rates', in *The Effects of Exchange Rate Adjustments*, eds. Clark, P. B. *et al.*, Washington, D.C., 1974, 151–178.

Haberler, G., *Der internationale Handel*, Berlin (Springer), 1933.

Kouri, P. J. K., 'The Exchange Rate and the Balance of Payments in the Short Run and in the Long Run: A Monetary Approach', *Scandinavian J. of Ecs*, 78 (*1976*), 280–304.

Krueger, A. O., 'The Impact of Alternative Government Policies under Varying Exchange Systems,' *Quart. J. of Ecs*, 79 (*1965*), 195–208.

Metzler, L. A., 'Wealth, Saving, and the Rate of Interest', *J. of Pol. Ec.*, 59 (*1951*), 93–116.

Mundell, R. A., 'Flexible Exchange Rates and Employment Policy', *Canadian J. of Ecs and Pol. Science*, 27 (*1961*), 509–517.

Mundell, R. A., 'Capital Mobility and Stabilization Policy under Fixed and Flexible Exchange Rates,' *Canadian J. of Ecs and Pol. Science*, 29 (*1963*), 475–485.

Niehans, J., 'Some Doubts about the Efficacy of Monetary Policy under Flexible Exchange Rates,' *J. of Int. Ecs*, 5 (*1975*), 275–281.

Niehans, J., 'Exchange Rate Dynamics with Stock/Flow Interaction,' *J. of Pol. Ec.* 85 (*1977*), 1245–1257.

Niehans, J., *The Theory of Money*, Baltimore (Johns Hopkins Press), 1978a.

271

Niehans, J., 'Dynamic Purchasing Power as a Monetary Rule', 1978b (Flexible Exchange Rates and the Balance of Payments: Essays in memory of Egon Sohmen, (forthcoming).

Niehans, J., 'Static Deviations from Purchasing-Power Parity', 1978c (*J. of Monetary Ecs*, (forthcoming).

Officer, L. H., 'The Purchasing-Power Parity Theory of Exchange Rates: A Review Article', *IMF Staff Papers, 23 (1976)*, 1–60.

OPTICA Report 1976, *Inflation and Exchange Rates: Evidence and Policy Guidelines for the European Community*, Brussels (Commission on the European Communities), 1977.

Samuelson, P. A., 'Theoretical Notes on Trade Problems,' *Rev of Ecs and Stats, 46 (1964)*, 145–154.

Sohmen, E., 'Fiscal and Monetary Policies under Alternative Exchange-Rate Systems', *Quart. J. of Ecs, 81 (1967)*, 515–523.

Chapter Fourteen

THE EQUIVALENCE OF REAL INTEREST RATES IN A MULTICURRENCY WORLD

*Robert Z. Aliber**

THE INTUITIVE presumption is that in an open international economy, real interest rates should not differ significantly across countries. The story is that funds flow toward countries offering higher interest rates and loans flow toward countries where interest rate differentials are no larger than transactions costs.

Intellectual support for this story has been provided by two recent developments, one in international money, one in finance. The monetary approach to the balance of payments implies that under a pegged exchange rate system the authorities determine the domestic component of the reserve base while the public determines the money supply; investors arbitrage funds among countries until the differences in interest rates are no greater than transactions costs. The counterpart proposition under a floating exchange rate system is that the authorities in each country determine the nominal reserves of the banking system while the public determines the 'real' money supply through its demand for money; if the reserves of the banking system grow rapidly, then the money supply and the price level increase correspondingly and the currency depreciates. The adjustment is based on the stability of the demand for money balances in real terms. Individuals 'arbitrage' their wealth among similar assets denominated in the several currencies in response to any anticipated differences in interest rates and changes in exchange rates on similar assets denominated in the several currencies. Differences in inflation rates and changes in exchange rates are the mechanisms by which the real interest rates in the various countries move toward equality.

* Richard Karplus and Stephen Schoess have provided substantial assistance with the data. Kaveh Alamouti provided helpful comment on an earlier draft.

THE EQUIVALENCE OF REAL INTEREST RATES

In finance, the theory of efficient markets stipulates that investors adjust their demands for various assets in response to new information so as to equalize their anticipated rates of return on a risk-adjusted basis. Each asset is valued in terms of its contribution to the risk and return of the investor's portfolio. If risk-adjusted interest rates on assets available in the several countries differ by more than transactions costs, investors would find it profitable to rearrange the currency mix of their assets; if they do not, an explanation would be needed for the apparent reluctance of investors to take advantage of a profit opportunity. To the extent that the international capital market is efficient, risk-adjusted real interest rates would be similar across countries.

While the story about similarity of real interest rates may be compelling in a world in which exchange rates do not change, much as in the regions within a unified currency area, the argument has less intuitive force if exchange rates may change. Then investors compare anticipated yield on domestic and on foreign assets, which includes a term for the anticipated change in the exchange rate as well as an interest rate term. The equality of anticipated yields implies the equality of real interest rates on similar assets denominated in the several currencies only if two conditions are satisfied: one involves the relationship between the rate of price level change and the money interest rate, while the other involves the relation between the change in the exchange rate and the interest rate differential.

Fisher noted that 'the rate of interest [the percentage premium of present goods over future goods of the same kind], is always relative to the standard in which it is expressed' (Fisher). He indicated that a cost of living index – a composite of consumption of goods and services – provides an absolute standard of value in terms of real interest rates could be expressed. While money interest rates tend to adjust to changes in the price level, the adjustment may be imperfect because of the 'universal lack of foresight,' and the real interest may differ over time and across countries.

However, unanticipated increases in commodity price levels lead to declines in the real interest rates received by lenders and paid by borrowers; similarly, increases in real interest rates follow from decreases in the commodity price levels. Changes in the real interest rates occur, however, only when changes in the commodity price level are unanticipated. Perhaps some investors make persistent errors so that, period by period, lenders subsidize borrowers; if not, the pattern of these errors between anticipated real rates and realized interest rates would be random rather than systematic.

One of the paradoxes is that many individuals who accept the story that real interest rates do not differ significantly across countries nevertheless also accept a number of propositions which implicitly assume that real interest rates do differ significantly. If real interest rates are always similar, then changes in national monetary policies would not have any effect on real variables. If real interest rates are not sensitive to the exchange-rate regime, then most of the issues in the debate between those who favor floating exchange rate regimes and those who favor pegged rate regimes are irrelevant. The proponents of floating exchange rates have suggested that differences in real interest rates across countries are no greater under floating exchange rate regimes than under pegged regimes. The proponents of pegged exchange rates respond that if there are no costs to segmentation of national money markets, no benefits are attached to segmentation and so national currencies should be merged to eliminate the nuisance costs of exchange transactions. If real interest rates are always similar, firms would then be indifferent about currencies in which they denominate their assets and liabilities. If real interest rates are more or less continuously similar, one of the important benefits of international diversification of portfolios would disappear, although real interest rates may be similar as a result of diversification. Finally, if real interest rates already do not differ significantly, then the unification of currencies would not be expected to lead to major welfare gains from the redistribution of the world's capital costs.

Casual empiricism suggests that real interest rates are not similar across countries. Under flexible exchange rate regimes, very sharp deviations from Purchasing Power Parity have occurred when changes in exchange rates have been large, either parity changes under the adjustable peg system or sharp movements in floating rates (Aliber). Purchasing Power Parity does not hold for selected short-run intervals, even if it holds for long-run intervals; the implication is that real interest rates in various countries are unlikely to be similar on a month-to-month or a quarter-to-quarter basis, even if they are not significantly different over the long-run intervals. Even if Purchasing Power Parity is valid as a long-run central tendency, it does not follow that real interest rates would be similar across countries; there may be persistent differences across countries in the levels of real interest rates. Money interest rates differed significantly even when parities were unchanged for

275

extended periods, which suggests that real interest rates differed even when exchange rates were pegged (Morgenstern, Homer).

This paper seeks to evaluate the empirical support for the equality of real interest rates across countries. The next section of the paper considers how interest rates adjust to various disturbances. The subsequent section deals with the empirical tests.

I. Real Disturbances and Real Interest Rates

Both structural and monetary disturbances may affect real interest rates, both the post-disturbance equilibrium levels and the paths to the new equilibrium. Within any one country, real interest rates tend toward equality across regions even though they might differ sharply across regions in the absence of arbitrage. Arbitrage equalizes nominal yields, and, since the deflators are similar if not identical, real interest rates are also equalized. Even if structural disturbances in any one region affect the nominal interest rates, arbitrage – changes in the volume of trade in securities – minimizes any regional impacts on interest rates.

Structural disturbances in one country in a multiple currency world may induce changes in exchange rates even while relative prices remain unchanged. The terms of trade change as a result of the structural disturbances; exports increase either because export prices fall or because profits on exports are higher. In both cases, the currency tends to appreciate, and the reduced price of imports and exports leads to downward pressure on the price level. If nominal interest rates are constant, real interest rates increase as the domestic prices decline. At this point, the distinction between nominal interest rates and nominal returns must be emphasized; the latter includes the return from the change in the exchange rate. However, if the nominal returns on domestic and foreign securities are to be similar after adjustment for the anticipated change in the exchange rate, then nominal interest rates must also decline.

Monetary disturbances are likely to lead to changes both in price levels and in exchange rates. Nominal interest rates on similar assets denominated in various currencies unambiguously differ if investors anticipate that exchange rates may change, with the difference equal to the anticipated rate of change in exchange rates. If, however, the changes in exchange rates reflect differences in the rates of price level change among countries, then the deflators for the money interest rates and for nominal price levels are the same; real rates of return will be continuously equal to investors in both countries even though nominal interest rates differ.

276

Thus, if

$$r_d - r_f = \left(\frac{\dot{e}}{e}\right)^*,$$

where r_d is the domestic interest rate, r_f the foreign interest rate, and $(\dot{e}/e)^*$ the anticipated rate of change in the exchange rate; and if

$$\left(\frac{\dot{e}}{e}\right)^* = \left(\frac{\dot{P}_d}{P_d}\right)^* - \left(\frac{\dot{P}_f}{P_f}\right)^*,$$

where $(\dot{P}_d/P_d)^*$ is the anticipated rate of change of domestic prices and $(\dot{P}_f/P_f)^*$ the anticipated rate of change of foreign or world prices, then

$$r_d - r_f = \left(\frac{\dot{P}_d}{P_d}\right)^* - \left(\frac{\dot{P}_f}{P_f}\right)^*$$

or

$$r_d - \left(\frac{\dot{P}_d}{P_d}\right)^* = r_f - \left(\frac{\dot{P}_f}{P_f}\right)^*.$$

In this case, the deflator used to adjust nominal interest rates to obtain real interest rates may be either the change in the domestic price level or the change in the world price level adjusted by the change in the exchange rate; both deflators lead to identical estimates of the real interest rate. By the same token, if Purchasing Power Parity does not hold continuously, the estimate of the real interest rate depends on whether domestic prices or adjusted world prices are used as the deflator.

If monetary disturbances lead to proportional changes in prices, nominal interest rates, and exchange rates, then real interest rates should not change. If, however, monetary disturbances have dissimilar impacts on these several variables, even if only in the short run, then monetary expansion could lead to a decline in interest rates (because of the liquidity effect), and a depreciation of the currency in the exchange market, without any significant direct effect on the price level. The more comprehensive statement is that real interest rates must differ across countries as long as the adjustment to a monetary disturbance is not consistent with a simple Fisherian model.

Several different relationships are possible as regards the equivalence of nominal interest rates and of real interest rates. One

277

is that real returns are not similar even though nominal returns are similar; a second is that both nominal and real returns are dissimilar; a third is that real returns are not significantly different even though nominal returns are.

Inevitably, some unforeseen events will cause real interest rates to differ *ex post* from anticipated values. Whether such events can cause real interest rates to differ persistently or only on a period-to-period basis is a key empirical question. A persistent difference might reflect a payment for bearing risk, although it would be inappropriate to regard all observed differences as payments for risk-bearing. In *The Theory of Interest*, Fisher noted that the variability of real interest rates was likely to be greater than the variability of nominal rates, because the variability in commodity price levels is greater than the variability of nominal interest rates. One explanation is that changes in price levels which are supposed to drive the nominal interest rates are unanticipated. Another explanation is that money interest rates cannot fall below zero, so that real interest rates can be large and positive whenever the price level is falling, because the decline in money interest rates has a lower bound. In contrast, real interest rates may become large and negative whenever there is a large unanticipated increase in commodity price levels; there is no limit to the amount by which they may become negative.

Within the international economy, one of the criticial questions is whether there have been substantial changes in real interest rates among countries when changes in exchange rates occur. Another is whether differences in real interest rates reflect differences in nominal interest rates even when exchange rates are pegged, perhaps reflecting differences in investor assessment of default risk (used in a generic sense). If all changes in exchange rates are only monetary in origin, then there should be no significant impact on the real interest rate, at least in the long run; the monetary assumption means that both Purchasing Power Parity and Fisher Open hold. But to argue that differences in inflation rates, or monetary phenomena, must necessarily lead to equivalent changes rates does not mean that all changes in exchange rates represent responses to monetary disturbances. Some may represent a response to a real or structural disturbance, such as the discovery or depletion of a raw material, a sudden change in wealth due to a change in terms of trade, or a sharp change in investor anticipation of inflation rates.

Nevertheless, while non-monetary disturbances which cause

278

changes in exchange rates might have the effect of reversing the relationship among real interest rates in the several countries, at least the pre-trade pattern of interest rates, arbitrage should equalize real interest rates once the system has attained equilibrium after adjustment to the structural disturbance. For example, there may have been a reversal of the real interest rate pattern as between sterling and the dollar in the early 1920s and, similarly, more recently, between the yen and the mark, and the yen and the dollar. The evidence for such changes, the sudden change in the direction of capital flows, is indirect. As a country's international investment position changes, its pre-trade real interest rate should change. If the proposition that changes in the relationship among the pre-trade levels of real interest rates in several countries is accepted, then it must follow logically that real interest rates may differ if an adjustment involves a change in exchange rates. Consequently, it would be expected that real interest rates are likely to differ across countries whenever a change in exchange rate occurs because of non-monetary disturbance or whenever the adjustment to a monetary disturbance involves departure from a simple Fisherian system.

II. *Measurement of Real Interest Rates*

Testing whether real interest rates are similar across countries is somewhat analogous to testing whether Purchasing Power Parity is valid. In both cases, predicted values must be compared with observed values. In both cases, the data used to generate the prediction must be adjusted by a deflator. The operational problems are similar. The time series used for the prediction must be selected; a choice must be made among possible deflators; a technique must be developed to obtain estimates of real values from nominal values; and a standard must be set to determine whether the observed values differ significantly from the predicted values.

The analogy, however, is less than complete. Tests of Purchasing Power Parity involve price indexes, which are composites either of goods or of goods and services. In contrast, tests of equivalence of real interest rates involve comparisons of individual interest rates in each country rather than of indexes of interest rates; in this sense the analogy is with the Law of One Price rather than with Purchasing Power Parity. Yet the Law of One Price involves identical commodities in different locations, while the national securities whose interest rates are to be compared may not be identical in the minds of investors, even though the names of the securities are identical;

279

U.S. Treasury bills may differ from U.K. Treasury bills in attributes other than currency of denomination.

Interest rates on four or five similar securities in each country, such as bank deposits, Treasury bills, and Treasury bonds, might be compared; such securities differ in terms of maturity, debtor (hence default risk), and liquidity as well as yield. The possible deflators include the consumer price index, the wholesale price index, a GNP deflator, and an international deflator which is the product of a world price index and the exchange rate.

Two approaches have been used to test Purchasing Power Parity. The absolute version involves the relationship between the levels of prices in various countries and the exchange rate; the relative version involves the relationship between *changes* in the price level relationships and *changes* in the exchange rates. The argument for not testing the absolute version is that, even though the Law of One Price holds for particular commodities, the level of the exchange rate is affected by transactions in services, investments, pensions and remittances, and military expenditures. Since the pattern of these transactions probably changes less extensively or less rapidly than relative commodity price levels, the relative version of Purchasing Power Parity may be valid even if the absolute version is not. If these factors changed more rapidly or extensively, the tests of the relative version of Purchasing Power Parity would not be successful (and neither would tests of the absolute version) because changes in the price level-exchange rate relationship would be dominated by changes in exchange rates attributable to factors other than changes in relative prices.

When Purchasing Power Parity is tested, analysts argue about whether wholesale price indexes or the consumer or retail indexes are more appropriate predictors of the exchange rate. Critics of using the wholesale price index argue that if goods in the several market baskets are identical, there can be no deviation greater than transaction costs (or else the Law of One Price will be violated), and so the tests of Purchasing Power Parity should be based on the retail or consumer price indexes.[1] Then the central question in testing Purchasing Power Parity is how long a disturbance in either the goods market or in the exchange market alters the traditional relationship between the price of tradeables and the price of non-tradeables in one or several countries; in effect, the test is of the consumption and production responses to changes in the relation between the price of tradeables and the price of non-tradeables in each country.

The financial market counterpart to the statement that Purchasing Power Parity should be calculated in absolute levels is that the real interest rate in each country should be the same; the 'prediction' is that deviations from the Law of One Price apply to securities just as they apply to commodities. The counterpart to the statement that the relative version of Purchasing Power Parity should be tested is to examine the relationship between the first differences of real interest rates rather than between their levels; the first differences may be similar while the levels differ. Both versions involve comparisons of holding period returns. One input to the measurement of holding period returns is the anticipation of changes in exchange rates attached to these currencies, and another is anticipation of any losses due to default. Comparisons of nominal interest rates involve estimation of at least two uncertain events and, as well, payments that investors may demand for bearing risk about one or both uncertainties.

The analogy between Purchasing Power Parity in the commodities market and its counterpart in the financial markets extends to the operational problems. One question, whose PPP counterpart is the choice of commodity price levels, involves the selection of assets for comparison; the possible choices include short-term and long-term government securities and corporate debt. The second question involves the choice of a deflator to use in adjusting nominal values to real values. For Purchasing Power Parity, the deflator is usually the parity or market exchange rate, although occasionally a black market exchange rate has been used. The alternatives for deflating nominal interest rates include the retail price indexes and the wholesale price indexes in each country and the world price indexes, or foreign price indexes. A third concern involves the horizon over which real interest rates should be computed, and whether the test uses monthly or quarterly data.

Nominal returns on riskless similar assets for the major countries are shown in Table 1, where the domestic interest rate, e.g., the interest rate on U.S. dollar securities, is compared with foreign interest rates adjusted for realized changes in exchange rates relative to the dollar. In a world of certainty, nominal interest rates on similar securities available in the several countries would be similar after adjustment for the anticipated (and realized) changes in the exchange rates. The means and standard deviations, based on monthly data, and the correlation coefficients based on monthly and quarterly data, are shown for two periods of comparable length, one during the pegged rate period and the second during the floating rate period.

Table 1. Comparisons of Nominal Interest Rates (Monthly Data).

	Pegged				Floating			
	M	SD	CCI	CC III	M	SD	CCI	CCIII
US	4.41 (0.09)	0.71	0.035	0.128	6.09 (0.18)	1.35	0.067	0.078
UK	2.72 (2.16)	16.50	0.918	0.917	3.19 (3.11)	24.07	0.654	0.721
BEL	3.14 (0.23)	1.82	0.229	0.239	10.51 (4.01)	30.70	0.934	0.959
FRA	4.23 (0.28)	2.15	0.251	0.318	9.63 (4.15)	31.98	0.825	0.783
GER	3.58 (0.40)	3.09	0.077	0.201	12.82 (4.78)	35.74	0.901	0.938
NET	5.19 (0.31)	2.37	0.223	0.331	11.40 (4.12)	31.67	0.922	0.932
CAN	4.86 (0.34)	2.57	0.421	0.462	5.26 (1.40)	10.51	0.025	−0.144
JAP	7.66 (0.35)	2.71	0.149	0.199	10.99 (3.13)	24.35	0.677	0.728
SAFR	4.08 (0.27)	2.05	−0.349	−0.405	4.00 (3.73)	28.91	0.312	0.523
World	4.087	2.05			5.95	17.26		

Source; IFS Tape

Note; The numbers in the parentheses under the means are their respective standard errors calculated as $\dfrac{SD}{\sqrt{N}}$ where N = 60.

CCI = Correlation Coefficients Monthly Data.
CCIII = Correlation Coefficients Quarterly Data.

Nominal interest rates are nearly one and one-half times as high in the floating period as in the pegged period, for the floating period is one of world inflation. The standard deviations of nominal interest rates are much higher in the floating period than in the pegged rate period. The increase in the mean interest rate is greater than the increase inferred from the increase in dollar interest rates for all countries except Great Britain and South Africa. Mean nominal interest rates differ substantially, with the highest mean about three times the magnitude of the lowest in the pegged rate period and four times the magnitude in the floating period. Nominal returns are compared with each other and with a world interest rate, which is an unweighted average of the means of national interest rates. The mean interest rates of two (out of eight) countries differ significantly from the U.S. interest rate during the pegged period. During the floating period, the standard errors are so large that one cannot be confident that any of the means are not drawn from the same population.

The correlation coefficients between the unweighted world average interest rate and the national rates are reasonably low in the pegged rate period, which suggests that period-to-period changes in the means are not significantly related. The correlation coefficients are higher for most currencies during the floating rate periods, at least for the countries in Europe; this 'regional interest rate factor' probably reflects the strong correlation of changes in the exchange rates of the countries in the joint float.

Nominal interest rates might differ across countries because the interest rate differentials 'predict' changes in exchange rates which do not occur, or alternatively, because changes in exchange rates occur which were not predicted by the interest rate differential. The intuitive presumption is that small differences in nominal interest rates will reflect anticipated changes in exchange rates which do not occur, whereas large changes in exchange rates will not be reflected in the interest rate differential, since such changes usually result from shocks which were unanticipated. Thus

$$r_d - r_f = \frac{S_t - S_{t+n}^*}{S_t},$$

where $\dfrac{S_t - S_{t+n}^*}{S_t}$ is the anticipated rate of change in the exchange rate.

Since

$$\frac{S_t - S_{t+n}}{S_t} = \text{the observed change in the exchange rate,}$$

then

$$\frac{S_t - S_{t+n}^*}{S_t} - \frac{S_t - S_{t+n}}{S_t} = \text{prediction error.}$$

The mean changes in the exchange rates and mean prediction errors are shown in Table 2. In the pegged rate period, the unanticipated changes in exchange rates were larger than the actual changes, which is consistent with *a priori* expectations. The results are less clear in the floating period. The standard deviations of the unanticipated changes are larger than the standard deviations of the actual changes, which is somewhat surprising. The implication is that the larger the unanticipated changes in the exchange rates, the more likely that real interest rates will not be continuously the same across countries.

Estimates of real interest rates for each of the major industrial countries are shown in Table 3, where the real interest rate is calculated as the reported interest rate on Treasury bills or call money for each time period deflated by the period-to-period change in both the domestic price level (the domestic deflator, DD) and

Table 2. Actual and Unanticipated Changes in Exchange Rates.

	Pegged		Floating	
	M Actual	M Unanticipated	M Actual	M Unanticipated
UK	0.788	2.420	2.380	1.310
BEL	0.039	0.317	−0.156	−0.342
FRA	0.054	−0.075	0.982	0.129
GER	0.049	0.219	0.328	−0.359
NET	0.026	−0.187	0.488	−0.677
CAN	−0.026	−0.104	0.388	0.042
JAP	−0.063	−0.803	0.079	−0.686
SAFR	0.017	0.073	1.613	1.700

	SD Actual	SD Unanticipated	SD Actual	SD Unanticipated
UK	2.914	2.935	4.47	4.63
BEL	0.272	0.416	5.18	5.45
FRA	0.342	0.462	5.03	5.25
GER	0.414	0.573	5.09	5.51
NET	0.317	0.427	5.05	5.34
CAN	0.410	0.472	1.91	1.86
JAP	0.317	0.636	3.04	3.69
SAFR	0.032	0.355	4.76	4.81

the world price level (meaning U.S. price level) adjusted for the change in the exchange rate (hereafter the international deflator, ID). In a Fisherian world, the real interest rates calculated by the two deflators should be similar.

In the pegged-rate period, the differences in real interest rates are modest; they are somewhat larger if the international deflator is used. Real interest rates are substantially below the nominal interest rates. The differences between nominal and real interest rates are smaller when the international deflator is used, which means, since rates were then pegged, that the world price level (the U.S. price level) rose by less than the price levels in Great Britain, France, etc. In the floating-rate period, real interest rates in each country except Germany have a negative mean when the domestic deflator is used, suggesting that domestic price increases were more or less continually unanticipated. When the international deflator is used, some of the real interest rates are positive, a result of the sharp appreciations of the several currencies. For example, the Belgian real interest rate has a mean of −2.99 per cent a year with the domestic deflator and a mean of 2.36 a year with the international deflator, which

Table 3. Comparisons of Real Interest Rates
(Monthly Data).

	Pegged				Floating			
	DD		ID		DD		ID	
	M	SD	M	SD	M	SD	M	SD
US	1.58 (0.27)	2.01	1.58 (0.27)	2.01	−1.45 (0.43)	3.34	−1.45 (0.43)	3.34
UK	1.71 (0.72)	5.54	−0.11 (2.30)	16.90	−5.18 (1.32)	9.99	−4.35 (3.10)	23.93
BEL	0.07 (0.50)	3.78	0.31 (0.42)	3.25	−2.99 (0.56)	4.35	2.56 (4.05)	31.32
FRA	1.56 (0.53)	3.93	1.90 (0.40)	3.05	−0.77 (0.41)	3.12	2.09 (4.20)	32.34
GER	1.41 (0.47)	3.40	0.75 (0.52)	4.02	0.88 (0.60)	4.60	5.28 (4.80)	36.38
NET	0.39 (1.40)	10.54	2.36 (0.41)	3.13	−2.38 (0.91)	7.15	−3.86 (4.18)	32.19
CAN	1.42 (0.41)	3.19	2.04 (0.43)	3.30	−1.49 (0.56)	4.31	−2.27 (1.48)	10.88
JAP	2.47 (1.30)	9.90	4.84 (0.48)	3.63	−3.47 (1.60)	12.84	3.45 (3.20)	24.56
SAFR	0.90 (0.48)	3.58	1.26 (0.38)	2.91	−5.22 (0.57)	4.43	−3.56 (3.80)	29.41

DD = domestic deflator.   ID = international deflator.

Table 4. Differences in Mean Interest Rates, Nominal and Real
(Monthly Data).

	Pegged Period						Floating Period					
	Nominal	SD	Real D	SD	Real I	SD	Nominal	SD	Real D	SD	Real I	SD
UK	-1.69	16.50	0.03	5.54	-1.69	16.90	-2.90	24.07	-3.73	9.99	-2.90	23.93
BEL	-1.27	1.82	-1.49	3.78	-1.23	3.25	4.42	30.70	-1.44	4.35	4.01	31.32
FRA	-0.18	2.15	-0.02	3.93	0.32	3.05	3.54	31.98	0.88	3.12	3.54	32.34
GER	-0.83	3.09	-0.17	3.40	-0.83	4.02	6.73	35.74	2.33	4.60	6.73	36.38
NET	0.68	2.37	-1.19	10.54	0.78	3.13	5.31	31.67	0.93	7.15	-2.41	32.19
CAN	0.45	2.57	-0.16	3.19	0.46	3.30	-0.83	10.51	-0.04	4.31	-0.89	10.88
JAP	3.25	2.71	0.89	9.90	3.26	3.63	4.90	24.35	-2.02	12.84	4.90	24.56
SAFR	-0.33	2.05	-0.68	3.58	-0.32	2.91	-2.09	28.91	-3.67	4.43	-2.11	29.51

Note: Since the difference in nominal interest rates is computed after an adjustment for the change in the exchange rate, and the same change is used with the international deflator, the nominal interest rates and the real rates obtained with the international deflator are similar.

Table 5A. Correlation of Changes in Interest Rates

(Monthly Data).

Nominal Pegged

	US	UK	BEL	FRA	GER	NET	CAN	JAP	SAFR
US	—								
UK	-0.03	—							
BEL	-0.27	0.05	—						
FRA	-0.04	0.05	0.34	—					
GER	0.04	-0.06	0.10	-0.16	—				
NET	0.09	-0.03	0.49	-0.36	0.04	—			
CAN	0.25	0.27	-0.10	0.09	-0.07	0.13	—		
JAP	-0.16	0.02	-0.07	0.07	-0.18	-0.01	0.15	—	
SAFR	0.24	-0.45	-0.10	0.09	-0.02	-0.03	-0.12	-0.08	—

Nominal Floating

	US	UK	BEL	FRA	GER	NET	CAN	JAP	SAFR
US	—								
UK	0.07	—							
BEL	0.01	0.55	—						
FRA	0.05	0.58	0.82	—					
GER	0.04	0.49	0.92	0.79	—				
NET	0.12	0.53	0.94	0.78	0.90	—			
CAN	0.18	-0.12	0.03	-0.08	0.07	0.07	—		
JAP	-0.17	0.52	0.61	0.58	0.58	0.57	0.02	—	
SAFR	-0.12	0.29	0.36	0.31	0.34	0.35	-0.07	0.38	—

287

Table 5A—continued

Real Pegged — DD

	US	UK	BEL	FRA	GER	NET	CAN	JAP	SAFR
US	—	0.06	0.14	0.21	0.02	−0.03	0.47	−0.19	−0.11
UK		—	0.23	−0.06	0.24	0.14	0.06	−0.01	−0.04
BEL			—	0.06	0.20	0.16	0.14	0.01	−0.01
FRA				—	0.34	0.09	0.05	0.18	−0.27
GER					—	0.11	0.15	0.02	−0.17
NET						—	0.03	0.16	0.14
CAN							—	−0.31	0.14
JAP								—	−0.01
SAFR									—

Real Floating – DD

	US	UK	BEL	FRA	GER	NET	CAN	JAP	SAFR
US	—	0.10	0.11	−0.13	−0.19	−0.02	0.47	−0.02	0.35
UK		—	0.16	0.22	0.31	0.28	0.03	0.12	−0.11
BEL			—	0.16	0.09	0.14	0.25	0.22	0.27
FRA				—	−0.13	0.26	−0.07	0.27	−0.15
GER					—	0.23	−0.24	−0.03	−0.05
NET						—	−0.06	0.18	0.16
CAN							—	−0.10	0.25
JAP								—	−0.01
SAFR									—

Table 5A—*continued*

Real Pegged — ID

	US	UK	BEL	FRA	GER	NET	CAN	JAP	SAFR
US	—	0.22	0.77	0.66	0.63	0.64	0.65	0.60	0.72
UK		—	0.21	0.20	0.09	0.13	0.35	0.16	-0.14
BEL			—	0.74	0.57	0.77	0.49	0.52	0.56
FRA				—	0.37	0.65	0.49	0.51	0.50
GER					—	0.45	0.36	0.32	0.45
NET						—	0.48	0.43	0.44
CAN							—	0.51	0.37
JAP								—	0.43
SAFR									—

Real Floating — ID

	US	UK	BEL	FRA	GER	NET	CAN	JAP	SAFR
US	—	0.04	0.23	0.17	0.24	0.25	0.32	0.05	0.15
UK		—	0.57	0.59	0.51	0.54	-0.12	0.52	0.30
BEL			—	0.82	0.92	0.95	0.09	0.63	0.39
FRA				—	0.80	0.79	-0.04	0.59	0.32
GER					—	0.90	0.12	0.60	0.36
NET						—	0.12	0.58	0.37
CAN							—	0.04	-0.02
JAP								—	0.39
SAFR									—

Table 5B. Correlation of Changes in Interest Rates

(Quarterly Data).

Nominal Fixed

	US	UK	BEL	FRA	GER	NET	CAN	JAP	SAFR
US	—	0.016	−0.321	0.062	0.057	0.161	0.326	−0.177	0.344
UK		—	0.084	0.165	0.077	0.042	0.345	0.070	−0.559
BEL			—	0.343	0.175	0.588	−0.191	−0.114	−0.107
FRA				—	−0.325	0.312	0.039	0.077	0.032
GER					—	0.259	−0.052	−0.197	0.016
NET						—	0.097	−0.052	0.140
CAN							—	0.202	−0.249
JAP								—	−0.148
SAFR									—

Nominal Floating

	US	UK	BEL	FRA	GER	NET	CAN	JAP	SAFR
US	—	0.174	0.023	0.161	0.056	0.149	0.205	−0.362	−0.404
UK		—	0.599	0.588	0.548	0.582	−0.263	0.537	0.284
BEL			—	0.737	0.944	0.949	−0.111	0.658	0.430
FRA				—	0.674	0.693	−0.407	0.515	0.235
GER					—	0.926	0.003	0.691	0.377
NET						—	−0.103	0.576	0.408
CAN							—	−0.128	−0.206
JAP								—	0.274
SAFR									—

Table 5B—*continued*

Real Pegged – DD

	US	UK	BEL	FRA	GER	NET	CAN	JAP	SAFR
US	—	0.012	0.146	0.333	−0.008	−0.024	0.414	−0.231	−0.187
UK		—	0.412	0.092	0.443	0.305	−0.052	−0.117	−0.095
BEL			—	0.232	0.368	0,176	0.251	−0.041	−0.111
FRA				—	0·386	0.017	0.040	0.288	−0.411
GER					—	0.343	0.120	−0.023	−0.189
NET						—	−0.002	0.174	0.062
CAN							—	−0.351	0.051
JAP								—	−0.156
SAFR									—

Real Floating – DD

	US	UK	BEL	FRA	GER	NET	CAN	JAP	SAFR
US	—	−0.114	0.243	−0.016	−0.405	−0.060	0.645	0.229	0.579
UK		—	0.100	−0.162	0.137	0.121	0.257	−0.176	−0.064
BEL			—	0.447	−0.096	0.328	0.491	0.232	0.548
FRA				—	−0.186	0.321	0.102	0.353	0.051
GER					—	0.074	−0.345	−0.155	−0.416
NET						—	0.004	−0.069	0.114
CAN							—	0.013	0.554
JAP								—	0.155
SAFR									—

Table 5B—continued

Real Pegged – ID

	US	UK	BEL	FRA	GER	NET	CAN	JAP	SAFR
US	—	0.286	0.804	0.583	0.684	0.706	0.489	0.559	0.701
UK		—	0.243	0.300	0.217	0.211	0.472	0.208	-0.216
BEL			—	0.726	0.641	0.841	0.398	0.507	0.596
FRA				—	0.259	0.624	0.307	0.473	0.439
GER					—	0.615	0.320	0.315	0.486
NET						—	0.398	0.430	0.552
CAN							—	0.485	0.096
JAP								—	0.371
SAFR									—

Real Floating – ID

	US	UK	BEL	FRA	GER	NET	CAN	JAP	SAFR
US	—	-0.093	0.185	0.077	0.159	0.156	0.486	0.146	0.118
UK		—	0.600	0.577	0.546	0.576	-0.278	0.529	0.275
BEL			—	0.741	0.945	0.951	-0.037	0.669	0.445
FRA				—	0.676	0.692	-0.364	0.518	0.238
GER					—	0.928	0.055	0.696	0.390
NET						—	-0.059	0.584	0.416
CAN							—	0.014	-0.127
JAP								—	0.310
SAFR									—

reflects the fact that the 'international price level' measured in Belgian francs was increasing less rapidly than the Belgian price level. The standard deviations, however, appear substantially greater when the international deflator is used, a result of the movement in exchange rates. Most real interest rates become less negative or positive with the international deflator, indicating that the appreciation of the foreign currencies was greater than would have been predicted from changes in price relatives alone; except in Canada, some non-price phenomena were driving the exchange rates. The difference means that variations in exchange rates are substantially larger than is suggested by changes in relative price levels. In the pegged-rate period, the real interest rates on dollar assets and on Belgian franc assets differ when the domestic deflator is used; when the international deflator is used, the real interest rates on dollar assets and Japanese yen assets differ. In the floating rate period, interest rates on dollar assets and South African assets differ when the domestic deflators are used; when the international deflators are used, the standard errors are so large that one cannot be confident that the means differ significantly.

In Table 4 the differences in nominal interest rates are compared with the differences in real interest rates for both the floating period and the pegged period. Not surprisingly, the differences in real interest rates are smaller than the differences in nominal interest rates. In the pegged-rate period, the standard deviation of real interest rates is larger than that of nominal interest rates with both deflators; the standard deviation is smaller when the international deflator is used. This finding appears to be an extension of Fisher's proposition that the variability of real interest rates is greater than that of nominal interest rates. During the floating period, the standard deviation of real interest rates when the domestic deflators are used is larger than the standard deviation of nominal interest rates, which suggests that the interest rates partially adjust to offset the variations in exchange rates.

The correlations of changes in nominal interest rates and of real nterest rates are shown for monthly data in Table 5A and for quarterly data in Table 5B. In the pegged-rate period, using nominal data, about half the values have the 'wrong' sign; this result is somewhat less marked using real interest rates and domestic deflators. The coefficients generally are substantially higher when the international deflator is used, especially for the countries which participate in the joint currency float. The values are only modestly higher when quarterly data are used. These values are not so high

Table 6A. Autocorrelations of Residuals of Real Interest Rates (Domestic Deflators).

	US P	US F	UK P	UK F	BEL P	BEL F	FRA P	FRA F	GER P	GER F	NET P	NET F	CAN P	CAN F	JAP P	JAP F	SAFR P	SAFR F
1	0.13	-0.02	0.04	0.31	0.13	0.42	-0.21	0.32	0.34	0.40	-0.16	0.39	0.14	0.42	0.01	0.19	-0.02	0.25
2	0.06	0.11	-0.02	0.05	-0.12	0.24	-0.06	0.05	0.12	0.09	-0.06	0.02	-0.24	0.23	-0.29	-0.02	0.15	-0.04
3	-0.05	0.04	-0.29	0.13	-0.20	0.26	0.05	-0.07	0.04	0.04	-0.06	-0.31	-0.17	0.23	-0.05	0.17	0.11	-0.70
4	-0.02	-0.07	-0.03	-0.08	-0.09	0.34	-0.02	-0.31	-0.16	-0.06	-0.02	-0.09	-0.03	0.23	-0.15	0.01	-0.02	0.08
5	-0.02	-0.01	0.02	-0.07	-0.01	0.29	0.04	-0.21	-0.17	-0.24	0.19	0.09	0.04	0.08	-0.03	0.07	0.11	0.15
6	-0.01	0.07	0.14	0.22	0.01	0.10	0.11	0.11	0.04	-0.19	-0.15	0.47	-0.00	0.11	0.12	0.11	0.08	0.16
7	-0.11	0.01	-0.06	-0.08	0.03	-0.05	0.10	0.00	-0.13	-0.04	-0.05	0.14	-0.03	0.14	-0.11	0.06	0.06	0.11
8	0.00	0.06	0.09	-0.17	-0.12	0.13	0.14	0.04	-0.16	-0.04	-0.08	-0.18	0.06	0.06	-0.01	0.09	0.24	-0.03
9	-0.03	0.09	-0.30	-0.05	-0.09	0.09	0.01	0.03	-0.04	0.03	-0.01	-0.41	-0.16	0.13	-0.00	0.20	0.03	0.09
10	-0.02	0.01	-0.01	-0.17	0.06	-0.08	0.01	-0.18	0.04	0.02	-0.01	-0.21	-0.23	0.08	-0.18	-0.05	-0.05	0.12
(s.e.)	(0.13)	(0.13)	(0.13)	(0.13)	(0.13)	(0.13)	(0.13)	(0.13)	(0.13)	(0.13)	(0.13)	(0.13)	(0.13)	(0.13)	(0.13)	(0.13)	(0.13)	(0.13)

Table 6B—Autocorrelations of Residuals of Real Interest Rates (International Deflators).

	US P	US F	UK P	UK F	BEL P	BEL F	FRA P	FRA F	GER P	GER F	NET P	NET F	CAN P	CAN F	JAP P	JAP F	SAFR P	SAFR F
1	0.13	-0.02	0.39	0.48	0.38	0.33	0.42	0.30	0.27	0.36	0.36	0.30	0.16	0.26	0.58	0.25	0.30	
2	0.06	0.11	-0.03	-0.02	0.25	0.04	0.16	-0.01	0.14	0.03	0.18	-0.07	-0.08	0.16	0.48	0.03	0.10	
3	-0.05	0.04	0.01	0.17	-0.31	0.02	0.09	-0.10	0.06	0.01	0.06	-0.03	-0.17	0.34	0.32	-0.11	0.03	
4	-0.02	-0.07	0.01	-0.08	0.17	-0.06	0.18	0.18	0.06	-0.10	0.07	-0.05	-0.11	0.28	0.32	-0.13	-0.17	
5	-0.02	-0.01	0.04	-0.02	0.06	-0.19	0.13	0.10	0.15	-0.19	0.06	-0.21	-0.22	-0.05	0.21	-0.08	-0.22	
6	-0.01	0.07	0.05	-0.14	0.06	-0.44	-0.03	-0.38	0.31	-0.32	0.09	-0.35	-0.10	0.01	0.17	-0.07	-0.21	
7	-0.11	0.06	-0.02	-0.17	0.26	-0.03	-0.18	-0.18	0.08	-0.06	0.03	0.08	-0.04	0.01	0.13	0.11	-0.22	
8	0.00	0.09	-0.07	-0.04	0.12	0.06	-0.18	-0.02	-0.03	0.06	-0.03	0.08	0.14	0.02	0.12	-0.10	0.12	
9	-0.03	0.09	-0.06	0.00	0.02	-0.05	-0.12	-0.11	0.04	0.07	-0.09	0.10	0.12	-0.24	0.13	-0.06	0.12	
10	-0.02	0.01	-0.06	0.12	0.11	0.01	-0.06	-0.14	0.02	0.09	0.03	-0.04	-0.12	-0.17	0.16	-0.07	0.08	
(s.e.)	(0.13)		(0.13)		(0.13)		(0.13)		(0.13)		(0.13)		(0.13)		(0.13)		(0.13)	

294

as to suggest that real interest rates in the several countries are strongly correlated on a period-to-period basis.

The autocorrelations of the residuals between the observed real interest rate and a predicted real interest rate are shown in Table 6A (where the real interest rate is based on the domestic deflator) and in Table 6B (where the international deflator is used). When the domestic deflator is used, the period-to-period residuals are correlated for seven of the nine countries when exchange rates were floating and for one country when exchange rates were pegged. The results are similar for the floating rate period when the international deflator is used and somewhat stronger for the pegged rate period. The inference is that interest rates adjust sluggishly to changes in price levels and, for several months at least, investors make systematic errors in forecasting movements in price levels.

III. Summary and Conclusions

This paper has examined whether real interest rates on similar assets denominated in various currencies differ significantly. The intuitive story is that nominal returns should not differ, because investors will shift funds to take advantage of differences in returns which exceed transaction costs. If nominal interest rates are similar, then real interest rates should also be similar. Casual empiricism suggests some doubts about the equality of both nominal and real interest rates.

Arbitrage tends to drive real interest rates toward equality. Arbitrage in financial markets differs from arbitrage in goods markets in several important ways. Investors are uncertain about future exchange rates. And while goods available in domestic and foreign markets may be perfect substitutes, domestic and foreign securities may be less than perfect substitutes because of differences in their risk characteristics.

In a multiple currency world, real interest rates will be affected by both structural disturbances and by monetary disturbances. The adjustment to structural disturbances is almost certain to involve a change in the relationship among real interest rates in the several countries. Similarly, many adjustments to monetary disturbances are likely to involve a change in the relationship among real interest rates, especially over short-run intervals of one to two years.

Testing whether real interest rates differ significantly is similar in many ways to testing whether Purchasing Power Parity holds; observed values must be compared with predicted values. Comparisons of the levels of real interest rates is analogous to testing the absolute version of Purchasing Power Parity. Comparisons of first-differences in real interest-rate levels is analogous to testing the relative version of Purchasing Power Parity. Nominal interest rates in the nine countries examined do not differ significantly after adjustment for observed changes in the exchange rates. The standard deviations of the mean interest rates are large, and although the observed means differ, the large standard errors lead to the conclusion that the means do not differ significantly. The correlation coefficients between changes in mean nominal interest rates and an unweighted mean world interest rate are reasonably low, which suggests that, in the short run at least, nominal interest rates differ significantly.

Real interest rates were obtained by deflating nominal interest rates both by changes in domestic price levels, the domestic deflator, and by changes in world price level adjusted for changes in the exchange rates, the international deflator. Both deflators result in levels of real interest rates substantially below the levels of nominal interest rates; the difference between nominal and real interest rates is greater when the international deflator is used. The differences among countries in real interest rates are greater than the differences in nominal interest rates.

Changes in the relationships among real interest rates are stronger than the changes in the relationships among nominal interest rates, more so with the use of quarterly data than with monthly data. Yet the value of these correlation coefficients is still low compared to the values that would be expected if arbitrage kept real interest rates continuously in line.

The relationship among successive observations of real interest rates was examined to determine whether the residuals were random or systematically related. For both pegged and floating periods, the residuals are correlated.

The variety of tests suggests that real interest rates do not move together on a month-to-month or quarter-to-quarter basis. The correlations generally are positive, but the values are low, much lower than would be expected if investors continuously altered the currency mix of their portfolios to take advantage of any deviations from the Law of One Price. While the findings do not permit the conclusion that the means are significantly different the data do not suggest that the means are likely to be identical. Hence, the story that investors arbitrage real interest rates into line, buttressed by the monetary approach and the theory of efficient markets, is not convincing.

ROBERT Z. ALIBER

NOTE

1. One view of Purchasing Power Parity examines the price of tradeables in the several countries. A second focuses on the relationship between the price of nontradeables, in the several countries, or between the price of tradeables and nontradeables, on the basis that the prices of tradeables in the several countries cannot significantly deviate from one another.

REFERENCES

Aliber, Robert Z., 'Equilibrium and Disequilibrium in the International Money Market', *Weltwirtschaftliches Archiv*, Vol. 112, 1976, pp. 73–90.
Aliber, Robert Z., *Exchange Risk and Corporate International Finance*, Macmillan, London, 1978.
Fisher, Irving, *The Theory of Interest*, Augustus M. Kelley, New York, 1965.
Fisher, Irving, *The Purchasing Power of Money*, Macmillan, New York, 1925.
Homer, Sidney, *A History of Interest Rates*, Rutgers University Press, New Brunswick, 1963.
Homer, Sidney and Richard I. Johannesen, *The Price of Money 1946–1969*, Rutgers University Press, New Brunswick, 1967.
Morgenstern, Oskar, *International Financial Transactions and Business Cycles*, Princeton University Press, Princeton, 1959.

Chapter Fifteen

EXCHANGE-RATE CHANGES AND THEIR EFFECT ON
EXPORT PRICES IN A DISEQUILIBRIUM MODEL OF
ITALY'S FOREIGN TRADE*

Giorgio Basevi and Renzo Orsi†

1. Introduction

This paper constitutes the first part of a study that aims at determining price and quantity of Italian commodity exports under the hypothesis of imperfectly clearing markets.

A common situation in many disequilibrium models – such as those built for the econometric analysis of financial markets – is that price (e.g., the interest rate) is set, or at least bound, by factors exogenous to the model (e.g., the monetary authorities), and that a rationing mechanism is supposed to allocate the difference between supply and demand at that price.[1]

In recent models of export behaviour, however, price is not exogenous to the model; and yet the assumption is made that it is not endogenized together with quantities exchanged at every moment in time. One reason for this failure of markets to adjust prices so as to clear continuously is typically identified in oligopolistic power on the part of exporters.[2] While adopting this

* We are grateful to Giovanni Pecci, whose research on the behaviour of Italian firms engaged in foreign trade we have here used as the basic data source on currency denomination and delivery lags in Italian export contracts. Both Pecci's work and partly our own have been financed by a Ford Foundation grant under a project directed by G. Basevi and A. Steinherr (Contract no. 775–0043). We have also benefited from the assistance of Guja Bacchilega in data collection and processing. A. S. Deaton and J. Frenkel provided constructive criticism and indications for further research when this paper was presented at the International Seminar in Macro-economics held at the Maison des Sciences de l'Homme in Paris (September 11–12, 1978).

† The authors are with the University of Bologna, and the Universities of Bologna and Modena, respectively.

hypothesis concerning the determination of *contract* export prices, we concentrate much of our study on an additional reason for the failure of actually *observed* price indices to correspond to market clearing prices. This reason is to be found in the short-run effect that changes in exchange rates have on the domestic-currency value of export unit values, as given in customs authorities data, when export contracts are denominated in foreign currencies.[3]

In Section 2 we set out our theoretical model. Section 3 deals with estimation procedures in the framework of our attempt to integrate micro- and macro-data on export price behaviour. Section 4 discusses the data and the empirical results. Section 5 contains a brief summary of our work and a few first conclusions, which will need to be reassessed and completed when the second part of our work – i.e. the one specifically aimed at discovering the export quantity determination process – has been accomplished.

2. The Model

While it may seem erroneous, even in a disequilibrium model, to separate the price and quantity determination processes, we assume a price-setting behaviour that does indeed abstract from the short-run development of the quantities demanded and actually exported.

2.1. Export price setting. Our hypothesis is that, because of greater uncertainty and imperfectly competitive positions in foreign markets, producers of exports do not allow their prices to change continuously so as to clear their share of those markets. Rather, they set them at a 'normal' level on the basis of longer-run considerations; namely, at a level consistent with the equality of long-run demand and supply, and normally modified only when required by factors affecting these long-run schedules. In the short run producers adjust quantities instead of prices, by either accumulating inventories, if demand is smaller than output, or by allowing the formation of queues, if output is below demand at the ruling 'normal' price.

According to this hypothesis, we first specify long-run supply and demand functions, and then solve simultaneously for price, so as to obtain an estimating function for 'normal' price. In order to justify the choice of variables determining our functions, we need to bear in mind that the model is built for the estimation of the quantity and price indices[4] of Italian exports of manufactures (i.e. those products that belong to groups 5–9 of the S.I.T.C.).

We assume that foreign demand for Italian exports of manufactures (X^d) depends upon the level of imports of manufactures by the main industrial countries (WTR), the unit value index of Italian exports calculated in lira terms (PX), and the export price index of the main competitors to Italian exporters in foreign markets converted into Italian lira (PWX). It is assumed that these are the basic variables that affect long-run demand, and that Italian exporters' evaluation of demand for the purpose of setting price is based on what they consider to be their 'normal' or long-run levels. Since we shall assume that exporters' price setting behaviour aims at controlling their share of the market, we shall specify the demand function in terms of market share.[5]

Thus, disregarding stochastic elements for the time being, we specify the following function with which Italian exporters estimate long-run demand for their products:

$$\frac{\bar{X}^d}{\overline{WTR}} = a_1 + a_2 PX + a_3 \overline{PWX} \tag{1}$$

where bars above the variables denote long-run equilibrium values as seen by Italian exporters. Because of our hypothesis on export price setting, PX does not bear a bar since it is assumed not to be subject to revision on the basis of short-run elements (i.e., $PX = \overline{PX}$). The expected signs of the coefficients are as follows:

$$a_1, a_3 > 0; a_2 < 0.$$

Italian exporters of manufactures are then assumed to set an export price (PX) such as to keep a share of the market consistent with the profitability of their production as determined by normal unit labour costs ($\overline{ULC}$) and their long-run estimate of the prices of imported raw materials in terms of lire ($\overline{PMRM}$). The latter are supposed to affect Italian exporters' normal offer, in so far as they weigh on them more or less than on their competitors' export prices ($\overline{PWX}$). In fact, whenever an increase in the price of Italian raw-material imports does not affect equally their competitors' prices, Italian exporters cannot increase their offer prices and are therefore negatively affected in their capacity to hold their market share. Thus, still disregarding stochastic elements, the Italian exporters' estimate of their market share as based on normal cost conditions can be described as follows:

$$\frac{\bar{X}^s}{\overline{WTR}} = b_1 + b_2 PX + b_3 \overline{ULC} + b_4 \frac{\overline{PMRM}}{\overline{PWX}} \tag{2}$$

where the expected signs of the coefficients are:

$$b_1, b_2 > 0; \ b_3, b_4 < 0.$$

Equating (1) with (2), and solving for the export price variable, we obtain:

$$PX = c_1 + c_2 \overline{PWX} + c_3 \overline{ULC} + c_4 \frac{\overline{PMRM}}{\overline{PWX}} \qquad (3)$$

where

$$c_1 = \frac{b_1 - a_1}{a_2 - b_2} \gtrless 0 \qquad\qquad c_3 = \frac{b_3}{a_2 - b_2} > 0$$

$$c_2 = \frac{-a_3}{a_2 - b_2} > 0 \qquad\qquad c_4 = \frac{b_4}{a_2 - b_2} > 0$$

Equation (3) is the basis for our estimation of normal *contract* prices of Italian exports of manufactures.[6]

2.2. Exchange rate changes and export price recording. If *recorded* prices were actual *contract* prices, we could proceed to the estimation of (3), but our results would not be very original. However, in addition to being determined at a normal level on the basis of the factors analysed in the preceding section, the price of exports is set in one or another currency, which may be that of the exporter, that of the importer, or a major third currency.[7]

In the preceding analysis it was implicitly assumed that the price was set in the exporter's currency. If it were so, no effect would result from a change in the exchange rate, besides those working directly through the variables PWX and PMRM (which, being expressed in lira terms, should be affected by the conversion into lira prices of their foreign currency counterparts), or indirectly through any other variable appearing in (3) and reacting with some lag to changes in the exchange rate (such as, in particular, ULC).

If, on the other hand, the export contract price was set in a foreign currency, its conversion into lira would be affected in an additional way by any change in the lira exchange rate vis-à-vis that particular currency. In fact recorded price indices are based on customs documents, whereby export contract values, if denominated in foreign currencies, are converted by customs officers into lira values at the exchange rate ruling at the time of the goods passing the border. Thus, if an export contract has been set at prices based on equation (3) at a moment preceding a change in the exchange rate, and if the goods covered by that contract pass the border at a moment following a change in the exchange rate, the Italian lira price actually recorded on the basis of the customs authorities' declarations will be increased (decreased) if the contract is dominated in the foreign currency vis-à-vis which the lira is devalued (revalued). This variation – which, it must be emphasized, does not take place for contracts denominated in lire– is the purely mechanical result of current customs statistics collection, and, as such, is wholly additional to the exchange-rate effects which are directly and indirectly incorporated into equation (3). This, however, means also that this effect is purely temporary, since it affects only goods crossing the border on the basis of contracts stipulated before the relevant change in the exchange rate has taken place. Goods crossing the border on the basis of contracts subsequent to an exchange-rate change will not be affected in this way.

The typical situation is represented in Figure 1 with reference

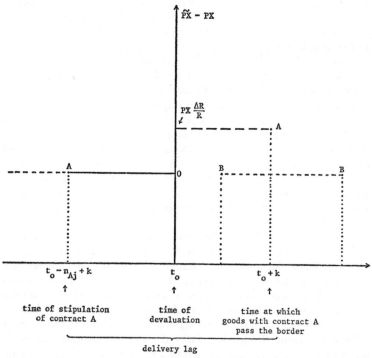

Figure 1.

302

to a representative exporting firm j. Along the vertical axis is measured the difference between the actual *recorded* export price index ($\widetilde{PX}$) for a shipment of goods under contract A and the value that it should have (PX) on the basis of an equation such as (3) when applied to this representative firm. We assume that this firm denominates its export contract A in a foreign currency. If at a time t_0 a devaluation of the domestic currency occurs in terms of this foreign currency and provided the contract was stipulated before time t_0, the passage of the goods at the border at time $t_0 + k$ is *recorded* in lire at a price $\widetilde{PX} = PX(1 + \Delta R/R)$, where R is the lira exchange rate vis-à-vis this particular currency and PX is the *contract* price converted into lira terms at the old exchange rate. In Figure 1, contract A was signed at time $(t_0 - n_{Aj} + k)$, where n_{Aj} is the delivery lag agreed upon in this contract by firm j. Contracts stipulated after time t_0 (such as one for shipment B in Figure 1) will quote prices that incorporate the new exchange rate in the basic determinant variables Z.

While Figure 1 pertains to individual contracts, and how they

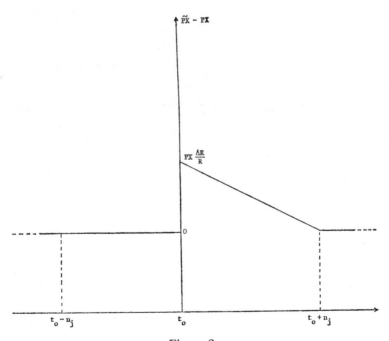

Figure 2.

303

are affected in their customs recording by an isolated change in the exchange rate, Figure 2 represents the situation of a firm j dealing with a flow of export contracts. If these are stipulated continuously, and if the delivery lag for all contracts is supposed constant and equal to n_j, the effect of a change in the exchange rate taking place at time t_0 (and still assuming denomination of all contracts in the foreign currency vis-à-vis which the lira is devalued) assumes the shape of a continuously declining rectangular frequency distribution, i.e. of a triangle with base equal to n_j as shown in Figure 2. All contracts stipulated between $(t_0 - n_j)$ and t_0 are subject to this 'customs conversion effect' (CCE); as the relative weight of contracts stipulated before time t_0 decreases with time,

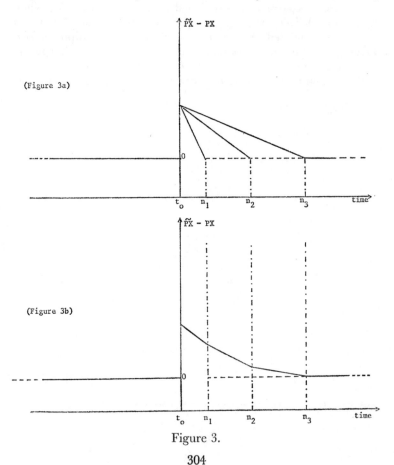

Figure 3.

their cumulated effects decrease also, and in a linear way under our assumptions.

In Figure 3, on the other hand, it is assumed that the delivery lag is not the same on all contracts made by the representative firm j (Figure 3a). In this case, the gradual expiration of contracts with various delivery lags turns our CCE into a discontinuously decreasing one (Figure 3b), which vanishes when the last goods delivered under a contract antedating the devaluation have finally been recorded at the border. With a continuous flow of contracts of various delivery lags the broken line in Figure 3b approximates a curve.

We shall deal with the problems of macro-aggregation in the next two sections. Even here, however, we may have a better understanding of the phenomenon that we intend to measure by looking at it in a graphical way which is familiar from the 'elasticity approach' to the exchange-rate effects on aggregate exports. In Figure 4 we represent the aggregate supply and demand schedules

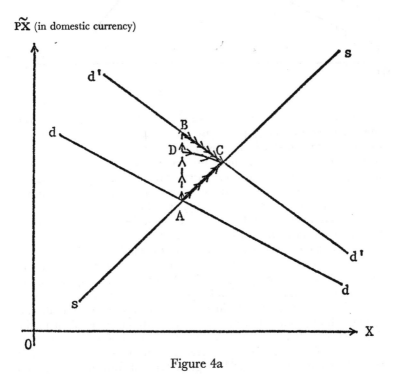

$\tilde{P}\tilde{X}$ (in domestic currency)

Figure 4a

$\widetilde{PX}$ (in foreign currency)

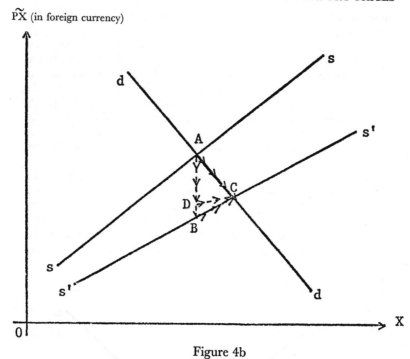

Figure 4b

that underlie our equation (3). We abstract for the time being from the quantity rationing problems that will be the object of our disequilibrium model in a subsequent paper; we do this in order to concentrate attention here on the CCE upon contracts pre-dating a variation in the exchange rate. We have assumed, in Figure 4, that the overall exchange rate of the lira (the 'effective' exchange rate) is increased, i.e. that the lira is devalued vis-à-vis a weighted average of foreign currencies. With the graph rep-resenting the lira price of exports on its vertical axis (Figure 4a), the textbook effect is to shift upward the demand for Italian exports. Now, if all export contracts were denominated in lire, we would move with some time lag from point A to point C along the supply curve. On the other hand, if all export contracts were denominated in foreign currency, we would immediately move to point B, and then gradually come down to C as the contracts antecedent to the devaluation faded away. Obviously, if only part of export contracts were denominated in foreign currencies, the vertical upward shift from A would stop short of B (e.g. at D) and from there it would

306

again move gradually to C. Figure 4b shows exactly the same three possibilities, but with the export price index on the vertical axis now denominated in foreign currency; in this case the textbook analysis describes the lira devaluation as a downward shift in the supply curve of Italian exports. Before moving to its final resting point C, short-run recorded price would immediately move to either B or D, depending upon whether the totality or only a fraction of export contracts were denominated in lire.

2·3. Aggregation. On the basis of our preceding analysis we can write the following equation for the customs recorded price of exports that the representative firm j denominates in currency i:

$$P\tilde{X}^i_{jt} = Z'_{jt}c_j \left(1 + \sum_{k=0}^{n^i_j} \frac{\Delta R_{i,\,t-k}}{R_{i,\,t-k-1}} \zeta^i_{kj} \right) \qquad (4)$$

where $Z'c$, for brevity, is the product of the vector of coefficients c in equation (3) and the vector of explanatory variables Z, and where the parameters ζ^i_{kj} are values for the decay function describing our 'customs conversion effect', such that $\zeta^i_{0j} = 1$ and $\zeta^i_{n^i_j j} = 0$, and n^i_j is the maximum delivery lag applying to the contracts made by firm j in currency i. Suppose now that a share w_{ij} of export contracts is denominated in currency i by firm j. Assuming that delivery lags are set by firm j independently of the currency of denomination of its contracts, [9] we can write:

$$P\tilde{X}_{jt} = Z'_{jt}c_j \left(1 + \sum_{i=1}^{m} \sum_{k=0}^{n_j} w_{ij} \frac{\Delta R_{i',\,t-k}}{R_{i,\,t-k-1}} \zeta_{kj} \right) \qquad (5)$$

where m is the number of currencies in which contracts are denominated, including the lira, such that $\sum_{i=1}^{m} w_{ij} = 1$.

Aggregation over firms is supposed to be perfect for the normal part of the equation, i.e. over the various $Z'_j c_j$, so that we may write:

$$P\tilde{X}_t = Z'_t c \left(1 + \sum_{j=1}^{s} \mu_j \sum_{i=1}^{m} \sum_{k=0}^{n_j} w_{ij} \frac{\Delta R_{i,\,t-k}}{R_{i,\,t-k-1}} \zeta_{kj} \right) \qquad (6)$$

where μ_j is the share of firm j in the total exports of Italian manu-

307

factures, for which $\widetilde{PX}$ is the recorded price index, such that $\sum_{j=1}^{s} \mu_j = 1$, where s is the number of firms in the population. This, together with equation (3), is our basic estimating equation.

3. Estimation Procedures

Obviously, our estimation procedures will be heavily dependent upon the availability and nature of the necessary data. While these will be discussed in more detail in Section 4, we intend to introduce the subject here in order to enable the reader to appreciate the various alternatives that were open to us with respect to estimating procedures.

3.1. With information on delivery lags.

Ideally, estimation of equations (3) and (6) would require full integration of macro- and micro-information. By this we mean that, besides the data necessary to estimate equation (3) – which is a macro-equation – we would need data from firms (or at least industrial sectors) on the denomination by currency of their contracts and on the time distribution of their delivery lags. Moreover, the two sources of data should be consistent, in the sense that the sample of firms or sectors should be representative of the macro-population, so that, in particular, the weights μ_j as they result from the sample, the currency distribution of contracts and their delivery lags should correspond to the distributions of the same variables in the total population of Italian exporters of manufactures.

If all these data were available in the form required, equation (6) would not add any problem of estimation to those presented by equation (3). In fact the parameters following the summation symbol in equation (6) would all be known, and we could estimate a corrected version of equation (3) as follows:

$$ PX \Bigg/ \left(1 + \sum_{j=1}^{s} \mu_j \sum_{i=1}^{m} \sum_{k=0}^{n_j} w_{ij} \frac{\Delta R_{i,\,t-k}}{R_{i,\,t-k-1}} \zeta_{kj}\right) = Z_i'c. \qquad (7) $$

In other words, we would previously be correcting the export-price figures on the basis of micro-data on currencies of denomination and on the distribution and maximum length of delivery lags, and we would then use the 'corrected' price variable as the new dependent variable in estimating equation (3). In terms of disequilibrium models, this means introducing explicitly the mechanism of adjustment that is necessary to re-establish equilibrium, at least with regard to the element of disequilibrium introduced into recorded export variables by customs conversion practices.

As described more fully in Section 4, we shall be able to follow this approach at least part of the way, because of our ability to tap both macro- and micro-data with characteristics closely resembling the ideal ones.

3.2. Without information on delivery lags. If micro-information on delivery lags is not available, or not fully available or not consistent with the population of the macro-data, we are in a situation where we can no longer consider as perfectly known all the parameters appearing after the summation sign in equation (6). As a consequence we are no longer able to correct the dependent variable in equation (3) before proceeding to estimate it, but shall rather have to proceed to a joint estimation of the macro-parameters of equation (3) and the micro-parameters of equation (6). For example, if the distribution of delivery lags by sectors is not fully known from the micro-data, we may have to estimate the decay function identified by the parameters ζ_{kj} in equation (6). As we shall see, it will be expedient to do so in our case, at least as a control test on the validity of the micro-information based on our sample of Italian exporting firms. Moreover, the consistency of our micro-data with the macro-aggregates appearing in equation (3) is not wholly satisfactory, for reasons that will be explained more fully in Section 4. In particular, the μ_j resulting from our micro-sample do not correspond to the weights resulting from aggregate statistics on Italian foreign trade. Also, data provided by the Bank of Italy on the currency distribution of Italian export receipts are, in some cases, excessively at variance with the currency distribution of export contract denomination.[10]

Because of these various failures of data and theoretical difficulties, we would like to estimate, in addition to equation (7), a linear approximation to equation (6), which takes the following form:

$$\widetilde{PX}_t = Z_t c + \left(\sum_{j=i}^{s} \mu_j \sum_{i=1}^{m} \sum_{k=0}^{n_j} w_{ij} \frac{\Delta R_{i,\,t-k}}{R_{i,\,t-k-1}} \zeta_{kj} \right) \widetilde{PX}_{t-1} \qquad (8)$$

3.3 Partial versus full aggregation. In Equation (8), although the parameters n_j and ζ_{kj} should be jointly estimated with the other parameters originally coming from equation (3), we would still keep the micro-basis of the information by not aggregating them over the whole population of the exporting sectors. This, however, is a great weakness from the point of view of econometric estimation, because it greatly reduces the degrees of freedom of our estimation. We are therefore strongly inclined, if for no other reason at least as a check on the validity of our assumptions and estimates based on micro-data, to take a bolder step towards full aggregation. This consists in assuming that perfect aggregation of the distribution of currency denomination and delivery lags can be performed over firms and sectors of Italian exporters, so as to enable us to write the following aggregate equation:

$$PX_t = Z_t'c + \left(\sum_{k=0}^{n} \zeta_k \sum_{j=1}^{s} \mu_j \sum_{i=0}^{m} w_{ij} \frac{\Delta R_{i,t-k}}{R_{i,\,t-k-1}} \right) \tilde{PX}_{t-1} \qquad (9)$$

where $n = \sum_{j=1}^{s} \mu_j n_j$ and where instead of a series of ζ_{kj} for every sector j, we estimate a unique set of ζ_k coefficients which, as we shall see later, correspond to the $\zeta_k = \sum_{j} \mu_j \zeta_{kj}$ appearing in Table IV.

4. Empirical Results

4.1. Sources of data. The sources for our macro-data were standard, being statistics published by international organizations (O.E.C.D. and I.M.F.) and by national authorities (the Bank of Italy and the Italian Statistical Office). These sources were used in order to obtain directly, or to construct, the indices of unit values of Italian exports of manufactures ($\tilde{PX}$) and those of Italy's export competitors (PWX),[11] the shares of the different commodity exporting sectors in the aggregate exports of manufactures (μ_j), the relevant series of lira exchange rates vis-à-vis a number of foreign currencies (R_i), the index of Italian unit labour costs in manufacturing (ULC), and the Italian price index of imported raw materials (PMRM).

More interesting, both theoretically and empirically, is the source of our micro-data. These were obtained from a study of the behaviour of Italian importers and exporters based on a sample survey of 408 Italian firms.[12] Both in that study and in our own use of it, the sample of firms has been aggregated into a number of sectors generally corresponding to the one-digit categories of the S.I.T.C. In what follows, we shall assume that this aggregation is without bias and we shall, from now on, substitute sectors for firms in the estimates of our disaggregated equations (3)–(8).

Table 1. Distribution by currency of contract denomination in a survey of Italian exporting firms – *Percentages*.

S.I.T.C. Categories	Years	Ital. L	U.S.$	D.M.	Brit. £	F.F.	Other E.E.C. Curren.	Other Curren.	Total
5	1970	36.9	15.1	9.8	13.1	10.6	8.1	6.4	100
	71–73	29.6	17.9	13.1	12.0	8.5	9.7	9.2	100
	1976	22.9	21.8	17.5	11.3	7.8	11.3	7.4	100
6.1–6.5	1970	64.3	9.2	10.1	5.2	6.0	4.5	1.7	100
	71–73	60.4	12.5	11.2	4.0	6.5	4.3	1.1	100
	1976	50.3	17.9	16.4	3.1	5.7	5.2	1.3	100
6.6–6.9	1970	37.6	13.8	12.5	12.6	12.1	7.0	4.4	100
	71–73	33.2	16.5	15.9	10.0	9.8	7.5	7.1	100
	1976	23.8	22.6	21.8	8.7	9.5	8.2	5.3	100
7.1	1970	46.2	18.7	7.5	10.4	8.9	5.1	3.2	100
	71–73	43.5	20.2	9.1	8.1	6.9	7.1	5.1	100
	1976	34.6	30.2	12.6	5.6	6.1	6.9	4.1	100
7.2	1970	40.8	16.6	11.9	9.1	12.1	7.3	2.2	100
	71–73	38.3	18.0	12.5	8.2	10.6	7.9	4.5	100
	1976	28.9	24.2	19.8	6.0	8.2	8.7	4.2	100
7.3	1970	26.8	15.9	12.1	16.1	14.4	6.1	8.6	100
	71–73	23.3	19.3	12.9	15.0	12.8	8.5	8.2	100
	1976	15.7	21.4	15.6	15.2	12.1	10.0	10.0	100
8–9	1970	42.3	16.1	10.0	8.0	8.2	6.5	8.9	100
	71–73	38.7	19.1	12.9	7.0	10.1	6.8	5.4	100
	1976	29.2	24.3	15.6	7.3	10.7	7.1	5.8	100

311

Out of the many questions asked in the survey questionnaire, two were particularly relevant to our study, namely (i) in which currency does the exporting firm denominate the contract price, and (ii) what is the length of the lag between the time at which the contract is stipulated and the time at which the goods are delivered.

The answers to the first question were directly usable for our purposes: the questionnaire provided precodified answers which detailed, in this case, the possibility of denominating in Italian lire, US $, DM, British £, FF, other EEC currencies, and all other currencies.

As for the second question, we have assumed that the time lag between contract stipulation and product delivery closely approximates that between contract stipulation and time at which the documents accompanying the goods at the border of exit are entered by customs authorities. It is this control which is the basis of foreign trade statistics over which unit value indices are constructed, and which gives rise to the CCE that we are trying to identify.

The answers to the first question gave rise to the data reported here in Table 1. These data are interesting in themselves, as they show how, comparing years before and after the move to fluctuating exchange rates, the role of the lira in the invoicing of exports dropped substantially, while that of the DM increased correspondingly. Be that as it may, we have used the information in Table 1 in order to construct series of sectoral 'effective' changes in the lira exchange rates, to be used as the changes in the variables R_i in equations (3) and (7). In order to do so, we have considered that the currency weights resulting from the survey as applying to 1970 also applied to the whole period of the sample before 1970; and those applying to 1976 similarly applied to our sample period from 1974 to 1976. We have then used these weights to construct sectoral series of 'effective' exchange-rate changes.

The answers to the second question produced the data reported here in Table 2. We report for each sector only the maximum lag that any answering firm in that sector declared to be its average delivery lag. In other words, we do not report average sector lags, because for our purpose of identifying the limit of the CCE distribution, it is the maximum lag (with respect to the sector) applied by any single firm that matters. It is noticeable from Table 2 that, although behaviour regarding *payments* lags changed significantly as between the period of fixed exchange rates (before February–March 1973) and that of floating rates, behaviour in

312

respect of *delivery* lags was not significantly affected. This is, in fact, essentially dependent on commercial practices and technological factors; and in any case, no clear incentive seems to exist for changing it in response to an increase or decrease in the degree of uncertainty about exchange rates. In any case, although extremely interesting for other purposes, the payment lags are not reported here because they are not relevant to our analysis. This is concerned with data on export unit values and real trade movements; an analysis of trade credit (capital movements) would, on the other hand, be highly dependent on information about payment lags and how they are affected by exchange-rate changes.

Table 2. Time lags between contract stipulation and delivery of goods in a survey of Italian exporting firms.

	Maximum time lags in days	
S.I.T.C. categories	*Before 1973*	*After 1973*
5	106	112
6.1–6.5	130	120
6.6–6.9	175	180
7.1	360	360
7.2	225	210
7.3	105	125
8–9	250	240

Note: the S.I.T.C. categories are as follows:

5	Chemicals
6.1 to 6.5	Other manufactured goods
6.6 to 6.9	Iron, steel and other metal manufactures
7.1	Machinery and non-electrical equipment
7.2	Machinery and electrical equipment
7.3	Transport products
8 to 9	Miscellaneous manufactured products.

4.2. Analysis of the estimates. In our estimates we proceeded in the following way.

(a) Our *first step* was to estimate the basic long-run equation (3), as if PX were not subject to our 'customs conversion' noise. The result is somewhat unsatisfactory because, as usual in applied econometric work, a best specification (in terms of how to estimate – through moving averages or lag structures – the 'normal' levels of the independent variables) was obtained by trial and error. This process was affected by the use of a dependent variable not yet corrected for our CCE. In order to eliminate this original bias, we returned subsequently to the search for a 'best' specification of our

Table 3. Summary of Estimation Results. (Quarterly data 1963.1–1976.4).

Explanatory Variables	$\overline{PWX}_t$	$\overline{ULC}_t$	$\sum_{i=0}^{3} w_i \dfrac{PMRM_{t-i}}{PWX_{t-i}}$ (*)	CCE before 1973	CCE after 1973	R^2	S.E.	D.W.
Equations *Basic Equation* (3)	0.905 (13.38)	0.631 (2.70)	−0.02 (−0.08)	not considered	not considered	0.99	3.72	1.03
Equation (7) With micro-survey information	0.823 (11.56)	0.576 (1.91)	0.046 (2.78)	a priori constraint	a priori constraint	0.99	3.45	1.31
Equation (9) (9.1) with n = 3 and ζ_o free	0.832 (13.05)	0.652 (3.12)	0.040 (1.36)	not significant	significant	0.99	3.32	1.14
(9.2) with n free, $\zeta_o = 1$ and other ζ on a linear decay function	0.676 (7.97)	1.022 (4.64)	0.109 (2.35)	not significant	significant	0.99	3.06	1.70
(9.3) with n free, $\zeta_o = 1$ and other ζ on a second-degree decay function	0.727 (8.22)	0.897 (3.92)	0.088 (1.87)	not significant	significant	0.99	3.00	1.64

Note: The figures in parentheses are t-values for estimated coefficients.
(*) These values are the sum of w_i distributed lag coefficients for a second-degree polynomial which are restricted to zero at the end of the period.

314

basic equation (3) after having completed a first series of exploratory estimates over the dependent variable corrected for the CCE.

The results of our estimates of equation (3) are reported in the first row of Table 3. The 'normal' values of the independent variables were obtained as moving averages over four periods for PWX and ULC, whereas in the case of PMRM/PWX we were compelled to use Almon distributed lags, because of the high degree of multicollinearity between variables. On the basis of our many provisional results, we can also attribute in large measure to multicollinearity the fact that the coefficient c_4 is not significantly different from zero. On the other hand, the coefficients c_2 and c_3 have the expected sign and are statistically significant. The constant c_1 could, theoretically, have any sign; our best estimates turned out to be those without it.

On the whole the statistics of the estimate reveal a good fit, except for the DW test, which indicates the presence of a certain positive autocorrelation of errors. This, however, was to be expected, since we know that the dependent variable is still subject to our CCE. It will indeed be interesting to see whether the DW test improves in the following estimates, where such noise is explicitly taken into account.

(b) Our *second step* involved exploiting the information provided by the micro-survey in order to compute the CCE, and constrain the dependent variable $\tilde{PX}$ to satisfy the structure of exchange-rate adjustments represented in equation (7). In other words, we recomputed a series of export-price indices and estimated over it our basic long-run equation as obtained from the first step. Because the sectoral weights μ_j that result from the micro-survey are sometimes substantially different from what they should be on the basis of macro-data of Italian exports, we computed this estimate using alternatively the survey data and the macro-data on the weights μ_j.[13] Since the results of these two alternative estimates are not significantly different, we report in Table 3 only the regression based on the micro-survey values of μ_j.

As for the coefficients ζ_{kj} of the decay function, their values, as revealed by the micro-survey, are reported in Table 4 for each sector j. In accordance with the data reported in Table 2, their values reach zero, for all sectors, before the fourth quarter after a change in the exchange rate.

The coefficients and statistics of this second-step estimate are reported in the second row of Table 3. It can be seen from this estimate of equation (7) that the use of our survey information on the CCE helps in reducing multicollinearity and residual autocorrelation. In fact, c_4, the coefficient of PMRM/PWX, becomes positive and significant, while the two other coefficients are not substantially different from the estimates of equation (3); moreover, the value of the DW statistic is increased. In addition, as we shall discuss in more detail in Section 5, the residual percentage errors of the estimate are noticeably reduced at critical points of the sample, when the effective exchange rate of the lira was subject to substantial shocks.

(c) Ideally, our *third step* should now lead to estimation of equation (8). This would mean trying to estimate, rather than impose, a series of sectoral decay functions for the CCE. While the information necessary for this procedure is available to us from the survey, we provisionally decided to postpone such an attempt, because of its demanding characteristics, particularly with respect to degrees of freedom and number of explanatory variables. Thus we directly moved to estimation of equation (9).

Table 4. Decay Functions for the CCE.

(A) Disaggregated weights from micro-survey data.

Weights ζ_{kj}	Before 1973				After 1973			
S.I.T.C.	0	1	2	3	0	1	2	3
5	1.0	0.19	—	—	1.0	0.14	—	—
6.1–6.5	1.0	0.30	—	—	1.0	0.24	—	—
6.6–6.9	1.0	0.48	—	—	1.0	0.49	—	—
7.1	1.0	0.75	0.49	0.24	1.0	0.75	0.49	0.24
7.2	1.0	0.59	0.19	—	1.0	0.57	0.13	—
7.3	1.0	0.13	—	—	1.0	0.27	—	—
8–9	1.0	0.64	0.27	—	1.0	0.63	0.24	—

(B) Aggregated weights over S.I.T.C. groups 5–9.

Weights ζ_k	Before 1973				After 1973			
	0	1	2	3	0	1	2	3
O.E.C.D. data on μ_j	1.0	0.48	0.17	0.05	1.0	0.48	0.16	0.05
Micro-survey data on μ_j	1.0	0.44	0.13	0.04	1.0	0.43	0.12	0.04

where $\zeta_k = \sum\limits_{j=1}^{s} \mu_j \zeta_{kj}$.

We do not present in Table 3, nor discuss here, the complete set of our results, but only those which seem interesting in the light of our theoretical analysis. Here too, moreover, for the sake of partially verifying the validity of the survey data, we performed all estimates in the two versions based on the alternative sources (survey or OECD) for weighting (with the μ_j) the sectoral information coming from the questionnaire sent to Italian foreign traders. However, because of substantial similarity of the results, we present only the versions pertaining to the micro-survey values of μ_j. In all cases, we want to emphasize that equation (9) implies that the weights of the decay function of the CCE are now estimated over the data, except for ζ_o which must theoretically be equal to unity. This constraint has been explicitly introduced into the estimating procedures of some versions of equation (9), whereas in others we have been interested in seeing whether its free estimate significantly differs from unity. In addition, in some cases, we have also checked through free estimation whether the time at which the CCE vanishes does indeed correspond to that resulting from the micro-survey (i.e., an aggregate $n = \sum \mu_j n_j$ lying between 180 and 270 days.

Table 3 presents a first version of equation (9), i.e., equation (9.1), in which ζ_o is left free but n is constrained at its aggregated survey value, and the decay function is compelled to assume a triangular form. In this case also, as previously in the case of equation (7), the estimates improve relative to the basic equation (3), both in terms of increased significance of the coefficients and somewhat reduced autocorrelation. Moreover, the coefficient on the new explanatory variable for the CCE is significant for the period of generalized exchange-rate fluctuation (after 1973). We are not surprised, on the other hand, that this variable is not significant before 1973, for two reasons. First, and most obviously, the lira effective exchange rate was relatively stable during that first part of the sample. Secondly, and quite interestingly from our point of view, it seems to have been the practice of the Italian customs authorities before 1971 to use the IMF fixed parities, rather than actual market rates, to convert into lira values the foreign-currency equivalent of export and import contracts. This practice, as far as we understand, was also followed by the statistical office of the OECD when translating into US$ values the original domestic-currency values of foreign trade for the purpose of compiling their statistical publications, on which our price indices are based. Thus, for both reasons, it is only after 1971–73 that our CCE should really have introduced predictable noise into the data of export price indices.

With respect to equation (7), where the weights of the decay function are predetermined on the basis of the survey information, we now see from Table 4 that, letting the data estimate the ζ_k over a straight line, does not substantially alter their values. In particular, the value of ζ_0 seems to be not significantly different from unity after 1973, as it should be. On the other hand, with respect to the structure of equation (7), the degree to which auto-correlation has been reduced is less satisfactory. This may be due to the fact that in equation (9.1) we constrained the aggregated weights ζ_k to lie on a straight line, even though theoretically they should dispose themselves along a curve as shown in Figure 3b. This theoretical feature was, on the other hand, satisfied by our estimate of equation (7).

In equation (9.2) we introduce the constraint that $\zeta_0 = 1$, while, on the other hand, we allow the data to identify the vanishing point of the CCE. As shown in detail by Table 4, the decay function in this case does not decrease immediately after time t_0: the first estimated coefficient ζ_1 is still not significantly different from unity, and only the subsequent values of ζ_k drop along a straight line to reach zero between the third and fourth quarters. While this second feature, being the free result of the data, confirms the length of the CCE as it emerged from the survey information, the first feature may seem surprising. Its economic meaning, and possible justification, would be that during the first quarter following a change in the exchange rate an insignificant amount of goods passes the border under contracts that have already incorporated the economic effects of the exchange rate. Since our data – being quarterly averages (for both prices and exchange rates) – do not fully correspond to what our theoretical apparatus would require – i.e., instantaneous observations over continuous time – this result may indeed be justifiable along such lines. In any case we notice that the estimate of (9.2) presents substantial improvements in the DW test.

Finally, the specification of equation (9.3) differs from that of (9.2) only with respect to the forms of the decay function, in the sense that we have tried to obtain an approximation to its theoretical shape by choosing a second-degree polynomial for the weights of the CCE. The empirical results, as shown particularly by Table 4, give again rise to the phenomenon just discussed, namely that ζ_1 is not significantly different from unity. In other words, it seems to take one quarter before goods under new contracts incorporating the exchange-rate changes come through the border. On the other hand, the subsequent form of the decay curve follows its theoretically expected shape, by decreasing smoothly at a decreasing rate. This feature, of course, was not allowed by our previous estimates of equation (9), since they were done with a first-degree polynomial. As for the other statistics, equation (9.3) presents substantially the same positive features as equation (9.2).

Notice, however, that in all estimates presented in Table 3 the very high values of R^2 suggest that, in addition to the purely economic relationship between $\tilde{PX}$ and the explanatory variables in the regressions, there might be at work the effect of other variables acting on both sides of the equations. This is another indication that the basic equation (3) still needs better theoretical specification.

5. Conclusions

Our general result is that, throughout the various ways in which we have attempted to correct for the basic export-price-setting equation in order to take into account the customs conversion effect, the estimates of the coefficients, as well as the overall statistics of the equations, improved. In addition, a scrutiny of the residual percentage errors of the estimates shows interesting aspects that cannot be captured in the overall analysis of the results conducted in the preceding section. In particular, considering that the lira depreciated substantially in effective terms in 1973, and then again in 1976, it is of interest to concentrate attention on errors of estimate during these periods.

Our basic, i.e. uncorrected, equation (3) has the following residual percentage errors in the four quarters of 1973: +1.44, +3.48, +2.17, −0.04. Our equation (9.3), one of the best, shows for the same period the following errors: +0.18, −0.39, −0.61, +0.12. The corresponding errors in 1976 are, for equation (3), −2.72, +5.75, +2.98, −0.35, while for equation (9.3) they are −5.02, −0.45, +1.68, +1.67. It is clear that, for these two periods of turbulence in the lira exchange rate, and particularly in 1973, our treatment of the customs conversion effect has substantially reduced the residual errors of the estimate. The only important exception seems to be that for the first quarter of 1976. Here, however, we have a clear explanation for our poor result. During a large part of that quarter the official foreign-exchange market was closed in Italy (from January 21 to February 27, 1976). While our series on exchange rates, being based on Bank of Italy data, refers for that period to the lira rates quoted in the

Frankfurt market, the customs authorities kept using, as their conversion rates in collecting export contract statistics, the official rates last quoted before the closing of the official market. As these could not take into account the substantial devaluation of the lira that intervened in foreign-exchange markets during that month, – whereas our series of exchange rates does – we introduce an element of excessive correction by applying also to this particular observation our customs conversion effect. And, indeed, whereas the uncorrected error of the estimate (from equation (3)) is only -2.7 in 1976.1, it increases *downwards* to -5.0 per cent in our 'corrected' estimates: a clear sign that we have excessively accounted for the CCE by using the true (Frankfurt) market rates instead of the rates adopted by Italian border authorities at that time.

Summarizing now the general characteristic of our treatment of the CCE, we may say that, when information about this phenomenon is wholly taken from the micro-survey sample and introduced as correction of our macro-data before estimating the price setting function (equation (7)), the results are good, relative to those based on uncorrected data, but they still suffer from a certain degree of autocorrelation of the residuals, albeit in a reduced amount.

On the other hand, when this information is used only partially by either imposing the initial value of the decay function or the length of it, but not imposing its shape to conform exactly to the one resulting from the micro-survey, then our results improve more substantially. This is true in particular when we impose $\zeta_0 = 1$ but let a second-degree polynomial adjust a best decay function. In this case the coefficients ζ_k dispose themselves along a theoretically predicted curve, and they also vanish at a point close to that indicated by the information of the micro-survey. Moreover, autocorrelation of the errors is further and substantially reduced.

Another interesting result, even though one that should have been expected on *a priori* grounds, is that in all cases the estimates of the CCE are significant only for the period of generalized fluctuation of exchange rates.

In conclusion, we feel confident in saying that correction for the customs conversion effect is worthwhile and even necessary to improve the basic estimate of the price-setting behaviour of Italian exporters of manufactures. Of course, there are limits to our analysis and results. The basic equation (3) does not yet fully conform to our *a priori* theoretical model, and we still expect to improve it, particularly by incorporating explicitly into the model the disequilibrium analysis of export quantity determination. In addition, the quality of the data, particularly with respect to export price indices (unit values), is far from satisfactory. The usual defects of these have probably been compounded, in our case, by the strong assumptions we have been compelled to introduce in order to ignore the problems generally arising from aggregation biases.

NOTES

1. See, for example, Melitz and Pardue (1973), and Laffont and Garcia (1977).
2. See, for example, Minford (1978), Chapter 3.
3. The extent to which our approach follows the path-breaking work by Magee (1973, 1974) will be apparent. However, we depart from Magee and the literature that has been built upon his work, by attempting to integrate econometrically the information that is available to us about micro-data on export contracts and delivery lags into a macroestimation of export price and quantity determination.
4. Although we are aware of the problems and errors connected with the use of unit values as proxies for export or import price indices, we shall ignore them in this paper. On this, see particularly Kravis and Lipsey (1971).
5. To be sure, this information has been almost imposed on us by the need to escape the heavy multicollinearity between the main export demand variable (WTR) and most of the price and cost variables, that has plagued our attempts to estimate export levels rather than shares.
6. Assuming that equations (1) and (2) are stochastic with errors characterized by the usual properties, the error term of equation (3) will also enjoy those properties, since it is a weighted average of the errors in (1) and (2).
7. On this phenomenon, see Grassman (1973a, 1973b, 1976) and Pecci (1978).
8. The figure, as is well known from the theory of international trade, suffers from the partial-equilibrium features of the 'elasticity approach'. Our formal model, however, need not be affected by this weakness, as all relevant elements should have been included in equation (3); this means that in reality both the demand and supply curve in Figures 4a and 4b are shifted in various ways by the direct and indirect effects of exchange-rate changes. Whatever these may be, and hence wherever will be point C relative to point A, our customs conversion effect is additional to these exchange-rate effects, and it shifts the normal adjustment path in the way described in Figures 4a and 4b with respect to its partial-equilibrium counterpart.
9. We are aware of the seriousness of this assumption, which we are however compelled to make for the sake of simplicity. We plan to correct for it in our subsequent study, where the full information provided by Pecci's research will be available.
10. While there is no need that the currency in which export receipts are obtained be the same as the currency in which export contracts are initially denominated, the correlation of their distributions should not be too low.
11. These indices were directly obtained from an unpublished O.E.C.D. source. Note that theoretically PWX, being a composite index of our competitors' export unit values, should also be adjusted for the customs conversion effects pertaining

to each of its component export unit values. We assume, however, that the various CCE wash out in the process of aggregation that leads to the composite index PWX.

12. See Pecci (1978). The sample chosen was originally made up of 1016 firms randomly drawn out of the list of addresses available from the Italian Institute for Foreign Trade. A total of 408 questionnaires were returned three months after their distribution (June 1977), but only 347 were fully satisfactory for the purposes of Pecci's research.

13. These differences may be due to the fact that, since the questionnaire presented the various sectors with the names given to them in the S.I.T.C., but without explicitly referring to this classification, it is possible that some firms misplaced themselves. In any case, we doubt that an explicit reference to the S.I.T.C. in the questionnaire would have improved the results: besides suspecting that many firms ignore this international classification, we also notice a tendency on their part lazily to place themselves in the residual categories of products.

REFERENCES

Grassman, S. (1973a), 'A Fundamental Symmetry in International Payments Patterns', *Journal of International Economics*, 3, 105–116.

Grassman, S. (1973b), *Exchange Reserves and the Financial Structure of Foreign Trade*, London, Saxon House & Lexington Books.

Grassman, S. (1976), 'Currency Distribution and Forward Cover in Foreign Trade', *Journal of International Economics*, 6, 215–221.

Kravis, I. B. and R. E. Lipsey (1971), *Price Competitiveness in Foreign Trade*, National Bureau of Economic Research, Columbia University Press.

Laffont, J. J. and Garcia, R. (1977), 'Disequilibrium Econometrics for Business Loans', *Econometrica*, 45, 1187–1204.

Magee, S. (1973), 'Currency Contracts, Pass-through and Devaluation', *Brookings Papers on Economic Activity*, 303–325.

Magee, S. (1974), 'U.S. Import Prices in the Currency–Contract Period', *Brookings Papers on Economic Activity*, 117–168.

Melitz, J. and Pardue, M. (1973), 'The Demand and Supply of Commercial Bank Loans', *Journal of Money, Credit and Banking*, 5, 669–692.

Minford, P. (1978), *Substitution Effects, Speculation and Exchange Rate Stability*, Amsterdam, North Holland Publishing Co.

Pecci, G. (1978), 'Commercio estero, imprese manifatturiere e svalutazione: indagine su un campione di imprese italiane nel passaggio dai cambi fissi ai cambi flessibili', *Prometeia, Rapporto di Previsione*, June.

EXCHANGE RATES AND EXPORT PRICES: A COMMENT

Marcus H. Miller

THE AUTHORS examine the way in which the prices of Italian manufactured exports are determined and consider in particular how export prices in lira will change when the external value of the lira changes. The hypothesis tested is that the price charged for any given volume of exports will reflect both demand factors and cost factors. Demand factors are represented by a measure of the size of this market (imports by the main industrial countries) and an index of the prices charged by the main competitors to Italian exporters: supply factors include the same measure of market size together with unit labour costs and the costs of imported raw materials. On the assumption that market size will affect demand and supply equally, the authors conclude that export prices in lira will be determined solely by the index of competitors' prices (converted into lira) and by the two cost indices, (see equation 3) and they assume that those factors will determine prices even before volumes have time to adjust.

When the chosen equation is fitted to data for Italian exporters from 1963–74, the role of competitors' prices and of labour costs is confirmed. However, the measure which is used to represent the cost of raw-material imports is generally not significant, so if labour costs do not react quickly to devaluation, the results suggest that there will be no very substantial 'cost-push' effect of devaluation on Italian export prices; export prices will rather be pulled up by competitors' prices. It should, however, be noted that in the empirical work the cost of raw materials appears only when deflated by the index of competitors' prices. Hence if both raw-material import costs and competitors' prices remain constant in foreign currency terms on devaluation, this import cost index would show no change, and any increase in lira export prices as a consequence of devaluation will have to be attributed to the 'demand-pull' of competitors' prices. As the way the import cost variable is defined seems likely to exaggerate the measured influence of competitors' prices relative to import costs, the rejection of import cost-push effects may be more apparent than real.

In their investigations of the impact of demand and cost factors on lira export prices the authors are very careful to take account of the extended delays between the time at which export contracts are agreed and the time that delivery is effected. If a devaluation of the lira occurs between the signing of the contract and the delivery of the goods, then such deliveries after devaluation will reflect pre-devaluation costs and prices.

If the contracts were agreed in lira then, it is argued, such deliveries would show no change in lira value due to the devaluation, but if the contracts were agreed in foreign currency, they will be revalued when the rate changes and will show a large change when the lira falls. The resulting difference in the value of the foreign currency contracts and their lira equivalents is what they call the customs conversion effect (CCE) and considerable attention is given to measuring it and to seeing whether allowing for CCE will reduce the serial correlation in the equation residuals which exists when the role of foreign-currency contracts is ignored. The influence of the effect is only reckoned to be temporary, lasting only as long as there are backlogged contracts to be delivered. When all such contracts have been delivered, the price of exports whether invoiced in lira or foreign currency will be the same and will reflect costs and foreign prices measured at the new, post-devaluation exchange rate.

The authors note that the share of exports invoiced in foreign currency expanded progressively over the sample period, a period in which the lira weakened considerably. *Prima facie* this would appear to imply that CCE must become a more important feature in determining lira earnings as time progresses and such trends continued. But such a conclusion is a little odd: if the CCE means that foreign buyers are paying more for Italian goods invoiced in foreign currency than they would if invoiced in lira, why do such importers condone an increase in this foreign-currency invoicing as the lira weakens? And, more fundamentally, if both parties to such contracts come to expect the lira to fall in value before delivery, would some allowance not be appropriate for this in drawing up the different invoices, an allowance which would tend to reduce the measured CCE?

In what follows use is made of an extremely simplified version of the equation fitted to the data to define CCE and to show how CCE will be affected if contracts are drawn up to allow for anticipation of exchange-rate change as embodied in the forward exchange rate.

In schematic form (and omitting the index of imported raw materials altogether) equation (3)

$$p = \alpha e p_w' + \beta c$$

where p is the price of exports (in lira)

p_w' is the index of competitors' prices (in foreign currency)

e is the spot exchange rate (foreign currency units/lira)

c is the index of unit labour costs (in lira).

Assuming that p_w' and c are constant, and that for the exports under consideration there is a *one-period delay* between contract and delivery, one may value contracts made just before a devaluation at the time of their actual delivery (post-devaluation) as follows:

$$V_1 = \alpha \, Lep_w' + \beta c$$

will be the lira value of a lira contract (where $Le \equiv e_{t-1}$) and

$$V_2 = e \left\{ \frac{\alpha Lep_w' + \beta c}{Le} \right\} = e\alpha p_w' + \frac{e}{Le} \beta c$$

will be the lira value of a foreign-currency contract. Hence the customs conversion effect may be determined as:

$$CCE = V_2 - V_1 = \left(\frac{e - Le}{Le} \right) \alpha Lep_w' + \left(\frac{e - Le}{Le} \right) \beta c = \left(\frac{e - Le}{Le} \right) V_1$$

So the customs conversion effect simply measures the change in the value of foreign-currency contracts relative to their lira counterparts as the relative price of foreign currency changes.

At the time the contracts were drawn up, however, there would have been forward exchange rates available, and, for purposes of illustration, one may assume that these rates could be used to convert lira and foreign-currency values at the time of signing the contract. Hence the price agreed in lira, for goods to be delivered one period hence, would be

$$p = \alpha f p_w' + \beta c$$

325

where f is the forward exchange rate (foreign currency/lira) and the contract price agreed in foreign currency (p') would be

$$p' = \frac{p}{f} = \alpha p'_w + \frac{\beta c}{f}$$

After a devaluation the value of these two contracts would be

$$V_1 = \alpha f p'_w + \beta c$$

$$V_2 = e \alpha p'_w + \frac{e \beta c}{f}$$

and so the customs conversion effect is

$$CCE = V_2 - V_1 = \left(\frac{e - Lf}{Lf}\right)(\alpha f p'_w + \beta c)$$

$$= \left\{\frac{(e - Le) - (Lf - Le)}{Lf}\right\} V_1$$

But now this effect can have either sign, and it will be positive only if the rise in the actual price of foreign currency exceeds the forward premium as it stood at contract time ($e - Le > Lf - Le$).

If the forward rate was an accurate predictor of the future spot exchange rate (so $e - Le = Lf - Le$) then there would be zero CCE, so both lira and foreign-currency contracts would have the same value at delivery time. But this is not to say that the lira value of deliveries remains constant when the lira falls; instead the lira value of contracts to deliver in the future is adjusted at contract time to ensure that the price on delivery will reflect the higher lira prices on export deliveries. The absence of the CCE resulting from such behaviour indicates the correct adjustment of lira prices to take account of the exchange-rate change.

In terms of the author's diagram 4, this means that if contracts are drawn up at a forward rate which is equal to the actual future spot rate then the recorded price will move directly to the new equilibrium level (shown as C in that diagram) and that this movement will *not* depend on the currency of denomination – as CCE will, in this circumstance, be zero. It is silly to suppose that the forward rate will typically forecast the future spot rate accurately but it is important to note that a jump at devaluation does not necessarily indicate the presence of CCE; that it is consistent with no CCE and accurate foresight. Is it not possible that some of the equation residuals being 'explained' by CCE are partly the result of assuming *no* 'forecasting' of devaluation? Could they not therefore be 'explained' by allowing for devaluation anticipations to have some effect on contracts for future delivery, in the way discussed above for example?

Lastly, one can argue that if contracts for future delivery are drawn up using information given by the forward rate, rather than the prevailing spot rate, then this *could* lead to a switch to foreign-currency invoicing for the exports of a country with a current deficit and a weak forward rate.

The argument is that for such a weak currency the forward discount may well *exceed* the amount of depreciation expected. Hence $e - Le < Lf - Le$ and CCE will be negative, *even when expectations are realised*. But if CCE is negative, foreign-currency contracts turn out to be less expensive than their lira equivalents; which explains why they will be attractive to foreign importers. As for Italian exporters, they could, by selling the foreign currency forward, attain the same amount of lira as they could have obtained by invoicing in lira. So the downward shading of the prices charged in foreign-currency contracts to reflect the weakness in the forward lira, together with the ability of Italian exporters to sell their foreign-currency earnings forward at a considerable forward premium, would make the shift towards foreign-currency invoicing (at a time of increasing lira weakness) more explicable than it is on the authors' working assumption that there is no shading of the price of goods when a strong foreign currency is chosen for invoicing.

Perhaps the authors' survey data could be used to check the working assumption that provides them with such pronounced customs conversion effects? Was there really no shading of the price charged to foreign buyers who agreed to be invoiced in a strong foreign currency?

A REJOINDER TO MILLER

Giorgio Basevi and Renzo Orsi

IN HIS EXCELLENT discussion of our paper, Marcus Miller raises two main questions connected with the role of exchange rate expectations in the process of setting export prices.

The first, and more fundamental, question is directly aimed at how exporters and their importing partners incorporate into contract prices their respective expectations about exchange rates. The second question is put in the form of a puzzle : why should foreign importers have accepted an increase in the share of contracts denominated in non-lira currency during a period when the lira was weakening?

On the first question, Miller rightly argues a point which had also been made clear to us by Jacob Frenkel during an earlier presentation of this paper: namely that, if changes in exchange rates were perfectly anticipated and incorporated into contract prices, there would be no CCE left to measure. Against this, we can only argue on empirical grounds. In fact it appears from our survey of Italian exporters' behaviour that even after the floating of most currencies in 1973 and the crises of the lira of 1973 and 1976, only about 48 per cent of exporters used some form of expected exchange rate different from the current or past average spot rate. True enough, this percentage had risen from a low of only about 6 per cent in 1970, to 11 per cent in 1971–73, to 48.5 per cent in 1976; but after so much turmoil in exchange markets only 22.8 per cent in 1976 used the forward exchange rate as a predictor of future spot rates (2 per cent in 1970). While we accept Miller's point that these data should be incorporated explicitly into the analysis of the CCE, we may provisionally argue that, in the absence of such explicit treatment, our estimates of the CCE could be taken as an empirical measure of the degree to which exchange rate expectations were indeed static. In particular, the fact that the first value of the ζ decay function stays, in our free estimates of it, consistently below unity (around 0.7), seems to indicate that the majority of Italian export contracts incorporate only static expectations about exchange rates. However, clearly more could and should be done with our data in order to provide a satisfactory answer to the question.

As to the second question, Miller himself provides an imaginative and theoretically appealing answer. Indeed, the forward rate for the lira seems to forecast future spot rates with a devaluation bias, which could explain the increasing share of foreign-currency denominated contracts along the lines suggested by Miller. As a partial confirmation of this we may again refer to the increasing role of forward exchange rates as a basis for setting Italian export prices. Although they had a weight in 1976 of only 22.8 per cent in the total of export contracts, their role had risen from the low of 2 per cent in 1970, and this was happening along with an increase in the share of export contracts denominated in foreign currency.

However, we could make use of other data from a set of questions in our survey, which were meant to identify whether during the sample period a significant change had occurred in the strength of the negotiating positions of Italian exporters vis-à-vis their foreign customers. A careful study of this information might qualify Miller's explanation of the phenomenon, in so far as it pointed to an increased awareness on the part of Italian exporters of the price and profit implications of changes in exchange rates, and/or an increased capacity for translating this into more favourably drawn contracts. Clearly, more work is necessary and possible on these aspects too, and we are grateful to Marcus Miller for the excellent suggestions he has given us.

Index

Names and page references to principal contributors are shown in bold type. Page references to bibliography are given in *italics* and text references in plain type.

INDEX

LIST OF PARTICIPANTS IN THE SYMPOSIUM

Professor R. Z. Aliber, Graduate School of Business, Chicago. Professor R. E. Baldwin, University of Wisconsin. Mr. A. Boltho, Magdalen College, Oxford. Professor G. Basevi, University of Bologna. Professor J. Black, University of Exeter. Mr. Christopher Bliss, Nuffield College, Oxford. Sir Alec Caincross, Oxford. Mr. Hugh Corbet, Trade Policy Research Centre, London. Professor W. M. Corden, Australian National University, Canberra. Professor J. B. Donges, Institut für Weltwirtschaft, Kiel. Mr. J. S. Flemming, Nuffield College, Oxford. Professor F. Gehrels, University of Munich. Mr. S. Golt, London. Professor S. Harris, Australian National University, Canberra. Professor H. Herberg, University of Mannheim. Mr. Brian Hindley, London School of Economics and Political Science. Ms. Helen Hughes, The World Bank, Washington, DC. Professor R. W. Jones, University of Rochester, NY. Mr. V. R. Joshi, Merton College, Oxford. Professor R. Komiya, University of Tokyo. Professor A. Krueger, University of Minnesota. Mr. I. M. D. Little, La Garde Freinet, France. Professor A. I. Macbean, University of Lancaster. Professor R. I. McKinnon, University of Stanford. Professor S. P. Magee, University of Texas at Austin. Professor J. E. Meade, Cambridge. Professor M. Michaely, Hebrew University of Jerusalem. Professor M. Miller, University of Warwick. Professor J. Niehans, University of Bern. Mr. P. M. Oppenheimer, Christ Church, Oxford. Professor T. Peters, University of Leuven, Belgium. Mr. T. M. Rybczynski, Lazard Bros. and Co. Ltd., London. Professor A. K. Sen, All Souls College, Oxford. Professor L. A. Sjaastad, University of Chicago. Professor M. Streit, University of Mannheim. Mr. J. Tumlir, GATT, Geneva. Professor H-J. Vosgerau, University of Konstanz, Germany. Mr. D. Wall, University of Sussex. Professor H. Willgerodt, University of Wiesbaden.